This is the third of three volumes containing papers presented in the invited symposium sessions of the Seventh World Congress of the Econometric Society. The papers summarize and interpret key recent developments and discuss current and future directions in a wide range of topics in economics and econometrics. They cover both theory and applications. Authored by leading specialists in their fields these volumes provide a unique survey of progress in the discipline.

Econometric Society Monographs No. 28

Advances in economics and econometrics: theory and applications

Volume III

Advances in economics and econometrics: theory and applications

Seventh World Congress
Volume III

Edited by

DAVID M. KREPS

and

KENNETH F. WALLIS

CAMBRIDGE
UNIVERSITY PRESS

Published by the Press Syndicate of the University of Cambridge
The Pitt Building, Trumpington Street, Cambridge CB2 1RP
40 West 20th Street, New York, NY 10011-4211, USA
10 Stamford Road, Oakleigh, Melbourne 3166, Australia

© Cambridge University Press 1997

First published 1997

Printed in Great Britain at the University Press, Cambridge

A catalogue record for this book is available from the British Library

A catalogue record is available from the Library of Congress

ISBN 0 521 580137 hardback
ISBN 0 521 589819 paperback

330.015195
A2442
1995
v.3

VN

Contents

viii   **Contents**

Contributors

Yuzo Hosoya
Tohoku University

James H. Stock
Harvard University

Timothy Bresnahan
Stanford University

Geert Ridder
Vrije Universiteit Amsterdam

Gerard J. van den Berg
Vrije Universiteit Amsterdam

John Geweke
University of Minnesota

Paul A. Ruud
University of California, Berkeley

Joel L. Horowitz
The University of Iowa

Eric Renault
Université des Sciences Sociales de Toulouse

George Tauchen
Duke University

Preface

This book contains papers presented in the invited symposium sessions of the Seventh World Congress of the Econometric Society, held at Keio University, Tokyo in August 1995, for which we were Program Co-Chairs. The papers summarize and interpret key recent developments and discuss current and future directions in a wide range of topics in economics and econometrics. These were chosen on the basis of their broad interest to members of the Society, and so cover both theory and applications, and demonstrate the progress made in the period since the previous World Congress. The program also reflected the fact that this was the first World Congress held outside Europe and North America. The authors are leading specialists in their fields, yet do not overemphasize their own research contributions. In one case, the two speakers in the session have combined their papers into a single chapter for this book – a long one, needless to say.

The more general objectives are reflected in the presentation of all the papers in a single book under a general title, with joint editorship, thus departing from the previous practice of separate "economic theory" and "econometrics" books. The size of the book has necessitated its division into three volumes, and thematic connections have suggested the contents of each volume. Within each volume the papers appear in the order of their presentation in Tokyo, which we hope will help readers who were there to remember what a marvellous occasion the Congress was.

We are grateful to the members of our Program Committee for much valuable advice, to the Chairs and discussants of the invited symposium sessions for their contributions, and to Patrick McCartan at Cambridge University Press for his guidance during the preparation and production of this book. More generally we wish to acknowledge the steadfast support we received in our task form Robert and Julie Gordon, respectively Treasurer and Secretary of the Society, and from Masahiro Okuno-Fujiwara, Chair of the Local Organizing Committee for the Congress.

David M. Kreps
Kenneth F. Wallis

CHAPTER 1

Causal analysis and statistical inference on possibly non-stationary time series

Yuzo Hosoya

1   INTRODUCTION

The purpose of this chapter is to provide a method of quantitative characterization of the interactive structure between a pair of possibly non-stationary vector time series by the means of causal measures (which consist of the measures of association, one-way effect, and reciprocity) and to consider the statistical inference problems involved in estimating those measures. Those measures were introduced in Hosoya (1991) in connection with the problem of extracting from each of a pair of stationary processes the component process which causes the other in purely one-way or feedback free manner in the sense of the Granger causality. All of the three measures have the advantage of frequency-wise decomposability and enable us to see how two time series interact in frequency bands of interest (see also Geweke (1982, 1984) for an important forerunner of this approach). We extend this approach to possibly non-stationary time series and deal with the related inference problems. By that extension, we are able to discern naturally the long-run and the short-run effects one series has on the other even when they contain stochastic trends, whereas as Stock and Watson (1988) pointed out, such distinctions are not feasible by means of time-domain representation of time series unless some convention is imposed.

The literature on statistical estimation and testing to deal with integrated or near-integrated time series, so far, seems to be limited to the unconditional inference with the exception of Basawa and Brockwell (1984), and besides not much attention seems to have been paid to the information amount aspect of estimates. This contribution investigates this aspect of inference and proposes conditional inference for possibly non-stationary processes based on conditional distributions of the maximum-likelihood (ML) estimate.

The chapter proceeds as follows: section 2 introduces the concept of reproducible processes and the standard harmonic analysis of stationary processes is extended to those processes. To be specific, section 2.1 discusses the concept, section 2.2. reviews the causal measures for stationary processes, and section 2.3 gives a prediction theory for reproducible processes. Section 3 introduces the causal measures to non-stationary ARMA processes and discusses statistical estimation and confidence-set construction of causal measure related functionals. Section 4 examines at first the information-loss problem in a general non-ergodic set-up and then shows that, for near-integrated models, the terminal observation is a first-order ancillary statistic which recovers the information loss suffered by the ML estimate. Section 4.2 provides the conditional characteristic function of the ML estimate, giving the Basawa–Brockwell result as the limiting case. Section 4.3 introduces the concept of the Ornstein–Uhlenbeck bridge and gives the conditional large-sample stochastic representation of the ML estimate. Section 5 deals with the conditional inference on vector autoregressive (VAR) processes; section 5.1 extends the result of section 4.3 to near-integrated VAR models. Section 5.2 shows the asymptotic normality of the ML estimate of cointegrating vectors given an appropriate first-order ancillary statistic. On the basis of cointegrated VAR models, section 6 exhibits some estimation results on the measure of the one-way effect for a few Japanese macroeconomic data.

We use the following notations and symbols. Let $\{x(t); t \in J\}$ and $\{y(t); t \in J\}$ (J: the set of all integers) be respectively real p and q dimensional stochastic processes with mean 0 with finite covariance defined on a same probability space. Let H be the Hilbert space which is the closure in the mean square of the linear hull of $\{x_j(t); t \in J, j = 1,\dots,p\}$ and $\{y_k(t); t \in J, k = 1,\dots,q\}$ in the space of all random variables with finite variance, where $x_j(t)$ denotes the jth component of the vector $x(t)$. $H\{x(s)\}$ and $H\{x(\infty)\}$ indicate respectively the linear closed subspace of H generated by $\{x_j(t); t \leq s; j = 1,\dots,p\}$ and $\{x_j(t); t \in J; j = 1,\dots,p\}$. In this contribution, the projection of a random vector $z = \{z_j; j = 1,\dots,r\}$ on to $H(\cdot)$ implies the component-wise projection; namely if $\bar{z}_j$ is the projection of z_j on to $H(\cdot)$, then the projection of z on to $H(\cdot)$ means the vector $\bar{z}$, whose jth component is in $H(\cdot)$. The determinant of a square matrix A is denoted as $\det A$, and the complex transpose of A is denoted by A^* (this notation is retained for a transpose of real matrix A). The partition of a $(p + q) \times (p + q)$ matrix A

$$A = \begin{bmatrix} A_{11} & A_{12} \\ A_{21} & A_{22} \end{bmatrix}$$

always implies that A_{11} is a $p \times p$ submatrix. I_r denotes the $r \times r$ identity matrix. The covariance matrix of a random vector z is denoted as $\mathrm{Cov}\{z\}$. If

Causal analysis and statistical inference 3

a sequence of random vectors $\{z^{(n)}, n = 1, 2, 3, \cdots\}$ tends weakly to a distribution P of a random vector z, it is denoted either by $z^{(n)} \Rightarrow P$ or by $z^{(n)} \Rightarrow z$. Two random variables which are equal with probability 1 are identified.

2 CAUSAL MEASURES FOR NON-STATIONARY PROCESSES

Second-order (or covariance) stationary processes have the nice property of isomorphism with the frequency domain representation, enabling the analysis of the frequency-domain properties. Explosive processes, on the other hand, lacking this property, are deprived of frequency-domain characterizations in general. The purpose of this section is to provide a device to bridge the gap between these two kinds of processes.

2.1 Reproducible processes

There turns out to be a class of possibly non-stationary processes to which the prediction theory of stationary processes naturally extends. The processes of this class are termed reproducible processes. To be formal, let $\{w(t), t \in J\}$ be a second-order stationary r-vector process and let $\{z(t), t = 1, 2, \cdots\}$ be another r-vector process with finite covariance. Throughout the chapter, the convention $z(t) = 0$ for $t \leq 0$ is used if $z(t)$ is originally defined only for $t \geq 1$ and extension is needed. Denote by $\varepsilon(t)$ the prediction error of $w(t)$ with respect to $H\{w(t-1)\}$; then the process $\{z(t)\}$ is said to be reproducible with respect to $\{w(t)\}$ if the prediction error of $z(t)$ with respect to $H\{z(t-1), w(0)\}$ is equal to $\varepsilon(t)$ for all $t \geq 1$. Namely, the respective prediction errors of $w(t)$ and $z(t)$ are identical. If a process $\{z(t)\}$ is reproducible with respect to $\{w(t)\}$, then it evidently follows that $H\{z(t), w(0)\} = H\{w(t)\}$. There are two cases of reproducible non-stationary processes which have wide application in econometric modeling. One is a class of time-dependent linear processes and the other is non-stationary autoregressive processes with dependent shocks.

Example 1 Let $A(L, t) = \Sigma_{j=0}^{s} A(j, t)L^j$ be a finite-order time-dependent linear filter where L is the backward-shift operator, the $A(j, t)$s are $r \times r$ matrices and $A(0, t) = I_r$ for all t. Given a second-order stationary process $\{w(t)\}$, suppose that $\{z(t), t \geq 1\}$ is generated by $A(L, t)z(t) = w(t)$. Then the process $\{z(t)\}$ is reproducible with respect to $\{w(t)\}$.

The Granger causality is defined for a pair of reproducible processes as follows. Suppose that the processes $\{x(t)\}$ and $\{y(t)\}$ are reproducible with respect to $\{u(t)\}$ and $\{v(t)\}$ respectively. If the respective prediction errors of $x(t)$ with respect to $H\{u(t-1), v(t-1)\}$ and with respect to $H\{u(t-1)\}$ are the same, $\{y(t)\}$ is said not to cause $\{x(t)\}$. Then the next theorem is an obvious consequence of this extended definition of the Granger non-causality.

Theorem 1 $\{y(t)\}$ *does not cause* $\{x(t)\}$ *if and only if* $\{v(t)\}$ *does not cause* $\{u(t)\}$.

Example 2 Suppose that the linear filter $A(L, t)$ has a block diagonal form

$$A(L, t) = \begin{bmatrix} A_{11}(L, t) & 0 \\ 0 & A_{22}(L, t) \end{bmatrix}$$

so that $(t) = (x(t)^*, y(t)^*)^*$ has the representation

$$\begin{bmatrix} A_{11}(L, t) & 0 \\ 0 & A_{22}(L, t) \end{bmatrix}\begin{bmatrix} x(t) \\ y(t) \end{bmatrix} = \begin{bmatrix} u(t) \\ v(t) \end{bmatrix} \equiv w(t).$$

Theorem 1 holds for the pair of $\{x(t)\}$ and $\{y(t)\}$.

Theorem 1 and example 1 illustrate the situations where Granger's non-causality between two non-stationary processes is determined by the corresponding relation between the generating processes. The question then is under what circumstances the causal measures in the frequency domain have meaningful extension to reproducible non-stationary processes.

2.2   Causal measures

There are three measures summarizing the causal relations between a pair of non-deterministic stationary processes. They are the measures of association, one-way effect and reciprocity, each of which is defined as overall as well as a frequency-wise measure. The measure of association is equal to the sum of the others.

Before giving the formal definitions, some intuitive exposition of those measures would be useful. Any stationary vector time series, say $\{u(t)\}$, can be regarded as a sum of sine and cosine curves of various frequencies with orthogonal random weights whose covariance at frequency λ is (roughly) proportional to the spectral density matrix $f_{11}(\lambda)$. Furthermore the one-step ahead prediction error which is denoted as $u_{-1.}(t)$ based only on the process itself has the property that the determinant of the covariance $\mathrm{Cov}\{u_{-1.}(t)\}$ is representable as the geometric mean of $\det f_{11}(\lambda)$, so that $\det f_{11}(\lambda)$ is a measure of the contribution of the frequency λ component to

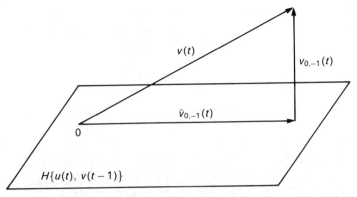

Figure 1.1 The one-way effect process $\{v_{0,-1}(t)\}$ as the residual of the projection of $v(t)$ on to $H\{u(t), v(t-1)\}$

the total one-step ahead prediction error. Granger's causality concept is concerned with how another process, say $\{v(s); s \leq t - 1\}$, if added as a predictor, contributes in the reduction of the one-step ahead prediction error of $u(t)$ (see Granger (1963, 1969, 1980) and Hosoya (1977)). Suppose the determinant of the covariance of the one-step ahead prediction error (denoted as $u_{-1,-1}(t)$) is expressible as the geometric mean of a function $g(\lambda)$. Then the ratio $\det f_{11}(\lambda)/\det g(\lambda)$ would measure the contribution of $\{v(t)\}$ in reducing the prediction error of $u(t)$ for frequency λ, namely the causal intensity from v to u at frequency λ.

The direct derivation of this ratio, however, does not work quite so well. Technically, there is no general way to represent $\det \text{Cov}\{u_{-1,-1}(t)\}$ as a geometric mean of some function $g(\lambda)$ such that $\det f_{11}(\lambda)/\det g(\lambda) \geq 1$. Secondly, even if it is possible, the effect from $\{v(s), s \leq t - 1\}$ to $u(t)$ contains also the feedback effect from $\{u(t)\}$ so that the ratio cannot be interpreted as the genuine one-way effect from $v(t)$ to $u(t)$. These two difficulties are solved by considering the joint process $\{u(t), v_{0,-1}(t)\}$ instead of $\{u(t), v(t)\}$ where $v_{0,-1}(t)$ is the one-way effect component of $\{v(t)\}$ as constructed in figure 1.1. The process $\{v_{0,-1}(t)\}$ does not contain the feedback effect and besides $\det \text{Cov}\{u'_{-1,-1}\}$ has the desirable decomposable property in the frequency domain as shown in (3) below so that the frequency-wise contribution of the process $\{v_{0,-1}(t)\}$ in prediction error reduction can be discerned.

Suppose that the $(p + q)$-vector process $\{u(t), v(t)\}$ is second-order stationary and has the spectral density matrix $f(\lambda)$ such that

$$\int_{-\pi}^{\pi} \log \det f(\lambda)\,d\lambda > -\infty, \tag{1}$$

so that the process has a positive-definite covariance matrix of the one-step ahead prediction error. This covariance matrix is denoted by Σ. The partitions of $f(\lambda)$ and Σ are denoted respectively by

$$f(\lambda) = \begin{bmatrix} f_{11}(\lambda) & f_{12}(\lambda) \\ f_{21}(\lambda) & f_{22}(\lambda) \end{bmatrix} \text{ and } \Sigma = \begin{bmatrix} \Sigma_{11} & \Sigma_{12} \\ \Sigma_{21} & \Sigma_{22} \end{bmatrix}.$$

For the sake of compact representation the following notations are used: $u_{-1,.}(t), u_{-1,-1}(t)$, and $u_{-1,0}(t)$ are the residuals of the projection of $u(t)$ on to $H\{u(t-1)\}$, $H\{u(t-1), v(t-1)\}$, and $H\{u(t-1), v(t)\}$ respectively. The prime indicates that $u(t)$ and $v(t)$ are projected on to the subspaces of $H\{u(\infty), v_{-1,0}(\infty)\}$, and $H\{u_{1,0}(\infty), v(\infty)\}$ respectively so that $u'_{-1,-1}(t)$ and $u'_{.,\infty}(t)$ are the residuals of the projection of $u(t)$ on to $H\{u(t-1), v_{0,-1}(t-1)\}$, and $H\{v_{0,-1}(\infty)\}$.

The process $\{v_{0,1}(t), t \in J\}$ can be regarded as the feedback-free component of $\{v(t)\}$ which acts upon $\{u(t)\}$ purely in a one-way manner. The processes $\{u_{-1,0}(t)\}$ and $\{v_{0,-1}(t)\}$ are thus termed the processes of one-way effect, and the causal measures are constructed based on those processes as follows. The overall measure of one-way effect from $\{v(t)\}$ to $\{u(t)\}$ is defined by

$$M_{v \to u} = \log[\det \mathrm{Cov}\{u_{-1,.}(t)\}/\det \mathrm{Cov}\{u'_{-1,-1}(t)\}], \tag{2}$$

and $M_{v \to u}$ is defined similarly (see figure 1.2 for the graphic display of prediction error reduction). The assumption (1) implies that the spectral density matrix f has a factorization

$$f(\lambda) = \frac{1}{2\pi} \Lambda(e^{-i\lambda})\Lambda(e^{-i\lambda})^*,$$

where $\Lambda(e^{-i\lambda})$ is the boundary value of a maximal analytic function $\Lambda(z)$ in the unit disc such that $\Lambda(0)\Lambda(0)^* = \Sigma$. Since f does not degenerate a.e., $\Lambda(e^{-i\lambda})^{-1}$ exists a.e. Now the measure of one-way effect at frequency λ is defined by

$$M_{v \to u}(\lambda) = \log[\det f_{11}(\lambda)/\det\{f_{11}(\lambda) - 2\pi \tilde{f}_{12}(\lambda)\tilde{\Sigma}_{22}^{-1}\tilde{f}_{21}(\lambda)\}], \quad -\pi < \lambda \le \pi, \tag{3}$$

where $\tilde{f}_{21}(\lambda) = [-\Sigma_{21}\Sigma_{11}^{-1}, I_q]\Lambda(0)\Lambda(e^{-i\lambda})^{-1}\begin{bmatrix} f_{11}(\lambda) \\ f_{21}(\lambda) \end{bmatrix}, \tilde{f}_{12} = \tilde{f}_{21}^*,$ and

$\tilde{\Sigma}_{22} = \Sigma_{22} - \Sigma_{21}\Sigma_{11}^{-1}\Sigma_{12}.$

For the purpose of introduction of the other measures, denote the joint spectral density matrix of $\{u'_{.,\infty}(t), v'_{\infty,.}(t)\}$ by

$$f'(\lambda) = \begin{bmatrix} f'_{11}(\lambda) & f'_{12}(\lambda) \\ f'_{21}(\lambda) & f'_{22}(\lambda) \end{bmatrix},$$

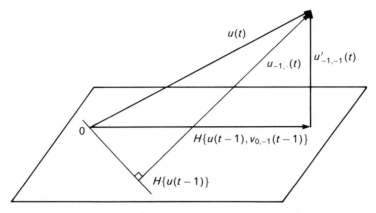

Figure 1.2 Comparison of the prediction errors $u'_{-1,-1}(t)$ and $u_{-1,\cdot}(t)$

where $u'_{\cdot,\infty}(t)$ and $v'_{\infty,\cdot}(t)$ are the residuals of projection of $u(t)$ and $v(t)$ on to $H\{v_{0,-1}(\infty)\}$ and $H\{u_{-1,0}(\infty)\}$ respectively. Removal of the parts explained by the one-way effect of each other process leaves only reciprocal interactions, and the intensity of reciprocity is measured by how one-step ahead prediction error is reduced by means of joint prediction, instead of separate prediction of each series. These considerations lead to the following definition of the measure of reciprocity $M_{u \cdot v}$ and the measure of association $M_{u,v}$ and their associated decompositions in the frequency domain. Namely, define the measure of association $M_{u,v}(\lambda)$ at frequency λ between the processes $\{u(t)\}$ and $\{v(t)\}$ by

$$M_{u,v}(\lambda) = \log[\det f_{11}(\lambda)\det f_{22}(\lambda)/\{\det f'(\lambda)\}] \qquad (4)$$

and define the measure of reciprocity by

$$M_{u \cdot v}(\lambda) = \log[\det f'_{11}(\lambda)\det f'_{22}(\lambda)/\{\det f'(\lambda)\}]. \qquad (5)$$

Furthermore define the corresponding overall measures $M_{u,v}$ and $M_{u \cdot v}$ by

$$M_{u,v} = \frac{1}{2\pi}\int_{-\pi}^{\pi} M_{u,v}(\lambda)d\lambda; \; M_{u \cdot v} = \frac{1}{2\pi}\int_{-\pi}^{\pi} M_{u \cdot v}(\lambda)d\lambda.$$

Then the following equalities hold between those causal measures

$$M_{u,v}(\lambda) = M_{u \to v}(\lambda) + M_{u \cdot v}(\lambda) + M_{v \to u}(\lambda),$$

and

$$M_{u,v} = M_{u \to v} + M_{u \cdot v} + M_{v \to u} \qquad (6)$$

(see Hosoya (1991) for the detail).

Example 3 There is an important case where filtering of stationary processes leaves those causal measures invariant. Let $d(L) = \Sigma_{j=0}^s d_j L^j$ be a filter with scalar coefficients such that $d_0 = 1$ and all the zeros of $\Sigma_{j=0}^s d_j z^j$ are outside the unit circle and let $\{x(t)\}$ and $\{y(t)\}$ be the stationary processes generated by $d(L)x(t) = u(t)$ and $d(L)y(t) = v(t)$. Then the joint process $\{x(t), y(t)\}$ has a spectral density matrix $g(\lambda) = |d(e^{-i\lambda})|^{-2} f(\lambda)$ which has a decomposition

$$g(\lambda) = \frac{1}{2\pi} \{d(e^{-i\lambda})^{-1} \Lambda(e^{-i\lambda})\}\{d(e^{-i\lambda})^{-1} \Lambda(e^{-i\lambda})\}^*$$

$$\equiv \frac{1}{2\pi} \Lambda'(e^{-\lambda}) \Lambda'(e^{-i\lambda})^*,$$

where $\Lambda'(0) = \Lambda'(0)^* = \Sigma$. The direct substitution of f and Λ by g and Λ' in (3), (4), and (5) shows that, under the transformation of $\{u(t), v(t)\}$ to $\{x(t), y(t)\}$, the frequency-wise as well as overall measures of the one-way effect, association, and reciprocity are all invariant.

Example 4 Set $D_{11}(L) = \Sigma_{j=0}^s D_{11}(j)L^j$ and $D_{22}(L) = \Sigma_{j=0}^s D_{22}(j)L^j$ where the $D_{11}(j)$s and the $D_{22}(j)$s are $p \times p$ and $q \times q$ matrices respectively and consider the transformation

$$\begin{bmatrix} D_{11}(L) & 0 \\ 0 & D_{22}(L) \end{bmatrix} \begin{bmatrix} x(t) \\ y(t) \end{bmatrix} = \begin{bmatrix} u(t) \\ v(t) \end{bmatrix}. \tag{7}$$

Suppose that all the zeros of $D_1(z)$ and $D_{22}(z)$ are all outside unit circle and $D_{11}(0)$ and $D_{22}(0)$ are identity matrices; then although the measures of the one-way effect between $\{x(t)\}$ and $\{y(t)\}$ are the same as those between $\{u(t)\}$ and $\{v(t)\}$, the other measures are not necessarily invariant.

2.3   Prediction theory for reproducible processes

Suppose $\{\varepsilon(t), t \in J\}$ is an r-vector white-noise process with mean 0 and with covariance matrix Σ and suppose that $\{z(t), t \geq 1\}$ is an r-vector linear process with time-varying coefficients generated by

$$z(t) = \sum_{j=0}^{\infty} A(j, t)\varepsilon(t - j), \tag{8}$$

where we assume that $A(0, t) = I_r$ and $\Sigma_{j=0}^{\infty} A(j,t)\Sigma A(j, t)^* < \infty$ for all $t \geq 1$ so that $z(t)$ has finite covariance matrix for all t. Suppose also that the process $\{z(t), t \geq 1\}$ in (8) is reproducible with respect to $\{\varepsilon(t)\}$; namely, $H\{z(t), \varepsilon(0)\} = H\{\varepsilon(t)\}$ for all $t \geq 1$. Now set

$$\Gamma(e^{-i\lambda}, t) = \sum_{j=0}^{\infty} A(j, t)e^{-i\lambda j}$$

and define the time-varying spectral density matrix $f^z(\lambda, t)(t \geq 1)$ of the process $\{z(t)\}$ by

$$f^z(\lambda, t) = \frac{1}{2\pi}\Gamma(e^{-i\lambda}, t)\Sigma\Gamma(e^{-i\lambda}, t)^*, \quad -\pi < \lambda \leq \pi.$$

As the next theorem shows, the prediction theory of second-order station-ary processes extends to this class of reproducible linear processes and the prediction error covariance is decomposable in the frequency domain.

Theorem 2 *If the reproducible process $\{z(t)\}$ in (8) has a time-varying density matrix f^z such that for all t*

$$\int_{-\infty}^{\infty} \log \det f^z(\lambda, t)d\lambda > -\infty; \tag{9}$$

then the relationship

$$\det \text{Cov}\{z_{-1}(t)\} = (2\pi)^r \exp\left\{\frac{1}{2\pi}\int_{-\pi}^{\pi} \log \det f^z(\lambda, t)d\lambda\right\} \tag{10}$$

holds, where $z_{-1}(t)$ is the residual of the projection of $z(t)$ on to $H\{z(t-1), \varepsilon(0)\}$.

Proof Fix t at $t = t_0$, say $(t_0 \geq 1)$. Since $\{z(t)\}$ is reproducible, the projection of $z(t_0)$ on to $H\{z(t_0 - 1), \varepsilon(0)\}$ is equal to the one on to $H\{\varepsilon(t_0 - 1)\}$. Consider the second-order stationary process $\{w(t)\}$ defined by

$$w(t) = \sum_{j=0}^{\infty} A(j, t_0)\varepsilon(t - j), t \in J,$$

which has the spectral density $f(\lambda, t_0)$. For that process, let $w_{-1}(t)$ be the one-step ahead projection error; then we have the equality

$$\text{Cov}\{w_{-1}(t)\} = \Sigma = (2\pi)^r \exp\left\{\frac{1}{2\pi}\int_{-\pi}^{\pi} \log \det f^z(\lambda, t_0)d\lambda\right\},$$

for all $t \in J$,

under assumption (9) (see Rozanov (1967)). Now the relationship (10) follows from the equality $w_{-1}(t_0) = z_{-1}(t_0)$, because t_0 is arbitrary. $\square$

Remark 1 In case $d(z) = 0$ has a unit root in example 3, the process $\{x(t)\}$ does not have spectral representation, but we can endow the formal improper density $g(\lambda) \equiv f_{11}(\lambda)/|\Sigma_{j=0}^{s}d(e^{-i\lambda j})|^2$ to that process. Since $\int_{-\pi}^{\pi}\log|1 - e^{i\lambda}|^2d\lambda = 0$, it follows

$$\int_{-\pi}^{\pi} \log\det\left\{f_{11}(\lambda)/|\sum_{j=0}^{s} d(e^{-i\lambda j})|^2\right\}d\lambda = \int_{-\pi}^{\pi} \log\det f_{11}(\lambda)d\lambda,$$

whence, quite in parallel to stationary cases, we have

$$\det\operatorname{Cov}\{x_{-1,.}(t)\} = (2\pi)^p\exp\left\{\frac{1}{2\pi}\int_{-\pi}^{\pi} \log\det g(\lambda)d\lambda\right\}.$$

The measure of the one-way effect is extended to the time-varying coefficient process in (8) as follows. Suppose $z(t)$ consists of two components $z(t) = (x(t)^*, y(t)^*)^*$.

Assumption A

(i) $\{x(t), t \geq 1\}$ has its own linear representation

$$x(t) = \sum_{j=0}^{\infty} B(j,t)\eta(t - j) \qquad (B(0,t) = I_p)$$

with respect to a white-noise process $\{\eta(t)\}$ with mean 0 and covariance Ω,

(ii) $\{x(t), t \geq 1\}$ is reproducible with respect to $\{\eta(t)\}$,

(iii) $f_{11}^z(\lambda, t) = f^x(\lambda, t)$, where

$$f^x(\lambda, t) = \frac{1}{2\pi}(\Sigma_{j=0}^{\infty}B(j,t)e^{-i\lambda j})\Omega(\Sigma_{j=0}^{\infty}B(j,t)e^{-i\lambda j})^*.$$

Denote by $y_{0,-1}(t)$ the residual of projection of $y(t)$ on to $H\{x(t), y(t-1), \varepsilon(0)\}$ and denote by $x'_{-1,-1}(t)$ the residual of projection of $x(t)$ on to $H\{x(t-1), y_{0,-1}(t-1), \varepsilon(0)\}$. Moreover, denote by $x_{-1,.}(t)$ the residual of projection of $x(t)$ on to $H\{x(t-1), \eta(0)\}$. Setting by $\tilde{f}^z(\lambda, t)$ the time-varying joint spectral density of $\{x(t), y_{0,-1}(t)\}$, define $M_{y\to x}(t)$ and $M_{y\to x}(\lambda, t)$ as in (2) and (3) respectively; in particular

$$M_{y\to x}(\lambda, t) = \log[\det f_{11}^z(\lambda, t)/\det\{f_{11}^z(\lambda, t) - \tilde{f}_{12}^z(\lambda, t)\tilde{\Sigma}_{22}^{-1}\tilde{f}_{21}^z(\lambda, t)\}],$$

where $\tilde{\Sigma}_{22} = \Sigma_{22} - \Sigma_{21}\Sigma_{11}^{-1}\Sigma_{12}$.

Theorem 3 *Suppose that Assumption A holds we have*

$$M_{y\to x}(t) = \frac{1}{2\pi}\int_{-\pi}^{\pi} M_{y\to x}(\lambda, t)d\lambda,$$

where $M_{y\to x}(t)$ and $M_{y\to x}(\lambda, t)$ are independent of t in effect.

The proof is quite in parallel to Hosoya (1991, pp. 440–2) thanks to theorem

2 and is omitted. The next section considers a special case for which assumption A holds and which has wide application in econometric time-series analysis.

3   POSSIBLY NON-STATIONARY ARMA PROCESSES AND INFERENCE

Let $d(L) = \Sigma_{j=0}^{s} d(j)L^{j}$ be a lag operator with scalar coefficients such that $d(0) = 1$ and the zeros of $\Sigma_{j=0}^{d} d(j)z^{j}$ are either on or outside the unit circle, and let $D(L)$ be the $(p + q) \times (p + q)$ diagonal matrix with $d(L)$ for all the diagonal elements. This section considers exclusively the type of possible non-stationary processes which are represented by

$$D(L)\begin{bmatrix} x(t) \\ y(t) \end{bmatrix} = \begin{bmatrix} u(t) \\ v(t) \end{bmatrix},$$

where the process $\{u(t), v(t)\}$ is a second-order stationary processes having a spectral density matrix $f(\lambda)$ which satisfies the condition (1) of section 2.2.

The processes $\{x(t)\}$ and $\{y(t)\}$ are determined solely by $\{u(t)\}$ and $\{v(t)\}$ respectively, satisfying assumption A. In this case, the causal concepts and measures are extended as follows. By the one-step ahead prediction errors of $x(t)$ and $y(t)$ by their own past values, we imply the residuals of the projection of $x(t)$ and $y(t)$ on to $H\{x(t-1), u(0)\}$ and $H\{y(t-1), v(0)\}$ respectively. The one-way effect component of $y(t)$ is the residual of the projection of $y(t)$ on to $H\{x(t), y(t-1), u(0), v(0)\}$ and this is equal to $v_{-1,0}(t)$. Similarly, that component of $x(t)$ is given by $u_{0,-1}(t)$. The residual of the projection of $x(t)$ on to $\{x(t-1), u(0), v_{-1,0}(t-1)\}$ is given by the corresponding quantity of $u(t)$ projected on to $\{u(t-1), v_{0,-1}(t-1)\}$; thus it is natural to define the extended measures of the one-way effect from $\{y(t)\}$ to $\{x(t)\}$ by the measures $M_{v \to u}(\lambda)$ and $M_{v \to u}$. In fact, there exists T such that for $t \geq T M_{y \to x}(\lambda, t) = M_{v \to u}(\lambda)$ and $M_{y \to x}(t) = M_{v \to u}$. Also $M_{x \to y}(\lambda, t)$ and $M_{x \to y}(t)$ are defined analogously.

Error correction models represent economic relationships which are dynamically in stable equilibrium in the presence of incessant incoming shocks, generating unit-root processes (see Engle and Granger (1987)). Typically such an r-vector process $\{z(t), t = 1, 2, \cdots\}$ is represented by a multivariate ARMA process

$$z(t) = \sum_{j=1}^{a} A(j)z(t-j) + \sum_{k=0}^{b} B(k)\varepsilon(t-k), \qquad z = 1, 2, \cdots \qquad (11)$$

in which $\{\varepsilon(t), t \in J\}$ is a white-noise process with mean 0 and covariance matrix Σ and the $A(j)$s and the $B(k)$s are $r \times r$ matrices such that the zeros of

$\det(\Sigma_{k=0}^{b}B(k)z^{k})$ are outside the unit circle and the zeros of $\det(I_{r} - \Sigma A(j)z^{j})$ are either $z = 1$ or outside the unit circle.

The causal measures introduced in the last section are evaluated for the cointegrated multivariate ARMA process (11) (see Granger and Lin (1995) for the original idea of the extension to cointegrated AR models and see Hosoya (1991, pp. 439–40) for stationary ARMA processes). Set $A(L) = I_{r} - \Sigma_{j=1}^{a}A_{j}L^{j}$ and denote by $C(L)$ the adjoint matrix of $A(L)$. Denote by $D(L)$ be the diagonal matrix whose diagonal elements are all equal to det $A(L)$. Since then we have

$$C(L)A(L) = D(L), \tag{12}$$

the application of the operator $C(L)$ to both sides of equation (11) gives

$$D(L)z_{t} = C(L)B(L)\varepsilon(t) \equiv w(t). \tag{13}$$

Note that $w(t)$ is a finite-order MA process and hence stationary. Moreover:

Lemma 1 *The zeros of* $\det\{C(z)B(z)\}$ *are either on or outside of the unit circle. Therefore, the covariance matrix of the one-step ahead prediction error of* $w(t)$ *is equal to* Σ.

Proof It follows from (12) that $\det C(z) = \{\det A(z)\}^{r-1}$, whence the zeros of $\det C(z)$ are either on or outside the unit circle. Since the zeros of $\det B(z)$ are either on or outside the unit circle, the first statement follows. In view of the property of the zeros, the second statement follows immediately. $\square$

Let $\Sigma^{1/2}\Sigma^{1/2} = \Sigma$ be a decomposition of Σ and set as above $w(t) = C(L)B(L)\varepsilon(t)$; then $w(t)$ is a second-order stationary process and the above lemma implies that $\Lambda(e^{-i\lambda}) = C(e^{-i\lambda})B(e^{-i\lambda})\Sigma^{1/2}$ satisfies the conditions for the causal measures introduced in section 2.2. The measures are defined between $\{x(t)\}$ and $\{y(t)\}$ by means of the corresponding measures between $\{u(t)\}$ and $\{v(t)\}$, where

$$z(t) = \begin{bmatrix} x(t) \\ y(t) \end{bmatrix} \text{ and } w(t) = \begin{bmatrix} u(t) \\ v(t) \end{bmatrix}.$$

Therefore the substitution

$$\Lambda(e^{-i\lambda}) = C(e^{-i\lambda})B(e^{-i\lambda})\Sigma^{1/2} \text{ and } f(\lambda) = \frac{1}{2\pi}\Lambda(e^{-i\lambda})\Lambda(e^{-i\lambda})^{*} \tag{14}$$

in the definitions of causal measures (5), (6), and (7) gives the corresponding causal measures for ARMA processes with possible unit roots.

A large part of asymptotic inference on the causal measures for cointegrated economic time series turns out to be executable by means of a standard asymptotic theory for stationary processes. Take the cointegrated multivariate ARMA model for instance. It is represented by

$$\Delta z(t) = \Gamma z(t-1) + \sum_{j=1}^{a-1} \Gamma(j)\Delta z(t-j) + \sum_{k=0}^{b} B(k)e(t-k)$$

with $\Gamma = \Gamma^{(1)}\Gamma^{(2)*}$ where $\Gamma^{(1)}$ and $\Gamma^{(2)}$ are $r \times r_1$ matrices $r_1 < r$ and it reduces to (11) by setting $I_r + \Gamma + \Gamma(1) = A(1)$, $\Gamma(j) - \Gamma(j-1) = A(j)$, $2 \leq j \leq a - 1$ and $-\Gamma(a) = A(a)$. Suppose that $\{e(t)\}$ is a Gaussian white-noise process with mean 0 and covariance matrix Σ. Also let θ be a vector of order $r \cdot r_1$ constituted of the elements of $\Gamma^{(2)}$ and let ψ be the vector which consists of the elements of $\Gamma^{(1)}$, the $\Gamma(j), j = 1, \cdots, a-1, B(k), k = 0, \cdots, b$ and the lower triangular matrix of $\Sigma^{1/2}$. The frequency response function and the spectral density matrix Λ and f are determined by (θ, ψ); namely, it follows from (14) that

$$\Lambda(e^{-i\lambda} | \theta, \psi) = C(e^{-i\lambda} | \theta, \psi)B(e^{-i\lambda} | \psi)\Sigma(\psi)^{1/2}$$

and

$$f(\lambda | \theta, \psi) = \frac{1}{2\pi}\Lambda(e^{-i\lambda} | \theta, \psi)\Lambda(e^{-\lambda} | \theta, \phi)^*. \tag{15}$$

In view of the definitions, the causal-measure related quantities are all functionals of $\Lambda(e^{-i\lambda} | \theta, \psi)$ and $f(\lambda | \theta, \psi)$. If $G(\Lambda, f)$ is such a quantity, as a vector-valued functional of Λ and f, it is determined in turn by (θ, ψ). Therefore we can write $G = G(\theta, \psi)$. For instance, the overall measure of one-way effect $M_{y \rightarrow x}$ is given by

$$G(\theta, \psi) = \frac{1}{2\pi}\int_{-\pi}^{\pi} M_{y \rightarrow x}(\lambda | \theta, \psi)d\lambda,$$

where $M_{y \rightarrow x}(\lambda | \theta, \psi)$ is evaluated according to the foregoing arguments; or one might be interested in the contribution of a long-run effect

$$G(\theta, \psi) = \int_{-\lambda_0}^{\lambda_0} M_{y \rightarrow x}(\theta, \psi)d\lambda / \int_{-\pi}^{\pi} M_{y \rightarrow x}(\lambda | \theta, \psi)d\lambda,$$

where λ_0 is a certain small positive number. Note that in these instances, $G(\theta, \psi)$ are smooth functions of (θ, ψ) in general.

Based on identifying restrictions on $\Gamma^{(2)}$ and the $\Gamma(j)$s and the $B(k)$s, the parameters θ, ψ are estimated by the ML method or the quasi ML method (see Johansen (1988) for the ML estimation in the AR case and see Hosoya and Taniguchi (1982, 1993) for the quasi-ML estimation which applies to general stationary linear processes). Denote by $(\hat{\theta}, \hat{\psi})$ the ML estimate. Johansen (1988) showed that, if (θ, ψ) is the true value, $n(\hat{\theta} - \theta)$ tends to have a mixed multivariate normal distribution and $\sqrt{n}(\hat{\psi} - \psi)$ tends to have a multivariate normal distribution as $n \to \infty$, so that $G(\hat{\theta}, \hat{\psi})$ is a $\sqrt{n}$ consistent estimate of $G(\theta, \psi)$ and $\sqrt{n}\{G(\hat{\theta}, \hat{\psi}) - G(\theta, \psi)\}$ is asymptotically normally distributed with mean 0 and with covariance matrix

$$H(\theta, \psi) = D_\psi G(\theta, \psi)^* \Psi(\theta, \psi) D_\psi G(\theta, \psi),$$

where $D_\psi G$ is the Jacobian matrix and Ψ is the asymptotic covariance matrix of $\sqrt{n}(\hat{\psi} - \hat{\psi})$. Note that the first-order asymptotic distribution of $G(\hat{\theta}, \hat{\psi})$ is completely determined by $\hat{\psi}$ and the non-standard limiting distribution of $\hat{\theta}$ is not involved. This is due to the fact that the sampling error of $\hat{\theta}$ is negligible in comparison with that of $\hat{\psi}$. As a consequence, the confidence set with a limiting confidence level is constructed by means of asymptotically χ^2 statistics of either

$$N\{G(\hat{\theta}, \hat{\psi}) - G(\theta, \psi)\} H(\theta, \psi)^{-1} \{G(\hat{\theta}, \hat{\psi}) - G(\theta, \psi)\}$$

or

$$N\{G(\hat{\theta}, \hat{\psi}) - G(\theta, \psi)\} H(\hat{\theta}, \hat{\psi})^{-1} \{G(\hat{\theta}, \hat{\psi}) - G(\theta, \psi)\}$$

where the degrees of freedom are equal to the dimension of ψ (see Lütkepohl and Reimers (1992) and Toda and Phillips (1994) for the Granger test for non-causality based on the cointegrated AR model). Section 6 will provide some empirical ML estimation results.

4   INFORMATION RECOVERY FOR NON-STATIONARY MODELS

As was seen in section 3, the first-order asymptotic theory for inference on causal-measure related statistics involves the asymptotic normality only, whereas the higher-order asymptotics or inference for the near-unit root or cointegration rank require further consideration. The rest of this chapter deals with inference problems of near-integrated or cointegrated processes from the viewpoint of information loss and its recovery, and for that purpose the conditional inference based on first-order asymptotically ancillary statistics.

Suppose that a parametric statistical model has the log-likelihood function $L_n(\theta, \phi)$ based on the observation $z_{(n)} \equiv (z(1), \cdots, z(n))$, where θ and ϕ are vector-valued parameters. Assume that L_n is sufficiently smooth with respect to θ and ϕ for each n (this condition is satisfied in the cases we consider below). Denote by $\hat{\theta}_n$ and $\hat{\phi}_n$ the ML estimate of θ and ϕ. Denote also by DL_n and D^2L_n the Jacobian and the Hessian matrix of L_n obtained as the derivatives with respect to (θ, ϕ). Then the Fisher information matrix of the observation $z_{(n)}$ is defined by

$$I_n(\theta, \phi \,|\, z_{(n)}) = E\{[DL_n(\theta, \phi)][DL_n(\theta, \phi)]^*\} = -E\{D^2L_n(\theta, \phi)\},$$

whereas the information matrix of the ML estimate $\hat{\theta}_n, \hat{\phi}_n$ is given by

$$I_n(\theta, \phi \,|\, \hat{\theta}_n, \hat{\phi}_n) = I_n(\theta, \phi \,|\, z_{(n)}) - E[\mathrm{Cov}\{DL_n(\theta, \phi) \,|\, \hat{\theta}_n, \hat{\phi}_n\}]$$

so that the expectation of the conditional covariance matrix $E\ \mathrm{Cov}\{DL_n(\theta, \phi) \,|\, \hat{\theta}_n, \hat{\phi}_n\}$ measures the amount of information loss due to the reduction of data to $\hat{\theta}_n, \hat{\phi}_n$ (see, for example, Hosoya (1988)). For standard ergodic models, $I_n(\theta, \phi \,|\, z_{(n)})$ is of order $O(n)$, and $I_n(\theta, \phi \,|\, \hat{\theta}_n, \hat{\phi}_n)/I_n(\theta, \phi \,|\, z_{(n)})$ tends to 1 as $n \to \infty$ in general, namely, the maximum-likelihood estimate is first-order asymptotically sufficient. Now suppose that the following weak convergences hold jointly

(B1) $[n(\hat{\theta}_n - \theta), \sqrt{n}(\hat{\phi}_n - \phi)] \Rightarrow (\tilde{\theta}, \tilde{\phi})$

(B2) $\begin{bmatrix} n^{-2}D_{\theta\theta}L_n & n^{-1}D_{\theta\phi}L_n \\ n^{-1}D_{\phi\theta} & n^{-1}D_{\phi\phi}L_n \end{bmatrix} \Rightarrow \begin{bmatrix} U & V^* \\ V & C \end{bmatrix}$,

where $\tilde{\theta}$ and $\tilde{\phi}$ are non-degenerated random variables, where $D_{..}$ denotes the second-order derivative evaluated at (θ, ϕ), and U, V, and C are random matrices such that U does not degenerate to a constant. Under the assumptions B1 and B2, the information matrix $I_n(\theta, \phi \,|\, x_{(n)})$ is of order $O(n^2)$ and thus the information loss of $\hat{\theta}_n, \hat{\phi}_n$ in the leading term of the asymptotic expansion of the information amount is obtained by evaluating

$$E[\mathrm{Cov}\{n^{-1}DL_n(\theta, \phi) \,|\, n(\hat{\theta}_n - \theta), \sqrt{n}(\hat{\phi}_n - \phi)\}]. \qquad (16)$$

Although the explicit evaluation of this quantity for finite n is not practicable, the asymptotic version of (16) is obtained instead based on the asymptotic joint distribution of $n^{-1}DL_n(\theta, \phi), n(\hat{\theta}_n - \theta)$, and $\sqrt{n}(\hat{\phi}_n - \phi)$. In order to make the difference explicit the notation

$$\underline{E}[\underline{\mathrm{Cov}}\{n^{-1}DL_n(\theta, \phi) \,|\, n(\hat{\theta}_n - \theta), \sqrt{n}(\hat{\phi}_n - \phi)\}] \qquad (17)$$

is used where underlined E and Cov indicate the expectation and covariance of the asymptotic distribution of the arguments involved. The matrix (17) is the first-order information loss. Since, in view of the Taylor expansion, we have

$$n^{-1}DL_n(\theta, \phi) = -\begin{bmatrix} n^{-2}D_{\theta\theta}L_n(\theta, \phi) & n^{-3/2}D_{\theta\phi}L_n(\theta, \phi) \\ n^{-3/2}D_{\phi\theta}L_n(\theta, \phi) & n^{-3/2}D_{\phi\phi}L_n(\theta, \phi) \end{bmatrix}$$

$$\cdot \begin{bmatrix} n(\hat{\theta}_n - \theta) \\ n^{1/2}(\hat{\phi}_n - \phi) \end{bmatrix} + o_p(1),$$

it follows from B1 and B2 that

$$\underline{E[\text{Cov}}\{n^{-1}DL_n(\theta, \phi) \,|\, n(\hat{\theta}_n - \theta), \sqrt{n}(\hat{\phi}_n - \phi)\}$$
$$= \begin{bmatrix} E[\text{Cov}\{U\tilde{\theta}\,|\,\tilde{\theta}\}] & 0 \\ 0 & 0 \end{bmatrix} \qquad (18)$$

so that, unless U is functionally completely determined by $\tilde{\theta}$, the maximum-likelihood estimate $\hat{\theta}_n$ and $\hat{\phi}_n$ suffer first-order information loss by which we imply henceforth the dominant matrix $E[\text{cov}\{U\tilde{\theta}\,|\,\tilde{\theta}\}]$ in the right-hand side matrix in (18).

Let $\eta_n(z(1), \cdots, z(n))$ be a statistic such that $\eta_n \Rightarrow \tilde{\eta}$ jointly with (B1) and (B2) above and suppose that η_n and $\tilde{\eta}$ satisfy:

(C1) the Fisher information of η_n is at most of order $O(n)$,
(C2) the conditional first-order information loss of $\tilde{\theta}$ conditioned on $\tilde{\eta}$ vanishes; namely, $E[\text{Cov}\{U\tilde{\theta}\,|\,\tilde{\theta}, \tilde{\eta}\}\,|\,\tilde{\eta}] = 0.$

The first condition implies that η_n is first-order ancillary; namely, conditioning statistical inference on η_n suffers no loss of first-order information which is of the order $O(n^2)$. In order to see this, let $L_n(\theta, \phi \,|\, \eta_n)$ be the conditional log-likelihood and $g_n(\eta_n \,|\, \theta, \phi)$ be the marginal-density function of η_n. If g_n is smooth with respect to (θ, ϕ), it follows from $L_n(\theta, \phi) = L_n(\theta, \phi \,|\, \eta_n) + \log g_n(\eta_n \,|\, \theta, \phi)$, that

$$\frac{1}{n^2}[E\{D^2 L_n(\theta, \phi) - E(D^2 L_n(\theta, \phi \,|\, \eta_n)\}]$$

$$= \frac{1}{n^2} E[D^2 \log g(\eta_n \,|\, \theta, \phi)] = O\left(\frac{1}{n}\right).$$

The condition (C2) implies that $\tilde{\eta}$ recovers completely the first-order information loss; in other words, conditioned on η_n, the ML estimate $\tilde{\theta}$ is asymptotically first-order sufficient, losing no first-order conditional information (see Hosoya, Tsukuda, and Terui (1989) for conditional inference for simultaneous structural equation models; their results are readily extendable to ergodic time-series models).

4.1   The case of scalar-valued autoregressive processes

Consider the case where an array of scalar-valued processes $\{x_n(t), t = 0, 1, \cdots, n\}$, $n = 1, 2, \cdots$, is generated by

$$x_n(t) = \alpha_n x_n(t - 1) + e(t), \qquad t = 0, 1, 2, \cdots, \qquad (19)$$

where $x_n(0) = 0$, $\alpha_n = \exp(\alpha/n)$ and $\{e(t)\}$ is a Gaussian white-noise process with mean 0 and variance σ^2. Let $L_n(\alpha_n, \sigma^2)$ be the log-likelihood based on the observations $x_n(1), \cdots, x_n(n)$, and denoted by $\hat{\alpha}_n, \hat{\sigma}_n^2$ the maximum-likelihood estimate of α_n and σ^2 based on the log-likelihood L_n. Let $\{b(t), 0 \le t \le 1\}$ be a Brownian motion such that $E(b(t)) = 0$ and $E(b(1)) = \sigma^2$ and let $\{u_\alpha(t), 0 \le t \le 1, u_\alpha(0) = 0\}$ be an Ornstein–Uhlenbeck (O–U) process generated by the stochastic differential equation

$$du_\alpha(t) = \alpha u_\alpha(t) + db(t).$$

Then the following weak convergence results hold jointly (see Chan and Wei (1987) and Phillips (1987))

$$\sum \varepsilon(t)x(t-1)/n \Rightarrow \int_0^1 u_\alpha(t)db(t)$$

and

$$\sum_{t=1}^n x_n(t-1)^2/(\sigma^2 n^2) \Rightarrow \int_0^1 u_\alpha(t)^2 dt,$$

so that

$$n(\hat{\alpha}_n - \alpha_n) \Rightarrow \int_0^1 u_\alpha(t)db(t)/\int_0^1 \{u_\alpha(t)\}^2 dr.$$

Since $\sqrt{n}(\hat{\sigma}_n^2 - \sigma^2) \Rightarrow N(0, 2\sigma^4)$, the pair $(\hat{\alpha}_n, \hat{\sigma}_n^2)$ satisfies the condition (B1). On the other hand, as for the Hessian matrix of L_n, we have

$$\begin{bmatrix} n^{-2}D_{\alpha_n\alpha_n}L_n & n^{-1}D_{\alpha_n\sigma^2}L_n \\ n^{-1}D_{\sigma^2\alpha_n}L_n & n^{-1}D_{\sigma^2\sigma^2}L_n \end{bmatrix} \Rightarrow \begin{bmatrix} -\int\{u_\alpha(t)\}^2 dt & \int u_\alpha db(t)/\sigma^2 \\ \int u_\alpha(t)db(t)/\sigma^2 & -1/(2\sigma^2) \end{bmatrix}. \quad (20)$$

The last weak convergence implies that the condition (B.2) is satisfied for the Hessian matrix. In view of (18), the first-order information loss of $(\hat{\alpha}_n, \hat{\sigma}^2)$ is equal to

$$E\left[[\mathrm{Cov}\left\{ \int_0^1 u_\alpha(t)db(t) | \int_0^1 u_\alpha(t)db(t)/\int_0^1 \{u_\alpha(t)\}^2 dt \right\} \right], \quad (21)$$

which is positive since the joint distribution of $\int u_\alpha(t)db(t)$ and $\int\{u_\alpha(t)\}^2 dt$ does not degenerate. To find an appropriate asymptotically ancillary statistic which recovers the information loss, note that, thanks to the relationship

$$\sum_{t=1}^n x(t-1)^2/n^2 = \{\hat{\sigma}_n^2 - (x(n)/\sqrt{n})^2\}/(2 - 2\hat{\sigma}_n^2), \quad (22)$$

$\Sigma x(t - 1)^2/n^2$ is completely determined by $\hat{\alpha}_n$, $x(n)/(\hat{\sigma}_n\sqrt{n})$ and $\hat{\sigma}_n^2$. Therefore set $\eta_n = x(n)/(\hat{\sigma}_n\sqrt{n})$. It follows from (22) that the first-order conditional information loss given η_n

$$E\left[\underline{\mathrm{Cov}\left\{\frac{1}{\sigma^2 n^2}\sum_{t=1}^{n} x_n(t - 1)^2 \cdot n(\hat{\alpha}_n - \alpha_n) \mid n(\hat{\alpha}_n - \alpha_n), \sqrt{n}(\sigma_n^2 - \sigma^2), \eta_n\right\}}\mid\eta_n\right]$$

is equal to zero, because the conditioning statistics completely determine $\Sigma x_n(t - 1)^2/n^2$. Namely, η_n satisfies the condition (C2). Since $x_n(n)/\sqrt{n}$ is asymptotically distributed as $N(0, \frac{1}{2}(\sigma^2/\alpha)(e^{2\alpha} - 1))$, η_n is exactly not asymptotically ancillary in general. However, it satisfies the condition (C1), because the Fisher information of η_n and $\hat{\sigma}^2$ are of order $O(1)$ and $O(n)$ respectively. Accordingly, it would pertain to use the conditional distribution of $\hat{\alpha}_n$ given $\eta_n = x_n(n)/(\sqrt{n}\hat{\sigma}_n)$ for statistical inference purposes on α_n.

4.2   Conditional distribution of the ML estimate

Let $\{x_n(t), t = 0, \cdots, n\}$ be the array as given in (19). Let $M(\lambda_1, \lambda_2, \lambda_3)$ be the joint moment generating function of the three statistics $\int_0^1 u_\alpha(t)db(t)$, $\int_0^1\{u_\alpha(t)\}^2 dt$ and $\{u_\alpha(1)\}^2/\sigma^2$; then $M(\lambda_1, \lambda_2, \lambda_3)$ has the following representation.

Lemma 2

$$M(\lambda_1, \lambda_2, \lambda_3) = \left[\frac{(U + R)\exp(U - R) - (U - R)\exp(U + R)}{2R}\right]^{-1/2}$$

$$\cdot[1 - 2\lambda_3 S]^{-1/2}, \tag{23}$$

where

$$R(\lambda_1, \lambda_2) = \{\alpha^2 + 2\lambda_1\alpha\sigma^2 - 2\lambda_2\sigma^2\}^{1/2}, \quad U(\lambda) = \alpha + \lambda\sigma^2$$

and

$$S(\lambda_1, \lambda_2) = \{\exp(R) - \exp(-R)\}/\{(U + R)\exp(-R) - (U - R)\exp(R)\}.$$

Proof Let $M_n(\lambda_1, \lambda_2, \lambda_3)$ be the joint moment generating function of $\Sigma_{t=1}^{n}\varepsilon(t)x_n(t - 1)/n$, $\Sigma_{t-1}^{n}x_n(t - 1)^2/n^2$, and $x_n^2/(n\sigma^2)$. Set $p_n = 2 + 2U/n + R^2/n^2$, $q_n = 1 - U/n$ and $r_n = 1 - 2\lambda_3/n$. Then a line of calculations parallel to White (1958) gives

$$M_n(\lambda_1, \lambda_2, \lambda_3) = [c_1 s_n^n + c_2 t_n^n]^{-1/2},$$

where

$$s_n, t_n = \{p_n \pm \sqrt{p_n^2 - 4q_n^2}\}/2$$

and

$$c_1 = (r_n - t_n)/(s_n - t_n), \; c_2 = -(r_n - s_n)/(s_n - t_n).$$

Since $\lim_{n \to \infty} s_n^n = \exp(U + R)$ and $\lim_{n \to \infty} t_n^n = \exp(U - R)$, the limit of $M_n(\lambda_1, \lambda_2, \lambda_3)$ is obtained as in the lemma. $\square$

Remark 2 Note that $S(\lambda_1, \lambda_2)$ is real and positive if $|\alpha| \neq 0$ and $|\lambda_1|$ and $|\lambda_2|$ are sufficiently small, or if $\alpha = 0$ and $\lambda_1 > 0$, $\lambda_2 < 0$ and $|\lambda_2|$ is sufficiently small. Also note that the substitution $\lambda_3 = 0, \alpha = 0, \sigma = 1$ leads to

$$\det D_n = \cos\sqrt{2\lambda_1} - \frac{\lambda_1}{\sqrt{2\lambda_2}} \sin\sqrt{2\lambda_2} \; .$$

The expression was originally given by White (1958).

The conditional asymptotic distribution of $n(\hat{\alpha}_n - \alpha_n)$ given $x_n^2(n)/(n\hat{\sigma}^2)$ is derived from the conditional joint moment generating function $M(\lambda_1, \lambda_2 \mid x)$ of $\int_0^1 u_\alpha db(t)$ and $\int_0^1 \{u_\alpha(t)\}^2 dt$ given $\{u_\alpha(1)/\sigma\}^2 = x$. Let $F(z \mid x)$ denote the asymptotic conditional distribution function; namely

$$F(z \mid x) = \Pr \left\{ \int_0^1 u_\alpha(t) db(t) / \int_0^1 \{u_\alpha(t)\}^2 dt < z \mid (u_\alpha(1)/\sigma)^2 = x \right\}.$$

Theorem 4 *We have*

$$M(\lambda_1, \lambda_2 \mid x) = \left[\frac{e^{2\alpha} - 1}{\alpha} \right]^{1/2} \left[\frac{R}{\exp(R) - \exp(-R)} \right]^{1/2}$$

$$\exp\left[-x \left\{ (2S)^{-1} - \frac{\alpha}{e^{2\alpha} - 1} \right\} \right] \qquad (24)$$

and

$$F(z \mid x) = \frac{1}{2} - \frac{1}{\pi} \int_0^\infty \frac{\mathscr{I}_m[M(i\lambda, -iz\lambda \mid x)]}{\lambda} d\lambda, \qquad (25)$$

where R and S are as defined in Lemma 2 and $\mathscr{I}_m$ indicates the imaginary part of the argument.

Proof Since $\{u_\alpha(1)/\sigma\}^2$ is distributed as $[(e^{2\alpha} - 1)/2\alpha]\chi^2(1)$, where $\chi^2(1)$ is a χ^2 random variable with one degree of freedom, it follows that the conditional joint moment generating function $M(\lambda_1, \lambda_2 \mid x)$ of $\int_0^1 u_\alpha(t) db(t)$ and $\int_0^1 \{u_\alpha(t)\}^2 dt$ given $\{u_\alpha(1)/\sigma\}^2 = x$ is expressed in view of the Bartlett formula (1938) as

$$M(\lambda_1, \lambda_2 \mid x) = \left[\frac{e^{2\alpha} - 1}{\alpha}\right]^{1/2} \left[\frac{R}{\exp(R) - \exp(-R)}\right]^{1/2}$$

$$\exp\left[-x\left\{(2S)^{-1} - \frac{\alpha}{e^{2\alpha} - 1}\right\}\right]. \tag{26}$$

The conditional distribution function is then obtained by inverting $M(i\lambda, -iz\lambda \mid x)$

$$F(z \mid x) = \lim_{\alpha \to \infty} \lim_{u \to \infty} \frac{1}{2\pi} \int_{-u}^{u} \frac{e^{-i\lambda\alpha} - 1}{i\lambda} M(i\lambda, -iz\lambda \mid x) d\lambda$$

$$= \frac{1}{2} - \frac{1}{\pi} \int_0^\infty \frac{\mathscr{I}_m[M(i\lambda, -iz\lambda \mid x)]}{\lambda} d\lambda$$

(see Kendall and Stuart (1977, p. 99)). □

Dealing with explosive autoregressive processes, Basawa and Brockwell (1984) showed that if the autoregressive coefficient α_n in (19) is fixed as $\alpha_n = c$ and $c > 1$, the conditional distribution of a suitably standardized ML estimate $\hat{\alpha}_n$ given $x(n)$ is asymptotically normal. This Basawa–Brockwell asymptotics is obtained as the limiting case of theorem 4 when $\alpha \to \infty$. Namely:

Theorem 5 *The conditional distribution of*

$$\alpha^{-1} e^\alpha \int_0^1 u_\alpha(t) db(t) / \int_0^1 \{u_\alpha(t)\}^2 dt$$

given $u_\alpha(1)^2 / \sigma^2 = \alpha^{-1}(e^{2\alpha} - 1)y$ tends to the normal distribution with mean 0 and variance σ^2/y as $\alpha \to \infty$.

Proof It follows from (24) by direct calculation that

$$\lim_{\alpha \to \infty} M\{0, \alpha^2 e^{-2\alpha}\lambda \mid \alpha^{-1}(e^{2\alpha} - 1)y\} = \exp\left(\frac{1}{2}\lambda\sigma^2 y\right).$$

Therefore given $u_\alpha(1)^2 = \alpha^{-1}(e^{2\alpha} - 1)y$, the conditional asymptotic distribution of $\int_0^1 u_\alpha(t)^2 dt$ as $\alpha \to \infty$ degenerates to the point $\frac{1}{2}\sigma^2 y$, whence, in order to derive the conditional asymptotic. distribution of $\alpha^{-1} e^\alpha \int_0^1 u_\alpha(t) db(t)/\int_0^1 \{u_\alpha(t)\}^2 dt$, it suffices to consider $\alpha e^{-\alpha} \int_0^1 u_\alpha(t) db(t)/(\frac{1}{2}\sigma^2 y)$, whose moment generating function is given by

$$M_\alpha(\lambda) = M(2\alpha e^{-\alpha}\lambda/(\sigma^2 y), 0 \mid \alpha^{-1}(e^{2\alpha} - 1)y).$$

Again by direct evaluation of (24) we have

$$\lim_{\alpha \to \infty} M_\alpha(\lambda) = \exp\left(\frac{1}{2}\frac{\sigma^2}{y}x^2\right),$$

where the right-hand side member is the moment generating function of normal distribution with mean 0 and variance σ^2/y. $\square$

4.3 Conditional stochastic representation

Numerical evaluation of the condition distribution $F(z\,|\,x)$ in theorem 4 requires numerical integration as given by Knight and Satchell (1993) who deal with the unconditional distribution function of $\hat{\alpha}_n$ for an AR(1) process. Although theorem 4 might be formally extended to multivariate near-integrated autoregressive processes, the numerical multiple integration involved would be intractable for higher-order multiplicity. This section gives the asymptotic conditional stochastic representation of $n(\hat{\alpha}_n - \alpha_n)$ given $(x(n)/\sigma^2)^2$ which has the merit of indicating Monte Carlo simulations for the asymptotic conditional distribution. The importance of stochastic representation and the Monte Carlo simulation based on it become evident especially when we must deal with higher-order multivariate distributions.

On the analogy of the Brownian bridge, define the Ornstein–Uhlenbeck (O–U) bridge $\{v_\alpha(t), 0 \le t \le 1\}$ with zero initial and terminal values by the stochastic integral

$$v_\alpha(t) = \exp(\alpha - t)[\exp(-2\alpha) - \exp(-2\alpha t)]$$

$$\cdot \int_0^t \frac{\exp(-s\alpha)}{\exp(-2\alpha) - \exp(-2\alpha s)} db(s), \tag{27}$$

where $b(t)$ is the Brownian motion with variance $\mathrm{Var}\{b(1)\} = \sigma^2$. In term of the stochastic differential equation, the process is expressed by

$$dv_\alpha(t) = \frac{\alpha[\exp(-\alpha t) + \exp(-2\alpha + \alpha t)]}{\exp(-2\alpha) - \exp(-2\alpha t)} v_\alpha(t) + db(t)$$

provided that $v_\alpha(0) = 0$. The next lemma is a straightforward consequence of the definition (27).

Lemma 3 *For t_1, t_2 such that $0 \le t_1 \le t_2 \le 1$, we have*

$$E\{v_\alpha(t_1)v_\alpha(t_2)\} = \frac{\sigma^2}{2\alpha}\exp\{\alpha(t_1 + t_2)\}\{1 - \exp(-2\alpha t_1)\}$$

$$\cdot \left[1 - \frac{1 - \exp(-2\alpha t_2)}{1 - \exp(-2\alpha)}\right].$$

Let $w(t)$ be the residual of the linear regression of $u_\alpha(t)$ on to $u_\alpha(1)$; namely

$$w_\alpha(t) = u_\alpha(t) - \beta(t)u_\alpha(1) \qquad 0 \le t \le 1,$$

where

$$\beta(t) = \{\exp(-2\alpha t) - 1\}\exp(-\alpha + \alpha t)/\{\exp(-2\alpha) - 1\}. \qquad (28)$$

Lemma 4 *The process* $\{w_\alpha(t)\}$ *is stochastically independent of* $u_\alpha(1)$ *and has the same covariance structure as* $\{v_\alpha(t)\}$. *Since they are Gaussian processes, this implies that* $\{w_\alpha(t)\}$ *and* $\{v_\alpha(t)\}$ *have the same finite-dimensional distributions.*

Proof The independence follows from the construction of $\{w_\alpha(t)\}$. The direct calculation leads to the second statement. $\square$

Set

$$\gamma(\alpha) = \frac{\exp(-2\alpha)}{\{\exp(-2\alpha) - 1\}^2}\left[\frac{\exp(2\alpha) - \exp(-2\alpha)}{2\alpha} - 2\right].$$

Theorem 6 *Given* $u_\alpha(1)/\sigma = x$, $n(\hat{\alpha}_n - \alpha_n) + \alpha$ *has asymptotically the same distribution as*

$$\frac{1}{2}\sigma^2(x-1)\Big/\left[\int_0^1 v_\alpha(t)^2 dt + 2\sigma x \int_0^1 \beta(t)v_\alpha(t)dt - \sigma^2 x^2\gamma(\alpha)\right], \qquad (29)$$

where $\{v_\alpha(t)\}$ *is the O–U bridge given in* (26).

Proof It follows from (28) that

$$\int_0^1 \beta(t)^2 dt = \frac{\exp(-2\alpha)}{\{\exp(-2\alpha) - 1\}^2}\left[\frac{\exp(2\alpha) - \exp(-2\alpha)}{2\alpha} - 2\right] = \gamma(\alpha).$$

The three statistics $\sum_{t=1}^n x_n(t-1)\varepsilon(t)/n$, $\sum_{t=1}^n x(t-1)^2/n^2$, and $x(n)^2/n\hat{\sigma}^2$ are asymptotically jointly distributed as $\int_0^1 u_\alpha(t)db(t)$, $\int_0^1 u_\alpha(t)^2 dt$, and $u_\alpha(1)^2/\sigma^2$ where $\int_0^1 u(t)db(t) = \frac{1}{2}[u(1)^2 - 2\alpha\int_0^1 u(t)^2 dt - \sigma^2]$. Therefore we have

$$n(\hat{\alpha}_n - \alpha_n) \Rightarrow \frac{\sigma^2(x-1)}{2\int_0^1 u_\alpha(t)^2 dt} - \alpha,$$

and also we have, in view of lemma 3

$$\int_0^1 u_\alpha(t)^2 dt = \int_0^1 w_\alpha(t)^2 dt + 2u_\alpha(1)\int_0^1 \beta(t)w_\alpha(t)dt + u_\alpha(1)^2\gamma(\alpha). \quad \square$$

5 POSSIBLY NON-STATIONARY VAR PROCESSES

This section considers two types of VAR processes; section 5.1 extends the results of the previous section to near-integrated VAR processes, introducing the multivariate Ornstein–Uhlenbeck bridges and section 5.2 deals with cointegrated VAR processes.

5.1 The near-integrated VAR model

Suppose this time $\{b(t), 0 \le t \le 1\}$ is an r-vector Brownian motion such that $b(0) = 0$ and $\text{Cov}\{b(1)\} = \Phi$. The r-vector O–U process $\{u(t), 0 \le t < \infty\}$ is defined by the stochastic differential equation

$$du(t) = \Gamma u(t)dt + db(t)$$

(Γ is an $r \times r$ matrix) so that it has the solution

$$u(t) = \exp(t\Gamma)u(0) + \int_0^t \exp\{\Gamma(t-s)\}db(s), \tag{30}$$

where $\exp\{t\Gamma\}$ is defined as the exponential of the matrix $t\Gamma$. The O–U process with $u(0) = 0$ has the covariance matrix such that for $t_1 \le t_2$

$$E\{u(t_1)u(t_2)^*\} = \exp(t_1\Gamma)\left[\int_0^{t_1} \exp(-s\Gamma)\Phi\exp(-s\Gamma^*)ds\right]\exp(t_2\Gamma^*).$$

Define the matrix-valued function $F(t)$ by

$$F(t) = \int_0^t \exp(-s\Gamma)\Phi\exp(-s\Gamma^*)ds;$$

and define the vector-valued O–U bridge $\{v(t), 0 \le t \le 1\}$ with zero initial and terminal values by the stochastic integral

$$v(t) = \exp(t\Gamma)\{F(1) - F(t)\}\int_0^t [\exp(s\Gamma)(F(1) - F(s))]^{-1}db(s). \tag{31}$$

Then the covariance of $\{v(t)\}$ is given as

$$\begin{aligned}
&E\{v(t_1)v(t_2)^*\} \\
&= \exp(t_1\Gamma)\{F(1) - F(t_1)\}[\{F(1) - F(t_1)\}^{-1} - F(1)^{-1}] \\
&\quad \cdot \{F(1) - F(t_2)\}\exp(t_2\Gamma^*) \\
&= \text{Cov}\{u(t_1), u(t_2)\} - \text{Cov}\{u(t_1), u(1)\}\text{Cov}\{u(1), u(1)\}^{-1}\text{Cov}\{u(1), u(t_2)\}
\end{aligned}$$

which is equal to the covariance between $u(t_1) - \beta(t_1)u(1)$ and

$u(t_2) - \beta(t_2)u(1)$, where $\beta(t)$ is the regression coefficient matrix, namely $\beta(t) = E\{u(t)u(1)^*\}[E\{u(1)u(1)^*\}]^{-1}$.

Suppose that $\{z_n(t), -a \le t \le n\}, n = 1, 2, \cdots$, is an array of r-vector AR processes generated by

$$\Delta z_n(t) = n^{-1}\Gamma z_n(t-1) + \sum_{j=1}^{a-1} \Gamma(j)\Delta z_n(t-j) + e(t), \tag{32}$$

where $z_n(-a), \cdots, z_n(0)$ are given and $\{e(t), t \in J\}$ is a Gaussian white-noise process with $E(e(t)) = 0$ and $E(e(t)e(t)^*) = \Sigma$. Suppose also that the zeros of $1 - \Sigma_{j=1}^{a-1}\Gamma(j)z^j$ are all outside of the unit circle. Let the symbol $[x]$ indicate the greatest integer not exceeding x and set $y_n(t) = z_n([nt]), 0 \le t \le 1$. The next theorem is a straightforward multi-dimensional extension of Chan and Wei (1987) and Phillips (1987) and the result is stated without proof.

Theorem 7 *The processes $\{y_n(t), 0 \le t \le 1\}$ weakly converge to the O–U process $\{u(t); 0 \le t \le 1\}$ which has the representation (31) for $u(0) = 0$ and for the Brownian motion $\{b(t)\}$ such that*

$$\text{Cov}\{b(1)\} = \{I_r - \Sigma_{j=1}^{a-1}\Gamma(j)\}^{-1}\Sigma\{I_r - \Sigma_{j=1}^{a-1}\Gamma^*(j)\}^{-1}.$$

Set $A_n = I_r + n^{-1}\Gamma$ and let $\hat{A}_n$ be the maximum-likelihood estimate of A_n.

Theorem 8 *The pair $\{\hat{A}_n, z_n(n)/\sqrt{n}\}$ constitutes an asymptotically first-order sufficient statistic and $z_n(n)/\sqrt{n}$ is a first-order ancillary statistic.*

Proof Define the statistic $\tilde{A}$ by

$$\tilde{A} = \int_0^1 db(t)u(t)^* \left[\int_0^1 u(t)u(t)^*dt\right]^{-1}.$$

Then, since $n(\hat{A}_n - A_n) = n^{-1}\Sigma e(t)z_n(t-1)^*[n^{-2}\Sigma z_n(t-1)z_n(t-1)^*]^{-1} + o_p(1)$, we have $n(\hat{A}_n - A_n) \Rightarrow \tilde{A}$, in view of theorem 7. Let P be the matrix

$$\frac{1}{2\pi}\int_{-\pi}^{\pi} \left\{\sum_{j=1}^{a-1}\Gamma(j)e^{-ij\lambda}\right\}\left\{I - \sum_{k=1}^{a-1}\Gamma(k)e^{-ik\lambda}\right\}^{-1}$$

$$\Sigma\left\{I - \sum_{k-1}^{a-1}\Gamma(k)^*e^{ik\lambda}\right\}^{-1}\left\{\sum_{j=1}^{a-1}\Gamma(j)^*e^{ij\lambda}\right\}d\lambda;$$

then in view of (31), we have

$$u(1)u(1)^* = \Gamma\int_0^1 u(t)u(t)^*dt + \int_0^1 u(t)u(t)^*dt\Gamma^* + \int_0^1 u(t)u(t)^*dt\tilde{A}^*$$

$$+ \tilde{A}\int_0^1 u(t)u(t)^*dt + (P + \Sigma). \tag{33}$$

Denote by $\otimes$ the Kronecker product and by Vec the operator which transforms a matrix into a column vector by stacking the column of the matrix one underneath the other. Then (33) implies that

$$\text{Vec}\left[\int_0^1 u(t)u(t)^*dt\right] = [I_r \otimes (\Gamma + \tilde{A})$$

$$+ (\tilde{A} + \Gamma) \otimes I_r]^{-1}\text{Vec}[u(1)u(1)^* - (P + \Sigma)];$$

that is to say, $\int_0^1 u(t)u(t)^*dt$ is determined by $u(1)$ and $\tilde{A}$. For a finite sample, this implies that, as far as the first-order asymptotic approximation is concerned, the sum of square $n^{-2}\Sigma_{t=1}^n z_n(t-1)z_n(t-1)^*$ is completely determined by the ML estimate $\hat{A}_n$ and the terminal value $n^{-1/2}z_n(n)$. Thus it follows from (17) that $\hat{A}_n$ and $n^{-1/2}z_n(n)$ constitute a first-order sufficient statistic. The second statement is evident. $\square$

It follows from (33) that

$$\text{Vec}[\tilde{A}] = \left[\int_0^1 u(t)u(t)^*dt \otimes I_r + I_r \otimes \int_0^1 u(t)u(t)^*dt\right]^{-1}$$

$$\cdot \text{Vec}\left[u(1)u(1)^* - \left\{\Gamma\int_0^1 u(t)u(t)^*dt + \int_0^1 u(t)u(t)^*dt\Gamma^*\right\} - (P + \Sigma)\right].$$

Since the process $v(t) = u(t) - \beta(t)u(1)$ is independent of $u(1)$, conditionally given $u(1) = c$, $\text{Vec}[\tilde{A}]$ has the same distribution as

$$[V(v,c) \otimes I_r + I_r \otimes V(v,c)]^{-1}\text{Vec}[cc^*$$

$$- \{\Gamma V(v,c) + V(v,c)\Gamma^*\} - (P + \Sigma)], \tag{34}$$

where

$$V(v,c) = \int_0^1 \{v(t) + \beta(t)c\}\{v(t) + \beta(t)c\}^*dt$$

and $v(t)$ is the O–U bridge given in (31) for $\Phi = \{1 - _{j=1}^{a-1}\Gamma(j)\}^{-1}$ $\Sigma\{I - \Sigma_{j=1}^{a-1}\Gamma(j)^*\}^{-1}$.

Although the numerical inversion of a higher-order multivariate characteristic function is formidable, the numerical evaluation of the conditional distribution of $\text{Vec}[\tilde{A}]$ is feasible by means of Monte Carlo simulations of $V(v,c)$ via the generation of the discretized version of the O–U bridge $\{v(t_k)\}$ for $t_k = k/m$, $k = 0, 1, \cdots, m-1$; namely, the $v(t_k)$s are generated by

$$v(t_k) = \exp(t_k\Gamma)\{F(1) - F(t_k)\}\sum_{l=0}^k \exp((l/m)\Gamma)[F(1)$$

$$- F(l/m)]^{-1}\Delta b(l+1),$$

where the $\Delta b(l)$; $l = 1, \cdots, m$, are i.i.d. pseudo-random numbers with $N[0, m^{-1/2}\{I - \Sigma_{j=1}^{a-1}\Gamma(j)\}^{-1}\Sigma\{I - \Sigma_{j=1}^{a-1}\Gamma(j)^*\}^{-1}]$.

5.2   Conditional inference for cointegrated time series

Let $\{z(t), t \geq -a\}$ be a Gaussian r-vector AR process generated by

$$\Delta z(t) = AB^* z(t-1) + \sum_{j=1}^{a-1} \Gamma(j)\Delta z(t-j) + e(t), \tag{35}$$

where A and B are full-rank $r \times r_1$ matrices $(0 < r_1 < r)$ and the $\Gamma(j)$s are $r \times r$ matrices and the $e(t)$s $(t \in J)$ are Gaussian white noise with $E\{e(t)\} = 0$ and $\text{Cov}\{e(t)\} = \Sigma$. As shown in Johansen (1988), $\{\Delta z(t), t \geq -p\}$ is stationary Gaussian process having the representation

$$\Delta z(t) = \sum_{j=0}^{\infty} G(j)e(t-j) \tag{36}$$

with exponentially decreasing coefficients $G(j)$. For the purpose of identification of B, assume that ith component of the ith column vector of B is equal to 1, for $i = 1, \cdots, r_1$. Set $r_2 = r - r_1$ and let Λ be the $r \times r_2$ matrix whose columns are obtained by the successive Schmidt orthogonalization by the projection of each unit vector $\lambda_j(j \geq r_1 + 1)$ on the linear space spanned by the column vectors of B and $\lambda_{r_1+1}, \cdots, \lambda_{j-1}$, where λ_j is the column unit vector with 1 for the jth component. This identification has the merit of determining B and Λ uniquely. Although this modeling is more restrictive than Johansen's, it is less so compared with Phillips' triangular model. In order to deal with the first-order information structure of this model, only the parameter B of the likelihood function matters.

As in (17), the first-order information loss of the ML estimate $\hat{B}$ with respect to B is given by

$$E[\text{Cov}\{n^{-1}\partial L_n(B)/\partial b_{ij} \mid T(\hat{B} - B)\}]. \tag{37}$$

Since the information amount of the ML estimates $\hat{A}$, $\hat{\Gamma}(j)$ and $\hat{\Sigma}$ are of order $O(n)$, they can be ignored. It follows from (36) that the process $\{\Delta z(t)\}$ has the spectral density matrix

$$f(\lambda) = \frac{1}{2\pi}\left(\sum_{j=0}^{\infty} G(j)e^{-i\lambda j}\right)\Sigma\left(\sum_{j=0}^{\infty} G(j)e^{-i\lambda j}\right)^*,$$

whence the serial covariances are obtained by

$$E(\Delta z(t)\Delta z(t-l)^*) = \int_{-\pi}^{\pi} e^{il\lambda}f(\lambda)d\lambda. \tag{38}$$

Set $y(t-1) = B^*z(t-1)$; then in view of the relationship (35), we have

$$E(y(t-1)\Delta z(t-l)^*) = (A^*A)^{-1}$$

$$\cdot \left\{ \int_{-\pi}^{\pi} A^* \left[I - \sum_{j=1}^{a-1} \Gamma(j)e^{-i\lambda j} \right] e^{il\lambda j} f(\lambda)d\lambda \right\} \tag{39}$$

and also

$$E(y(t-1)y(t-1)^*) = (A^*A)^{-1}$$

$$\cdot \left[A^*\mathrm{Cov}\{\Delta z(t), y(t-1)\} - \sum_{j=1}^{a-1} A^*\Gamma(j)\mathrm{Cov}\{\Delta z(t-j), y(t)\} \right]. \tag{40}$$

Denote the partial covariance between $\Delta z(t)$ and $y(t-1)$, after elimination of the effects due to $\Delta z(t-1), \cdots, \Delta z(t-a+1)$, by

$$\text{Partial Cov}\{\Delta z(t), y(t-1)\} = \begin{bmatrix} \Omega_{11} & \Omega_{12} \\ \Omega_{21} & \Omega_{22} \end{bmatrix},$$

where the Ω_{ij} $(i,j = 1,2)$ are determined by the relationships (37) through (38). Set $G = \Sigma_{j=0}^{\infty} G(j)$ and let $\{b(t)\}$ be an r-vector Brownian motion such that $\mathrm{Cov}\{b(1)\} = \Sigma$. As Johansen (1988) showed, we have

$$T(\hat{B} - B) \Rightarrow I(u,v) \equiv \Lambda\left(\int_0^1 u(t)u(t)^*dt \int_0^1 u(t)dv(t)^* \right)^{-1},$$

where $u(t) = \Lambda^*Gb(t)$ and $v(t) = \Omega_{22}(\Omega_{21}\Omega_{11}^{-1}\Omega_{12})\Omega_{21}\Omega_{11}^{-1}b(t)$. We have then

$$\underline{\mathrm{Var}} \left\{ \frac{\partial L(B)}{n\partial B_{ij}} \Big| n(\hat{B} - B) \right\}$$

$$= \mathrm{Var}\left\{ \sum_{k,l=1}^{r} I_{kl}(u,v) \int_0^1 (Gw(t))_i (Gw(t))_k^* dt (A^*\Sigma^{-1}A)_{jl} \Big| I(u,v) \right\}. \tag{41}$$

The right-hand side member of (41) is in general positive since $I(u,v)$ does not functionally determine $(Gb(t))_i(Gb(t))_k^*$. For this cointegration model, the information loss is recovered by means of conditioning on $C_n = n^{-2}\Sigma_{t=1}^{n}\{\hat{\Lambda}_n^*z(t)\}\{\hat{\Lambda}_n^*z(t)\}^*$, where $\hat{\Lambda}$ is the ML estimate of Λ. Since we have

$$\frac{1}{n^2} \sum_{t=1}^{n} z(t)z(t)^* \Rightarrow [(B,\Lambda)^*]^{-1}$$

$$\cdot \begin{bmatrix} 0 & 0 \\ 0 & \Lambda^*\int_0^1 [Gb(t)(Gb(t))^*]dt\Lambda \end{bmatrix} [(B,\Lambda)]^{-1},$$

and since $\hat{\Lambda}$ tends to Λ in probability in view of the construction of $\hat{\Lambda}$ and Λ,

$$C_n \Rightarrow \Lambda^* \int_{-\pi}^{\pi} [Gw(t)(Gw(t))^*]dt\Lambda.$$

Consequently, given $n(\hat{B} - B)$ and C_n, we have

$$\underline{\text{Var}} \left\{ \frac{\partial L(B)}{n\partial B_{ij}} \mid n(\hat{B} - B), C_n \right\} = 0,$$

which implies that $\hat{B}$ and C_n are first-order sufficient. Set

$$D_n = [\hat{\Lambda}^* \hat{G} \hat{\Sigma} \hat{G}^* \hat{\Lambda}]^{-1/2} C_n [\hat{\Lambda}^* \hat{G} \hat{\Sigma} \hat{G}^* \hat{\Lambda}]^{-1/2}$$

where

$$\hat{G} = G(\hat{A}, \hat{B}, \hat{\Gamma}(1), \cdots, \hat{\Gamma}(a - 1)).$$

Then

$$D_n \Rightarrow [\Lambda^* G\Sigma G^* \Lambda]^{-1/2} \Lambda^* \int_{-\pi}^{\pi} [Gb(t)(Gb(t))^*]dt\Lambda[\Lambda^* G\Sigma G^* \Lambda]^{-1/2}$$

and the distribution of the right-hand side member is independent of the model parameters. Thus D_n is a first-order ancillary statistic which recovers the information loss of $\hat{B}$. It follows from Johansen (1988, lemma 8) that, given D_n, we have

$$T(\hat{B} - B) \Rightarrow N\left[0, \Lambda \int_0^1 u(t)u(t)^* dt\Lambda^* \otimes \text{Cov}\{v(1)\} \right].$$

6   EMPIRICAL ANALYSIS

For the purpose of illustration, this section gives some estimation results of the measure of one-way effects. The used data are the quarterly observations of gross domestic production (GDP), call rates, $M_2 + CD$, and exports and imports in Japan during the period of the first quarter of 1975 through the fourth quarter of 1994 (all variables are nominal and in logarithmic scale except for call rates). The fitted model is the cointegrated AR(5) process; namely, for $t = 0, 1, 2, \cdots$

$$\Delta z(t) = A_0 + \sum_{j=1}^{3} A_j D_j(t) + \Pi z(t - 1) + \sum_{k=1}^{4} \Pi_k \Delta z(t - k) + e(t), \quad (42)$$

where the $e(t)$s are Gaussian white noise with mean 0 and covariance matrix Σ, the D_js are the seasonal dummy variables, and $\Pi = AB^*$. The cointegration ranks (denoted by r_1 in figures 1.3) are determined by means of the stepwise application of Johansen and Juselius's (1990) τ trace test with a 10 percent significance level for each step (starting from zero rank). The parameters are estimated by the ML method and the estimates are denoted by $\hat{\Pi}$, $\hat{\Pi}_j$, $\hat{\Sigma}$, respectively. Let $\hat{C}(e^{-i\lambda})$ be the adjoint matrix of

$$I_r - I_r e^{-i\lambda} - \hat{\Pi}e^{-i\lambda} - \sum_{j=1}^{4} \hat{\Pi}_j(e^{-ik\lambda} - e^{-i(k+1)\lambda})$$

as given in section 3 and then the measures of one-way effect from $\{y(t)\}$ to $\{x(t)\}$ are estimated based on the frequency response estimate $\hat{\Lambda}(e^{-i\lambda}) = \hat{C}(e^{-i\lambda})\hat{\Sigma}^{1/2}$ and on the spectral density estimate $\hat{f}(\lambda) = \frac{1}{2\pi}\hat{\Lambda}(e^{-i\lambda})\hat{\Lambda}(e^{-i\lambda})^*$.

Figures 1.3a through 1.3h show the estimated $M_{y\to x}(\lambda)$ and $M_{y\to x}$ for respective pairs of x and y, where $z(t) = (x(t)^*, y(t)^*)^*$. Although the estimation of $M_{y\to x}(\lambda)$ was actually conducted on possible combinations of (x, y) for the five variables, only a few are exhibited because of the space. Notable findings are as follows:

(1) The one-way effects from call rates to other variables are comparatively strong in general; the overall measures from call rates to GDP, $M_2 + CD$, exports and imports are 4.38, 4.48, 8.64, and 4.15 respectively. In contrast, the one-way effects from GDP or imports to call rates are as small as 0.001 or 0.01 respectively.

(2) Neither effects from GDP to $M_2 + CD$ nor from $M_2 + CD$ to GDP are notable.

(3) The one-way effects from money supply to exports or imports are weak whereas the effects from exports or imports to money supply are strong. The overall measure of GDP and exports to $M_2 + CD$ is 1.73 whereas GDP and imports to $M_2 + CD$ is 3.20.

(4) The causal characteristics in three- or four-variable models are mostly similar to the two-variable models; but sometimes inconsistency appears. For example, the measure of one-way effect from call rates and money supply to GDP is estimated as $M_{y\to x} = 4.01$. It is notably strong but not quite consistent with the measure when y is call rates only where $M_{y\to x} = 4.38$ as given in (1). The reason for this is that the estimations are based on different models.

(5) Peak at the zero frequency occurs for some frequency-wise measures, but in all such cases the contribution of $M_{y\to x}(\lambda)$ near the zero frequency turns out to be small.

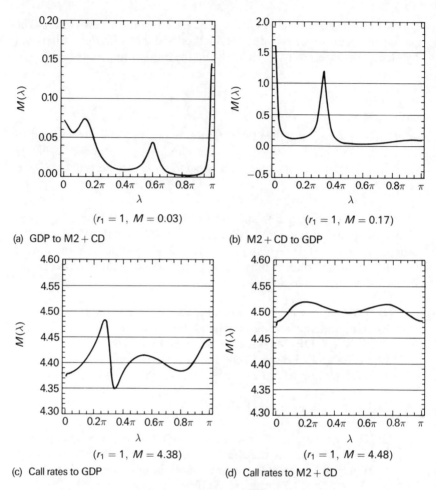

Figure 1.3 Estimated measures of one-way effect (r_1 is the cointegration rank and M is the overall measure)

The presented analysis of this section is exclusively based on point estimation and hence is still of limited scope. Such issues as partial causal analysis or statistical significance of the estimates remain to be investigated.

7   CONCLUSION

Recent proliferation of econometric literature on non-stationary time-series analysis is enriching our way of looking at and interpreting economic time-series data. Aiming at accommodating non-stationary time series, this

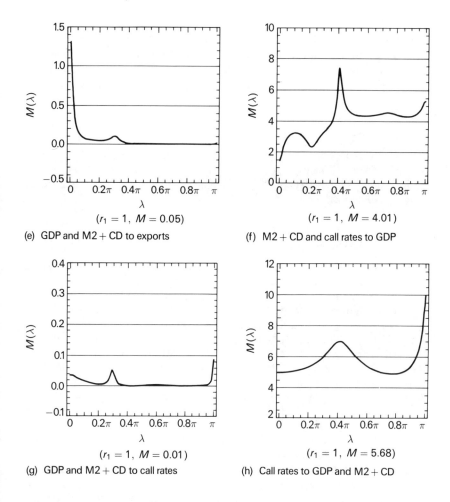

(e) GDP and M2 + CD to exports

($r_1 = 1$, $M = 0.05$)

(f) M2 + CD and call rates to GDP

($r_1 = 1$, $M = 4.01$)

(g) GDP and M2 + CD to call rates

($r_1 = 1$, $M = 0.01$)

(h) Call rates to GDP and M2 + CD

($r_1 = 1$, $M = 5.68$)

chapter extended to non-stationary processes the conventional frequency domain analysis of causal relations between stationary processes. The extension enables isolating and measuring long-run effects between stochastic-trended economic time series. Also the chapter gave a statistical estimation procedure for such measures and showed related empirical applications.

The ML estimate is no longer asymptotically sufficient for non-ergodic models in contrast to standard ergodic parametric models for which it is asymptotically first-order sufficient. For such models, we proposed inference based on the conditional distribution of the ML estimate given a pertinent ancillary statistic which fills the information loss the ML estimate suffers from. We also introduced a family of vector-valued Ornstein–Uhlenbeck bridges for the purpose of conditional stochastic representation of the ML estimate for near-integrated processes.

Note

The research was supported in part by the Scientific Research Grant No. C0763019 of the Japanese Ministry of Education and Science. I am very grateful to Professors H. K. van Dijk and J. H. Stock for helpful comments and to Yao Feng for computational assistance.

References

Bartlett, M. S. (1938). "The characteristic function of a conditional statistic." *Journal of the London Mathematical Society*, 13(1): 62–7.
Basawa, I. V. and Brockwell, P. J. (1984). "Asymptotic conditional inference for regular nonergodic models with an application to autoregressive processes." *The Annals of Statistics*, 12(1): 161–71.
Chan, N. H. and Wei, C. Z. (1987). "Asymptotic inference for nearly nonstationary AR(1) processes." *The Annals of Statistics*, 15(3): 1050–63.
Engle, R. F. and Granger, C. W. J. (1987). "Co-integration and error-correction: representation, estimation and testing." *Econometrica*, 55(2): 251–76.
Geweke, J. (1982). "Measurement of linear dependence and feedback between multiple time series." *Journal of the American Statistical Association*, 77(378): 304–13.
(1984). "Measures of conditional linear dependence and feedback between time series." *Journal of the American Statistical Association*, 79(388): 907–15.
Granger, C. W. J. (1963). "Economic process involving feedback." *Information and Control*, 6(1): 28–48.
(1969). "Investigating causal relations by cross-spectrum methods." *Econometrica*, 39(3): 424–38.
(1980). "Testing for causality: a personal viewpoint." *Journal of Economic Dynamics and Control*, 2(4): 329–52.
Granger, C. W. J. and Lin, J. L. (1995). "Causality in the long run." *Econometric Theory*, 11(3): 530–6.
Hosoya, Y. (1977). "On the Granger condition for non-causality." *Econometrica*, 45(7): 1735–6.
(1988). "The second-order Fisher information." *Biometrika*, 75(2): 265–74.
(1991). "The decomposition and measurement of the interdependency between second-order stationary processes." *Probability Theory and Related Fields*, 88: 429–44.
Hosoya, Y. and Taniguchi, M. (1982). "A central limit theorem for stationary

processes and the parameter estimation of linear processes." *The Annals of Statistics*, 10(1): 132–53; (1993). "Correction." *The Annals of Statistics*, 21(2): 1155–7.

Hosoya, Y., Tsukuda, Y., and Terui, N. (1989). "Ancillarity and the limited information maximum-likelihood estimation of a structural equation in a simultaneous equation system." *Econometric Theory*, 5(3): 385–404.

Johansen, S. (1988). "Statistical analysis of cointegration vectors." *Journal of Economic Dynamics and Control*, 12(213): 231–54.

Johansen, S. and Juselius, K. (1990). "Maximum likelihood estimation and inference on cointegration with application to the demand for money." *Oxford Bulletin of Economics and Statistics*, 52(2): 169–210.

Kendall, M. and Stuart, A. (1977). *The Advanced Theory of Statistics*, vol. I, 4th edn. London: Charles Griffin & Co.

Knight, J. L. and Satchell, S.E. (1993). "Asymptotic expansions for random walks with normal errors." *Econometric Theory*, 9(3): 363–76.

Lütkepohl, H. and Reimers, H.-E. (1992). "Granger-causality in cointegrated VAR processes." *Economics Letters*, 40(3): 263–8.

Phillips, P. C. B. (1987). "Towards a unified asymptotic theory for autoregression." *Biometrika*, 74(3): 535–47.

Phillips, P. C. B. and Durlauf, S. N. (1986). "Multiple time series regression with integrated processes." *Review of Economic Studies*, 53(175): 473–95.

Rozanov, Y. A. (1967). *Stationary Random Processes*. San Francisco: Holden-Day.

Stock, J. H. and Watson, M. W. (1988). "Variable trends in economic time series." *Journal of Economic Perspectives*, 2(3): 147–74.

Toda, H. and Phillips, P. C. B. (1994). "Vector autoregressions and causality." *Econometrica*, 61(6): 1367–93.

White, J. S. (1958). "The limiting distribution of the serial correlation coefficient in the explosive case." *The Annals of Mathematical Statistics*, 29(4): 1188–97.

CHAPTER 2

Cointegration, long-run comovements, and long-horizon forecasting

James H. Stock

1   INTRODUCTION

Over the past decade, methodological advances in modeling and analyzing long-run relations have produced fundamental changes in the way that econometricians approach economic time-series data. Prior to these advances, econometric analysis of time-series data either ignored the problems which arise when regressors are highly persistent, or used a preliminary transformation to induce stationarity followed by analysis of the transformed variables. Now, the concept of cointegration, developed by Granger (1981), Granger and Weiss (1983), and Engle and Granger (1987), which builds on work on error correction models (Sargan (1964) and Davidson, Hendry, Srba, and Yeo (1978)), provides a powerful and widely adopted framework for studying long-run as well as short-run relations.

This chapter undertakes a selective survey of some recent theoretical work and focuses on some problems which remain in this area.[1] The thesis of this chapter is that, although the modern methodology of cointegration/unit root analysis provides a compelling framework for some problems, such as short-term forecasting using long-run information, for some applications this methodology has important limitations. The limitations of concern here arise when some of the regressors have an autoregressive root which is large but, in contrast to the basic assumption of cointegration analysis, not exactly one.

In empirical work it is common that an econometrician has evidence that the largest autoregressive root α in a series x_t is nearly one. For example, confidence intervals for the largest autoregressive root are given in table 2.1 for three economic time series (the confidence intervals are computed by inverting the Dickey–Fuller (1979) t-statistic using the method in Stock (1991)). While the Dickey–Fuller test fails to reject a unit root for all three

Table 2.1. *Largest autoregressive roots of three economic time series*

Series	#Obs.	DF t-stat	OLS estimate of sum of lags	Median-unbiased estimate of α	90% Confidence interval
US real GDP, 70:I–94:IV (quarterly)	100	−2.96	0.887	0.872	(0.744, 1.029)
Australian wool price 74:3–94:12 (monthly)	250	−2.28	0.959	0.989	(0.940, 1.015)
90-day US Treasury bill rate, 61:9–94:12 (monthly)	400	−2.12	0.971	0.985	(0.962, 1.006)

Notes: The "DF *t*-stat" is the Dickey–Fuller (1979) *t*-statistic testing the unit root hypothesis. The OLS estimate of the sum of the lag coefficients is one plus the coefficient on the lagged level term in the Dickey–Fuller regression. The median-unbiased estimate and the 90 percent confidence interval were computed by inverting the Dickey–Fuller test statistic using the method of Stock (1991). The number of lags in the Dickey–Fuller regression was selected by the Bayes information criterion (BIC). For the 90-day US Treasury bill rate, a constant was included and the BIC chose 12 lags; for US real GDP and Australian wool prices, a constant and a time trend were included and BIC chose 1 and 0 lags, respectively.

series, neither do we reject roots close to one. Absent economic theory that specifies a particular value of α, the confidence interval in table 2.1 provides no objective basis for inferring, for example, that for the Australian wool price series α = 1.00 rather than 0.98.

This chapter is organized around three of the practical problems which motivated much of the original theoretical work on unit roots and cointegration:

A Tests of the hypothesis that x_{t-1} does not predict y_t when x_t is serially correlated and possibly has a unit autoregressive root. A leading example is tests in linear rational expectations models with highly autocorrelated regressors, for example, tests of whether stock returns are predictable by lagged variables such as the dividend yield (cf. Mankiw and Shapiro (1985), Fama (1991)).

B Inference about the parameters of long-run relationships. A classic example is construction of a confidence interval for the income elasticity in a levels consumption function relating log consumption and log income.

C Long-run forecasting and the construction of forecast intervals for y_{T+k} or x_{T+k}, where the forecast horizon k is long in the sense that it is a non-trivial fraction λ (e.g., $\lambda \geq 0.1$) of the sample size T.

In each of these problems, if x_t is I(1) ($\alpha = 1$) then the methods of stationary time-series econometrics will generally be inappropriate but these three problems are well handled (asymptotically) using the technology of integration and cointegration. However, if α is large but not exactly one, then both the I(0) approach, which treats x_t as stationary, and the I(1) approach, which treats x_t as having an exact unit root, can produce systematic errors in inference.

In each of these three problems, the relevant distributions depend on the nuisance parameter α. A common method for handling this nuisance parameter is first to pretest for unit roots and/or cointegration and, when indicated, to impose a unit root and/or cointegration. Assuming the pretest is ideal in the sense that type I errors tend to zero in large samples, this yields asymptotically valid inference when $\alpha = 1$.[2] If, however, α is large but not necessarily one, this pretest strategy will not deliver reliable inference in problems A, B, or C, even with an ideal pretest. For example, in problem A, controlling size asymptotically means that, under the null hypothesis, the limit of the supremum (taken over α) of the rejection rate should be at most 5 percent, say. Although the supremum of the limit of the rejection rates under this pretest procedure is controlled when α is fixed, the limit of the supremum is not, and this results in size distortions which persist asymptotically. A Monte Carlo experiment in section 3 demonstrates that these size distortions can be large, particularly in problem B.

Section 2 gives precise definitions of concepts related to I(1) regression and briefly reviews the modern approach to problems A, B, and C; this will be referred to as the "I(1)" methodology. Section 3 examines the performance of the I(1) approach to problems A, B, and C when α is large but not exactly one. While perhaps this could be done using finite sample techniques, such a treatment would be cumbersome at best. Because the key source of difficulties is the single nuisance parameter α when it is large, the analysis of section 3 uses an asymptotic approach which provides great simplifications over a finite-sample treatment, yet retains the essential dependence on α. This is done by modeling the largest autoregressive root as local to unity, specifically, in a T^{-1} neighborhood of one. It has been

documented elsewhere (see Stock (1994a) for references) that this device
provides good approximations to finite sample distributions when α is large
and there are 100 or more observations. Thus, these asymptotics provide a
magnifying glass which focuses on the problematic dependence of the
finite-sample distributions on α.

Section 5 contains a review of several alternative, currently unconven-
tional approaches to problems A–C. One general conclusion, presented in
section 6, is that, despite the significant advances in this literature,
state-of-the-art techniques fail to provide acceptable inference in these
important applications. This should not be taken as a sweeping indictment
of research on cointegration and unit roots, for indeed much of value has
been learned. However, the conclusion suggests that current techniques
typically do not address adequately some of the problems which originally
motivated this line of research, and this in turns suggests directions for
future work.[3]

2 THE I(1) APPROACH TO PROBLEMS A, B, AND C

In this chapter, a univariate time series $u_t, t = 1, \ldots, T$, is said to be I(0) if the
sequence of its rescaled partial sums, $T^{-\frac{1}{2}}\Sigma_{t=1}^{[Ts]}u_t$ (where $[\cdot]$ denotes the
greatest lesser integer function), obeys a functional central limit theorem
and converges weakly to a stochastic process which is proportional to a
Brownian motion. This is implied by various primitive assumptions
including mixing conditions (Herrndorf (1984)) or by u_t being a one-
summable linear moving average of martingale difference sequences (Hall
and Heyde (1980), Phillips and Solo (1992)). In this section, attention is
limited to the case that the stochastic component of x_t is I(1).[4]

2.1 Problem A: regression when x_t is I(1)

When x_t is I(1), problem A is a special case of the more general regression
problem

$$y_t = \delta_1'z_{1t} + \delta_2 + \delta_3'z_{3t} + \xi_t, \tag{1}$$

where ξ_t is a martingale difference sequence with respect to its lags and to
$(z_{1t}', z_{3t}')'$ and its lags, $E\xi_t^2 = \sigma_\xi^2, z_{1t}$ consists of I(0) variables (taken without
loss of generality to have mean zero), and z_{3t} consists of I(1) variables which
are not themselves cointegrated (the spectral density of Δz_{3t} at frequency
zero has full rank). Problem A is nested in (1) by letting $z_{1t} = x_{t-1}$ if x_t is I(0)
and omitting z_{3t}, or by letting $z_{3t} = x_{t-1}$ if x_t is I(1) and omitting z_{1t}.

Another example of a regression nested in (1) is the augmented Dickey–Fuller (1979) regression, which is obtained by setting $z_{1t} = (\Delta y_{t-1}, \ldots, \Delta y_{t-p})$ and $z_{3t} = y_{t-1}$.

Asymptotic distribution theory for ordinary least squares (OLS) estimation of (1) has been developed by Chan and Wei (1988), Park and Phillips (1988), and Sims, Stock, and Watson (1990). Asymptotically, the moment matrix of the regressors is block diagonal; $\{T^{\frac{1}{2}}(\hat{\delta}_1 - \delta_1),$ $T^{\frac{1}{2}}(\hat{\delta}_2 - \delta_2), T(\hat{\delta}_3 - \delta_3)\}$ have a joint limiting distribution where $T^{\frac{1}{2}}(\hat{\delta}_1 - \delta_1)$ is independent of $\{T^{\frac{1}{2}}(\hat{\delta}_2 - \delta_2), T(\hat{\delta}_3 - \delta_3)\}$; and $T^{\frac{1}{2}}(\hat{\delta}_1 - \delta_1)$ $\xrightarrow{d} N(0, (Ez_{1t}z'_{1t})^{-1}\sigma_\xi^2)$. Although tests involving only δ_1 have conventional χ^2 distributions, in general, the limiting distribution of the Wald tests involving δ_3 is non-standard (an exception is when the cross spectral density of $(\Delta z_{3t}, \xi_t)$ is zero at frequency zero, in which case the distribution is χ^2). In general, the Wald test statistic has a representation as a functional of Brownian motion. For example, in the augmented Dickey–Fuller example above, the t-statistic testing $\delta_3 = 1$ has the Dickey–Fuller (1979) "$\hat{t}_\mu$" distribution. When the distribution depends on nuisance parameters, such as a spectral density at frequency zero, it typically can be computed by simulation using consistent estimators of the nuisance parameters.

The implication of these results for application A is that the distribution of the t-statistic testing whether x_{t-1} predicts y_t will in general have either a $N(0,1)$ distribution if $|\alpha| < 1$, or a non-standard distribution if $\alpha = 1$. The non-standard distribution is readily computed by Monte Carlo simulation.

2.2   Problem B: cointegrating regressions

Let Y_t be an $n \times 1$ vector time series. Engle and Granger (1987) defined Y_t to be cointegrated if each element of Y_t is I(1) but there exists an $n \times r$ matrix β of full column rank with $1 \le r < n$ such that $\beta' Y_t$ is I(0). Various forms are available for representing cointegrated variables. Three useful, equivalent forms are the levels vector autoregression (VAR) representation, the vector error correction model (VECM) form (Engle and Granger (1987)), and the triangular form (Campbell and Shiller (1987), Phillips (1991)); for discussion see Engle and Yoo (1991) and Watson (1994). Here, we work with the triangular form, in which Y_t is partitioned into an $r \times 1$ vector y_t and a $k \times 1$ vector x_t where $k = n - r$, and the cointegrating matrix is conformably normalized as $\beta = (I_r, -\theta)'$, where θ is $r \times k$. Including a constant term, the triangular form is

$$x_t = \mu_x + v_t, \Delta v_t = u_{1t}, \tag{2a}$$

$$y_t - \theta x_t = \mu_y + u_{2t}, \tag{2b}$$

where $u_t = (u'_{1t}, u'_{2t})'$ is a I(0) vector process, the spectral density of which at frequency zero, Ω, has full rank. It is assumed throughout that v_0 is $O_p(1)$.

Various estimators are available for estimation of the cointegrating parameter θ. Although the OLS estimator of the regression of y_t on x_t is consistent, in general it has bias of order $O(T^{-1})$ and in finite samples this bias can be large (Stock (1987)). This $O(T^{-1})$ bias can be avoided by using an asymptotically efficient estimator. Many such estimators have been proposed (see Hargreaves (1994) for a partial list). Some are readily motivated as Gaussian maximum likelihood estimators (MLEs), or approximate MLEs, in one of the representations above. One of the most common MLEs is the Johansen (1988)/Ahn and Reinsel (1990) estimator, which is the Gaussian MLE in a finite order VECM; see Watson (1994) for further discussion.

The triangular form provides a convenient alternative starting point for developing efficient estimators. As a motivation, suppose that u_t is Gaussian, and orthogonalize the system by projecting u_{2t} on to u_{1t}, that is, write $u_{2t} = E(u_{2t} \mid \{u_{1t}\}) + \tilde{u}_{2t} = d(L)u_{1t} + \tilde{u}_{2t}$, where $d(L)$ is two sided. By construction, $\{\tilde{u}_{2t}\}$ and u_{1t} are independent. Thus (2b) becomes, $y_t = \theta x_t + d(L)\Delta x_t + \tilde{u}_{2t}$. Thus, if $d(L)$ has finite order, by the theory of seemingly unrelated regressions, θ can be estimated efficiently by generalized least squares (GLS) regression of y_t onto x_t and leads and lags of Δx_t. However, because x_t is I(1), the GLS and OLS estimators of θ in this regression are asymptotically equivalent, so OLS estimation of this augmented regression asymptotically yields the MLE. This approach can be thought of as OLS with additional variables and variants of it have been studied by Phillips and Loretan (1991), Saikkonen (1991), and Stock and Watson (1993); the particular estimator just described is the "dynamic OLS" (DOLS) estimator of Stock and Watson (1993).

The various efficient estimators of cointegrating vectors have the same asymptotic distribution, which is a random mixture of normals (Johansen (1988), Phillips (1991)). Importantly, standard Wald statistics testing q restrictions on θ, based on an efficient estimator $\hat{\theta}$, have asymptotic χ^2_q distributions. Thus, despite the non-standard nature of the problem and the non-standard distribution of the OLS estimator and the MLE, hypothesis tests on θ and confidence intervals for θ can be constructed using standard techniques. These powerful yet simple methods for inference on θ are arguably the greatest single accomplishment of cointegration theory. These results are the foundation of the now-conventional cointegration approach to problem B, in which an efficient estimator is used to estimate the cointegration coefficients and confidence intervals are constructed based on this estimate and its standard error.

2.3   Problem C: long-run forecasting

Depending on the orders of integration and cointegration, standard models for generating forecasts are the levels VAR (stationary series), the VECM (cointegrated series), and the differences VAR (I(1), no cointegration). If the series being forecast do not contain deterministic trends, then computation of asymptotic prediction intervals conditional on the chosen model is straightforward. Parameter uncertainty becomes more important when the series contain deterministic trend components (Sampson (1991)).

3   DISTRIBUTIONS WHEN α IS LOCAL TO UNITY

This section analyzes the behavior of the I(1) procedures of the previous section when α is large but not necessarily one. As discussed in the introduction, in theory this could be done using finite sample techniques, but a simpler and more incisive treatment is possible by focusing on the problematic large root, in particular setting $\alpha = 1 + c/T$, where c is a constant, and using asymptotic approximations. In this case, the stochastic part of $T^{-\frac{1}{2}}x_{[Ts]}$ converges to an Ornstein–Uhlenbeck process (Bobkoski (1983), Cavanagh (1985), Chan (1988), Chan and Wei (1987), and Phillips (1987)). Distributions of functionals of the Ornstein–Uhlenbeck process are described by the single parameter c; however, c is not consistently estimable, although confidence intervals for c can be constructed (Stock (1991), Andrews (1993)).

The asymptotic power of efficient tests of an autoregressive unit root with fixed size against the alternative $\bar{a} = 1 + \bar{c}/T$ is strictly less than one (Elliott, Rothenberg and Stock (1996), Rothenberg and Stock (1995)). It follows that if the critical value tends to infinity with the sample size, as needed if the test is to distinguish I(1) from I(0) processes consistently, then the asymptotic power of the test against the local-to-unity alternative is zero.[5]

3.1   Problem A with local-to-unity regressors[6]

Consider the bivariate model

$$x_t = \mu_x + v_t, (1 - \alpha L)v_t = u_{1t}, u_{1t} = a(L)^{-1}\varepsilon_{1t} \tag{3a}$$

$$y_t = \mu_y + \gamma x_{t-1} + u_{2t}, u_{2t} = \varepsilon_{2t}, \tag{3b}$$

where $a(L) = \Sigma_i^k = a_i L^i, a_0 = 1$. Suppose interest is in testing the hypothesis $\gamma = \gamma_0$; in the linear rational expectations application discussed in the introduction, $\gamma_0 = 0$. Further suppose that $\varepsilon_t = (\varepsilon_{1t}, \varepsilon_{2t})'$ is a martingale difference sequence with $E(\varepsilon_t \varepsilon_t' | \varepsilon_{t-1}, \varepsilon_{t-2}, \dots) = \Sigma = [\sigma_{ij}], \sup_t E\varepsilon_{it}^4 < \infty, i = 1, 2, Ev_0^2 < \infty$, and the roots of $a(L)$ are fixed and greater than one.

Let $\Omega = [\omega_{ij}]$ be 2π times the spectral density of $u_t = (u_{1t}, u_{2t})'$ at frequency zero, so $\omega_{11} = \sigma_{11}/a(1)^2$ and $\omega_{22} = \sigma_{22}$. Assume that the functional central limit theorem $T^{-\frac{1}{2}}\Sigma_{t=1}^{[T\lambda]}(u_{1t}/\omega_{11}^{\frac{1}{2}}, u_{2t}/\omega_{22}^{\frac{1}{2}})' \Rightarrow W$ is satisfied, where "$\Rightarrow$" denotes weak convergence on $D[0,1]$, where $W = (W_1, W_2)'$ is a two-dimensional Brownian motion with covariance matrix $\bar{\Omega} = [\bar{\omega}_{ij}]$, where $\bar{\omega}_{11} = \bar{\omega}_{22} = 1$ and $\bar{\omega}_{12} = \bar{\omega}_{21} = \delta = \omega_{12}/(\omega_{11}\omega_{22})^{\frac{1}{2}}$.

Let t_γ denote the t-statistic testing the $\gamma = \gamma_0$ in (3b). Then, under the null

$$t_\gamma \Rightarrow \tau_{2,c} = \delta\tau_{1,c} + (1-\delta^2)^{\frac{1}{2}}z \tag{4}$$

where $\tau_{1,c} = (\int J_c^{\mu 2})^{-\frac{1}{2}}\int J_c^\mu dW_1, \tau_{2,c} = (\int J_c^{\mu 2})^{-\frac{1}{2}}\int J_c^\mu dW_2, J_c^\mu(s) = J_c(s) - \int_0^1 J_c$ $(r)dr, J_c$ is the Ornstein–Uhlenbeck process which obeys $dJ_c(s) = cJ_c(s) + dW_1(s)$, and z is a standard normal random variable distributed independently of (W_1, J_c).

Evidently the limiting distribution of t_γ depends on both c and δ. Because δ is consistently estimable (in general, by the sample cross-spectral correlation of u_t at frequency zero, here by the sample correlation between the OLS residuals $\hat{\varepsilon}_{1t}$ and $\hat{\varepsilon}_{2t}$), δ will be treated as known. However, c is not consistently estimable, and, if $\delta \neq 0, t_\gamma$ has a non-standard asymptotic distribution. Thus asymptotic inference cannot in general rely on simply substituting a suitable estimator $\hat{c}$ for c when selecting critical values for tests of γ.

Suppose the test based on t_γ is performed following a consistent pretest for a unit root in x_t: if the unit root test rejects, the $N(0,1)$ distribution is used, if not, (4) is used. Evidently, the size of this procedure is $\sup_c P[\delta\tau_{1c} + (1-\delta^2)^{\frac{1}{2}}z \notin (d_0, d_1)]$, where (d_0, d_1) are the critical values of $\tau_{2,0}$. Numerical evaluation indicates that the size can be large. For example, for tests with nominal level 5 percent, if $\delta = 0.9$ the size is 0.33 if a constant is included in the regression (3b), and is 0.64 if a constant and time trend are included.

3.2   Problem B with local-to-unity regressors

Consider the triangular form in the bivariate case with intercepts and where α is the largest root of x_t

$$x_t = \mu_x + v_t, (1 - \alpha L)v_t = u_{1t} \tag{5a}$$

$$y_t = \mu_y + \theta x_t + u_{2t} \tag{5b}$$

where the value of θ, θ_0, is taken to be non-zero. As in (3), let u_t have spectral density Ω and assume $T^{-\frac{1}{2}}\Sigma_{t=1}^{[T\lambda]}(u_{1t}/\omega_{11}^{\frac{1}{2}}, u_{2t}/\omega_{22}^{\frac{1}{2}}) \Rightarrow W$, where W is defined following (3). Note that, in contrast to (3b), in (5b) u_{2t} is not restricted to be a martingale difference sequence but rather is a general I(0) process.

If α is local to unity, then consistent pretests for unit roots and cointegration in (x_t, y_t) would lead one to conclude that x_t and y_t are I(1) and cointegrated, so that θ should be estimated using an efficient cointegration estimator $\hat{\theta}$. However, Elliott (1994) showed that, even if u_t has a parametric structure of known order, if $\alpha = 1 + c/T$ and θ is a scalar, $\hat{\theta}$ and its t-statistic t_θ testing $\theta = \theta_0$ have the limits

$$\{T(\hat{\theta} - \theta_0), t_\theta\} \Rightarrow \{ - \omega_{11}^{-\frac{1}{2}}\omega_{2.1}^{\frac{1}{2}}\int J_c^\mu dW_{2.1}(\int J_c^{\mu 2})^{-1}$$
$$- c\delta\omega_{11}^{-\frac{1}{2}}\omega_{22}^{\frac{1}{2}}, z - c\delta(1 - \delta^2)^{-\frac{1}{2}}(\int J_c^{\mu 2})^{\frac{1}{2}}\}, \qquad (6)$$

where $W_{2.1}$ is a standard Brownian motion, $w_{2.1} = w_{22} - w_{21}^2/w_{11}$, and z is a standard normal random variable, where $(z, W_{2.1})$ are independent of (W_1, J_c). As in problem A, the limiting random variables in (6) have distributions which depend on c.

The implications parallel those for problem A. Tests of $\theta = \theta_0$ typically exhibit size distortions, even asymptotically, and confidence intervals for θ can have coverage rates less than their nominal asymptotic value. In fact, the asymptotic size of the Wald test of $\theta = \theta_0$ based on t_θ with standard normal critical values is arbitrarily close to one, depending on δ.

3.3   Problem C with local-to-unity regressors

The presence of a large but not necessarily unit root substantially complicates the problem of making long-run point and interval forecasts.[7] To be concrete, consider the bivariate cointegrating model (5), where it is further supposed that (u_{1t}, u_{2t}) obeys a VAR(p) with all roots strictly outside the unit circle and where $Ev_0^2 < \infty$. Then in levels, (x_t, y_t) obeys a VAR($p + 1$) with one root local to the unit circle.

Consider two alternative forecasting strategies. In the first, the econometrician computes forecasts from a levels VAR. In the second, the econometrician pretests for the number of unit roots in the system, after which forecasts are constructed using the levels VAR (no unit roots detected), a VECM with $\alpha = 1$ imposed (one unit root), or a differences VAR (two unit roots). To simplify the analysis, suppose that a consistent I(0)/I(1) classification procedure is used, so that in sufficiently large samples the pretest strategy, applied to (5), delivers a VECM with probability approaching one. Finally, suppose that p is known.

At short horizons, the levels VAR and the pretest procedures yield asymptotically equivalent forecasts and asymptotically valid prediction intervals when $\alpha = 1 + c/T$.[8] However, the problem of long-term forecasting is more complicated. Specifically, model the forecast horizon k as being a constant fraction λ of the sample size, so $k = [T\lambda]$. Let $x_{s|t}$ denote the conditional mean of x_s given $(x_t, y_t, x_{t-1}, y_{t-1}, \ldots)$. Then $T^{-\frac{1}{2}}(x_{T+k|T}, y_{T+k|T}) = T^{-\frac{1}{2}}e^{c\lambda}(x_T, \theta x_T) + o_p(1)$. Moreover, $T^{-\frac{1}{2}}x_{T+k} \Rightarrow e^{c\lambda}J_c(1) + \phi_c(\lambda)$ and $T^{-\frac{1}{2}}(y_{T+k} - \theta x_{T+k}) \xrightarrow{p} 0$, where J_c is as defined in section 3.1, $\phi_c(\lambda)$ is $N(0, \omega_{11}(1 - e^{2c\lambda})/(1 - e^{2c}))$, and ϕ_c and J_c are independent.

First consider the levels VAR procedure, with forecasts $(\hat{x}_{T+k|T}, \hat{y}_{T+k|T})$. Then $T^{-\frac{1}{2}}(x_{T+k} - \hat{x}_{T+k|T}) \Rightarrow [1 - e^{(c^*-c)\lambda}]e^{c\lambda}J_c(1) + \phi_c(\lambda)$, where c^* is a $O_p(1)$ random variable which depends on J_c; thus the long-run levels VAR forecast is conditionally biased of order $O(T^{\frac{1}{2}})$, with conditional bias $E[T^{-\frac{1}{2}}(x_{t+k} - \hat{x}_{T+k|T})|x_T] \to E[(1 - e^{(c^*-c)\lambda})|J_c(1)]e^{c\lambda}J_c(1)$. The magnitude of this bias depends on the distribution of c^* which depends on nuisance parameters. Typically, however, c^* will be biased toward zero, so the forecast will be biased toward zero as well. Moreover, because the conditional distribution of x_{T+k} depends on c but c is not consistently estimated, prediction intervals computed using standard (stationary) first-order asymptotics will have incorrect tolerance levels.

The pretest estimator is also conditionally biased and produces invalid long-run prediction intervals. For the pretest forecast, $T^{-\frac{1}{2}}(x_{T+k} - \hat{x}_{T+k|T}) \Rightarrow (1 - e^{c\lambda})J_c(1) + \phi_c(\lambda)$. The limiting conditional bias is $E[T^{-\frac{1}{2}}(x_{T+k} - \hat{x}_{T+k|T})|x_T] \to (1 - e^{c\lambda})J_c(1)$, which for $c < 0$ is biased away from zero. Imposition of the unit root produces incorrect inference on $e^{c\lambda}$ and $\phi_c(\lambda)$ which results in prediction intervals with an incorrect tolerance level.

As in problems A and B, the central difficulty is the dependence of a key distribution (here, the conditional distribution of (x_{T+k}, y_{T+k})) on c, which cannot be consistently estimated.

3.4 Finite sample simulation

A small Monte Carlo experiment was performed to assess whether these issues are important in sample sizes typically encountered in econometric applications. The design consists of equations for income (y_t), consumption (c_t), and the unforecastable excess returns (r_t) on a portfolio of equities. The parameters of the income autoregression were chosen to be similar to those estimated for US real GDP, 70:I–94:IV (the first series in table 2.1). Accordingly

$$\tilde{\Delta} y_t = 0.3\tilde{\Delta} y_{t-1} + \zeta_{1t}, \tag{7a}$$

$$c_t = \theta y_t + \zeta_{2t}, \tag{7b}$$

$$r_t = \zeta_{3t} \tag{7c}$$

Table 2.2. *Monte Carlo results*

T	α	c	I(0) methodology			I(1) methodology		
			(A)	(B)	(C)	(A)	(B)	(C)
100	1.00	0	0.25	0.83	0.35	0.05	0.94	0.67
	0.975	−2.5	0.15	0.90	0.50	0.07	0.83	0.72
	0.95	−5	0.12	0.93	0.56	0.11	0.66	0.78
	0.90	−10	0.08	0.95	0.62	0.16	0.38	0.86
400	1.00	0	0.25	0.80	0.36	0.05	0.94	0.68
	0.99375	−2.5	0.15	0.88	0.50	0.07	0.84	0.75
	0.9875	−5	0.11	0.91	0.55	0.11	0.63	0.80
	0.975	−10	0.09	0.92	0.62	0.16	0.32	0.90
Nominal			0.05	0.95	0.68	0.05	0.95	0.68

Notes: Columns (A) contain Monte Carlo rejection rates of tests with nominal level 5 percent. Columns (B) contain Monte Carlo coverage rates of confidence intervals with nominal coverage rate 95 percent. Columns (C) contain Monte Carlo coverage rates of prediction intervals with nominal coverage rate 68 percent. The design, statistics and methodologies are described in the text. All regressions are run including a constant, except for the first-differences regression used to generate the I(1) forecasts, in which the constant was supressed. Results are based on 10,000 Monte Carlo replications.

where $\tilde{\Delta} = 1 - \alpha L$, ζ_t is i.i.d. $N(0, \Sigma)$ with $\Sigma_{ii} = 1$, $i = 1, \ldots, 3$, $\Sigma_{12} = 0.8$, $\Sigma_{13} = 0.9$, $\Sigma_{23} = 0.5$, and $\theta = 1$. For $T = 100$, the chosen values of α (1, ·975, ·95, ·90) fall within the 90 percent confidence interval for α for real GDP given in table 2.1; for $T = 400$, the chosen values (1, ·99375, ·9875, ·975) fall within the 90 percent confidence interval for α for the 90-day Treasury bill rate. For both sample sizes, $c = T(\alpha - 1)$ is 0, −2.5, −5 and −10.

Stylized versions of problems A, B, and C are examined by: (A) testing whether y_{t-1} forecasts r_t at the 5 percent significance level in a regression of r_t onto y_{t-1}; (B) constructing a 95 percent confidence interval for θ; and (C) constructing a 68 percent prediction interval for y_{T+k} based on a univariate forecast, where $k = 0.25T$. These problems were analyzed using two methodologies. In the "I(0)" methodology, unit root issues are ignored: in problem A, $N(0, 1)$ critical values were employed to test $\gamma = 0$ using t_γ; in problem B, the confidence intervals for θ were constructed using two stage least squares (TSLS) with y_{t-1} as an instrument (this is asymptotically full information maximum likelihood in (7) when α is unknown); and in problem C the 68 percent prediction interval for y_{T+k} is computed using standard methods after estimating an AR(2) in levels.

In the "I(1)" methodology, the econometrician assumes that $\alpha = 1$ and that (c_t, y_t) are cointegrated.[9] Accordingly, in problem A, the representation (4) is used to obtain critical values for t_y; in problem B, the hypothesis $\theta = 1$ is tested using the Wald test statistic from the MLE for the (c_t, y_t) system (the MLE is the DOLS estimator with contemporaneous Δy_t only); and in problem C, 68 percent prediction intervals for y_{T+k} are computed from OLS estimation of an AR(1) in first differences.

The results are summarized in table 2.2. In confirmation of findings by numerous researchers, when $\alpha = 1$ the I(0) methodology does poorly, with large size distortions in problems A and B and prediction intervals which have low coverage, while the I(1) methodology does well. However, when the root is slightly less than one, the I(1) methodology fails. Confidence intervals for θ based on the efficient cointegrating estimator have low probabilities of containing the true value, and prediction intervals based on $c = 0$ are too wide (they do not reflect long-run mean reversion when $c < 0$). It should be stressed that these problems occur for values of α within the 90 percent confidence intervals for US real GDP and the 90-day Treasury bill rate in table 2.1. Under the local-to-unity nesting, the distortions are relatively stable as the sample size increases for fixed c, which accords with results elsewhere that the local-to-unity asymptotics provide a good guide to the finite distributions.

4   POTENTIAL SOLUTIONS: PROBLEMS A AND B

This section reviews alternative approaches to problems A and B which solve the size distortion problems in certain cases. This discussion focuses on the case of no deterministic terms in either the data generation process or the various statistics, although some remarks are made about extension to the case of deterministic terms. The four approaches reviewed here are conservative tests based on least squares statistics, non-parametric tests based on sign and/or rank statistics, tests of whether the regression errors are I(0), and variable augmentation schemes.[10] A detailed analysis of finite-sample and asymptotic power of these approaches is beyond the scope of this survey (see however Campbell and Dufour (1994, 1995) for problem A).

4.1   Asymptotically conservative intervals and tests

An alternative approach to inference is to use the limiting distributions of the relevant t-statistics, which depend on c, and then to evaluate these for a range of c. Cavanagh, Elliott, and Stock (1995) considered bounds tests in problem A, and their results are briefly reviewed here (also see Dufour (1990), who derived exact bounds tests for regression parameters with Gaussian AR(1) errors and strictly exogenous regressors). The extension of this approach to problem B is then briefly discussed.

First consider problem A, so that (3) holds with $\mu_x = \mu_y = 0$. Critical values for a sup-bound test are chosen so that the test based on t_y has size no more than the prescribed level, uniformly in c. For example, 5 percent critical values can be obtained as the extrema (over c) of the 2.5 percent quantiles of the limiting random variable in (4). Alternatively, valid and less-conservative critical values can be obtained by choosing the upper and lower critical values so that the supremum (over c) of the rejection rate equals the desired level of the test. This test will be conservative in the sense that, for some c, the rejection rate under the null will be less than the level of the test. Tests which are potentially less conservative can be constructed by first computing a $100(1 - \eta_1)$ percent confidence set for c (using Stock's (1991) or Andrews' (1993) method), and then rejecting if t_y rejects using a $100\eta_2$ percent two-sided test based on critical values from (4) for every c in the first-stage confidence set. By Bonferroni's inequality, the combined procedure has size no more than $\eta_1 + \eta_2$. As with the sup-bound tests, η_1 and η_2 can be chosen so that the asymptotic size equals the desired level. Extension of this approach to additional deterministic terms is straightforward.

In theory, the Bonferroni approach can be extended to problem B with some modifications. To be concrete, suppose that θ is estimated using an efficient cointegration estimator which incorrectly imposes $\alpha = 1$ when in fact $\alpha = 1 + c/T$, so that the associated t-statistic testing $\theta = \theta_0$ has the limiting representation in (6). As in (4), the only nuisance parameters entering the second expression in (6) are δ, which is consistently estimable, and c. This permits construction of asymptotic confidence sets for θ given c. A first-stage confidence set for c can be constructed from univariate methods as discussed above. Unlike (4), however, the quantiles of (6) are not bounded in c, so the sup-bound test for the cointegration problem has infinite critical values. It also seems likely that Bonferroni confidence regions based on an efficient cointegration estimator will be quite wide, making this approach less appealing in problem B.

4.2   Non-parametric tests

Campbell and Dufour (1995) consider problem A (with no intercept term) and show that non-parametric tests achieve the desired size under weak conditions on x_t. For example, consider the sign test statistic

$$S(\gamma) = T^{-\frac{1}{2}}\Sigma_{t=2}^{T}\{\mathbf{1}[(y_t - \gamma x_{t-1})x_{t-1} > 0] - \tfrac{1}{2}\}. \tag{8}$$

If the conditional distribution of ε_{2t} given x_{t-1} has median zero, $\{\mathbf{1}(\varepsilon_{2t}x_{t-1} \geq 0)\}$ are i.i.d. Bernoulli random variables under general conditions on x_t, including but not limited to x_t being stationary, I(1), or local to I(1). Thus, under the null $\gamma = \gamma_0$, $S(\gamma_0)$ is a binomial random variable with an asymptotic $N(0, 1/4)$ distribution.

The local asymptotic power function of the sign test can be derived assuming that α is local to one. Specifically, suppose that (3) holds. If $\delta = 0$, the asymptotic power of the sign test of level η (with standard normal critical value d_η) against the alternative $\gamma = b/T$ is

$$P[|2S| > d_\eta] \rightarrow E[\Phi(-d_\eta - 2bf(0)\omega_{11}^{\frac{1}{2}}\int|J_c|)$$
$$+ \Phi(-d_\eta + 2bf(0)\omega_{11}^{\frac{1}{2}}\int|J_c|)], \tag{9}$$

where f is the p.d.f. of ε_{2t} conditional on x_{t-1}.

This approach can be extended to problem B by considering an instrumental variables version of the sign test statistic (8). In the cointegration context, in general x_t is endogenous and u_{2t} is serially correlated, so $\{\mathbf{1}(u_{2t}x_t > 0\}$ are not independent Bernoullis. Suppose, however, that u_{2t} is a $(q-1)$th order moving average process, specifically, that the distribution (with p.d.f. f) of u_{2t} conditional on x_{t-q} has median zero. Accordingly, let

$$R_q(\theta) = T^{-\frac{1}{2}}\Sigma_{t-q}^{T}\{\mathbf{1}[(y_t - \theta x_t)x_{t=q} > 0] - \tfrac{1}{2}\}. \tag{10}$$

Under the null $\theta = \theta_0$, if $\alpha = 1 + c/T$ then $R_q(\theta_0) \xrightarrow{d} N(0, V)$, where $V = \Sigma_{i=-q}^{q}\{\tfrac{1}{2}P[\mathrm{sgn}(u_{2t}) = \mathrm{sgn}(u_{2t-i})] - 1/4\}$, where $\mathrm{sgn}(z)$ is the sign of z. This distribution does not depend on c and thus holds if x_t is I(1) or has a local-to-unit root. A natural estimator for V is $\hat{V}(\theta) = \Sigma_{i=-q}^{q}\mathrm{cov}(\mathbf{1}[(y_t - \theta x_t)x_{t-q} > 0], \mathbf{1}[(y_{t-i} - \theta x_{t-i})x_{t-q-i} > 0])$; then $\hat{V}(\theta_0) \xrightarrow{p} V$ uniformly in c. In (10), x_{t-q} serves the role of an instrument for x_t.

The extension of this approach to a non-zero intercept μ_y in (5b) is not automatic and appears to require joint or preliminary inference about μ_y; cf. Campbell and Dufour (1994).

4.3   Tests for residuals being I(0)

In problem A, y_t has two components, ε_{2t} which is serially uncorrelated and γx_{t-1} which is local to I(1). This suggests testing the hypothesis $\gamma = 0$ by testing whether y_t is a martingale difference sequence against the alternative that it is a random walk plus noise. Results in King (1980) and King and

Hillier (1985) can be used to derive the family of efficient tests of the null that y_t is i.i.d. Gaussian against the alternative that it is the sum of an i.i.d. Gaussian process and an independent (unobserved) Gaussian random walk (Shively (1988)). In the case that the intercept is possibly non-zero, Nyblom and Mäkeläinen (1983) showed that the locally most powerful invariant (LMPI) test of this hypothesis rejects for large values of $L^\mu = T^{-2}\Sigma_{t=1}^T(\Sigma_{s=1}^t y_s^\mu)^2/\hat{\sigma}_y^2$, where $y_s^\mu = y_s - \bar{y}$ and $\hat{\sigma}_y^2 = T^{-1}\Sigma_{t=1}^T y_s^{\mu 2}$, where $\bar{y}$ is the sample mean of y_t (also see Nyblom (1986), Nabeya and Tanaka (1988), Tanaka (1990), and Saikkonen and Luukkonen (1993a)). Under the null, the test has a limiting distribution which is free of nuisance parameters and is the mean square of a scalar Brownian bridge (Anderson and Darling (1952), MacNeill (1978); critical values are tabulated by Nyblom and Mäkeläinen (1983, table 1)).

The L^μ test is valid when μ_y is non-zero and unknown. For comparability to the previous discussion, it is useful to consider a test which imposes $\mu_y = 0$. Saikkonen and Luukkonen (1993a) show that, in the closely related problem of testing for a unit moving average root when the intercept is known to be zero, the LMPI test rejects for large values of

$$L = T\bar{y}^2/(T^{-1}\Sigma_{t=1}^T y_t^2), \qquad (11)$$

which has a χ_1^2 null asymptotic distribution.

Although L and L^μ are derived assuming that x_t is unobserved and is I(1), these tests have power against (3) with $\alpha = 1 + c/T$. The asymptotic representation of L against the alternative $\gamma = b/T$ when (x_t, y_t) satisfy (3) with $\mu_x = \mu_y = 0$ is (Wright (1996))

$$L \Rightarrow [W_2(1) + b(\omega_{11}/\omega_{22})^{\frac{1}{2}}\int J_c]^2. \qquad (12)$$

Note that this limiting distribution depends on δ through the dependence of W_2 and J_c.

The extension of this approach to problem B is straightforward. Here the approach has the intuitive interpretation of testing directly the premise of cointegration that $y_t - \theta x_t$ is I(0) against it being I(1). A technical complication is that, under problem B, the null is that the error correction term is a general I(0) process, whereas in problem A the corresponding error is a martingale difference sequence under the null. However, this complication can be handled either by estimating the spectral density at frequency zero (cf. Park and Choi (1988), Tanaka (1990), and Kwiatkowski et al. (1992)) or by suitable prefiltering (cf. Saikkonen and Luukkonen (1993a, 1993b)). Here, we focus on the first of these approaches.

Specifically, consider (5) with $\mu_y = 0$ and let $u_{2t}(\theta) = y_t - \theta x_t$ and $\tilde{\omega}_{22} = \Sigma_{m=-l_T}^{l_T} k(m/l_T)\hat{\gamma}_{\hat{u}_2}(m)$, where $\hat{\gamma}_x(m) = (T-m)^{-1}\Sigma_{t=|m|+1}^T(x_t - \bar{x})$ $(x_{t-m} - \bar{x})$, k is a kernel weighting function (see Andrews (1991) for a discussion of kernel choice), and $\hat{u}_{2t} = y_t - \hat{\theta}x_t$, where $\hat{\theta}$ is a T-consistent estimator of θ uniformly in c, for example the static OLS estimator or one of the many efficient estimators which impose $\alpha = 1$. Then the suitably modified L statistic is

$$L(\theta) = T\bar{u}(\theta)^2/\tilde{\omega}_{22}. \tag{13}$$

Under suitable conditions on u_{2t} and the truncation parameter l_T (cf. Kwiatkowski *et al.* (1992), Stock (1994b)), if x_t is local to unity then $\tilde{\omega}_{22} \xrightarrow{p} \omega_{22}$ uniformly in c. Thus, under the null hypothesis, $L(\theta_0) \Rightarrow \chi_1^2$, and, under the alternative, $\theta = \theta_0 + b/T$, $L(\theta)$ has the limiting representation (12). It is straightforward to extend these results to the case of an intercept in (5b) using L^μ.

Evidently, when $\mu_y = 0$, $L(\theta)$ can be used to test the null that $\theta = \theta_0$ is a cointegrating vector, and confidence regions for θ can be constructed as the acceptance region of this test. Note that this test has a somewhat different interpretation than the other tests discussed for problem B because the null is the joint null that $\theta = \theta_0$ *and* that the relation is cointegrating, whereas the previous tests maintain the hypothesis that a cointegrating relation exists for $\theta = \theta_0$. In theory, confidence regions for θ_0 constructed using the modified Nyblom–Mäkeläinen statistic can be infinite or empty, either because of a type I error or because no such cointegrating relation exists.[11]

4.4   Variable augmentation schemes

Another approach to problem A is to augment the equation of interest (3b) with additional lags of x_t and then test the significance of the coefficients on all but the final lag. Choi (1993) proposed this approach in the univariate AR(1) model (a test for a unit root), and Toda and Yamamoto (1995) and Dolado and Lutkepohl (1996) proposed it for a general VAR(p). The theoretical justification of this approach is the result summarized in section 2.1 that standard t- and F-tests can be used to test restrictions on coefficients which can be rewritten as coefficients on mean-zero stationary regressors, which can be done for scalar x_t if there are at most $p - d$ linear restrictions, where d is the maximum (integer) order of integration of the regresser. Thus, Wald tests of all but one coefficient have the usual χ^2 asymptotic distribution. Although the results in Toda and Yamamoto (1995) and Dolado and Lutkepohl (1996) are for the exact $\alpha = 1$ case, calculations similar to those in Elliott (1994) can be used to extend this asymptotic χ^2 result to the case that variables are either I(1) or have a local-to-unit root.

Although these variable augmentation tests have correct size for problem A, they have poor power in the direction of a "levels effect," specifically

$\gamma \neq 0$ in (3b). Dolado and Lutkepohl (1996) show that the test has power less than one against alternatives in a $T^{-\frac{1}{2}}$ neighborhood of the null. The procedures in the previous three sections all had non-trivial power against $1/T$ alternatives, so the asymptotic relative efficiency (ARE) of the variable-augmentation test is zero. Of course, if deviations from the null are not in the direction of a levels effect, variable augmentation tests could perform satisfactorily. Currently there appears to be no finite sample study that compares this approach to the previous three approaches.[12]

5   POTENTIAL SOLUTIONS: PROBLEM C

The problem of forecasting in systems with possibly large roots has received less attention than have problems A and B. The treatment here is correspondingly brief and draws on Stock (1995). The discussion focuses on the point forecasting problem, in which the objective is to produce point forecasts which have desirable properties for a range of values of c. Precisely what constitutes a desirable property of a point forecast arguably depends on the application and, potentially, the ultimate user of the forecast. If the forecast is to be the basis of a decision by a private party, then a desirable forecast would be tailored to that individual's loss function and would incorporate the individual's prior beliefs, in accordance with decision theory. Alternatively, if the forecasts are produced on an ongoing basis and are used in general discussions of business plans and public policy, as is typically the case with government forecasts, then it is arguably desirable that the forecasts be unbiased and perform well under some standard loss function, for example squared error loss. This discussion will focus on this second case and concentrate on unbiased forecasting. In the cointegrated VAR considered in section 3.4, the conditional distributions of x_{T+k} and y_{T+k} are $O_p(T^{\frac{1}{2}})$ but $y_{T+k} - \theta x_{T+k}$ is $O_p(1)$. Moreover, the only parameter entering the asymptotic distribution of $T^{-\frac{1}{2}}(x_{T+k} - x_{T+k|T})$ which is not consistently estimable is c. Therefore, little is lost by restricting attention to a univariate AR(1) with a single large root, and this is done for the rest of this section.

Consider the problem of unbiased long-run forecasting. If $\{x_t\}$ is symmetrically distributed around zero, then any odd function of the data is unconditionally unbiased (cf. Magnus and Pesaran (1991)). Because the forecaster knows x_T, however, it seems of little solace that a forecast of, say, $0.5x_T$ is unconditionally unbiased because the forecaster could equally well have observed $-x_T$ as x_T. We therefore adopt the view, enunciated in Phillips (1979), that unconditional unbiasedness is of limited practical interest in forecasting applications, and instead we focus on forecasts which are unbiased conditional on $x_T \geq 0$. In particular, we consider the construction of median unbiased forecasts conditional on $x_T \geq 0$.

In principle, many median unbiased forecasts exist. Let τ_T be a statistic which has an asymptotic distribution that depends only on the true value c. Most if not all asymptotically similar unit root test statistics have this property; cf. Stock (1994a). Let $m(c)$ denote the median of this distribution as a function of c, and let m^{-1} denote its inverse function. If m is monotone then by definition $\hat{c}_m = m^{-1}(\tau_T)$ will exceed c one-half of the time and will be less than c one-half of the time; that is, $\hat{c}_m$ is a median unbiased estimator of c. Suppose τ_T is an even function of the data. Because $e^{c\lambda}$ is non-negative and is monotone in c, $P[e^{\hat{c}_m\lambda}x_T > e^{c\lambda}x_T | x_T \geq 0] = P[\hat{c}_m > c] \rightarrow \frac{1}{2}$, so $e^{\hat{c}_m\lambda}x_T$ is an asymptotically median unbiased long-run forecast of $x_{T+k|T}$ conditional on $x_T \geq 0$ for $k/T = \lambda$.

In practice this requires constructing the median function, a task which can be computationally intensive. This has been done for the Dickey–Fuller (1979) t-statistic and the Sargan–Bhargava (1983)/Bhargava (1986) statistics by Stock (1991) using local-to-unity asymptotics; for the OLS root estimator in an AR(1) by Andrews (1993) using exact sampling results for the Gaussian AR(1); and for Elliott, Rothenberg, and Stock's (1996) family of efficient unit root tests by Stock (1995). Here, we consider the performance of the median unbiased forecast based on one of these test statistics, the Dickey–Fuller t-statistic. For comparison purposes we also consider a levels OLS forecast and a pretest forecast (a 5 percent Dickey–Fuller test is used to decide whether $\{x_t\}$ has a unit root; if it rejects, the levels OLS forecast is used, otherwise $\alpha = 1$ is imposed).

Numerical results are summarized in table 2.3 for a forecast horizon equal to 25 percent of the sample size. The first three columns of results report the fraction of forecasts which fall below the true conditional mean, both as a function of $J_c(1)$ and conditional only on $J_c(1)$ being positive; the final three columns report the root mean squared error (RMSE) around the true conditional mean. Computations were performed using pseudo-random realizations of J_c with 500 observations per draw. The results are presented both conditional on $J_c(1) = j$ and on $J_c(1) > 0$. Results for distributions conditional on $J_c(1)$ were computed by writing the relevant statistics in terms of $J_c(1)$ and (independent) functionals of V_c, where $V_c(s) = J_c(s) - b(s)J_c(1)$, where $b(s) = e^{c(1-s)}(e^{2cs} - 1)/(e^{2c} - 1)$ for c non-zero and $b(s) = s$ for $c = 0$, where V_c and $J_c(1)$ are independent. Results for fixed $J_c(1)$ are based on 5,000 replications; results for $J_c(1) > 0$ are based on 20,000 replications.

These results reveal several features of these forecasts. The OLS forecast is increasingly shifted toward zero as $J_c(1)$ increases. While it is most often biased for c near zero, even for $c = -10$ it is biased toward zero nearly three-quarters of the time. The bias of the pretest procedure is not

Table 2.3. *Performance of various long-term forecasts, univariate* AR(1)

c	$J_c(1)$	% forecasts $< x_{T+k|T}$			RMSE of forecast minus conditional mean		
		OLS	PRE	MUF	OLS	PRE	MUF
0	0.2	1.000	0.538	0.709	0.160	0.055	0.123
	0.4	1.000	0.535	0.631	0.308	0.105	0.238
	0.6	0.997	0.530	0.542	0.432	0.143	0.344
	1.5	0.865	0.511	0.281	0.711	0.195	0.812
	>0	0.96	0.52	0.50	0.50	0.14	0.54
−2.5	0.2	0.977	0.087	0.613	0.077	0.094	0.088
	0.4	0.935	0.061	0.485	0.142	0.187	0.202
	0.6	0.844	0.036	0.338	0.186	0.280	0.359
	>0	0.90	0.07	0.50	0.14	0.21	0.30
−5	0.2	0.888	0.137	0.570	0.040	0.134	0.078
	0.4	0.783	0.074	0.379	0.072	0.276	0.219
	>0	0.83	0.12	0.50	0.07	0.22	0.22
−10	0.2	0.770	0.294	0.503	0.013	0.155	0.041
	0.4	0.570	0.099	0.222	0.033	0.349	0.168
	>0	0.74	0.29	0.50	0.03	0.19	0.11

Notes: The forecasting procedures are: OLS = levels OLS; PRE = pretest using 5 percent Dickey–Fuller (1979) demeaned t-statistic; MUF = forecast using median-unbiased estimator $\tilde{c}$. The procedures are described in the text. Entries are for the distribution conditional on $J_c(1)$ taking on the value in the second column; >0 indicates the distribution is conditional on $J_c(1) > 0$.

monotone in c. For c near zero, the unit root is rarely rejected and the pretest procedure is biased up. As c becomes more negative, the percent of unit root forecasts decreases. The MUF is biased away from zero as $J_c(1)$ increases, a consequence of the positive shift in the conditional distribution of the Dickey–Fuller t-statistic as $J_c(1)$ increases (the series appears more non-stationary). Conditional only on $J_c(1) > 0$, these forecasts are of course median unbiased (within simulation error), although they can have strong conditional bias.

No single estimator has uniformly lowest RMSE. The OLS forecast works well for $c \ll 0$. The MUF is preferable to OLS for $c = 0$ and small terminal values, although it is worse than OLS unconditional on J_c for all c considered. The pretest forecast works well for c nearly zero, but its RMSE increases substantially as c becomes more negative.

Additional research is needed. Although the MUF forecast is median unbiased on average, for certain terminal values it can be badly biased, and it fails to have the smallest RMSE of the three procedures for all c considered. Also, these results apply to point forecasts and do not address prediction intervals.

6   DISCUSSION AND CONCLUSIONS

This chapter has two main points. First, despite important advances over the past decade in our ability to model long-run economic relations, commonly used techniques fail to provide satisfactory solutions to some specific problems of long-run inference, in particular the construction of confidence intervals for and tests of coefficients on regressors which have large autoregressive roots, and to long-run point and interval forecasting. In these applications, the satisfactory performance of existing techniques, which are optimal for the unit root case, hinges critically on the untestable assumption of an exact unit root. This is not to imply that the current unit root and cointegration technology has no valid applications; indeed, consistent point estimation and first-order short-run forecasting are immune to the criticisms made here. However, departures from the unit root assumption which are so small as to be detectable with only low probability can nonetheless produce substantial distortions in inference and forecasts, at least when a regressor is endogenous.

The second point of this chapter is that some new techniques are emerging which are robust to whether the largest root is exactly one. This research is, however, incomplete in several ways. The techniques are disparate and in some cases ad hoc, and as yet there is not a unifying theory. Some of the approaches are closely tied to the linear autoregressive model with large roots, and it might be desirable to consider procedures valid under broader concepts of persistence. This suggests that these and related problems could prove fruitful areas for future research.

A natural question is what lessons for empirical practice arise from this ongoing research. Although any answer is necessarily speculative, this survey provides some clues. At a minimum, researchers using current unit root/cointegration methodology should be cognizant of the sensitivity of long-run forecasts, and of tests and confidence intervals for long-run coefficients, to the empirically untestable assumption of an exact unit root when the regressor in question is endogenous. Unless there are compeling a priori reasons for believing an exact unit root is present, certain empirical conclusions, such as confidence intervals for cointegrating parameters, can be delicate and in the end should be unconvincing to an appropriately skeptical audience. The broader promise of this research is less reliance on unit root and cointegration econometrics as currently conceived, and more credible statements of the uncertainty associated with long-run forecasts and with the parameters in long-run relations. In some cases, this uncertainty might actually be less than is implied by current techniques, such as long-run forecasting using a VECM when roots are in fact (just) stationary, although one suspects it typically will exceed that estimated by current procedures. More precise measures of uncertainty in turn should facilitate achieving the ultimate goal of more reliable inference about economic relations and policy choices.

Notes

This chapter was prepared for presentation at the Seventh World Congress of the Econometric Society, Tokyo, Japan, August 23, 1995. The author thanks Ronald Bewley, Juan Dolado, Graham Elliott, Max King, Thomas Rothenberg, Victor Solo, Herman van Dijk, Mark Watson, Kenneth Wallis, and workshop participants at the University of New South Wales, Sydney, Australia for helpful suggestions and/or comments on an earlier draft. Jeffrey Amato and Jonathan Wright provided excellent research assistance. This research was supported in part by National Science Foundation grant no. SBR-9409629.

1 A complete review of the literature is not attempted here; rather, the interested reader is referred to the survey and/or textbook treatments of including Banerjee *et al.* (1993), Hamilton (1994, chapters 18 and 19), Johansen (1995), and Watson (1994). The theory of inference about cointegrating relations is developed in (*inter alia*) Engle and Granger (1987), Phillips and Durlauf (1986), Stock (1987), Johansen (1988, 1991), Ahn and Reinsel (1990), Stock and Watson (1988, 1993), Engle and Yoo (1991), Phillips and Ouliaris (1990), Phillips (1991, 1995a), and Saikkonen (1991, 1992). The theory of testing for autoregressive unit roots in univariate time series is well developed and is reviewed in Banerjee *et al.* (1993) and Stock (1994a). Tests for cointegration are reviewed in Banerjee *et al.* (1993) and Watson (1994). For recent Monte Carlo evidence on tests for cointegration, see Gregory (1994), Haug (1993, 1996), and Ho and Sørenson (1996).

2 Deviations of the pretest from this ideal can result in finite sample distortions even if $\alpha = 1$; cf. Elliott and Stock (1994) and Toda and Yamamoto (1995).

3 This survey focuses solely on classical (frequentist) methods. From a Bayesian perspective, these problems are conceptually straightforward and simply require integration over α with respect to a suitable prior, although in this model the results can be highly sensitive to the choice of prior. Relevant readings can be found in the special issues of the *Journal of Applied Econometrics* (October–December 1991) and *Econometric Theory* (August–October 1994); also see Sims and Zha (1994).

4 Watson (1994) provides references for the case of higher orders of integration.

5 The remarks in this paragraph extend to the more general category of processes for which $T^{-\frac{1}{2}}x_{[Ts]}$ converges weakly to $Z(s)$, an $O_p(1)$ stochastic process which is

not proportional to a Brownian motion. One example of a "local-to-$I(1)$" model is an autoregression with $\alpha = 1 + c/T$. Another example is the error components model, $\Delta x_t = \zeta_{1t} + hT^{-1}\zeta_{2t}$, where $(\zeta_{1t}, \Delta\zeta_{2t})$ are jointly stationary processes, $\mathrm{var}(\Delta\zeta_{2t})$ is fixed, and $Ex_0^2 < \infty$; cf. Nyblom and Mäkeläinen (1983).

6 The discussion here follows Cavanagh, Elliott, and Stock (1995).

7 The results in this section are taken from Stock (1995). The literature on long-run forecasting with large roots is small. Phillips (1995b) considers forecast errors from VARs specified in levels and estimated by OLS when there are multiple unit or local-to-units roots, and generalizations of the levels of VAR results in this subsection can be found there. Remarks similar in spirit on the topic of VAR impulse response functions can be found in Sims and Zha (1994).

8 There can be, however, substantial finite problems for OLS forecasts from stable autoregressions; see for example Breidt, Davis, and Dunsmuir (1995), Kemp (1991, 1992), Maekawa (1987), Magnus and Pesaran (1991), Phillips (1979), and Stine (1987).

9 One could alternatively include unit root and cointegration pretests and use the $I(1)$ or $I(0)$ methodology depending on the outcome. If however $\alpha = 1 + c/T$ and the pretest is a consistent decision rule, then for reasons which parallel the discussion in section 2, the pretest will result in the $I(1)$ methodology with probability tending to one.

10 One might conjecture that another alternative would be to compute the distributions in question using the bootstrap. However, in the AR(1) model with $\alpha = 1$ (a special case of problems A and C), Basawa et al. (1991) showed that the parametric bootstrap, based on the OLS estimate of α, is not consistent for the distribution of the OLS estimator of α. The bootstrap fails because it requires consistent initial estimation of c, which is not possible.

11 Tests related to these which test only for the existence of cointegration and do not involve a hypothesized value of θ have been developed by Shin (1994) and Harris and Inder (1994). The approach in section 4.3 is due to Wright (1996).

12 Extension of this approach to the case of deterministic terms is straightforward; cf. Toda and Yamamoto (1995) and Dolado and Lutkepohl (1995).

References

Ahn, S. K. and Reinsel, G. C. (1990). "Estimation for partially nonstationary multivariate autoregressive models." *Journal of the American Statistical Association*, 85: 813–23.

Anderson, T. W. and Darling, D. (1952). "Asymptotic theory of certain 'goodness of fit' criteria based on stochastic processes." *Annals of Mathematical Statistics*, 23: 193–212.

Andrews, D. W. K. (1991). "Heteroskedasticity and autocorrelation consistent covariance matrix estimation." *Econometrica*, 59: 817–58.

(1993). "Exactly median-unbiased estimation of first order autoregressive/unit root model." *Econometrica*, 61: 139–66.

Banerjee, A., Dolado, J., Galbraith, J. W., and Hendry, D. F. (1993). *Co-Integration,*

Error Correction, and the Econometric Analysis of Non-Stationary Data. Oxford: Oxford University Press.

Basawa, I. V., Mallik, A. K., McCormick, W. P., Reeves, J. H., and Taylor, R. L. (1991). "Bootstrapping unstable first-order autoregressive processes." *Annals of Statistics,* 19: 1098–101.

Bhargava, A. (1986). "On the theory of testing for unit roots in observed time series." *Review of Economic Studies,* 53: 369–84.

Bobkoski, M. J. (1983). "Hypothesis Testing in Nonstationary Time Series." Unpublished Ph.D Thesis, Department of Statistics, University of Wisconsin.

Breidt, F. J., Davis, R. A., and Dunsmuir, W. T. M. (1995). "Improved bootstrap prediction intervals for autoregression." *Journal of Time Series Analysis,* 16: 177–200.

Campbell, B. and Dufour, J.-M. (1994). "Exact nonparametric tests of orthogonality and random walk in the presence of a drift parameter." Manuscript, CRDE, University of Montreal.

(1995). "Exact nonparametric orthogonality and random walk tests." *The Review of Economics and Statistics,* 78: 1–16.

Campbell, J. Y. and Shiller, R. J. (1987). "Cointegration tests of present value models." *Journal of Political Economy,* 95: 1062–88.

(1988). "Stock prices, earnings and expected dividends." *Journal of Finance,* 43: 661–76.

Cavanagh, C. L. (1985). "Roots local to unity." Manuscript, Department of Economics, Harvard University.

Cavanagh, C. L., Elliott, G. and Stock, J. H. (1995). "Inference in models with nearly integrated regressors." *Econometric Theory,* 11: 1131–47.

Chan, N. H. (1988). "On the parameter inference for nearly nonstationary time series." *Journal of the American Statistical Association,* 83: 857–62.

Chan, N. H. and Wei, C. Z. (1987). "Asymptotic inference for nearly nonstationary AR(1) processes." *Annals of Statistics,* 15: 1050–63.

(1988). "Limiting distributions of least squares estimates of unstable autoregressive processes." *Annals of Statistics,* 16: 367–401.

Choi, I. (1993). "Asymptotic normality of the least-squares estimates for higher order autoregressive integrated processes with some applications." *Econometric Theory,* 9: 263–82.

Davidson, J. E. H., Hendry, D. F., Srba, F., and Yeo, S. (1978). "Econometric modelling of the aggregate time-series relationship between consumers' expenditure and income in the United Kingdom." *Economic Journal,* 88: 661–92.

Dickey, D. A. and Fuller, W. A. (1979). "Distribution of the estimators for autoregressive time series with a unit root." *Journal of the American Statistical Association,* 74: 427–31.

Dolado, Juan J. and Lutkepohl, Helmut (1996). "Making Wald tests work for cointegrated VAR systems." *Econometric Reviews,* 15.

Dufour, J. M. (1990). "Exact tests and confidence sets in linear regressions with autocorrelated errors." *Econometrica,* 58: 475–94.

Elliott, G. (1994). "Application of Local to Unity Asymptotic Theory to Time Series

Regression." Unpublished Ph.D. Dissertation, Department of Economics, Harvard University.

Elliott, G., Rothenberg, T. J., and Stock, J. H. (1996). "Efficient tests for an autoregressive unit root." *Econometrica*, 64: 813–36.

Elliott, G. and Stock, J. H. (1994). "Inference in time series regression when the order of integration of a regressor is unknown." *Econometric Theory*, 10: 672–700.

Engle, R. F. and Granger, C. W. J. (1987). "Cointegration and error correction: representation, estimation, and testing." *Econometrica*, 55: 251–76.

Engle, R. F. and Yoo, B. S. (1987). "Forecasting and testing in co-integrated systems." *Journal of Econometrics*, 35: 143–59.

  (1991). "Cointegrated economic time series: an overview with new results." In Engle, R. F. and Granger, C. W. J. (eds.), *Long-Run Economic Relationships*. Oxford: Oxford University Press, pp. 237–66.

Fama, E. F. (1991). "Efficient capital markets II." *Journal of Finance*, 46: 1575–617.

Granger, C. W. J. (1981). "Some properties of time series data and their use in econometric model specification." *Journal of Econometrics*, 16: 121–30.

Granger, C. W. J. and Weiss, A. A. (1983). "Time series analysis of error correcting models." In Karlin, S., Amemiya, T., and Goodman, L. A. (eds.), *Studies in Econometrics, Time Series and Multivariate Statistics*. New York: Academic Press.

Gregory, A. W. (1994). "Testing for cointegration in linear quadratic models." *Journal of Business and Economic Statistics*, 12: 347–60.

Hall, P. and Heyde, C. C. (1980). *Martingale Limit Theory and its Applications*. New York: Academic Press.

Hamilton, J. D. (1994). *Time Series Analysis*. Princeton: Princeton University Press.

Hargreaves, C. P. (1994). "A review of methods of estimating cointegrating relationships." In Hargreaves, C. P. (ed.), *Nonstationary Time Series Analysis and Cointegration*. Oxford: Oxford University Press, pp. 87–132.

Harris, D. and Inder, B. (1994). "A test of the null hypothesis of cointegration." In Hargreaves, C. P. (ed.), *Nonstationary Time Series Analysis and Cointegration*. Oxford: Oxford University Press, pp. 133–52.

Haug, A. A. (1993). "Residual based tests for cointegration." *Economics Letters*, 41: 345–51.

  (1996). "Tests for cointegration: a Monte Carlo comparison." *Journal of Econometrics*, 71.

Herrndorf, N. A. (1984). "A functional central limit theorem for weakly dependent sequences of random variables." *Annals of Probability*, 12: 141–53.

Ho, M. S. and Sørenson, B. (1996). "Finding cointegration rank in high dimensional systems using the Johansen test." *The Review of Economics and Statistics*.

Johansen, S. (1988). "Statistical analysis of cointegrating vectors." *Journal of Economic Dynamics and Control*, 12: 231–54.

  (1991). "Estimation and hypothesis testing of cointegration vectors in Gaussian vector autoregressive models." *Econometrica*, 59: 1551–80.

  (1995). *Likelihood Based Inference in Cointegrated Vector Autoregressive Models*. Oxford: Oxford University Press.

Kemp, G. C. R. (1991). "The joint distribution of forecast errors in the AR(1) model." *Econometric Theory*, 7: 497–518.

(1992). "The distribution of forecast errors from an estimated random walk." Manuscript, University of Essex.

King, M. L. (1980). "Robust tests for spherical symmetry and their application to least squares regression." *Annals of Statistics*, 8: 1265–71.

King, M. L. and Hillier, H. (1985). "Locally best invariant tests of the error covariance matrix of the linear regression model." *Journal of the Royal Statistical Society, Series B*, 47: 98–102.

Kwiatkowski, D., Phillips, P. C. B., Schmidt, P., and Shin, Y. (1992). "Testing the null hypothesis of stationarity against the alternatives of a unit root: how sure are we that economic time series have a unit root?" *Journal of Econometrics*, 54: 159–78.

MacNeill, I. B. (1978). "Properties of sequences of partial sums of polyomial regression residuals with applications to tests for change of regression at unknown times." *Annals of Statistics*, 6: 422–33.

Maekawa, K. (1987). "Finite sample properties of several predictors from an autoregressive model." *Econometric Theory*, 3: 359–70.

Magnus, J. R. and Pesaran, B. (1991). "The bias of forecasts from a first-order autoregression." *Econometric Theory*, 7: 222–35.

Mankiw, N. G. and Shapiro, M. D. (1985). "Trends, random walks and tests of the permanent income hypothesis." *Journal of Monetary Economics*, 16: 165–74.

Nabeya, S. and Tanaka, K. (1988). "Asymptotic theory of a test for the constancy of regression coefficients against the random walk alternative." *Annals of Statistics*, 16: 218–35.

Nyblom, J. (1986). "Testing for deterministic linear trend in time series." *Journal of the American Statistical Association*, 81: 545–9.

Nyblom, J. and Mäkeläinen, T. (1983). "Comparisons of tests for the presence of random walk coefficients in a simple linear model." *Journal of the American Statistical Association*, 78: 856–64.

Park, J. and Choi, C. (1988). "A new approach to testing for a unit root." Working Paper No. 88-23, Center for Analytical Economics, Cornell University.

Park, J. Y. and Phillips, P. C. B. (1988). "Statistical inference in regressions with integrated processes: Part I," *Econometric Theory*, 4: 468–97.

Phillips, P. C. B. (1979). "The sampling distribution of forecasts from a first-order autoregression." *Journal of Econometrics*, 9: 241–61.

(1987). "Toward a unified asymptotic theory for autoregression." *Biometrika*, 74: 535–47.

(1991). "Optimal inference in co-integrated systems." *Econometrica*, 59: 282–306.

(1995a). "Fully modified least squares and vector autoregression." *Econometrica*, 63: 1023–79.

(1995b). "Impulse response and forecast error variance asymptotics in nonstationary VARs." Manuscript, Cowles Foundation, Yale University.

Phillips, P. C. B. and Durlauf, S. N. (1986). "Multiple time series regression with integrated processes." *Review of Economic Studies*, 53: 473–96.

Phillips, P. C. B. and Loretan, M. (1991). "Estimating long-run economic equilibria." *Review of Economic Studies*, 58: 407–36.

Phillips, P. C. B. and Ouliaris, S. (1990). "Asymptotic properties of residual based tests for cointegration." *Econometrica*, 58: 165–94.

Phillips, P. C. B. and Solo, V. (1992). "Asymptotic for linear processes." *Annals of Statistics*, 20(2): 971–1001.

Rothenberg, T. J. and Stock, J. H. (1995). "Inference in a nearly integrated autoregressive model with nonnormal innovations." Manuscript, University of California, Berkeley.

Saikkonen, P. (1991). "Asymptotically efficient estimation of cointegrating regressions." *Econometric Theory*, 7: 1–21.

(1992). "Estimation and testing of cointegrated systems by an autoregressive approximation." *Econometric Theory*, 8: 1–27.

Saikkonen, P. and Luukkonen, R. (1993a). "Testing for moving average unit root in autoregressive integrated moving average models." *Journal of the American Statistical Association*, 88: 596–601.

(1993b). "Point optimal tests for the moving average unit root hypothesis." *Econometric Theory*, 9: 343–62.

Sampson, M. (1991). "The effect of parameter uncertainty on forecast variances and confidence intervals for unit root and trend stationary time-series models." *Journal of Applied Econometrics*, 6: 67–76.

Sargan, J. D. (1964). "Wages and prices in the United Kingdom: a study in econometric methodology." In Hart, P. E., Mills, G., and Whitaker, J. K. (eds.), *Econometric Analysis for National Economic Planning*. London: Butterworth. Reprinted in Hendry, D. F. and Wallis, K. F. (eds.), *Econometrics and Quantitative Economics*. Oxford: Basil Blackwell, 1984.

Sargan, J. D. and Bhargava, A. (1983). "Testing for residuals from least squares regression for being generated by the Gaussian random walk." *Econometrica*, 51: 153–74.

Shin, Y. (1994). "A residual-based test of the null of cointegration against the alternative of no cointegration." *Econometric Theory*, 10: 91–116.

Shively, T. S. (1988). "An exact test for a stochastic coefficient in a time series regression model." *Journal of Time Series Analysis*, 9: 81–8.

Sims, C. A., Stock, J. H., and Watson, M. W. (1990). "Inference in linear time series models with some unit roots." *Econometrica*, 58: 113–44.

Sims, Christopher A. and Zha, Tao (1994). "Error Bands for Impulse Responses." Manuscript, Cowles Foundation, Yale University.

Stine, R. A. (1987). "Estimating properties of autoregressive forecasts." *Journal of the American Statistical Association*, 82: 1072–8.

Stock, J. H. (1987). "Asymptotic properties of least squares estimators of cointegrating vectors." *Econometrica*, 55: 1035–56.

(1991). "Confidence intervals for the largest autoregressive root in U.S. economic time series." *Journal of Monetary Economics*, 28: 435–60.

(1994a). "Unit roots, structural breaks and trends." In. Engle, R. F. and McFadden, D. (eds.), *Handbook of Econometrics, Vol. IV*. Amsterdam: Elsevier, chapter 46.

(1994b). "Deciding between I(1) and I(0)." *Journal of Econometrics*, 63: 105–31.

(1995). "Long Run Forecasting." Manuscript, Kennedy School of Government, Harvard University.

Stock, J. H. and Watson, M. W. (1988). "Testing for common trends." *Journal of the American Statistical Association*, 83: 1097–107.

(1993). "A simple estimator of cointegrating vectors in higher-order integrated systems." *Econometrica*, 61: 783–820.

Tanaka, K. (1990). "Testing for a moving average unit root." *Econometric Theory*, 6: 433–44.

Toda, Hiro Y. and Yamamoto, Taku (1995). "Statistical inference in vector autoregressions with possibly integrated processes." *Journal of Econometrics*, 66: 225–50.

Watson, M. W. (1994). "Vector autoregressions and cointegration." In Engle, R. F. and McFadden, D. (eds.), *Handbook of Econometrics, Vol. IV*. Amsterdam: Elsevier, chapter 47.

Wright, J. H. (1996). "Confidence intervals in a cointegrative regression based on stationarity tests." Manuscript, Harvard University.

CHAPTER 3

Testing and measurement in competition models

Timothy Bresnahan

What is market power? Where is it found in late twentieth century markets? Has increasing internationalization destroyed it? What mechanisms support firms' attempts to build market-power positions for themselves? What are its proximate causes? What are its deep causes? These are some of the questions on which economic theory has made the most rapid progress in the last two decades. In sharp contrast to the situation beforehand, we now understand at a deep level when to expect price to exceed marginal cost. Significant advances in the theory of imperfectly competitive supply tell us under what circumstances an industry will sell less than the perfectly competitive quantity at more than the perfectly competitive price. Perhaps more importantly, formal theories of imperfect competition, overwhelmingly based in the game theory, offer precise and therefore testable characterizations of the behavior supporting the non-competitive outcomes. This short-run supply theory is necessarily incomplete. It takes as given the degree to which firms' products within an industry are substitutes, the degree to which firms' cost circumstances are similar, the information structures under which prices and/or quantities are set, the number of firms competing, and so on. Theories of the determination of all these objects have been another area of very rapid progress.

The time for empirical work testing all this marvelous theory seems to have arrived. Yet the same ideas which permitted a theoretical revolution strategy, commitment, and imperfect information in the theory of games, have produced a body of theory dauntingly difficult to test. Game-theoretic ideas seem particularly suitable for the generation of COUNTER EXAMPLES, followed by counter examples, until all too soon they are *counter examples.*[1] Empirical work has responded to this situation in several ways. Some work has very tight integration of theory, econometric model, and data analysis. Other work eschews this tight integration, instead identifying key implications to test. Still other work largely ignores strategic theory or lumps very different (we thought!) theories into equivalence classes.

All of these different modes of using theory appear in very successful empirical work. In what follows, I look at some exemplary papers in three very different literatures; auctions, oligopoly pricing, and entry. I have picked the papers and the literatures to illuminate the variety of ways in which theory can be useful. Also, their centrality has led to empirical work with a great deal of attention paid to econometrics and economic theory. Finally, I picked these literatures because they contain an important shift from "testing theory" to "measuring economically important quantities," a topic to which I return in the conclusion.

1   BUYERS' BEHAVIOR IN AUCTIONS

Auctions are a reasonably common institutional mechanism for price determination in markets. They are used by government entities (as in the famous spectrum auctions in the US recently) and also in many private contexts. Auction practitioners have, over the years, built up a set of specific rules for bidding, sellers' reservation prices, etc. Often the participants in any particular auction understand these rules in a deep way. These formalized and well-understood rules have made the analysis of auctions a fertile field for equilibrium game-theoretic methods.

The theory of competitive bidding at auction is very compelling.[2] There is a tight correspondence between the real world auctions' stated rules and auction theory's rules of the game.[3] Almost all auctions have rules such that the game among buyers would be quite trivial if buyers knew everything there is to know about one another and about the object for sale. The essence of the auction is bidders' incomplete information. Auction theory, drawing on the theory of games with incomplete information, has been very successful in modeling descriptions of what bidders know and do not know and of the bidding rules to bidding strategies and therefore outcomes.

There is still considerable work left for empirical studies. First, even though the rules of the game are obvious in auctions, the distribution of bidders' private information and valuation is not. There are large differences between the case where bidders have the same guess about an unknown but "common" value for the for-sale object and the other case where each bidder has her own "private" value. Even more difficult, the shape of the bidder's valuation distribution matters in a very important but complex way. And it is not possible to learn about these kinds of issues by examining the institutions theoretically. They must be measured and tested. Fortunately, the theory gives very precise and quantitative guidance on how to map from the underlying private information to strategies.

The other task for empirical work, of course, is that the theory might just be wrong. Two potentially troubling parts of the theory are (1) the assumption of non-cooperative behavior – what about collusive bid rigging? And (2) the assumption of a high degree of rationality – can bidders really make calculations as complex as those in the theory?[4] In either case, the task of empirical work is to test idiosyncratic implications of the important parts of the theory – in particular, the "Nash" part of Bayesian Nash equilibrium against collusive bid rigging and the "Bayesian" part against the not-rational-enough alternative.

Let us now examine empirical work on auctions of two very different types. "Structuralist" empirical work specifies everything in economic agents' environment explicitly. In auction work, that means that the distribution of bidders' valuations forms an explicit part of the specification of the econometric model. Further, it is the equilibrium of an explicitly stated economic model which maps the underlying economic environment to observable data. Structuralist econometric models can be complex and difficult to construct, for the high degree of integration of theory and econometrics prevents shortcuts. Yet the econometrics also have a beautiful transparency, as there is literally not any part of the data analysis, not even the error term, without an explicit economic foundation. In "implication-ist" work, on the other hand, theory and data analysis have more separate roles. The testable implications of a theory, or a cluster of theories, are drawn out. The exact form of the empirical procedure is not derived from a specific theory, the error term especially may be "tacked on" to the model. Implicationist methods pick up in robustness some of what they lose in integratedness, as we shall see in the auctions work.

1.1   Structuralist studies of auctions

Consider first Laffont, Ossard, and Vuong's (1995) very structuralist approach to descending auctions for eggplants in Marmande, France. These are auctions in which sellers are farmers and buyers are various traders in agricultural goods. They are modeled as first price sealed bid auctions among risk-neutral bidders with independent private values drawn from the same distribution, $F(\ )$. Each auction is taken to be independent of all others. (The sample is selected to make the latter assumption more plausible.) In these circumstances, the solution concept is Bayesian Nash equilibrium. Each buyer's bidding strategy determines her bid, b^i as a function of her value, v^i, the reservation price, ρ^0, set by the seller, the distribution function for other bidders' valuations, and the number of bidders, I. The form of the strategy is actually quite simple for the bidder to calculate, assuming that she knows what game she is playing and that she knows the distribution of all other bidders' valuations or bids

$$b^i = e(v^i, I, p^o, F) = v^i - \frac{1}{(F(v^i))^{I-1}} \int_{p^0}^{v^i} (F(x))^{I-1} dx. \tag{1}$$

This same equilibrium notion provides non-trivial challenges for the structuralist econometrician. One would like to estimate the function $F(\ )$ in (1). More realistically, there may be exogenous variables, X (perhaps seasons in this agricultural example), and one would like to estimate $F(\cdot; x)$, a family of CDFs. Further, one would like to do this without putting too much restriction on the shape of $F(\ )$. The problem is, what is observed is the distribution of bids, not the distribution of underlying values. And those are linked to the data by the behavioral equation of the bidder, which depends itself upon the unknown distribution. Suddenly the problem seems more complex, as the mapping from the objects we are trying to estimate – distribution functions – to what we can observe – distribution functions of another object – is an integral. The mapping is extremely non-linear and has other associated numerical complexities. This calls for some quite elegant econometrics.[5] In their paper, Laffont et al. (1995) use a simulation estimator.[6]

This structuralist approach does not really offer much of a test of the relevant theory, at least not at this stage. Instead, the approach offers a way to measure the underlying objects in the theory, taking the theory as given.[7] What we *do* have at the end of papers like this are estimates that completely characterize the economic (including informational and strategic) behavior and environment of the bidders. Thus, calculations based on these estimates are not subject to any "Lucas critique" caveats. In this regard, the structuralist approaches to the empirical study of auctions reach a high level of integration of economic theory, econometric method, and data analysis.

1.2   Implications of auction theory

The implications of asymmetric information auction theory are not confined to a description of the equation determining equilibrium. Instead, the theory is quite full of results! Testing some of these results, by implications methods, has been another rich vein for empirical work. An interesting example is Hendricks and Porter (1988). They focus on common-value auctions in which some bidders are better informed than others about the underlying value. These auctions have the feature that, in equilibrium, the uninformed bidders are not as effective competitors as the informed bidders. They also have the feature that the structuralist approach described above would be vastly more difficult, as the distribution of both informed and uninformed bidders' information would form part of the integral equation for equilibrium bids.[8]

Hendricks and Porter proceed by identifying six distinct implications of the theory for empirical test. Many of these are tightly linked to the information economics part of the theory. Some of them are that:

> the informed firm wins the bid at least half the time
> and makes an expected profit,

> that uninformed firms earn zero profits on average,
> but lose when the informed firm bids (it is a secret who bids),

> the informed firm's strategy does not depend on the (expected) number of uninformed bidders, and

> the informed firm bids higher when public information is more positive (even though the informed firm's information is strictly better).

Taken together, these and a few other implications have a strong information economics, equilibrium, and rational actor flavor.

Hendricks and Porter proceed with a very thorough statistical examination of the observed bids on offshore oil leases and how they are shifted by a variety of environmental variables. Of particular importance is the assumption about the informed firm. The oil leases are auctioned off in a series of "tracts." Hendricks and Porter take a firm which has already drilled wells on adjacent tracts to be (potentially) better informed than those who have simply been able to perform above-ground research. This key assumption permits testing of many of the key implications of the theory. In particular, they find that the informed bidders make profits, that uninformed bidders bid conservatively to avoid the winner's curse, that informed firms respond somewhat to the (weak) competition from uninformed firms, and several other non-obvious implications of the theory. Given testing of the long list of implications, many tightly linked to the underlying economics of strategy and private information, powerful evidence for the full theory has been assembled.

Auctions: Summary

At the end of these empirical auctions papers, one feels very good about the theoretical revolution in Industrial Organization. The theory of auctions has been a success, not only in helping us think better about auctions in the abstract, but in predicting phenomena in real auctions. Realization of the theory in empirical papers has taken on two very different forms, each of which has been very successful. Structuralist methods have used theory as a factor of production in measuring deep economic parameters. Implicationist methods have tested the theory, including some non-obvious implications.

Of course, there are some worrisome notes and some things we do not understand yet. Some very interesting papers about bid-rigging in auctions suggest that the phenomenon is empirically important.[9] But the relevant evidence is much less satisfactorily tied to theory. Partly, this is a problem of theory; we do not, and probably cannot, have a theory of bid rigging which is as clean as the theory of competitive bidding. At best, we can hope for a theory of bid rigging which is about as clean as the theory of cartels, one topic of my next section. Another area of difficulty concerns the auctioning of multiple objects and buyer dynamics. Interestingly, this appears to be a topic on which stubborn fact is leading theory.[10] For example, difficult-to-explain price falls for objects auctioned later in the same day. Similarly, the topic of seller behavior at auctions is likely to be thornier than the topic of buyer behavior. But these are simply the boundaries of success; within the boundary, it is hard to have anything but positive feelings about the economic literature on auctions.

The success in empirical studies of auctions is something of an outlier in Industrial Organization (and I suspect in economics generally). The theory of games and the facts of auctions are particularly well aligned. The task of deciding what game-theoretic model goes with the world, out of the thousands of different ways to make models of the world, is reasonably direct in auctions. Discovering those same correspondences in other areas is more difficult.

2   OLIGOPOLY PRICING BEHAVIOR

Let us now turn to a problem that is closely related, oligopoly pricing behavior. In oligopoly, as in bidding at auction, prices are set by complex strategic interaction. The equilibrium observed arises from firms' interactions, which may well be characterized by gaming and all that implies. An auction has rules; these form many of the "rules of the game" which are at the heart of the competitive bidding model. In an open market place, however, it is rare that the "rules of the game" will be visible and obvious in market institutions.[11]

This is an embarrassment of riches for the empicial researcher looking at competition among the few. Which of the dozens of available theories to use? What econometric procedures might test for the theory actually in place in an industry? Alternatively, what can be accomplished in market power measurement robustly, i.e., without determining the exact theory of supply? Once again, these questions about the role of economic theory in empirical work appear in the literature as econometric modeling decisions.

2.1 Old work

One response to this challenge has been to limit attention to a small number of explicitly game-theoretic models of competition. These can then be tested, each against the other. Holding the model of demand fixed, a variety of econometric models of supply are introduced, each derived from an explicitly stated game.

To the best of my knowledge, my dissertation was the first attempt at this method. In it, there is a vertical product-differentiation model of the demand for automobiles. This leads to a demand system

$$Q_j = F_j(P, X, \beta) + \varepsilon_j, \tag{1}$$

where Q_j is the quantity demand of vehicle j, P is the vector of prices of all automobiles, X is the matrix of observable attributes of all automobiles, β are the parameters, and ε_j is the demand error. There is one such equation for each product, j. In the empirical work, the model actually estimated is very restrictive. The vertical product-differentiation theoretical model is imposed in a very structural way; each product's demand is a function only of its own and two other products' prices. The defense of this very restrictive specification came from (1) a reading of the automobile literature, (2) conversations with marketers in automobile companies, and (3) pure expedience.

Expedience dictated simple demand because the supply side was modeled in a very complex way. Costs were simple: the marginal cost of automobile j was constant, and depended on observed quality attributes plus an unobserved error as $MC_j = MC(X_j\gamma) + \eta_j$. Supply of each product is modeled by competing competitive interaction models, including Collusion (2) and Bertrand (3)

$$P_j = \arg\max_{P_j} \sum_{\text{all } k} (P_k - MC(X_k\gamma) - \eta_k) \cdot (F_j(P, X, B) + \varepsilon_j) \tag{2}$$

versus

$$P_j = \arg\max_{P_j} \sum_{k \in B_j} (P_k - MC(X_k\gamma) - \eta_k) \cdot (F_j(P, X, B) + \varepsilon_j), \tag{3}$$

where B_j is the set of products sold by the firm selling j. The goal of the empirical work is to test among competing game-theoretic models of supply, i.e., tell (1) and (2) from (1) and (3).

The principal empirical findings are two. First, as theory predicts for a vertically product-differentiated industry, price–cost margins are much larger for larger automobiles whether (2) or (3) is in effect.[12] The other is that both collusive and competitive pricing regimes were observed (in different years) in the period under study, the mid 1950s. The latter finding follows from non-nested tests of the model with Bertrand pricing against the model with Collusive pricing, and vice versa. Very similar ideas, and better method for testing among the distinct theories, have been used by Gasmi, Laffont, and Vuong (1992) in a study of the packaged soft drink industry covering strategic advertising as well as strategic pricing.

These papers investigate the consequences of strategic interaction for pricing one period at a time. The methods work well for theories that are quite distinct: Bertrand versus Collusion versus Stackelberg leadership by a specific firm are good candidates. Also, the methods can detect large shifts in the pricing rule over time.

2.2   Early work on repeated play

Once those different theories of supply in any particular period can be distinguished, we can turn to the dynamics. Switches between competitive and collusive regimes are a core element of dynamic oligopoly theory under uncertainty, a key insight of Green and Porter (1984). Substantial progress was made in detecting such switches by Porter (1984), who measured two distinct pricing regimes, each repeated many times, in his study.

In Porter's study of an 1880s railroad cartel, Q_t is grain shipped by rail from Chicago to the East Coast, measured in tons. The time index t refers to a week between the first week of 1880 and the sixteenth week of 1886. The price data, P_t, are based on a weekly poll taken by the cartel of its members; given the possibility of secret price cutting, P_t is probably to be interpreted as if it were a weighted average of list prices. The demand function takes the constant elasticity form.

Since there is some entry and some acquisition activity during the sample period, Porter adds structural dummies S_t to supply. Furthermore, it is assumed that the probability of a successful collusion is $1 - \pi$. After transformation, the supply relation ultimately estimated takes the form:

Supply relation$\qquad\qquad\qquad\qquad\qquad\qquad$Probability
$$\log P_t = \Gamma_0 + \alpha^a + \Gamma_1 \log Q_t + (\Gamma_2, S_t) + \varepsilon_{cit} \qquad \pi \qquad (4)$$
$$\log P_t = \Gamma_0 + \alpha^a + \alpha^b + \Gamma_1 \log Q_t + (\Gamma_2, S_t) + \varepsilon_{cit} \quad 1 - \pi$$

where α^a is a transformation of the conduct parameter in periods of successful collusion, and α^b measures the change in conduct when collusion breaks down. Of course, it is clear that α^a cannot be separately estimated from Γ_0 on the basis of estimating these equations, but there is considerable interest in estimating α^b, the percentage amount by which a breakdown in the cartel changes prices. As the form of (4) suggests, Porter estimates the supply and demand system by "switching equations" methods, in which the probability π as well as the regular parameters are estimated from the data. He finds that there are two pricing/quantity determination regimes, and that they correspond to very distinct supply behavior.

I recount this early history of the field not just to remember our youthful excitement at actually testing theories. The many compromises embedded in the econometric specifications of the papers left important economic issues unresolved. The two sources of market power are steep (firm and industry) demand curves and less-than-competitive conduct. Even my brief account of these early papers shows restrictive demand systems and an incomplete model of conduct. Ensuing work has attacked both problems with widely varying results.

2.3   Moving toward testing dynamic implications

Those papers tested only a subject of the implications of modern oligopoly theory. On the positive side, they provide evidence for switches among different pricing regimes in highly concentrated oligopolies. The gross size of the changes in supply behavior within the same industry over time, with reversals, itself provides strong evidence for the importance of strategic considerations as a part of oligopoly supply. More critically, however, the papers did not examine the causes of these changes in behavior over time. It is reasonable to look within the dynamic-oligopoly framework and ask whether the full implications of the Stigler theory of oligopoly, as realized by Green and Porter (1984) or Abreu *et al.* (1990), have been tested. Since incomplete information about demand is at the heart of the theory, one could ask whether it was really true that downward demand shocks predict changes to a "punishment" regime. Since there are alternative theories (as one should always expect with dynamic games in an incomplete information environment), such as that of Rotemberg and Saloner, one could ask which of the theories is true. Since the theories turn on repeated play to enforce the cartel contract, one could ask whether the changes in regime are frequent enough, endogenous enough, and matter enough for flow profitability to enforce cartel compliance. One could ask, somewhat outside the box defined by the theories, whether firms appear to be observing the contract (e.g., is there actual secret price cutting in equilibrium?) or whether some "social" rather than rational mechanism enforces the market power. All of these things are well worth asking.

They are, however, very difficult to answer.

The basic difficulty here lies in the theory itself. Dynamic game theory, at least for oligopoly, has had strong elements of "threat/enforcement" logic. This arises directly from the structure of oligopoly pricing, in which firms have individual incentives to depart from the high prices that are collectively profit maximizing. It is harder to measure a threat (probabilistic reversion to a low-price regime[13]) than it is to measure the behavior that the threat enforces (cooperation in the high-price regime). The distinction is empirically important. The behavior that the threats enforce, or more generally play in the stage game of a repeated game, are first-order implications of the theory. We can see these behaviors, test for them, measure them. The threats themselves may be much less visible implications of the theory. We see them only when they are actually carried out, as when the regime changes. In the specific circumstances of dynamic oligopoly, there are two problems: regime switches in a reasonably successful cartel will be rare, and the events that cause the regime switch are theorized to be invisible. These are unpromising conditions for systematic statistical investigation.

The importance of these more dynamic and information-intensive issues has drawn scholarships to the problem regardless. Roberts and Samuelson (1988) have investigated firms' dynamic responses to one another's advertising decisions, using a dynamic-games framework. Baker (1989) has examined what may be a cartel enforcement scheme in steel, using the special circumstances of the Great Depression as a backdrop to distinguish between the threat and the high-markup behavior enforced by the threat. A series of papers has followed up on Porter's railroad study.[14] A second basic implication of the theory, that the pricing regimes tend to persist over time, was verified by Cosslett and Lee (1985). The question of what triggers price wars, perhaps the key one in understanding the game dynamics, has been taken up by Porter (1985) and Ellison (1994). Since the railroad cartel used a quota system, Porter's idea was to see if deviations of market shares from the nominal quotas predict price wars; there seemed to be inadequate information in the data to determine whether this is the case. Ellison, using a more unified measurement framework based on close attention to the Markov structure of regime transformations, and to the dynamics of the serially correlated demand error, is able to go farther. Though the amount of information in the data somewhat undercuts the empirical finding, there do appear to be trigger strategies at work. Interestingly, there also appears to be some actual cheating on the cartel of the secret price cutting form.

These papers, taken as a group, are not all that encouraging about the future of testing dynamical, informational implications of oligopoly theory. The railroad-cartel dataset, just over a century old, is by far the best we have, and approaches the limits of what we could hope to have. Weekly data, public information, and a cartel that acted above board (it was then legal) are extraordinary assets. Yet, even with this data richness, the ultimate statistical evidence about the different hypotheses is more "consistent with" than "compelling for" a theory. Another century might well pass without a dataset that supports a better statistical investigation of cartel enforcement.

There are some first-order implications of oligopoly theory that are quite testable in real-world data environments. Collusive oligopolies will have monopoly-like pricing behavior (i.e., pricing behavior that depends on marginal revenue) in their cartel regime. Collusive oligopolies working in imperfect information environments will sometimes revert to more competitive pricing regimes. Since we have built measurement methods that are good at (1) telling static monopoly from more competitive static supply behaviors (like Cournot or Bertrand or perfect competition) and (2) detecting regime switches in supply behavior, these implications of the theory can be seen in reasonable data environments. These are also the first-order implications of the theory for welfare analysis. It is an accomplishment worth having to know how much like monopoly, and how often like monopoly, oligopolies are. We will know less, by statistical means at least, about the reasons for oligopoly cooperation.

All this points to a shift in scholarly emphasis from the intensive margin of industries where a theory may be deeply tested to the extensive margin of investigating strategic pricing outcomes in a wide variety of interesting and important contexts.

2.4   More flexible demand systems with product differentiation

Market power measurement with flexible demand assumptions has been an area of rapid and convincing progress. Consider again the demand systems in the papers discussed. One paper uses an extreme version of the VDP model, in which only three prices affect the demand for any particular product in a product-differentiated industry. The other assumes a constant-elasticity demand curve (in a market-power assessment context!) While these types of illustrative functional form assumptions may be fine for theoretical purposes, they are very restrictive for use in empirical work.

Attention to the demand side of the specification also derives from some important realities of modern economic life. The driving forces of economic and industrial change, at least in the developed world, in the late twentieth century have not particularly centered on cheaper production of the same body of goods. Instead, a steady process of new-goods and new-industries creation has been a critical shaper of events. As a result, the places in the modern economy where one would most like to assess market power are in product-differentiated industries. Consumer products industries with brand names; information technology industries with technical standards; pharmaceuticals and the health care sector itself, with complex therapeutic outcomes; retail trade with service and stockouts; these are fairly good representatives of likely locuses of market power in the present. Whether one thinks that the market power in them is a social ill, because of deadweight losses, or a social good, because the monopoly profits pay for the economic change, is of little import for the question of appropriate empirical methods. The fact is, this part of the economy is where the action is.[15]

Accordingly, a series of recent papers has estimated very complex oligopoly demand and pricing models. This includes some papers that are innovative in terms of measurement methodology, including those by Goldberg (1992), Berry, Levinsohn, and Pakes (1992), Trajtenberg (1986), and Hausman (1994). The first two of these papers consider the automobile market, and both bring substantially more data and a substantially less restricted specification to the demand side than the work discussed above. Hausman and Trajtenberg, working in very different industries and with different purposes, are also careful to make unrestrictive demand assumptions.

In Goldberg's paper, individual household microdata are used. This already permits a less restrictive specification of the aggregate demand elasticities. Different kinds of households are permitted to prefer different kinds of vehicles. The rich like big, fancy cars; young families show more of a preference for station wagons over convertibles than do young singles, and *vice versa*. Parameters that measure the impact of the observable heterogeneity in demand behavior, plus the sampling distribution of household types, permit an extremely unrestricted specification of the elasticities of substitution between products of different types.

Berry, Levinsohn, and Pakes are more concerned with the flexibility of the functional form for the demand system, since they use aggregate data on quantity demanded. Their approach is to start from an individual-choice demand model, but to permit the unobserved heterogeneity of consumer preferences to lie in a five-dimensional space. Thus, different automobiles can be "neighbors" in the product space in any of five dimensions. (The dimensions are defined by observable characteristics of the automobiles.) The work is careful to demonstrate that the pattern of elasticities of substitution and cross elasticities of substitution among different products is unrestricted, showing the resulting implications for the patterns of which products and firms compete with which. These elasticities also determine the equilibrium market power, measured by markups, in Bertrand equilibrium.

We see the same set of concerns in a closely related literature on assessing the contributions of a new good to social welfare.[16] A steep single-product demand curve is the hallmark of market power in product-differentiated industries. It is also the hallmark of large consumer surplus from the invention of a new good.

This literature has turned away from game-theoretic models of the supply side. Sellers are modeled either by static multi-product Bertrand, or go unmodeled.[17] There are three main reasons for this. First, these papers are difficult enough econometrically as it is; we progress by steps. Second, it is a perfectly reasonable position that, in product-differentiated industries, the slope of the single firm demand curve is the main source of market power.[18] Third, and most important, is the idea that strategy *is* important in these industries; product introduction strategy, advertising strategy, and product positioning strategy, not pricing.

3   STUDIES OF EQUILIBRIUM INDUSTRY STRUCTURE

Let us now turn to a third area of enquiry. This is the area of studies of the determinants of industry structure. Its relationships to the immediately preceding body of knowledge is one of complementarity. Given that competition among the few can be quite uncompetitive as a pricing mechanism, what determines the "few"?

The part of economic theory supporting this area of enquiry is difficult and complex. It includes the theory of entry barriers, of predation, and (before we forget) of non-strategic competitive entry. This is a set of literatures in which a great deal rides on specific strategic interactions. Large differences in outcomes may very well turn on small differences in circumstances, ones that are obvious to industry participants but very difficult to detect by the analyst. John Sutton, in a landmark book and in chapter 4 of volume I, ably describes the difficulty of this body of theory, so I will not repeat the argument here.

Empirical researchers, cognizant of the difficulties of a direct statistical attack on the objects central to the theory, have used eclectically implicationist methods. Sutton, building upon his synthesis of a wide variety of theories set out to test their implications using a "bounds" approach. This means attempting to characterize the robust implications of a wide variety of strategic theories. The theories themselves are thrown into an observational equivalence class – distinctions not related to the robust implications are neither tested nor measured. Sutton's two equivalence classes are industries with Endogenous Sunk Cost (ESC) and Exogenous Sunk Cost (XSC) characteristics. Roughly, in the ESC industries some strategic variable offers very considerable room for strategic interplay in the entry game. In XSC industries, only the rate at which competition causes prices to fall, the "toughness of price competition," matters for equilibrium industry structure (fixed costs in both contexts).

Sutton argued that a key implication of ESC was that, even in very large markets, concentrated structure will arise. Further, an important implication of the bounds approach is that no such relationship exists for XSC industries. For this core idea, then, Sutton pursued the empirical analogy; could failure of industry structure to converge to competition be found in larger markets, and would it be found in contrast to XSC industries? In his study of consumer products industries, he found that the behavior of different classes of industries was indeed quite different. As a systematic matter, XSC industries tend to be far less concentrated in large national economies. ESC industries are roughly equally concentrated across a wide range of market sizes.

Industry narratives, rather than systematic statistical work, pursued some of the details of the synthesis. By examining a wide variety in the toughness of price competition induced by government intervention, Sutton was able to verify that the toughness of price competition did indeed matter greatly in XSC industries. Further, he provides a series of narratives about market structure determination in the ESC industries. These suggest (1) that the forces at work are indeed those suggested by the theory and (2) that the primary problem of the theory, very subtle differences in strategic interaction in similar circumstances, also arises in the world. A wide variety of strategic mechanisms seemed to come into play in very similar industries, e.g., in the same industry in different countries.

In a related approach to the same issues, Peter Reiss and I and Stephen Berry took up the problem of equilibrium market structure determination statistically. Here, the guiding concept in the model was a latent profitability variable, Π_n, for the nth firm into a market. We applied the model to a sample of very concentrated markets, so it was Π_1, Π_2, etc., literally monopoly, duopoly, and triopoly profit that were modeled and estimated. Working independently of Sutton, we also focused on the size of the market as the key regressor.

In this framework, it is possible to examine specific entry games. Holding constant the cost and demand environment, specific models of entry and entry deterrence have distinct implications for observables. Examples in the literature include detecting leader–follower models with an observably distinct class of leaders (Bresnahan and Reiss (1990)) and discriminating among potential entrants of different types (Berry (1992)). These examples, in which strong assumptions about the *normal* form of the game linked to observable variety in potential entrants, reveal as much of the difficulties of modeling the game among entrants as they do about its potential payoffs.

The framework uses the size of the market, S, as the key exogenous observable. The latent profit to the nth firm into the market is modeled as

$$\Pi_n = (P(n) - mc)q(n){\cdot}S - F - B(N).$$

The first term is per-firm variable profit, modeled as linear in S.[19] The variable q is unit sales to the representative consumer made by each firm, so $q{\cdot}S$ is per-firm unit sales. The toughness of price competition appears as $P(n)$ (with $q(n)$ following along by a demand calculation). The outcome of the entry game is buried in the to-be-estimated parameters $B(n)$. If $B(2) > B(1)$, we infer that something is going on to keep second firms out of the market, but cannot say much about what it is.

These statistical models have two interpretations. The first one is structuralist. If the entry game can be written in normal form, hypotheses about simultaneous-move versus leader–follower equilibrium, or more generally about strategic heterogeneity among potential entrants, can be stated and tested.[20] The problem here is that much of the relevant theory resists statement in normal form; the underlying extensive forms are quite complex. This leads to an implicational reinterpretation. The parameter $B(N)$ is taken to be the reduced form of the theoretical model: whatever strategic interaction leads to unnaturally concentrated structure, we measure it. Obviously, this idea of $B(N)$ as a portmanteau statistic is closely related to Sutton's bounds idea.

The portmanteau statistic and the bound strike many as diffuse. Yet, quite a good deal has been learned. It may be very hard to learn (statistically) *how* sunk costs permit strategic manipulation of entry, exit, etc. Yet we have very good evidence, from very different contexts, *that* sunk cost, especially ESC, permit it.

There have been several analytical advances in knowledge despite these difficulties. We now know that there are a variety of industries in which the determination of entry and industry structure is strategic. Sunk costs have been implicated in the strategy, in the sense that industries where costs are more sunk and/or the sunk costs are more endogenous tend to have more concentrated structure. The latter inference, however, has a very reduced-form flavor. Little progress has been made in illuminating the exact mechanisms by which sunk costs, or exogenous sunk costs, enable strategic determination of market structure. Indeed, the very logic of the "bounds" approach is that it may not be possible to learn the exact mechanism.

Second, there may be alternative hypotheses of great power that are extremely difficult to reject. In both my paper with Peter Reiss (1990) and Berry (1992), consideration is given to the possibility that different potential entrants' profits (should they enter) are correlated. The correlation parameter is quite badly estimated in both analyses. Worse, the correlation parameter is very difficult to distinguish from the parameters measuring the extent of strategic limitations on competition. While this may sound like an econometric detail, the correlation is actually an important parameter. If entry calls for a great deal of skill or rare firm capabilities, that would appear in this context as weakly correlated profits across potential entrants. Potential entrants' profits will be strongly correlated if there are many firms with the capacity to enter. Presence or absence of a large body of capable entrants is an alternative, purely efficiency-based, theory of concentrated structure.

Despite these difficulties, we have learned a bit about some of the causes of concentrated industry structure. Certainly, the toughness of price competition is capable of measurement. Accordingly, we could move to systematic statistical work more of the task of measuring the extent to which industry structure is concentrated because of purely strategic considerations arising in the entry game. For this purpose, concentrated structure that arises because prices fall with entry would not count. This promising line is already associated with a small literature.[21]

Another method by which we could learn more about the causes of concentrated structure, and investigate more specifically the mechanisms, would be the use of the insider perspective. This is the approach of Burns (1986). He searched the records of the tobacco trust of a century ago for internal admissions that the trust was engaged in predation. (Predation was thought to be legal at the time; the records come down to us through the lawsuit which changed that.) He then regresses the price paid by the trust for various competitors it acquired, and finds that predation led to cheaper acquisitions. Similarly, many of Sutton's detailed industry studies in his chapters tell us the story of how strategy worked to lead to, or not lead to, concentrated structure in the industries he covers. I am not yet convinced that "bounds" is all we can get.

Of course, these more detailed studies have gone forward in extremely fact-rich environments. With modern antitrust laws, we will not frequently be able to collect data the way Burns did. Nor do many scholars have Sutton's exquisite timing, undertaking field research in a body of industries just as the business people who built its structure are contemplating retirement. The use of case studies and other insider-perspective methodologies may be a very promising route to deeper knowledge.

4   THE STATE OF KNOWLEDGE

The recent theoretical advances in Industrial Organization established the theoretical possibility of strategic forces mattering in industry economics.

No longer could the possibility that entrants were too few, prices too high, or strategy relevant be ruled out as a matter of pure logic. The literatures reviewed here have pushed that frontier farther. For some specific industries, we know that these are more than theoretical possibilities, they are marketplace realities.

In this chapter, I have examined three areas in which strategic interaction theories have been tested or strategic aspects of competition have been measured. One striking feature is the widely varying role of formal theory in the analysis. In some of the auction studies, there is a very high level of integration; every object in the theory is measured, every object in the empirical work has an explicit structural foundation in the Bayesian Nash Equilibrium theory. In the oligopoly pricing work, an initial phase of empirical work focused on testing strategic supply theories, also with game-theoretic foundations. More recent efforts have shifted emphasis to the demand side, however, and the vast majority of recent developments in the theory play no role. In the industry structure work, theories are grouped into (large!) equivalence classes, and analytical distinctions once taken to be important are suppressed. Only the robust, common implications of a wide variety of theories are tested. The second striking thing about these literatures is their emphasis on appropriate data analysis; a single industry or a group of closely related industries, price, quantity, entry and exit (not profit) as the dependent variables, and a focus on measurement method.[22]

Why did empirical work in Industrial Organization move from a model of theory testing to a model of using theories to interpret measures of economic quantities? Why haven't the deepest dynamic and informational aspects of the theory been tested? When we were working out strategic competition theory using models based on the theory of games, it was appropriate to put large weight on certain logical distinctions. As we turn to using the theory as one of the tools in making knowledge, the emphasis shifts. Theories are elegant when they clearly make right the logical distinctions; useful when they predict the important phenomena. I view it as a sign of maturity in our subdiscipline that a wide variety of approaches to studying phenomena, drawing on theory in a wide variety of ways, are in use.

For all the accomplishments of the papers covered here, they and others like them cover only a tiny fraction of the economy. That fraction has also been selected more for analytical convenience than, necessarily, for economic importance.[23] The challenge of going beyond them is twofold. First, there is work to do. Second, we will need to be more careful about the welfare economics as well as the positive economics, a topic which will take us back to the formal theory for more help.

Notes

I am indebted to many people for comments at the World Congress and thereafter. Jacques Cremer's wise suggestions deserve special notice.

1 Franklin Fisher has been a strong critic of the resulting "exemplifying theory" and its corrosive impact on empirical work: "The principal result of theory is that nearly anything can happen. This is confirmed by the inconclusive results of empirical studies. Theoretical models are oversimplified and provide questionable guidance in real situations. Empirical work is not informed by theory and is often without a sound analytic foundation. The field needs to study the ways in which the rich context of real situations affects behavior and results." One goal of this chapter is to take this challenge head on.

2 McAfee and McMillan (1987), Milgrom (1989), and Wilson (1992) survey the theoretical literature.

3 Where there may be gaps, these often relate to the behavior of *sellers*, which is a much more difficult subject for both theory and empirical work. Empirical scholars have tended to examine what sellers actually do in practice and make that part of the model of the game buyers play. Another important gap is the theory of complex, multi-object auctions, like those for parts of the electromagnetic spectrum recently conducted in the US.

4 With appropriate humility, we might also say that the behavior in the theory looks pretty compelling to us as economists but that there might be other elements of human behavior we do not understand yet which belong in the true theory.

5 Similarly, the need for elegant econometrics arises in other structuralist approaches to private-information games in very different contexts. See Wolak (1994) for a structuralist principal/agent model of regulation.

6 They simulate the first moment of the observed distribution of winning bids.

7 Paarsch (1992) offers a test between common-value and private-value variants. Laffont et al. (1995) offer some remarks on future testing in their conclusion, and we can hope for developments in that direction.

8 While it is wise not to say never, it seems unlikely that any structuralist investigation of the full Hendricks–Porter model will overcome these difficulties anytime soon.

9 See Porter and Zona (1993).

10 For example, Ashenfelter (1989).

11 A great deal of effort has been expended in attempting to work out the relationship between market institutions and the rules of the oligopoly game. It has proved difficult to take advantage of this in empirical work. A change in an institution's conditions of commitment or in the exact structure of the information it reveals can have profound implications for the game being played. There was for a while some hope that these subtleties might be resolved by purely logical arguments, but now the "refinement" agenda seems more like the quest for the holy grail than for the unified field theory. Even had the theory succeeded, we would still face the inherent difficulty of mapping institutions-in-the-world to institutions-in-the-

theory. Game-theory models are purely logical objects; they are linked to the world by correspondences between key assumptions and features of observable institutions that might be the same as the assumptions. That correspondence will be, in a real industry, subject to multiple interpretations.

12 This finding was later replicated from another more recent period by Bresnahan (1981). More importantly, it has been replicated by Berry, Levinsohn, and Pakes (1995) in a model which does not impose the vertical product-differentiation structure. Indeed, the Berry, Levinsohn, and Pakes model imposes only very weak restrictions on the pattern of substitutability. This superior structure comes with the requirement of more difficult econometrics.

13 Or of continuation in it, in the fully optimal version of the theory provided by Abreu *et al.* (1990).

14 See Porter and Lee (1985), Berry and Briggs (1988), and Hajivassilou (1989).

15 In the next section, when I turn to the LR analysis of the determinants of market structure, this same remark will return in force.

16 See Trajtenberg (1986) and Hausman (1994).

17 With the observation that product differentiation is the key, why do we need new measurement methods in Industrial Organization? The focus of these papers is on measuring buyer behavior, not testing seller behavior. While the outcome of that process is a market power or similar assessment, the process itself would seem to belong in another field. The answer arises because of the potential endogeneity of prices (or of other marketing variables) in the demand system. There is a substantial role for the industrial organization theory of supply to play in revealing why it is that the demand system is identified and how it should be estimated. Without an assumed model of supply, none of the demand systems would be identified. See Bresnahan, Stern, and Trajtenberg (1995).

18 This idea has even become fairly important to US antitrust enforcers, stirred by Baker and Bresnahan (1986).

19 The linearity is relaxed in later papers, but I retain it here for clarity in exposition.

20 Bresnahan and Reiss take up the question, in a study of rural automobile dealerships, of whether General Motors dealers are more frequent monopolists because they are leaders in a game where Ford dealers are followers. Berry examines the variety induced in airlines' entry behavior by their distinct pre-entry positions.

21 This literature was originated by Reiss and Spiller (1989). Bresnahan and Reiss (1991) provides further data along these lines.

22 One of the more valuable offshoots of the new IO theory has been this re-focus on careful industry studies. The theory leads us to expect both SR and LR competition to be complex, and to vary complexity across industries. It also leads us to expect industry details and institutions to be important. Now, competition studies are starting to catch up to regulatory ones in scholars' depth of knowledge of their industries.

23 This criticism applies to me, author of a study on rural dentists' exit, as much as to anyone.

References

Abreu, Dilip, Pearce, David, and Stacchetti, Enni (1990). "Toward a theory of discounted repeated games with imperfect monitoring." *Econometrica*, 58 (5) (September): 1041–63.

Ashenfelter, Orley (1989). "How auctions work for wine and art." *Journal of Economic Perspectives*, 3 (3): 23–36.

Baker, Jonathan (1985). *The Gains from Merger or Collusion in Product Differentiated Industries.* Oxford and New York: Blackwell.

 (1989). "Identifying cartel policing under uncertainty: The US steel industry, 1933–1939." *Journal of Law and Economics*, 32 (2): 47–76.

Berry, Steven (1992). "Estimation of a model of entry in the airline industry." *Econometrica*, 60 (4): 889–917.

Berry, Steven and Briggs, Hugh (1988). "A non-parametric test of a first-order Markov process for regimes in a non-cooperatively collusive industry." *Economics Letters*, 27 (1): 73–7.

Berry, Steven, Levinsohn, J., and Pakes, Ariel (1995). "Automobile prices in market equilibrium." *Econometrica*, 63 (4): 841–90.

Bresnahan, Timothy (1981). "Departures from marginal cost pricing in American automobile industry: estimates for 1977–1978." *Journal of Econometrics*, 17 (2): 201–27.

 (1995). "Competition and collusion in the American automobile industry." *Journal of Industrial Economics*, 35 (4): 457–82.

Bresnahan, Timothy, and Reiss, Peter (1987). "Do entry conditions vary across markets?" *Brooking Papers on Economic Activity: Microeconomics*, 3 (0): 833–71.

 (1990). "Entry in monopoly markets." *Review of Economic Studies*, 57 (4): 531–53.

 (1991). "Entry and competition in concentrated markets." *Journal of Political Economy*, 99 (5): 977–1009.

Bresnahan, Timothy, Stern, Scott, and Trajtenberg, Manuel (1995). "Market segmentation and the sources of rents from innovation: personal computers in the late 1980s." Stanford Center for Economic Research Research.

Burns, M. (1986). "Predatory pricing and the acquisition costs of competitors." *Journal of Political Economy*, 94: 266–96.

Cosslett, Stephen R. and Lee, Lung-Fei (1985). "Serial correlation in latent discrete variable models." *Journal of Econometrics*, 27 (1): 37–57.

Ellison, Glenn (1994). "Theories of cartel stability and the joint executive committee." *RAND Journal of Economics*, 25 (1): 37–57.

Fisher, Franklin (1991). "Organizing industrial organization: Reflections on the handbook of industrial organization." *Brooking Papers on Economic Activity: Microeconomics*, pp 210–25.

Gasmi, F., Laffont, J.J., and Vuong, Quang (1992). "Econometric analysis of collusive behavior in a soft drink market." *Journal of Economics and Management Strategy*, 1 (2): 277–311.

Goldberg, Pinelope (1995). "Product differentiation and oligopoly in international markets: the case of the US automobile industry." *Econometrica*, 63 (4): 891–951.

Green, Edward J. and Porter, Robert (1984). "Noncooperative collusion under imperfect price information." *Econometrica*, 52 (1): 87–100.

Hajivassiliou, Vassilis A. (1989). "Testing game-theoretic models of price fixing behavior." Yale Cowles Foundation Discussion Paper: 935, p. 36.

Hausman, Jerry A. (1994). "Valuation of new goods under perfect and imperfect competition." MIT Mimeo.

Hendricks, Kenneth and Porter, Robert (1988). "An empirical study of an auction with asymmetric information." *American Economic Review*, 78 (5): 865–83.

Hendricks, Kenneth, Porter, Robert and Boudreau, Byran (1987). "Information, returns, and bidding behavior in OCS auctions: 1954–1969." *Journal of Industrial Economics*, 35 (4): pp 517–42.

Laffont, Jean-Jacques, Ossard, Herve, and Vuong, Quang (1995). "Econometrics of first-price auctions." *Econometrica*, 63 (4): 953–80.

Lee, Lung-Fei and Porter, Robert (1984). "Switching regression models with imperfect sample separation information – with an application on cartel stability." *Econometrica*, 52 (2): 391–418.

McAfee, Preston and McMilan, John (1987). "Auctions and bidding." *Journal of Economic Literature*, 25 (2): 699–738.

Milgrom, Paul (1989). "Auctions and bidding: a primer." *Journal of Economic Perspectives*; 3 (3): 3–22.

Paarsch, Harry J. (1992). "Deciding between the common and private value paradigms in empirical models of auctions." *Journal of Econometrics*, 51 (1–2): 191–215.

Porter, Robert (1983). "A study of cartel stability: the joint executive committee, 1880–1886." *Journal of Economics*, 14 (2): 301–14.

(1985). "On the incidence and duration of price wars." *Journal of Industrial Economics*, 33 (4): 415–26.

Porter, Robert and Zona, J. Douglas (1993). "Detection of bid rigging in procurement auctions." *Journal of Political Economy*, 101 (3): 518–38.

Reiss, Peter and Spiller, Pablo (1989). "Competition and entry in small airline markets." *Journal of Law and Economics*, 32: 179–202.

Roberts, M. and Samuelson, L. (1988). "An empirical analysis of dynamic, nonprice competition in an oligopolistic industry." *RAND Journal of Economics*, 19: 200–20.

Sutton, John (1991). *Sunk costs and Market Structure: Price Competition, Advertising, and the Evolution of Concentration.* Cambridge, MA: MIT Press.

Trajtenberg, Manuel (1989). "The welfare analysis of product innovations, with an application to computed tomography scanners." *Journal of Political Economy*, 97 (2): 444–79.

Wilson, Robert (1992). "Strategic analysis of auctions." In Auman, Robert J. and Hart, Sergiu (eds.), *Handbook of Game Theory with Economic Applications*. Vol. 1.

Wolak, Frank A. (1994). "An econometric analysis of the asymmetric information, regulator-utility interaction." *Annales d'Economie et de Statistique*, 0 (34): 13–69.

CHAPTER 4

Empirical equilibrium search models

Geert Ridder and Gerard J. van den Berg

1   INTRODUCTION AND MOTIVATION

The labor market shows more resemblance to a busy street market than to a well-organized auction. As in a street market, there are many distinct buyers and sellers of a similar commodity, and the turnover of these agents prevents that complete knowledge of supply and demand is ever attained. Agents search for good deals, and in doing so they evaluate offers on the basis of their impression of the alternatives in the market. If we observe the actions of the agents in such a market, we may hope to learn which strategies they use. Moreover, trade occurs even between agents who do not have complete knowledge of supply and demand, and our observations may be informative on the determination of the terms of the transactions in such a market.

In labor economics, research on decentralized search markets has been and still is very active. This research is mainly theoretical. Only recently, researchers have used models from the vast theoretical literature in empirical studies. There are a number of reasons for this delay. First, theoretical models need to be adapted to empirical research, and this requires often considerable effort. Second, market models seem to require information on both sides of the market. In the previous decades, labor economists have invested heavily in the collection of data on the suppliers of labor. Efforts to collect comparable data for firms had less success. Without these data the estimation of market models seems to be pointless.

In this chapter we survey search market models that can be estimated from information on the supply side only. Of course, this comes at a price. First, we need quite extensive information on the suppliers of labor. Fortunately, the type of data that is needed is now available for many countries. Second, we need to close the model by assumptions on the behavior of the firms. This can be done in various ways. In this chapter, we shall use results of Burdett and Mortensen (Mortensen (1990), Burdett and Mortensen (1995)), who give an elegant analysis of search markets, that is particularly suited to empirical research. One attractive feature of their model is that it has a closed-form equilibrium solution. This solution depends on a set of parameters that can be estimated from individual labor-market histories. There are few theoretical contributions that are equally useful for empiricists.

We refer to the type of models considered in this chapter as equilibrium search models. These models are an important tool in understanding the joint distribution of wages and spells, as obtained from individual labor-market histories. Partial search models, i.e. search models that only model one side of the market, have been an important tool in understanding spell distributions. Hence, the present chapter goes one step further. The empirical analysis of equilibrium search models is a new development, and we can only report on the progress that has been made until now.

In search market models wages need not equal the marginal value product of workers. In the past decade empirical research has uncovered some facts that are not easily explained in standard competitive models of the labor market. It is not surprising, that the more realistic search models can accommodate these facts. As we shall see, search market models also have implications for the effectiveness of policy interventions, and, in some cases, the conclusions differ markedly from those obtained with competitive models.

The plan of the chapter is as follows. In section 2 we give a short overview of the history of search market models. Section 3 describes the type of data that is needed, and documents empirical regularities that the models should explain. The Burdett–Mortensen search-market model is introduced in section 4. Section 5 relaxes a number of counterfactual assumptions. The search-market model for homogeneous agents is estimated in section 6. The results lead to extensions that give a better fit to the observations. These are considered in section 7. Section 8 discusses some unresolved issues.

2   SOME HISTORY

Before we discuss the type of equilibrium search models that are considered in this chapter, it is instructive to see how the concept of equilibrium search has emerged and how it has evolved over time. In this short history, we shall stress those developments that have affected empirical work.

In most markets it takes effort to complete a transaction. Usually, a buyer and a seller have to meet and they must agree on the terms of the transaction, e.g., on the price. In the labor market, there are many potential employers of a job seeker, and many potential employees of an employer who has a job opening. Although there are intermediaries that match job seekers and job openings, job seekers and employers do not have complete information, and must search to meet potential employers c.q. employees. This observation is the starting point of search theory, and it is hardly surprising that search theory has become an important tool in the study of labor markets.

The first application of search theory was to the labor-supply decision of unemployed workers. The theoretical and empirical literature on this particular application is large. Mortensen (1986) surveys the theory, and Devine and Kiefer (1991) and Wolpin (1994) give an overview of the many empirical studies. Some of these empirical studies use models that are derived from search theory, while others use the theory to interpret the results obtained from reduced-form hazard rate analyses.[1] Search theory has also been used to study other labor-supply decisions under imperfect information, in particular job search by the employed (Mortensen and Neumann (1988) and Van den Berg (1992)). This is an important extension, because it is unlikely that workers will ignore job offers received while employed.

The supply-side search models are asymmetric, because it is assumed that only the (un)employed workers search, while the employers are passive. Indeed, there is evidence that employers, if they engage in search at all, employ strategies that differ from those used by workers (Van Ours and Ridder (1992)). Because of this disregard of employer behavior, labor-market search theory has sometimes been referred to as a partial-partial theory. It deals only with the supply side of a single market. Shortly after the introduction of search theory in economics, it became clear that this is unsatisfactory.

There are two problems with the concentration on the supply side, and these two problems have led to two types of equilibrium models: equilibrium contact rate models and equilibrium wage offer models. In the one-sided model, job seekers receive job offers according to a stochastic process, usually a Poisson process. It is unlikely, that the rate at which job seekers locate job openings is independent of the total number of job seekers and job openings. There may be congestion effects as the number of job seekers increases, and in general one expects that the total number of contacts in the market increases with the number of job seekers and job openings. The view that contacts may be considered as the outcome of a production process with the numbers of job seekers and job openings as inputs is since Blanchard and Diamond (1989) widespread among macro-economists. In the search literature, this observation has led to the consideration of the efficiency of search. Because it is likely, that the individual job seekers ignore the effect of their behavior on the contact rate, there is an externality that may result in a suboptimal level of unemployment. Although much effort has been invested in the development of models that acknowledge this search externality (recent contributions are Pissarides (1990) and Mortensen and Wright (1995)), it plays a smaller role in microeconometric studies. The reason is that these ignore the dependence of the arrival rates on aggregate conditions. Job seekers are assumed to be arrival-rate-takers, whose individual influence on the contact rate is negligible. Hence, if aggregate conditions do not change too much, this dependence can be ignored in studies of individual behavior. This is similar to ignoring the interaction of demand and supply in studies of individual behavior. This is similar to ignoring the interaction of demand and supply in studies of consumer demand. Of course, if the arrival rate depends on the number of active agents in the market, models that ignore this dependence may give misleading estimates of effects of policy interventions. We shall return to this point later.

The second problem with the one-sided approach touches the heart of the search model. It is clear that search will only occur if there is a gain from search. Although there may be a gain from unemployment search even if all jobs pay the same wage, this not true for search while employed. In other words, labor-market search requires the existence of a dispersed wage offer distribution. However, as Diamond already observed in 1971 (Diamond (1971)), the simple sequential search model, in which identical unemployed workers who face identical firms accept/reject wage offers one at a time, is not consistent with a dispersed wage equilibrium. His argument is simple: the optimal strategy with sequential search is a reservation wage strategy; for the employers it is suboptimal to offer a wage that is larger than the common reservation wage, and, hence, the equilibrium wage offer distribution is concentrated at this reservation wage; finally, this common reservation wage must be equal to the lowest wage that is acceptable to the unemployed, i.e., their value of leisure. The unique equilibrium is the monopsony equilibrium.

Diamond's observation stimulated research on the equilibrium wage offer distribution in a search market where (identical) job seekers employ an optimal search strategy, and (identical) employers set wages, taking account of these search strategies and the wages offered by other firms. This research has clarified the effect of the search method on the equilibrium offer distribution. Assume for instance that job seekers always receive two wage offers. In that case, the lower offer is rejected, and this rejection leads to a degenerate equilibrium wage offer distribution, which is concentrated at the highest wage that is acceptable to the employers, i.e., the common marginal value product of the job seekers. Hence, the equilibrium is the competitive equilibrium (Burdett (1990b)). A dispersed wage offer distribution results if the number of job offers at any contact is a random variable, which takes the values 1 or 2 (or more) with some probability (Burdett and Judd (1983)).

Diamond's result also does not hold if we allow for search while employed. The reason is that job seekers no longer have a common reservation wage, as the reservation wage of an employed job seeker is equal to his or her current wage. This insight was first used by Burdett and Mortensen (1995). In this chapter we consider models that follow their lead.

In search markets with heterogeneous workers and firms, we obtain a dispersed equilibrium wage offer distribution even if there is only unemployed search. As noted, wage offers must be equal to the reservation wages of job seekers. If among (unemployed) job seekers the reservation wages are dispersed, e.g., because values of leisure vary, *and* if the marginal value products differ among firms, then a dispersed wage offer distribution results (Albrecht and Axell (1984)). The dispersion in the value of products is necessary for a dispersed equilibrium: if all firms are equally productive, and the employers cannot discriminate between workers, then in general the wage offer distribution is degenerate, and the offered wage is determined by maximizing the profit function, where the supply of labor is equal to the number of unemployed workers whose value of leisure is smaller than the offered wage. Again this is the monopsony equilibrium. A model with heterogeneous workers and firms has been estimated by Eckstein and Wolpin (1990).

The attempts to obtain a dispersed wage offer distribution in a market equilibrium are not only of theoretical interest. They also have important implications for policy analysis and empirical research in the search framework. As noted, if only the unemployed search, then wage offers are equal to the reservation wage(s) of the unemployed. Hence, policy interventions that affect the reservation wages change the wage offer distribution as well. Job search models have been used to study the effect of unemployment benefits on the search strategy of the unemployed. If such models ignore the effect of changes in benefits on the wages set by the employers, the derived policy effects may be misleading.

Although search theory has inspired a vast amount of empirical work, its usefulness has been challenged. A major criticism has been that the wage offer distribution cannot be identified by the type of data that are usually collected. These data consist of durations and accepted wages. If all job seekers have a common reservation wage and a common wage offer distribution, then this amounts to a sample from a truncated distribution, where the reservation wage is the lower boundary of the support. If the common reservation wage is denoted by r and the wage offer distribution has density f which is positive for wages $w \geq 0$, then the density of the truncated distribution is

$$f(w \mid w \geq r) = \frac{f(w)}{1 - F(r)}, \quad w \geq r \tag{1}$$

with F the distribution function. A second wage offer density is defined using f

$$g(w) = \frac{1 - \pi}{1 - F(r)} f(w), \quad w \geq r \tag{2}$$

$$= h(w), \quad w < r \tag{3}$$

in which h satisfies $\int_0^r h(w)dw = \pi$ and is arbitrary otherwise. It is easily seen, that g is a proper density and that $g(w \mid w \geq r) = f(w \mid w \geq r)$ for all $w \geq r$. Hence, the distributions of accepted wages corresponding to f and g coincide, while the probability mass below the truncation point can be arbitrarily different. Because h is arbitrary, the wage offer density g can be chosen to be differentiable at r.

Accepted wages are not sufficient to identify the wage offer distribution. In particular, we cannot identify the probability mass below the reservation wage. This is a serious problem, because that probability mass is the probability that a job seeker rejects a wage offer, and therefore is a measure of the choosiness of the job seeker. One of the questions, that empirical studies try to answer is whether the length of a search spell is determined by the availability of job offers or by the rejection probability of offers. Partial-partial job search theory cannot answer this question without untestable distributional assumptions. Of course, we can identify the wage offer distribution if rejected offers are available. However, such data are rare. A possible solution is to restrict f to a class of densities that is closed under the operation in (2). Partial-partial search theory provides no guidance in the choice of the wage offer distribution, so that we can only trust results that do not require the untruncated wage offer distribution (Lancaster and Chesher (1983)). Because the wage offer distribution is endogenous to the equilibrium search models, that are considered in this chapter, these models do provide guidance on the choice of the wage offer distribution.

3   EMPIRICAL REGULARITIES

3.1   Data requirements

Because equilibrium search models concern the joint distribution of (unemployment and job) spells, and (accepted and earned) wages, they are estimated from data on individual labor-market histories. Individual labor-market histories are obtained by following a sample of individuals during some period of time, recording the dates at which transitions between labor-market positions occur, as well as other information pertaining to these positions. Often three positions or states are distinguished: unemployment, employment, and non-participation. In the employment state one usually records transitions between jobs, but we shall not distinguish between types of jobs. Equilibrium search theory does not purport to describe the participation decision, although it can be easily extended to allow for transitions to non-participation. For that reason, we concentrate on the states of unemployment and employment. Besides the dates of transitions, we assume that the income in these states is recorded, i.e., unemployment benefits in the unemployment state and wages in the jobs held in the employment state.

To summarize, we assume that for a sample of individuals and for some observation period, we observe the dates of transitions between the unemployment and employment states, and within the employment state the dates of job changes, and that for each spell of unemployment and each job we observe the associated income. The minimal data that allow for the estimation of an equilibrium search model are for each individual either an unemployment spell or a job spell with the incomes during these spells, and in case of a job spell the type of state occupied after the current spell, i.e., either another job spell or an unemployment spell. This just suffices to obtain the joint distribution of unemployment and job spells, the destination state after a job, and the wage earned in a job. The unemployment income is exogenous to the equilibrium search model.

These minimal data are available for many countries, mainly because of efforts to collect panel data on individual labor-market behavior. It must be stressed that, although equilibrium search models describe the behavior of workers and firms, they can be estimated from data obtained by surveying only workers. This is convenient, because matched individual-firm data are not easily obtained. If such data were widely available, they could also be interpreted in an equilibrium search framework, and indeed such data would allow us to make considerable progress, as we shall argue below.

We make a distinction between the joint distribution of spells and wages as derived from the theory and the *observed* distribution of these variables, obtained by some observation plan. They only coincide, if we observe the labor-market histories for new entrants. In theory, we could follow new entrants until retirement, but usually the observation period is restricted to a few years. In that case, it may be preferable to obtain labor-market histories for a random sample of individuals. An additional advantage is that it may be difficult to sample from the new entrants, while in most countries sampling frames for the whole population are readily available. By interviewing or by obtaining records from administrative sources, we determine the labor-market position at some reference date. Starting at the reference date, we reconstruct the labor-market history in the past, and we follow the individuals until the end of the observation period. The correspondence between the labor-market histories obtained by this observation plan, and the distributions derived from the theory is well known (e.g., Ridder (1984)). In most countries, labor-market histories are obtained by this observation plan.

The data used in this chapter are obtained by the OSA[2] Labor Supply Panel (OLSP). The first wave of this panel was in April–May 1985. Since then there have been three more waves in August–October 1986, August–October 1988, and August–November 1990. In the OLSP a sample of households in The Netherlands is followed over time. In 1985 this sample of 2,132 households was drawn at random from all households with at least one member in the age bracket 16–60. All individuals who were between 16 and 60 years of age were interviewed, in 1985, 4,020 individuals. Despite efforts to keep track of households that moved, some households were lost during subsequent waves. To keep the sample size constant, these were replaced by randomly selected households. In 1990, 1,384 (34 percent) of the individuals of the first wave were still in the panel. The replacement of lost households led to an increase in the number of individuals under observation, in 1990, 4,438 individuals. Although the OLSP is a panel of households, we treat it as a panel of individuals.[3]

From the OLSP we obtained the labor-market histories of the respondents. The reference date in the observation plan is the date of the first interview in April–May 1985. The data allow us to reconstruct the sojourn time in the labor-market state occupied at that date. Moreover, we can follow the individual until the last completed interview. This allows us to determine the period that the individual stays in the labor-market state of the first interview. In other words, from the OLSP we can obtain the minimal data needed to estimate the equilibrium search model. Most of the time we shall use a subsample. We exclude individuals who during the observation period have been self-employed, have been non-participant or have worked part-time, i.e., less than 30 hours per week. This selection consists of 1,949 individuals. Of those, 34 percent participated in all waves, while 33 percent dropped out after the first.

3.2 Wage regressions and distributions

Because wages, job spells, and unemployment spells are the endogenous variables of the equilibrium search model, it is important to study their distributions. First, we consider the wages. Labor economists have run numerous wage regressions, and it is not our intention to replicate those. We only want to show that the wage data in the OLSP are similar to those in many other studies. The wage data in OLSP are net wages. It would be preferable to have gross wages. In table 4.1 we report the results of a regression of the net hourly wage, in guilders, and the net monthly wage, in 1,000 guilders, for all individuals who had a job at the date of the first interview, and of the net monthly wage of the individuals in our subsample who had a job at that date. The regressors are

Industry: classification on the first digit of the standard industry classification.

Firm characteristics: number of employees divided by 1,000.

Job characteristics: contractual working hours and overtime in hours per week; job level.

Work history: self-reported work experience in years; total number of previous employers; total number of unemployment spells; tenure on the current job in years.

Education: level and orientation.

Demographics: age in years; born outside The Netherlands; region: city indicates the four main cities in The Netherlands.

Labor market: unemployment rate (percentage) by occupation, age, and gender.

Because the dependent variable in the equilibrium search models is the wage and not the logarithm of the wage, we do not apply a transformation to the wage.

The estimates replicate results in the literature. We find significant industry effects (Krueger and Summers (1988)) and employer size effects (Brown and Medoff (1989)). The effects of the job level and the level of education of the employee are pronounced. The coefficients of experience, tenure, and the number of previous employers are small and insignificant, except for the hourly wage regression in which the experience coefficient is significantly positive. This is surprising, but the estimates may be biased because of measurement error. The measure of work experience was obtained from a single question, and not from more detailed information on jobs held before January 1, 1980. The demographic variables have the expected sign. Note that employees who were not born in The Netherlands do not earn less, while women earn significantly less. The latter result may be due to the poor quality of the experience variable. Finally, there are significant differences between the regions, and the unemployment rate of employees of the same age, occupation, and gender has also a significantly negative effect on wages. As expected, monthly wages are positively related to working hours. The hourly wage is negatively related to working hours, but this is most likely due to the higher tax rate on full-time incomes.

Table 4.1. *Wage regressions: monthly (in 1000 guilders) and hourly net wage in 1985; standard errors in parentheses*

Variable	Hourly wage, full sample		Monthly wage, full sample		Monthly wage, subsample	
Industry						
Agriculture	-1.02	(1.01)	-0.18	(0.14)	-0.17	(0.16)
Mining	-1.64	(1.66)	-0.17	(0.23)	0.011	(0.27)
Heavy industry						
Processing	-1.19	(0.43)	-0.14	(0.060)	-0.13	(0.070)
Utilities	0.50	(0.90)	0.19	(0.13)	0.14	(0.14)
Construction	-0.48	(0.47)	-0.093	(0.066)	-0.12	(0.075)
Trade/repair	-1.15	(0.41)	-0.15	(0.057)	-0.16	(0.066)
Transportation	-0.74	(0.49)	-0.089	(0.068)	-0.10	(0.081)
Services	0.045	(0.44)	-0.034	(0.061)	0.055	(0.072)
Health/education	0.74	(0.39)	-0.11	(0.054)	-0.13	(0.064)
Firm characteristics						
Firm size	0.32	(0.11)	0.056	(0.016)	0.065	(0.018)
Job characteristics						
Working week	-0.095	(0.012)	0.041	(0.0017)	0.035	(0.0032)
Overtime	0.034	(0.025)	0.012	(0.0035)	0.014	(0.0038)
No skill required	-0.37	(0.40)	-0.082	(0.056)	-0.095	(0.072)
Semi-skilled	-0.25	(0.30)	-0.038	(0.042)	-0.046	(0.052)
Skilled						
Skilled, experience	0.21	(0.28)	-0.0037	(0.039)	-0.020	(0.048)
Specialized, some theory	1.09	(0.33)	0.16	(0.046)	0.17	(0.053)
Specialized, more theory	3.37	(0.34)	0.47	(0.047)	0.46	(0.056)
Scientific	4.23	(0.47)	0.54	(0.066)	0.51	(0078).

Table 4.1. continued

Variable	Hourly wage, full sample		Monthly wage, full sample		Monthly wage, subsample	
Work history						
Experience	0.050	(0.019)	0.0032	(0.0027)	−0.0028	(0.0040)
No. of employers	0.013	(0.036)	−0.0019	(0.0050)	0.0042	(0.0066)
No. of unemployment spells	−0.64	(0.27)	−0.084	(0.038)	−0.11	(0.045)
Tenure	0.000024	(0.18)	0.0050	(0.025)	−0.0040	(0.031)
Education						
Basic	−1.52	(0.88)	−0.29	(0.12)	−0.35	(0.15)
Extended	−0.60	(0.35)	−0.10	(0.050)	−0.13	(0.063)
Intermediate						
Professional	0.87	(0.26)	0.098	(0.036)	0.081	(0.044)
Higher professional	2.41	(0.33)	0.32	(0.047)	0.32	(0.056)
University	4.95	(0.57)	0.76	(0.080)	0.79	(0.096)
General	0.71	(0.28)	0.10	(0.040)	0.085	(0.047)
Humanities	−2.33	(1.05)	−0.38	(0.15)	−0.39	(0.17)
Agricultural	−0.63	(0.72)	−0.089	(0.10)	−0.12	(0.12)
Technical						
Transportation	−0.012	(0.65)	0.044	(0.091)	0.0094	(0.10)
Medical	0.43	(0.60)	0.054	(0.084)	0.049	(0.11)
Administrative	0.61	(0.31)	0.14	(0.043)	0.12	(0.050)
Social	−0.93	(0.56)	−0.089	(0.079)	−0.14	(0.10)
Care	−0.33	(0.42)	0.017	(0.058)	−0.0028	(0.075)
Public safety	−0.56	(0.82)	−0.097	(0.11)	−0.079	(0.13)

	(1)		(2)		(3)	
Demographic						
Age	0.057	(0.019)	0.015	(0.0027)	0.024	(0.0041)
Foreign born	0.22	(0.46)	−0.045	(0.065)	−0.10	(0.079)
Female	−2.01	(0.27)	−0.33	(0.038)	−0.29	(0.046)
North	0.081	(0.32)	−0.020	(0.045)	−0.015	(0.056)
East	−0.29	(0.26)	−0.094	(0.036)	−0.10	(0.043)
West						
South	−0.39	(0.24)	−0.062	(0.034)	−0.051	(0.041)
City	−0.50	(0.28)	−0.097	(0.040)	−0.11	(0.049)
Labor market						
Unemployment rate	−0.034	(0.011)	−0.0068	(0.0016)	−0.0071	(0.0020)
Constant	12.79	(0.86)	−0.11	(0.12)	−0.070	(0.18)
Mean of dep. var.	12.22		1.849		2.092	
R^2	0.43		0.66		0.54	
No. of observations	1679		1679		1270	

The differences between the estimates for the subsample and the full OLSP are small. Although the extensive list of explanatory variables given a better fit than usual, the R^2 does not exceed 0.66. We experimented with adding even more explanatory variables, e.g., working conditions, but we never obtained an R^2 larger than 0.70. Productive characteristics of the employees and job, firm, and labor-market characteristics do not fully explain the dispersion in wages. We are not the first to find evidence of unexplained wage or price dispersion. Bowlus, Kiefer, and Neumann (1995) report unexplained wage variation of 18–28 percent for full-time employees in narrowly defined job categories in a regional labor market. Earlier, Pratt, Wise, and Zeckhauser (1979) found evidence of significant price dispersion for 39 randomly selected consumer goods. We conclude that the wage regressions reported here, and those reported elsewhere, cast doubt on competitive wage setting. Whether alternative models fare better remains to be seen, but there is at least a case for trying alternatives to the standard competitive model.

As the models that we consider make specific predictions on the shape of the wage distribution, figure 4.1 plots kernel estimates of the wage densities in our subsample.[4] We give both the estimated density of wages of individuals working at the date of the first interview in April–May 1985, and that of the wages accepted by individuals who were unemployed at that date. The density of the wages earned is concentrated at higher wages than the density of the accepted wages.

3.3   Unemployment and job durations

Next we consider the distributions of the unemployment and job durations. Because the unemployment and job durations are interrupted at the date of the first interview, long job and unemployment durations are overrepresented in our sample, and simple summary statistics as empirical hazard functions are uninformative. For that reason we estimate reduced-form duration models of the mixed proportional hazards type. The results are taken from Van den Berg and Ridder (1993). The hazard is specified as

$$\theta(t \mid x, v) = \alpha t^{\alpha - 1} \exp(\beta' x) v \tag{4}$$

i.e., we estimate a mixed proportional hazards model of the Weibull type. The unobserved heterogeneity v is specified to have a discrete distribution with two points of support v_1, v_2. The mean of the distribution of v is normalized to 1. The likelihood function takes account of the length bias in the durations and is based on the joint distribution of the elapsed and residual durations relative to the date of the first interview. This joint

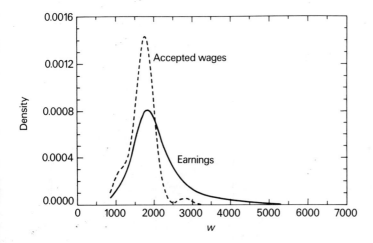

Figure 4.1 Kernel estimates of earnings and wage offer density

distribution can be found in, e.g., Ridder (1984). The results for the unemployment spells are in table 4.2, and those for the job spells in table 4.3.

The results agree with prior expectations. The age effect dominates and higher educated individuals have a larger re-employment hazard. Here, we are mainly interested in duration dependence in the re-employment hazard. If we allow for unobserved heterogeneity, there is some evidence of positive but insignificant duration dependence. As we shall see, the equilibrium search models can accommodate heterogeneity in the re-employment hazard, but duration dependence is less easily accounted for.

We also computed the correlation between the accepted wages of the unemployed and the residual unemployment duration measured from the date of the first interview. This correlation is 0.033, and is not significantly different from 0. If the reservation wages of the unemployed varied over the population, one would expect a significantly positive correlation between the duration of unemployment and the accepted wage. It seems that the re-employment hazard is not much affected by the reservation wage, and this is consistent with acceptance of the first offer that is received.

The results for the job spells show that younger, higher educated, and low wage individuals are more likely to leave their jobs. Again there is not much to choose between unobserved heterogeneity and duration dependence.

Table 4.2. *Proportional hazard models for unemployment spells (N = 217); standard errors in parentheses*

Variable	Exponential model		Two point unobs. heterogeneity		Unobs. heterogeneity, Weibull	
Education						
Primary						
Secondary	−0.21	(0.20)	−0.31	(0.24)	−0.39	(0.30)
Higher vocational	0.097	(0.30)	0.046	(0.26)	0.0086	(0.20)
University	0.57	(0.56)	0.47	(0.55)	0.49	(0.65)
Age						
−29						
30−8	−0.46	(0.21)	−0.49	(0.28)	−0.71	(0.44)
39−	−0.65	(0.19)	−0.63	(0.23)	−0.80	(0.35)
Job level						
Unskilled						
Semi-skilled	0.081	(0.20)	0.11	(0.21)	0.087	(0.28)
Skilled	−0.79	(0.41)	−0.77	(0.52)	−0.95	(0.80)
Specialized	−0.12	(0.47)	−0.031	(0.20)	−0.0005	(0.093)
Constant	−3.58	(0.18)	−2.56	(0.46)	−3.59	(1.13)
v_1			0.28		0.13	
v_2			1.63	(0.32)	1.55	(0.18)
$\Pr(v = v_2)$			0.53	(0.27)	0.61	(0.18)
α					1.39	(0.38)
Ln(likelihood)	−785.56		−780.42		−779.94	

Table 4.3. *Proportional hazard models for job durations (N = 1,614); standard errors in parentheses*

Variable	Exponential model		Two point unobs. heterogeneity		Unobs. heterogeneity, Weibull	
Education						
Primary						
Secondary	0.14	(0.086)	0.15	(0.10)	0.11	(0.087)
Higher vocational	0.42	(0.12)	0.45	(0.15)	0.32	(0.17)
University	0.70	(0.19)	0.80	(0.21)	0.55	(0.27)
Age						
-22						
23–9	-0.25	(0.12)	-0.24	(0.16)	-0.18	(0.13)
30–8	-1.02	(0.14)	-1.07	(0.17)	-0.78	(0.33)
39–	-1.62	(0.16)	-1.72	(0.19)	-1.26	(0.51)
Job level						
Unskilled						
Semi-skilled	0.045	(0.064)	0.029	(0.11)	0.020	(0.080)
Skilled	0.13	(0.13)	0.11	(0.16)	0.096	(0.12)
Specialized	0.20	(0.13)	0.14	(0.16)	0.13	(0.12)
Wage/1000	-0.21	(0.084)	-0.21	(0.086)	-0.14	(0.086)
Constant	-4.16	(0.16)	-3.52	(0.23)	-2.55	(0.80)
v_1			0.32		0.68	
v_2			1.40	(0.23)	1.18	(2.84)
$\Pr(v = v_2)$			0.63	(0.15)	0.64	(4.49)
α					0.72	(0.29)
Ln(likelihood)	-4683.8		-4668.3		-4667.1	

4.   STRUCTURAL MODELS FOR TRANSITIONS AND WAGE OFFERS: IDENTICAL WORKERS AND FIRMS

4.1   The basic model

Our starting point is the equilibrium search model introduced by Burdett and Mortensen (Burdett and Mortensen (1995), Mortensen (1990)). This model has a dispersed wage offer distribution as an equilibrium outcome, even if all workers and firms are identical. Moreover, it allows for job-to-job transitions, which cannot occur in some other equilibrium models. An interesting feature is that the model gives explicit solutions for the wage offer distribution and the distribution of wages paid in a cross-section of employees, and that it specifies all relevant transition intensities up to a vector of parameters. There are few theoretical contributions that are as helpful to the empirical researcher. Of course, such sharp implications are a mixed blessing because they can be rejected in empirical tests.

We consider a labor market consisting of a continuum of workers and firms. Firms set wages and unemployed *and* employed workers search among firms. The unemployed are looking for an acceptable job, the employed for a better job. Jobs do not last forever but terminate at an exogenous rate. Firms compete for employees, and set their wages taking account of the wages offered by other firms and the acceptance strategies of the (un)employed. Workers use the resulting wage offer distribution to determine their acceptance strategies. In such a labor market there are flows of workers who change jobs, who are unemployed and find a job, and who become unemployed. In a steady state the flows to and from a particular labor market position are equal. We assume that the labor market is in this steady state. The model does not consider how this steady state is reached.

We use the following notation:

λ_0 = arrival of job offers while unemployed
λ_1 = arrival rate of job offers while employed
δ = rate at which jobs terminate
w = wage rate
p = marginal value product of employee
b = value of leisure
m = number (measure) of workers
u = number (measure) of the unemployed
$F(w)$ = distribution function of wage offer distribution
$G(w)$ = distribution function of earnings distribution
r = reservation wage of unemployed job seekers

The distribution functions F and G have the usual properties: they are right-continuous. The left-hand limit of F at w is denoted by $F(w-)$. Initially, we allow for discontinuities in F, i.e., there may be wages with $F(w) - F(w-) > 0$. This is important, because we must entertain the possibility that the wage offer distribution is degenerate.

First, we consider the workers. The unemployed obtain wage offers from $F(w)$ at an exogenous rate λ_0. The optimal acceptance strategy maximizes the expected wealth of the unemployed, assuming that the time horizon is infinite. It can be characterized by a reservation wage r (Mortensen and Neumann (1988)).

$$r = b + (\lambda_0 - \lambda_1) \int_r^\infty \frac{1 - F(w)}{\delta + \lambda_1(1 - F(w))} \, dw. \tag{5}$$

This reservation wage takes account of continued search for a better job. As a result, it depends on the difference between the arrival rates while unemployed and employed. In particular, the reservation wage is equal to the value of leisure if the arrival rates are equal. The unemployed may accept offers below b if $\lambda_1 > \lambda_0$. Here, and in the sequel, we assume that future income is not discounted. A comparison of equation (5) with the usual expression for the reservation wage in the infinite horizon case, shows that wage offers are implicitly discounted at a rate $\delta + \lambda_1(1 - F(w))$, which is the job-leaving rate as we shall see shortly.

The acceptance strategy of the employed workers is simple. They accept any wage offer that exceeds their current wage. We assume that job-to-job transitions are costless.

Next, we consider the flows of workers that result from these acceptance strategies. The flow from unemployment to employment is $\lambda_0(1 - F(r-))u$, the product of the offer arrival rate, the acceptance probability, and the measure of unemployed workers. The flow from employment to unemployment is $\delta(m - u)$. In a steady state these flows are equal and the resulting measure of unemployed workers is

$$u = \frac{m\delta}{\delta + \lambda_0(1 - F(r-))}. \tag{6}$$

Let the distribution of wages paid to a cross-section of employees have distribution function G. We refer to this distribution as the *earnings* distribution. This terminology is somewhat confusing, because it suggests that working hours play a role. In the model the hours decision is not considered, but we stick to the terminology because it is used in the literature. The wages paid to a cross-section of employees are on average higher than the wages offered, because of the flow of employees to higher paying jobs. In a steady state G and F are related. Consider the employees with a wage less than or equal to w, who have measure $G(w)(m - u)$. The flow into this group consists of the unemployed that accept wage less than or equal to w, and this flow is equal to $\lambda_0(F(w) - F(r-))u$ if $w \geq r$ and is 0 otherwise. The flow out of this group consists of those who become unemployed $\delta G(w)(m - u)$ and those who receive a job offer that exceeds $w, \lambda_1(1 - F(w))G(w)(m - u)$. In a steady state the inflow and outflow are equal, and we can express G as a function of F

$$G(w) = \frac{F(w) - F(r-)}{1 - F(r-)} \frac{\delta}{\delta + \lambda_1(1 - F(w))}, \tag{7}$$

where we have substituted for u from equation (6). This equation holds if $w \geq r$, and $G(w) = 0$ otherwise. Note that if jobs last forever, i.e., $\delta = 0$, the steady-state unemployment rate is 0, and transitions to higher-paying jobs would continue until all workers have a wage equal to p. In the sequel we only consider the case that $\delta > 0$.

From the two wage distributions we derive the supply of labor to an employer who offers wage w. There are $(G(w) - G(w - h))(m - u)$ employees who earn a wage in the interval $[w - h, w]$, and there are $F(w) - F(w - h)$ employers who offer a wage in that interval. Because firms that offer the same wage have the same employment level, the supply of labor to a firm that offers w is obtained by dividing the number of employees by the number of firms and letting h approach 0. This supply is denoted by $l(w \mid r, F)$ where we explicitly indicate its dependence on the acceptance strategy of the unemployed and the wages offered by other firms that compete for the same workers.

$$l(w \mid r, F) = \lim_{h \to 0} \frac{(G(w) - G(w - h))(m - u)}{F(w) - F(w - h)}$$

$$= \frac{\dfrac{m\delta\lambda_0(\delta + \lambda_1(1 - F(r-)))}{\delta + \lambda_0(1 - F(r-))}}{(\delta + \lambda_1(1 - F(w)))(\delta + \lambda_1(1 - F(w-)))}, \text{ for } w \geq r$$

$$= 0, \text{ for } w < r. \tag{8}$$

Note that it is allowed that a positive measure of employers offer w. It is easily seen that l increases with w. Due to search frictions and competition for workers, employers face an upward-sloping supply curve for labor with a finite wage elasticity. The supply function is discontinuous at points of discontinuity of F.

Finally, we consider optimal wage setting by the employer. We assume that the marginal value product p is constant, i.e., we assume that the production function is linear in employment. In that case the profit flow of the firm that pays wage w is $(p - w)l(w \mid r, F)$. The wage offer of the firm maximizes this profit flow

$$w = \arg_s \max[(p - s)l(s \mid r, F)]. \tag{9}$$

We make the implicit assumption that the firm is only interested in the steady-state profit flow. Hence, in setting its wage the firm does not try to smooth its level of employment in response to short-run random fluctuations in the level of employment. Because all workers and all firms are identical, each worker is equally productive at each firm. This completes our description of the search market.

Next, we characterize equilibrium in this search market. Because firms that offer wages that are strictly smaller than r have no employees and 0 profits, while a firm that offers r has strictly positive profits, we have $F(r -) = 0$, i.e., there are no wage offers below r. Because firms that offer a wage equal to p have 0 profits, and again a firm that offers r has strictly positive profits, wage offers are bounded above by p. The fact that the profit per employee $p - w$ is continuous in w, puts restrictions on the equilibrium wage offer distribution: for let w be offered by a positive measure of firms i.e., $F(w) - F(w -) > 0$, then $l(w +) - l(w -) > 0$, i.e., there is a positive measure of workers employed at wage w. If one of the firms that offer w increases its wage offer by a small amount, it will in the long run attract all the workers employed at firms with wage offer w. Because the profit per employee is continuous in w, the firm increases its profit rate by $[l(w +) - l(w -)](p - w) > 0$. Hence, competition for employees eliminates the discontinuities in the wage offer distribution. An equilibrium wage offer distribution has no mass points, and, in particular, it cannot be degenerate. We have already noted that we also need $\delta > 0$ to preclude that the wage offer distribution is degenerate at p. The wage offers also are a connected set. Firms that offer a wage at the upper bound of a gap in the set of wage offers can lower their wage to the lower bound of the gap without losing any employees, because l is constant if F is. In doing so they increase their profits. Hence, profit maximization eliminates the gaps in the set of wage offers. As a consequence F is strictly increasing for all wage offers.

Finally, we derive an expression for F. In equilibrium, firms have no incentive to change their wage offer. This implies that all wage offers must give the same profit flow π. We already know that the lowest wage offer is equal to r. Firms that offer r only attract unemployed workers. Their profits are equal to

$$\pi = (p - r)l(r \mid r, F) = \frac{m\delta\lambda_0}{(\delta + \lambda_0)} \frac{p - r}{(\delta + \lambda_1)}. \tag{10}$$

This equation expresses the common profit rate as a function of the arrival rates, p and r. All equilibrium wage offers yield the same profit rate π.

$$\pi = \frac{m\delta\lambda_0(\delta + \lambda_1)}{\delta + \lambda_0} \frac{p - w}{(\delta + \lambda_1(1 - F(w)))^2}. \tag{11}$$

Substituting for π from equation (10) we can solve for F

$$F(w) = \frac{\delta + \lambda_1}{\lambda_1}\left(1 - \sqrt{\frac{p - w}{p - r}}\right). \tag{12}$$

This expression holds for all equilibrium wage offers. The lowest wage offer is r. By setting F equal to 1 we obtain the highest offer $\bar{w}$

$$\bar{w} = \left(\frac{\delta}{\delta + \lambda_1}\right)^2 r + \left(1 - \left(\frac{\delta}{\delta + \lambda_1}\right)^2\right)p. \tag{13}$$

Of course, $F(w)$ is 0 for $w < r$ and 1 for $w > \bar{w}$. Note that F is differentiable. The density function is

$$f(w) = \frac{\delta + \lambda_1}{2\lambda_1\sqrt{p - r}} \frac{1}{\sqrt{p - w}} \text{ for } r < w < \bar{w}, \tag{14}$$

$$= 0 \text{ otherwise.}$$

We substitute the equilibrium wage offer distribution in equations (5), (6), (7), and (8) to obtain the equilibrium reservation wage, unemployment rate, earnings distribution, and employment.

$$r = \frac{(\delta + \lambda_1)^2 b + (\lambda_0 - \lambda_1)\lambda_1 p}{(\delta + \lambda_1)^2 + (\lambda_0 - \lambda_1)\lambda_1} \tag{15}$$

$$u = \frac{\delta m}{\delta + \lambda_0} \tag{16}$$

$$G(w) = \frac{\delta}{\lambda_1}\left(\sqrt{\frac{p - r}{p - w}} - 1\right), \text{ for } r < w < \bar{w} \tag{17}$$

$$g(w) = \frac{\delta\sqrt{p - r}}{2\lambda_1} \frac{1}{(p - w)^{1.5}}, \text{ for } r < w < \bar{w} \tag{18}$$

$$l(w \mid r, F) = \frac{m\delta\lambda_0}{(\delta + \lambda_0)(\delta + \lambda_1)} \frac{p - r}{p - w}, \text{ for } r < w < \bar{w} \tag{19}$$

4.2 Implications of the basic model

In equilibrium the lowest wage offer is equal to the reservation wage of the unemployed. All job offers are acceptable to the unemployed, and the re-employment hazard is equal to the offer arrival rate. Equilibrium unemployment is due to search frictions. The homogeneous model does not allow for structural unemployment. Below we discuss extensions that have structural unemployment. The reservation wage is a weighted average of the value of leisure and productivity. It is always increasing in b. It decreases with p if $\lambda_1 > \lambda_0$. An increase in p makes search on the job more attractive, and hence the unemployed respond by lowering their reservation wage.

It is easily seen that the earnings distribution stochastically dominates the wage offer distribution. If λ_0 approaches ∞, i.e., if the unemployed find jobs instantaneously, then the wage offer and earnings distributions degenerate in p. This is the competitive equilibrium in the search market. If λ_1 approaches 0, i.e., if the employed do not receive alternative job offers, then the distributions degenerate at b, and this is the monopsonistic equilibrium if the labor supply is infinitely elastic at b. For $\delta > 0$ the maximum offer $\bar{w}$ is strictly smaller than p, and for $\lambda_1 > 0$ it is also strictly larger than b. Hence, the equilibrium offers are those of firms that have a finitely elastic labor supply. This is confirmed by the wage elasticity of $l(w \,|\, r, F)$, which is equal to $(p - w)/w$, as it is for a monopsonistic firm. Note also that in equilibrium there is a positive association between firm size and wage.

The wage offer and earnings distributions have an increasing density. The shape of these densities is mainly determined by λ_1 and δ. In figure 4.2 these densities are drawn. The densities become more concentrated near $\bar{w}$, if δ becomes smaller. If λ_1 increases, only the earnings density becomes more concentrated near $\bar{w}$, which in both cases converges to p.

Upon substitution of equation (12) in the job-leaving rate we obtain

$$\delta + \lambda_1(1 - F(w)) = (\delta + \lambda_1)\sqrt{\frac{p - w}{p - r}}. \tag{20}$$

Because the equilibrium wage-offer distribution is dispersed, the job-leaving rate decreases with w.

Are these implications of the equilibrium search model with identical agents consistent with the empirical evidence on labor-market transitions and wage (offer) distributions? Let us stress in advance, that consistency with all known empirical regularities is not expected. Firms and workers are not identical, and some allowance for this fact must be needed to obtain an acceptable description of the data. However, it is surprising that so many

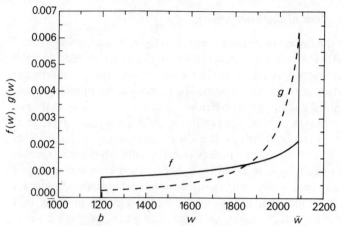

Figure 4.2 Earnings and wage offer density: $\lambda_0 = \lambda_1 = 0.047$,
$\delta = 0.025$, $b = 1129$, $p = 2208$

predictions of the model are in agreement with the outcomes of empirical research. The model predicts that the acceptance probability of the unemployed is 1. This is the found in many empirical studies (Devine and Kiefer (1991) survey the evidence for the US, and Van den Berg (1990) obtains the same result for The Netherlands). As we shall see, the model can be extended to deal with rejection of job offers, but the empirical evidence does not suggest that this is empirically important. The insignificant correlation between the length of unemployment spells and the accepted wages that was found in section 3 shows that it is also unimportant in our data.

The model also implies, that there is no duration dependence in the unemployment and job duration hazards. Again this is in agreement with the evidence in section 3. Of course, this is not a prediction, but an assumption. If we had found that there is significant duration dependence in the hazard rates, then we would expect the model to be a poor description of transitions and wages. The results in section 3 indicate that there is heterogeneity in the transition rates. As we shall see, we can allow for this by an extension of the basic model. The negative relationship between the wage and tenure on the job is also confirmed in section 3, as is the positive relation between wages and firm size.

The main problem is with the wage offer and the earnings densities. Both densities are increasing in the wage. This is clearly at odds with the empirical earnings and wage offer densities of figure 4.1. We are not aware of any study that has found an earnings distribution that resembles that in figure 4.2. Hence, attempts to estimate the parameters of the model from data should allow for a discrepancy between the observed and predicted distribution of earnings and wage offers.

Of course, there are other empirical regularities that the model cannot describe. In labor economics there has been lively debate on the positive relation between wages and labor-market experience. Although the debate is still active, the available evidence suggests that wage growth is due to both wage growth on the job and wage increases that are associated with transitions from lower to higher paying jobs (Abraham and Farber (1987), Altonji and Shakatko (1987), Topel (1991), Wolpin (1994)). The present model only allows for the second type of wage growth. Attempts have been made to construct an equilibrium search model in which firms offer a wage path, but thus far the resulting models are unappealing from an empirical viewpoint, because they do not allow for direct job-to-job transitions, and as a consequence have counterfactual implications for the relation between wages and firm size.

4.3   A closer look at the earnings and wage offer distributions

The equilibrium search model for homogeneous agents describes the labor market as a job ladder. At the bottom are the unemployed, who wait for an opportunity to start climbing the ladder. Upon receipt of an offer they start climbing. However, at any stage there is the possibility that one is kicked off the ladder, and, in that case, the worker has to start at the bottom again.

Let

$$y = \frac{p - w}{p - r} \tag{21}$$

with w either the accepted or the earned wage. The density of y is

$$f_y(y) = \frac{1}{2(1 - \psi)} y^{-0.5}, \text{ for } \psi^2 \leq y \leq 1 \tag{22}$$

for the wage offer distribution, and

$$g_y(y) = \frac{\psi}{2(1 - \psi)} y^{-1.5}, \text{ for } \psi^2 \leq y \leq 1 \tag{23}$$

for the earnings distribution, with $\psi = \delta/(\delta + \lambda_1)$. Here $y = 1$ corresponds to the bottom and $y = \psi^2$ to the top of the job ladder. The distribution of the random position on the ladder y only depends on λ_1/δ, the expected number of job offers during an employment spell, and this is clearly a measure of the speed at which employees climb the ladder.

If we rewrite equation (21) as

$$w - r = (1 - y)(p - r) \tag{24}$$

we see that in equilibrium the value of the match $p - r$ is split between the worker and the firm, and that $1 - y$ is the worker share. The worker share is a random variable with a distribution that depends on the speed at which alternative offers are obtained. Because y is strictly greater than 0, the worker never receives a wage equal to the value of his (marginal) product.

Finally, using the square root of the transformation in equation (21), we obtain the marginal density of a job duration, t_1, for a cross-section of employees

$$f_{t_1}(t_1) = \frac{\delta(\delta + \lambda_1)}{\lambda_1} \int_\psi^1 \exp(-(\lambda_1 + \delta)yt_1)\frac{1}{y}dy. \tag{25}$$

This is an exponential mixture with a specified heterogeneity distribution. The marginal density of t_1 does not depend on p. Although the wage is not equal to the marginal value product, it is a sufficient statistic for the productivity of the employee.

5   SOME EXTENSIONS OF THE BASIC MODEL

5.1   Counterfactual assumptions in the basic model

In section 4 we made some counterfactual assumptions. Here we investigate the robustness of the equilibrium solution to alternative assumptions. This shows that the model can be made more realistic without losing the benefit of a closed-form equilibrium solution. We consider

> Non-participation as an additional labor-market state
> Transitions to a job with a lower wage
> Wage-dependent layoff rate
> Non-linear production function

5.2   Flows into and out of non-participation

The basic equilibrium search model does not allow for non-participants, or more precisely it does not allow for transitions into and out of the state of non-participation. In observed labor-market histories such transitions occur for some individuals. In this subsection we extent the model by introducing a state of non-participation and allowing for transitions into and out of this state.

Transitions into and out of non-participation may be the result of an individual decision, e.g., the decision to dedicate all available time to household activities. They can also be forced, for example if the individual is conscripted for military service or if he becomes disabled. Let ζ_0, ζ_1, and ζ_2 denote the transition rates from unemployment to non-participation, from employment to non-participation, and from non-participation to unemployment, respectively. We do not aim to provide a structural model for these rates. Hence we assume that, to the extent that they are influenced by individual behavior, the variables that affect this behavior are distinct from the variables that affect the transitions in the basic model. For some transitions this may be a questionable assumption. For instance, the decision to devote one's time to household activities may be based on a comparison between the value of time in the home and the (potential) wage rate. We can allow for this by making ζ_1 dependent on the current wage. The resulting equilibrium solution is similar to that in subsection 5.4 in which δ is allowed to depend on the current wage.

The optimal strategy of unemployed and employed individuals again has the reservation wage property. For an individual in a job with wage w, it is again optimal to accept any wage offer larger than w.

In equilibrium, the inflow into non-participation equals the outflow from that state

$$\zeta_0 u + \zeta_1(m - u - n) = \zeta_2 n. \tag{26}$$

Here n denotes the measure of individuals in the state of non-participation. For unemployment, the equilibrium condition is

$$\delta(m - u - n) + \zeta_2 n = (\lambda_0 + \zeta_0)u. \tag{27}$$

Finally, for firms offering a wage no larger than w we have

$$\begin{aligned}\lambda_0 F(w)u &= (m - u - n)(\delta + \zeta_1)G(w) \\ &+ \lambda_1(1 - F(w))(m - u - n)G(w).\end{aligned} \tag{28}$$

By adding (26) to (27) (or by $w \to \infty$ in (28)) it follows that

$$(\delta + \zeta_1)(m - u - n) = \lambda_0 u \tag{29}$$

which is the steady-state condition for employment. If we substitute δ for $\delta + \zeta_1$, u for $u + n$, and λ_0 for $\lambda_0 u/(u + n)$ in equations (28) and (29), then these equations reduce to the steady-state conditions of the model of section 4.[5] Because the expressions for $F(w)$ and $G(w)$ follow from the steady-state conditions (28) and (29) and the equal profit conditions, this implies that, given r, $F(w)$ and $G(w)$ are equal to the corresponding expressions in the basic model, provided we replace δ by $\delta + \zeta_1$.[6] It follows that the shapes of the wage offer and earnings distributions in the present model are identical to those in the basic model.

It should be noted that the equation for r is not the same as in the basic model. In particular, r now depends on the difference Δ of the present value of being a non-participant and the present value of being unemployed

$$r = b + (\lambda_0 - \lambda_1) \int_r^\infty \frac{\bar{F}(w)}{\delta + \lambda_1 \bar{F}(w) + \zeta_1} dw + (\zeta_0 - \zeta_1)\Delta. \qquad (30)$$

Note that even though r is only relevant for transitions from unemployment to employment, and we do not model the decisions underlying transitions to and from non-participation, the utility of being a non-participant enters the equation for the reservation wage. This is because the individual compares the returns from different options. If the instantaneous utility of being a non-participant is a random draw from a distribution with mean x, then $\Delta = x/\zeta_2$.[7] Van den Berg (1990) estimates a partial job search model that allows for transitions into non-participation. He assumes that $x = b$.

5.3   Transitions to jobs with a lower wage

The basic equilibrium search model does not allow for job-to-job transitions that involve wage losses. However, in observed labor-market histories, such transitions do occur occasionally. Van den Berg and Ridder (1993) find that 11 percent of the direct job transitions result in a lower wage. Such transitions may be attributed to measurement error in wages or to the presence of non-wage benefits. Indeed, the latter can be treated as additive measurement error under the assumption that the worker valuation equals the constant marginal cost of provision. In that case the wages in the basic model can be reinterpreted as total compensation, including the unobserved non-wage benefits.[8]

We cannot exclude the possibility that transitions to a lower wage reflect optimal behavior resulting from another motive than the wish to earn a higher wage. For example, one may have to change jobs because the household moves to another location, which in turn may occur because one's partner has found a job there. In this subsection we generalize the model to deal with such transitions. Rather than incorporating the whole decision process underlying transitions to jobs with a lower wage, we shall simply assume that there is a certain rate at which job offers are accepted regardless of the wage offer.

Let η denote the rate at which, for employed individuals, transitions occur to jobs with a wage that is a random draw from the wage offer distribution. So, for employed individuals, job offers arrive with arrival rate λ_1, but, in addition, jobs arrive with arrival rate η. Both types of arrivals are characterized by random draws from $F(w)$. However, the latter always results in a transition, whereas the former need not. It is clear that the optimal strategy of unemployed and employed individuals still has the reservation wage property. For an individual in a job with wage w, it is again optimal to accept any wage offer larger than w. In equilibrium, the inflow into firms offering a wage no larger than w must equal the outflow from these firms

$$\lambda_0 F(w)u + \eta F(w)(1 - G(w))(m - u) = \delta G(w)(m - u) \\ + \lambda_1(1 - F(w))G(w)(m - u) + \eta(1 - F(w))G(w)(m - u). \tag{31}$$

The equilibrium solution in the present model can be derived as in Burdett and Mortensen (1995). We get

$$r = b + (p - b)\frac{\lambda_1(\lambda_0 - \lambda_1 - \eta)}{(\delta + \lambda_1 + \eta)^2 + \lambda_1(\lambda_0 - \lambda_1 - \eta)} \tag{32}$$

$$\bar{w} = p - (p - b)\frac{(\delta + \eta)^2}{(\delta + \lambda_1 + \eta)^2 + \lambda_1(\lambda_0 - \lambda_1 - \eta)} \tag{33}$$

$$F(w) = \frac{\delta + \lambda_1 + \eta}{\lambda_1}\left[1 - \sqrt{\frac{p - w}{p - r}}\right] \text{ for } r \leq w \leq \bar{w} \tag{34}$$

$$G(w) = \frac{\delta + \eta}{\lambda_1}\left[\sqrt{\frac{p - r}{p - w}} - 1\right] \text{ for } r \leq w \leq \bar{w}. \tag{35}$$

If $\eta = 0$ we obtain the expressions for the basic model. It follows that the shapes of $F(w)$ and $G(w)$ are as in the basic model. Except for multiplicative constants and somewhat different intervals of support, the distributions are identical.

5.4   Layoff rate dependent on the wage

In the basic model, it is assumed that the transition rate δ from employment to unemployment is independent of the wage w earned in the current job. This assumption may not hold. In particular, δ and w may be inversely related (see e.g., Mincer (1991)). Rather than providing a model in which the dependence on w is an implication of optimal behavior by firms or workers, we simply allow the parameter δ to be a function of w.

For simplicity, we take the job offer arrival rates in unemployment and employment to be equal, so $\lambda_0 = \lambda_1 \equiv \lambda$. We assume that $\delta(w)$ is positive, differentiable and non-increasing in w for all $b \leq w \leq p$. The assumption that δ does not increase in w ensures that individuals prefer jobs with high wages over jobs with low wages.[9] So, the optimal strategy of unemployed and employed individuals still is that a job is acceptable if and only if the wage offer exceeds the current income level, b for the unemployed, and w for individuals earning that wage. Moreover, the assumption that δ does not increase in w ensures that the job-leaving rate decreases with w.

In equilibrium, the inflow into firms offering a wage not larger than w must equal the outflow from these firms

$$\lambda F(w)u = (m - u)\int_b^w \delta(x)\mathrm{d}G(x) + \lambda(1 - F(w))G(w)(m - u). \qquad (36)$$

For the flows into and out of unemployment we obtain

$$\lambda u = (m - u)\mathrm{E}_G(\delta(w)), \qquad (37)$$

where E_G denotes the expectation and respect to the earnings distribution. Now assume that $\delta(w)$ is linear for $b \leq w \leq p$, i.e.,

$$\delta(w) = c_0 + c_1 w \qquad (38)$$

with $c_1 \leq 0$ and $c_0 + c_1 p > 0$. If $c_1 = 0$, the model simplifies to the basic model. The equilibrium in the present model can be derived as before. We find

$$\bar{w} = p - (p - b)\frac{(c_0 + c_1 p)^2}{(c_0 + c_1 p + \lambda)^2} \qquad (39)$$

$$F(w) = \frac{c_0 + c_1 p + \lambda}{\lambda}\left[1 - \sqrt{\frac{p - w}{p - b}}\right] \text{ for } b \leq w \leq \bar{w} \qquad (40)$$

$$G(w) = \frac{c_0 + c_1 p}{\lambda}\left[\sqrt{\frac{p - b}{p - w}} - 1\right] \text{ for } b \leq w \leq \bar{w}. \qquad (41)$$

Note that $c_0 + c_1 p = \delta(p)$. Thus, the equilibrium solutions for $F(w)$ and $G(w)$ are the same as in the basic model, if we substitute $\delta(p)$ for δ. It follows that the shapes of the wage offer distribution and the earnings distribution are exactly the same as in the basic model. It should be noted that the same substitution does not give the equilibrium u. By substituting equation (41) into equation (37) we obtain

$$u = \frac{\delta(p)(\lambda + \delta(b))}{\delta(p)(\lambda + \delta(b)) + \lambda(\delta(p) + \lambda)}. \qquad (42)$$

This has the striking implication that, even though the unemployed accept all job offers irrespective of b, the value of leisure has a negative impact on unemployment. This is because, as b increases, the earnings distribution shifts to the right, and, as a consequence, the average layoff rate decreases.

5.5   Non-linear production functions

The basic model assumes that the production technology is linear, so that the marginal value product of a worker is independent of the number of workers of the firm. This may be counterfactual. In particular, the marginal revenue product may be a decreasing function of the number of workers, i.e., the production function H may be concave in the number of employees n. The unit product price is denoted by p, so total revenue equals $pH(n)$ and marginal revenue product equals $pH'(n)$. We assume that H is differentiable, strictly increasing, and strictly concave, with $H(0) = 0$. For simplicity, we again take $\lambda_0 = \lambda_1 \equiv \lambda$.

Models with a concave production function are examined by Mortensen and Vishwanath (1993) and, subsequently, by Manning (1993) and Mortensen and Vishwanath (1994). In this subsection we summarize and extend some of their results, and we give closed-form solutions for special cases. Furthermore, we pay attention to empirically relevant aspects of the models.

Let, as before, $l(w)$ denote the steady-state number of workers of a firm that pays w. The employers choose w and the steady-state number of employees n to maximize

$$pH(n) - wn \text{ subject to } n \le l(w). \tag{43}$$

Note that, because of the non-linearity of H, the objective function $pH(n) - wn$ is not the steady-state profit flow. This is a deviation from the analysis in the basic model.

The most important implication of the convacity of $H(n)$ is that there exists a wage w^* such that for firms paying w^* it is not optimal to increase their workforce. This implies that $F(w)$ and $G(w)$ may have a mass point at w^*. For a firm offering w^* it is not optimal to increase the wage, since additional workers would cost more than they would produce. The equilibrium wage offer and earnings distribution both consist of at most two parts: a positive density on the interval $[b, \tilde{w}]$ and a mass point at $\bar{w}$. The mass point corresponds to the wage at which firms do not want to expand, so $\bar{w} = w^*$. In general, $b \le \tilde{w} \le \bar{w}$. If the probability mass associated with these two parts are both positive then $b < \tilde{w} < \bar{w}$; if not, it is possible that $\bar{w} = b$, or that there is no production at all.

Let us consider the model in more detail. First of all, the steady-state conditions are as in the basic model. However, if there is a mass point, then it is sensible to allow the inflow into jobs with wage $\bar{w}$ to be larger than the outflow from these jobs, which leads to excess supply and rationing of jobs with wage $\bar{w}$ (see Manning (1993)). For the moment we assume that in- and outflow are equal.

We distinguish between the five different types of equilibrium solutions.

I   *no production*
II $\Pr(w = b) = 1$, *so* $\bar{w} = b$
III $\Pr(w = \bar{w}) = 1$ *with* $\bar{w} > b$
IV *w has a positive density on* $[b, \tilde{w}]$ *and*
    $0 < F(\tilde{w}) = 1 - \Pr(w = \bar{w}) < 1$
V   *w has a positive density on* $[b, \tilde{w}]$ *and* $F(\tilde{w}) = 1$

Each of these can, depending on the values of the structural parameters δ, λ, p, b, m, and the shape of the production function H. We shall give necessary and sufficient conditions in terms of these parameters and H, and in doing so add to the theoretical results in the literature.

Consider a situation in which all firms offer a wage b. The steady-state workforce $l(b)$ of each firm is then $\lambda m/(\delta + \lambda)$. Cases I and II occur if and only if, with wage b, firms would prefer to have a smaller workforce than $m\lambda/(\delta + \lambda)$. This is equivalent to

$$pH'\left[\frac{\lambda m}{\delta + \lambda}\right] < b. \tag{44}$$

In these cases, there is production, i.e., we are in Case II, if and only if the value of the objective function (43) is positive. This means that Case I occurs if and only if

$$pH\left[\frac{\lambda m}{\delta + \lambda}\right] - b\frac{\lambda m}{\delta + \lambda} < 0. \tag{45}$$

Now suppose there is wage dispersion. The smallest wage offer is b. As in the basic model, the steady-state conditions imply that wherever $F(w)$ is continuous, i.e., for $b < w < \tilde{w}$

$$l(w) = \frac{\delta\lambda m}{(\delta + \lambda 1 - F(w))^2}. \tag{46}$$

From this it follows that $l(b) = \delta\lambda m/(\delta + \lambda)^2$. This determines the common value π of the objective function

$$\pi = pH\left[\frac{\delta\lambda m}{(\delta + \lambda)^2}\right] - b\frac{\delta\lambda m}{(\delta + \lambda)^2}. \tag{47}$$

There is dispersion, i.e., we are in Cases IV and V if and only if π exceeds the value of (43) for a single wage equilibrium. For Case III, $\bar{w} = pH'(l(\bar{w})) = pH'(\lambda m/(\delta + \lambda)) > b$. The corresponding value of (43) is $pH(\lambda m/(\lambda + \delta)) - \bar{w}\lambda m/(\delta + \lambda)$. The latter is smaller than π, i.e., we are in Case IV or Case V, if and only if

$$pH\left[\frac{\lambda m}{\delta + \lambda}\right] - pH'\left[\frac{\lambda m}{\delta + \lambda}\right]\frac{\lambda m}{\delta + \lambda}$$

$$< pH\left[\frac{\delta \lambda m}{(\delta + \lambda)^2}\right] - b\frac{\delta \lambda m}{(\delta + \lambda)^2}. \tag{48}$$

For Cases IV–V the equilibrium solutions are obtained in the standard way, with the qualification that we have to allow for a potential mass point at $\bar{w}$. Denote $\mathrm{Pr}(w = \bar{w})$ by γ. The steady-state condition for a firm paying $\bar{w}$ is

$$\delta l(\bar{w}) = \lambda(m - \gamma l(\bar{w})). \tag{49}$$

So, if there is a mass point, i.e., if we are in Case IV, then

$$\bar{w} = pH'\left[\frac{\lambda m}{\delta + \lambda \gamma}\right]. \tag{50}$$

By equating π in (47) to the value of (43) in $\bar{w}$ we obtain the following expression for γ

$$pH\left[\frac{\delta \lambda m}{(\delta + \lambda)^2}\right] - b\frac{\delta \lambda m}{(\delta + \lambda)^2}$$

$$= pH\left[\frac{\lambda m}{\delta + \lambda \gamma}\right] - pH'\left[\frac{\lambda m}{\delta + \lambda \gamma}\right]\frac{\lambda m}{\delta + \lambda \gamma}. \tag{51}$$

We are in Case V if the solution γ to this equation is smaller than zero, and in Case IV if it is between zero and one. This completes the characterization of Cases I–V. Note that the equilibrium is unique.

It remains to solve for $F(w)$ and $G(w)$ for the cases with wage dispersion. In general it is not possible to derive closed-form solutions. To see this, substitute first of all $l(w)$ into the equal profit conditions, i.e., the condition that, in equilibrium, for every w, (43) equals π. We obtain

$$\pi = pH(l(w)) - wl(w) \tag{52}$$

with $l(w)$ as in (46). A closed-form solution for $F(w)$ can only be obtained for specific production functions H.

Recall that for a linear production function the equilibrium densities $f(w)$ and $g(w)$ are increasing in w, and this property is not shared by their estimates. Intuitively, the equilibrium densities will be more increasing in a model with a concave production function. To see this, let us perform the following thought experiment. Suppose that $l(w)$ is as in the model with a linear production model, but that H is concave. Then the right-hand side of (52) will be decreasing in w. To restore equal profitability of firms with different w, it is necessary to make $l(w)$ increase faster with w. A concave production function decreases the profit per worker for large firms, and to restore equal profitability the number of workers in large firms has to be larger than in the linear production function model. From (46), it follows that $F(w)$ must be more convex, or, in other words, that $f(w)$ (and therefore $g(w)$) must be increasing more than in the linear production function model.

A closed-form solution can be obtained if $H(n) = \sqrt{n}$. Although this is a specific production function, many characteristics of the solution carry over to models with other concave H.

For Cases IV–V we have for $b \leq w \leq \tilde{w}$. We now present the solution

$$f(w) = \sqrt{\frac{\delta m}{\lambda}} \frac{1}{\sqrt{p^2 - 4\pi w}}. \tag{53}$$

The value of $\tilde{w}$ is determined by $F(\tilde{w}) = 1 - \gamma$ (in Case IV) or by $F(\tilde{w}) = 1$ (in Case V).

It is striking that the shape of $f(w)$ is virtually the same as in the linear production function model. In both models, $f(w)$ behaves like $(p - w)^{-1/2}$, with p suitably defined. Indeed, by suitably redefining p and choosing m, both densities coincide. This result does not always hold in models with other concave production functions. Also, in general, the ratio m of the measure of workers and the measure of firms enters the equilibrium solutions.

We now introduce the following parameters

$$b^* = \frac{b}{p}\sqrt{\frac{\lambda m}{\delta}} \tag{54}$$

$$c = \frac{\delta + \lambda}{\delta}. \tag{55}$$

Cases I–V can now be characterized as follows:

I $b^* > \sqrt{c}$
II $\sqrt{\gamma} > b^* > \frac{1}{2}\sqrt{c}$
III $\frac{1}{2}\sqrt{c} > b^* > c - \frac{1}{2}c^{3/2}$
IV $c - \frac{1}{2}c^{3/2} > b^* > c - \frac{1}{2}c^2$
V $c - \frac{1}{2}c^2 > b^*$

Note that the inequality in I, the second inequality in II, and the first inequality in IV coincide with (45), (44), and (48), respectively. It is easily verified that the four boundaries do not intersect as functions of c, for $c > 1$.

If $c > 4$ then Cases IV and V are not possible. In other words, if $\lambda > 3\delta$

then there cannot be wage dispersion in equilibrium. Indeed, given a priori plausible values of b/p and $\lambda/\delta, m$ must be quite small in order to have any production at all. In empirical studies, it is usually found that δ is more than five times as large as δ. All this can be interpreted as indicating that the specification $H(n) = \sqrt{n}$ is "too concave." Consider, for example, the class of functions $H(n) = n^\alpha$ with $0 < \alpha < 1$. There is positive production if $(b/p).(\lambda m/\delta)^{1-\alpha} < c^{1-\alpha}$, and there is wage dispersion if $(b/p).(\lambda m/\delta)^{1-\alpha} < c^{2-2\alpha} - (1-\alpha)c^{2-\alpha}$. Both conditions reduce to $b < p$ if α goes to one.

As noted above, in case of a mass point it may make sense to allow the inflow into jobs with $\bar{w}$ to exceed the outflow from such jobs. Consider the model in Case II. In this case, firms prefer to have a smaller steady-state workforce than they actually have. Given $w = b$, the optimal workforce $l^*(b)$ follows from the equation $pH'(l^*(b)) = b$ and is smaller than the workforce $\lambda m/(\delta + \lambda)$. For $H(n) \equiv \sqrt{n}$ we get $l^*(b) = p^2/(4b^2)$.

Now suppose firms can ration jobs, and that they accept only a fraction ϕ of the individuals applying for jobs, with $0 \le \phi \le 1$ and ϕ endogenous. For a given firm, the outflow of workers equals $\delta l^*(b)$ while the inflow equals $\phi\lambda(m - l^*(b))$. It follows that

$$\phi = \frac{\delta l^*(b)}{\lambda(m - l^*(b))} \tag{56}$$

with $0 < \phi < 1$. The steady-state condition for unemployment now states that $\delta(m - u) = \phi\lambda u$. As a result

$$u = m - l^*(b). \tag{57}$$

For $H(n) \equiv \sqrt{n}$ we get $u = p^2/(4b^2)$.

Other than before b has a positive effect on u. If $w = b$ and b increases then firms find it optimal to decrease their workforce.

Manning (1993) presents a model in which rationing of jobs with the highest wage is allowed for in all cases. From his results it follows that the model has multiple equilibria in our Cases III and IV. In those cases, firms offering $\bar{w}$ are indifferent between offering the $\bar{w}$ given above, and offering a slightly higher $\bar{w}$ while at the same time rationing the inflow of workers into their jobs. In Case II rationing leads to a higher value of the objective function, while in Cases III and IV there are equilibria with rationing that give the same value of the objective function. Above we normalized the equilibrium by taking $\phi = 1$.

We end this subsection by briefly considering a model in which the production function is convex. If H is convex then, as in the linear production function model, firms want to expand indefinitely. Consequently, $F(w)$ and $G(w)$ do not have mass points, and the equilibrium solution can be derived in the standard way. However, as in the extension above, explicit expressions can only be obtained for specific H.

Let $H(n) \equiv n^2$. To have any production, it is necessary and sufficient that the value of the objective function value at $w = b$ is positive. This means that π as defined in (47) with $H(n) \equiv n^2$ must be positive. In that case we get

$$f(w) = \frac{1}{2\lambda\sqrt{w^2 + 4\pi p}} \sqrt{\frac{\delta\lambda m}{2\pi}(-w + \sqrt{w^2 + 4\pi p})} \tag{58}$$

in which π is as above. The upper bound of the support is determined by the condition that $f(w)$ integrates to one.

The density $f(w)$ is decreasing in w. In fact, for plausible parameter values, it has an appealing shape. This can be regarded as an advantage from an empirical point of view. However, the underlying assumption that the production function is strongly convex is unrealistic.

6   ESTIMATION OF THE BASIC MODEL

The equilibrium search model with identical workers and firms of section 4.1 specifies the joint distribution of wages and spells up to a vector of parameters: the arrival rates λ_0, λ_1, the job termination rate δ, the marginal value product p, and the value of leisure b. With the minimal data described in section 3 these parameters can be estimated.

Here, and in the sequel, we use the following notation

x = position at date of first interview (1 if unemployed)
t_{0b} = elapsed unemployment spell (months) at date of first interview
t_{0f} = residual unemployment spell (months) at date of first interview
d_{0b}, d_{0f} = censoring indicators (1 if spell is censored)
t_{1b} = elapsed job spell (months) at date of first interview
t_{1f} = residual job spell (months) at date of first interview
d_{1b}, d_{1f} = censoring indicators (1 if spell is censored)
w_0 = accepted wage (guilders per month)
d_1 = observation indicator w_0 (= 1 if not observed)
w_1 = wage earned (guilders per month) at date of first interview
d_2 = observation indicator w_1 (= 1 if not observed)
v = indicator position after job (1 if unemployed)
d_3 = observation indicator v (= 1 if not observed)

We assume that censoring is independent, and also that all missing observations are missing at random. The model specifies the density functions of the "dependent" variables x, t_{0b}, t_{0f}, t_{1b}, t_{1f}, w_0, w_1, v.

$$f_x(x) = \left(\frac{\delta}{\lambda_0 + \delta}\right)^x \left(\frac{\lambda_0}{\lambda_0 + \delta}\right)^{1-x} \tag{59}$$

$$f_{t0}(t_{0b}, t_{0f} \mid x = 1) = [\lambda_0^{2-d_{0b}-d_{0f}}\exp(-\lambda_0(t_{0b} + t_{0f}))]^x \tag{60}$$

$$f_{w0}(w_0 \mid x = 1, d_{0f} = 0, d_1 = 0)$$

$$= \left[\frac{\delta + \lambda_1}{2\lambda_1\sqrt{p-r}\sqrt{p-w_0}}\right]^{x(1-d_{0f})(1-d_1)} \tag{61}$$

$$f_{t1}(t_{1b}, t_{1f} \mid x = 0, d_2 = 0) =$$

$$\left[\left((\lambda_1 + \delta)\sqrt{\frac{p-w_1}{p-r}}\right)^{2-d_{1b}-d_{1f}}\right.$$

$$\left.\exp\left\{-(\lambda_1 + \delta)\sqrt{\frac{p-w_1}{p-r}}(t_{1b} + t_{1f})\right\}\right]^{(1-x)(1-d_2)} \tag{62}$$

$$f_v(v \mid x = 0, d_2 = 0, d_3 = 0) = \tag{63}$$

$$\left[\left(\frac{\delta}{(\lambda_1 + \delta)\sqrt{\frac{p-w_1}{p-r}}}\right)^v \left(\frac{(\lambda_1 + \delta)\sqrt{\frac{p-w_1}{p-r}} - \delta}{(\lambda_1 + \delta)\sqrt{\frac{p-w_1}{p-r}}}\right)^{1-v}\right]^{(1-x)(1-d_2)(1-d_3)}$$

The joint density of x, t_{0b}, t_{0f}, t_{1b}, t_{1f}, w_0, w_1, v is obtained by multiplication of the conditional densities, and the likelihood function results from multiplication of the joint densities over the individual observations, $i = 1, \ldots, N$.

The accepted and earned wages satisfy the inequalities

$$r \le w_{0i}, w_{1i} \le \bar{w}, \text{ for } i = 1, \ldots, N. \tag{64}$$

Kiefer and Neumann (1993) observed that the sample maximum and minimum are consistent estimators of r and $\bar{w}$. In fact, these estimators converge at a faster rate than is usual for maximum-likelihood estimators, the rate being N instead of $\sqrt{N}$. Hence, if we estimate r instead of b, we obtain from equation (13)

$$\hat{r} = \min_{i=1,\dots,N} \{w_{0i}, w_{1i}\} \tag{65}$$

$$\hat{p} = \frac{\max_{i=1,\dots,N}\{w_{0i}, w_{1i}\} - \left(\dfrac{\delta}{\delta + \lambda_1}\right)^2 \hat{r}}{1 - \left(\dfrac{\delta}{\delta + \lambda_1}\right)^2}. \tag{66}$$

Upon substitution in the likelihood, we obtain an expression that only depends on $\lambda_0, \lambda_1, \delta$, and maximization gives ML estimates of these parameters. Because of the faster rate of convergence of the sample minimum and maximum, we can treat these estimates as known constants, and, as a consequence, the ML estimates have the usual asymptotic distribution. Christensen and Kiefer (1995) discuss these issues at length.

A criticism of this estimation method is that sample maxima and minima are sensitive to measurement error. Kiefer and Neumann (1993) argue that measurement error actually reduces the upward bias in the estimator of r. A more fundamental problem is that the method seems to perform badly in markets that are not really homogeneous. Kiefer and Neumann use a selection from the National Longitudinal Survey Youth Cohort (NLSY) to estimate the parameters, and they subdivide their sample by ethnicity and level of education. The ratio of the estimates of λ_1 and λ_0 is on average about 5. Jensen and Rosholm (1995) apply the same method to Danish data and obtain a ratio of more than 10. If we apply the method to the OLSP data, after deleting the 200 lowest and highest wages, we obtain the estimates in table 4.4.

The estimated earnings density is compared with the sample density in figure 4.3. The support of the empirical density is larger, because low and high wages have been omitted in the estimation of the homogeneous model. It is clear that the estimated density of the homogeneous model does not fit the earned wages. Of course, the estimates in table 4.4 are biased, because a method that is intended for a homogeneous labor market is applied to a labor market with heterogeneous agents. Indeed, stratification on observed variables reduces the ratio of the arrival rates. However, even after stratification it is not clear whether the observations refer to a homogeneous labor market. The fact that with the homogeneous model λ_1 is consistently much smaller than λ_0 makes one wonder whether stratification on observables is sufficient to create a homogeneous market. Instead, it is preferable to allow for heterogeneity from the outset.

Table 4.4. *Maximum-likelihood estimates with substitution of sample minimum and maximum* ($N = 1,561$)

	λ_0	λ_1	δ	r	p	$\bar{w}$
Estimate	0.024	0.00024	0.0047	1,450	15,691	2,800
Standard error	0.0012	0.000046	0.00018			

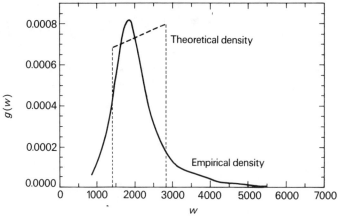

Figure 4.3 Kernel estimates of earnings density and earnings density implied by the ML estimates for the homogeneous model

7   EQUILIBRIUM SEARCH WITH HETEROGENEITY

7.1   Introducing heterogeneity in equilibrium search models

The equilibrium search model with homogeneous agents does not give an acceptable fit to the data. In particular, it does not give an acceptable description of the distribution of wages. Because, as was seen in section 5, the equilibrium solution is remarkably robust to removing counterfactual assumptions, we can only make progress by introducing heterogeneity in the model. A common practice in microeconometric models is to make the parameters of the theory dependent on the characteristics of the agents. In a market model this requires more thought, because the equilibrium solution for a market with heterogeneous agents differs from the solution for a market with identical agents. For that reason we distinguish between two types of heterogeneity: between-market heterogeneity and within-market heterogeneity. With the first type of heterogeneity we assume that there is a (possibly large) number of separate markets, which may be distinguished by observable and/or unobservable characteristics. The second type assumes that heterogeneous agents interact on a single market. At present there is more experience with between-market heterogeneity, and we concentrate on this type. With between-market heterogeneity we cannot use all conceivable characteristics to distinguish between markets. For instance, in most countries the labor markets for men and women are not segregated, and gender cannot be used to define separate labor markets. Of course, completely separate markets do not exist, but it seems reasonable to stratify the markets on age, education, and/or occupation/job level.

Can between-market heterogeneity give an acceptable fit to the data, in particular the wage data? To answer that question, we return to section 4.3, where we derived an alternative representation of the equilibrium earnings and wage offer distributions. From equations (24) and (15) we obtain

$$w - b = (1 - \mu y)(p - b) \tag{67}$$

with

$$\mu = \frac{(\delta + \lambda_1)^2}{(\delta + \lambda_1)^2 + (\lambda_0 - \lambda_1)\lambda_1} \tag{68}$$

with y a random variable with a distribution as in equations (22) or (23). This distribution does not depend on p or b.

The representation in equation (67) shows that there are two seemingly equivalent ways to generalize the wage (offer) distribution: assume a distribution over b or over p. However, there are reasons to prefer a distribution over p. First, if the unemployed receive unemployment benefits, it is reasonable to set b equal to these benefits. Because the observed variation in unemployment benefits between separate markets is usually small, variation in b does not help much in obtaining a better fit to the wage distribution. Second, most countries have mandatory minimum wages, and in a labor market where the lowest wage is equal to the minimum wage, the wage distribution does not depend on b. Again, variation in b does not produce a better fit to the wage data.

Now, let us assume that b is fixed and known, and let us assume that we have an empirical distribution of earned wages. Also assume, that λ_0, λ_1, and δ are known. We have already seen that these parameters are determined by the marginal distribution of the unemployment spells, job spells, and destination after a job spell. Then equation (67) shows that we can choose the moments of the distribution of p such that we obtain a perfect fit to the distribution of w. Note that if we have matched the moments of the earnings distribution, we cannot do the same for the wage offer distribution, and the relations between the two distributions provide a test of the model. A first attempt in this direction is in Van den Berg and Ridder (1993).

7.2 Heterogeneity in productivity

The next step is to allow for between-market heterogeneity in p in the estimation. We assume that the productivity p follows a distribution with density $k(p)$. The main difference with the analysis in section 6, is that we must integrate with respect to the distribution of p. To see what is involved, make the dependence of the lowest and highest wage on p explicit by writing $r(p)$ and $\bar{w}(p)$, and note that the observed wages satisfy the restriction

$$r(p) \leq w_{0i}, w_{1i} \leq \bar{w}(p).$$ (69)

Hence, the observed wages put restrictions on the range of p. If $\lambda_0 > \lambda_1$ both the lowest and the highest wage increase with p. If $\lambda_0 = \lambda_1$ the lowest wage decreases with p, but the highest wage still increases with p. In all cases, the lowest and the highest wage are both equal to b if $p = b$. We conclude that in markets with more productive activities, the average wage is higher. This is consistent with the existence of industry wage effects. Of course, $p > b$ is a necessary condition for the viability of the market. If $p < b$, workers prefer to be unemployed. The range of p is for $\lambda_0 > \lambda_1$

$$\frac{w_i - \mu b}{1 - \mu} \leq p \leq \frac{w_i - vb}{1 - v}$$ (70)

and for $\lambda_0 < \lambda_1$

$$p \geq \frac{w_i - \mu p}{1 - \mu}, \text{ for } w \geq b$$

$$p \geq \frac{w_i - vp}{1 - v}, \text{ for } w \geq b$$ (71)

with $v = \delta^2/((\delta + \lambda_1)^2 + (\lambda_0 - \lambda_1)\lambda_1)$, μ as defined in (68), and w_i either an accepted or earned wage.

The likelihood is obtained by integrating the likelihood of section 6 with respect to p, taking account of the integration boundaries in equations (70) and (71). This approach is used by Koning, Ridder, and Van den Berg (1995). They specify a lognormal distribution for p. The results that are comparable with the estimates in table 4.4 can be found in table 4.5.

Table 4.5. *Maximum-likelihood estimates with between market heterogeneity in productivity* $(N = 1,767)$

	λ_0	λ_1	δ	$E(r)$	$E(p)$	st.dev.(p)
Estimate	0.036	0.023	0.0033	1,538	2,274	455
Standard error	0.0019	0.0024	0.00015			

We find that λ_0 is still slightly larger than λ_1, but the ratio is more acceptable. The average productivity is also more in line with prior expectations. The predicted and empirical earnings density are compared in figure 4.4. Although the fit is still not perfect, it is clearly better than in figure 4.3.

We can decompose the variance of the earnings distribution into variation due to productivity differences and variation due to search frictions. We find that 73 percent of the wage variance is due to productivity variation and 27 percent is due to search frictions. This is in line with the R^2 of the wage regression. Koning, Ridder, and Van den Berg also stratify their sample according to age category and education, where the categories are as in the duration regression of section 3. They find that the job offer arrival rates decrease strongly with age, in particular the offer arrival rate in a job. Similar results are found by Van den Berg and Ridder (1993), who assume that the productivity distribution is discrete, and allow for measurement error in wages.

7.3   Heterogeneity within a single market

It is more realistic to assume that heterogeneous agents interact in a single market. The equilibrium solution in such models differs from that in section 4. Two types of within-market heterogeneity have been studied: heterogeneity in b and heterogeneity in p. Burdett and Mortensen (1995) derive the solution for the case of a continuous distribution in b, and Mortensen (1990) considers the case of discrete heterogeneity in p.

Heterogeneity in b implies that in equilibrium not all unemployed have the same reservation wage, and that there are wage offers below the reservation wage. Hence, models with heterogeneity in b have positive equilibrium (voluntary) search unemployment. In models with heterogeneity in p it is assumed that differences in productivity are associated with jobs and not with workers. In other words, two different workers are equally productive on the same job. In equilibrium, firms have different profit rates,

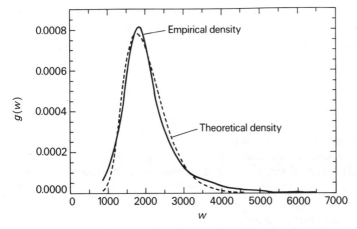

Figure 4.4 Kernel estimates of earnings density and earnings density implied by the ML estimates for the model productivity heterogeneity

with more productive firms having a higher profit rate. Inefficient firms survive because of the search frictions.

Models with a discrete heterogeneity in p have equilibrium wage offer and earnings densities with discontinuities. Such a model has been estimated by Bowlus, Kiefer, and Neumann (1995), using a method that generalizes that of section 6. The equilibrium solution for the case of continuously distributed p has been obtained by Bontemps, Robin, and Van den Berg (1995). They estimate a model with a lognormal distribution of p, but conclude that the fit to the wage data is not satisfactory. Because there is little experience with these models, it is too early to draw firm conclusions. A model with heterogeneity in b and p has the Albrecht and Axell (1984) model, which has been estimated by Eckstein and Wolpin (1990) as a special case (if the offer arrival rate in a job is 0).

8 SOME DIRECTIONS FOR FUTURE RESEARCH

Until now we have been silent on the implications of the models for policy. An obvious application is to the effect of unemployment benefits and minimum wages on the labor market. Indeed, in their book Card and Krueger (1995) refer to the basic model of section 4 as a possible explanation for the lack of a minimum wage effect on employment, and Burdett (1990) already pointed at this potential use of the model in policy analysis. However, as shown by Koning, Ridder, and Van den Berg (1995), this insensitivity does not extend to the model with heterogeneity in p. In that model, the minimum wage can lead to permanent unemployment, and they show that the equilibrium search framework improves on the estimates of the minimum wage effect obtained by fitting truncated distributions to wage data as in Meyer and Wise (1983). In models with within-market heterogeneity in productivity, the insensitivity holds again. Hence, a strong point of the equilibrium search approach is that it allows for a study of the effect of minimum wages without an a priori committal to a particular outcome. Indeed, although the equilibrium search model has a monopsonistic equilibrium, it is flexible enough to give an outcome that is close to a competitive equilibrium (see section 7).

Although we have shown that heterogeneous equilibrium search models can fit the joint distribution of wages and durations, this does not mean that we are fully satisfied with the results obtained thus far. However, because of its ability to describe the data reasonably well, additional data are needed to make progress. First, observed labor-market histories contain more information than the minimal information needed to estimate the model. In the OLSP we observe for some individuals several direct job-to-job transitions. This allows us to check the assumption that all direct job transitions are to higher paying jobs. Moreover, the models with within- and between-market heterogeneity in productivity have different implications for the correlation between subsequent wages, and longer labor-market histories may help in distinguishing between these types of heterogeneity. Second, data that combine observations on individual labor-market histories with information on the firms that employ these individuals (see Abowd, Kramarz, and Margolis (1994) for France, and Leth-Sorensen (1995) for Denmark) are becoming available. Hopefully, this allows us to obtain direct measures of the value of a match. In the models considered above, the value of the job to the employer is inferred from the wage. This is possible, because the model is explicit on the division of the value of the match between worker and firm, as in equations (22), (23), and (24). With direct estimates of the value of the match, we may be able to relax the assumptions on the division of the match value.

On the theoretical side, the model relies heavily on steady-state assumptions. A generalization of the model to a non-stationary environment is still ahead. A simple empirical strategy to deal with fluctuations is to make the arrival rates and the job destruction rate dependent on the aggregate unemployment rate. This is consistent with the theory, because these rates are taken as given by the agents. Of course, one needs to observe labor-market histories over a relatively long (calendar) time interval to obtain meaningful results. This approach resembles the estimation of price effects in demand systems, for which time-series data are needed.

Despite these shortcomings, we think that the type of equilibrium search models, as developed by Burdett and Mortensen, provide a useful focus for the study of the joint distribution of spells and wages in labor-market histories. Because of the relatively modest data requirements, the model has been estimated for a number of countries (Denmark, France, The Netherlands, and the US), and it may provide an interesting tool in the comparison of these and other labor markets (Germany, UK) for which the model has not yet been estimated.

Notes

This chapter was presented at an invited symposium at the Econometric Society 7th World Meeting in Tokyo, 1995. We thank our discussant Yoram Weiss for his comments. Gerard J. van den Berg acknowledges the Royal Netherlands Academy of Arts and Sciences for financial support. The Organization for Strategic Labour Market Research (OSA) allowed us to use the OSA panel data.

1 Wolpin (1994) contrasts these two approaches.
2 Organisatie voor Strategisch Arbeidsmarktonderzoek (Organization for Strategic Labor Market Research).
3 A full description of the OLSP can be found in Allaart *et al.* (1991).
4 We use a standard normal kernel. The bandwidth is as suggested by Silverman (1986).
5 This amounts to merging the states of unemployment and non-participation in the relevant equations of section 2.
6 Note that $F(w)$ and $G(w)$ given r in the basic model do not depend on u or λ_0.
7 There is no discounting.
8 Burdett and Mortensen (1995) consider the case that the cost of provision is a convex function of the level.
9 There is an analogy with the on-the-job search model in Van den Berg (1992) in which there are positive and wage-dependent costs of going from one job to another.

References

Abowd, J. M., Kramarz, F., and Margolis, D. N. (1994). "High-wage workers and high-wage firms." Mimeo, CREST-INSEE, Paris.
Abraham, K. G. and Farber, H. S. (1987). "Job duration, seniority, and earnings." *American Economic Review*, 77 (3): 278–97.
Albrecht, J. W. and Axell, B. (1984). "An equilibrium model of search unemployment." *Journal of Political Economy*, 92: 824–40.
Allaart, P. C. *et al.* (1991). "Trendrapport aanbod van arbeid." OSA Report No. 12, SDU.
Altonji, J. and Shakatko, R. (1987). "Do wages rise with job seniority?" *Review of Economic Studies*, 54: 437–59.
(1992). "A structural dynamic analysis of job turnover and the costs associated with moving to another job." *Economic Journal*, 102: 1116–33.

126   Geert Ridder and Gerard J. van den Berg

Van den Berg, G. J. and Ridder, G. (1993). "An empirical equilibrium search model of the labour market." Research Memorandum 1993-39, Faculty of Economics and Economometrics, Vrije Universiteit Amsterdam.

Blanchard, O. and Diamond, P. (1989). "The Beveridge curve." *Brookings Papers on Economic Activity*, no. 1: 1–74.

Bontemps, C., Robin, J. M., and van den Berg, G. J. (1995). "Equilibrium search with on-the-job search." Mimeo, CREST-INSEE Vrije Universiteit Amsterdam.

Bowlus, A. J., Kiefer, N. M., and Neumann, G. R. (1995). "Estimation of equilibrium wage distributions with heterogeneity." Working paper no. 95–11, Centre for Labour Market and Social Research. University of Aarhus and Aarhus School of Business.

Brown, C. and Medoff, J. (1989). "The employer size wage effect." *Journal of Political Economy*, 87: 1027–59.

Burdett, K. (1990a). "Empirical wage distributions: a framework for labor market policy analysis." In *Panel Data and Labor Market Studies*. (eds.), Hartog, J., Ridder, G. and Theeuwes, J. pp. 297–312.

    (1990b). "Search market models: a survey." Discussion Paper No. 354, Department of Economics, University of Essex.

Burdett, K. and Judd, K. (1983). "Equilibrium price distributions." *Econometrica*, 51: 995–69.

Burdett, K. and Mortensen, D. T. (1995). "Equilibrium wage differentials and employer size." Working Paper, Northwestern University.

Card, D. E. and Krueger, A. B. (1995). *Myth and Measurement: The New Economics of the Minimum Wage*. Princeton: Princeton University Press.

Christensen, B. J. and Kiefer, N. M. (1995). "Local cuts and separate inference." *Scandinavian Journal of Statistics*.

Devine, T. J. and Kiefer, N. M. (1991). *Empirical Labor Economics*. New York: Oxford University Press.

Diamond, P. A. (1971). "A model of price adjustment." *Journal of Economic Theory*, 3: 156–68.

Eckstein, Z. and Wolpin, K. I. (1990). 'Estimating a market equilibrium search model from panel data on individuals." *Econometrica*, 58: 783–808.

Flinn, C. and Heckman, J. J. (1982). "New methods for analyzing structural models of labor force dynamics." *Journal of Econometrics*, 18: 115–68.

Jensen, P. and Rosholm, M. (1995). "Estimating an equilibrium search model using Danish data." Mimeo, Centre for Labour Market and Social Research, University of Aarhus.

Kiefer, N. M. and Neumann, G. (1993). 'Wage dispersion with homogeneity: The empirical equilibrium search model." In *Panel Data and Labour Market Dynamics*. (eds.), Bunzel, H., Jensen, P. and Westergard-Nielsen, N., pp. 57–74. Amsterdam: North-Holland.

Koning, P., Ridder, G., and Van den Berg, G. J. (1995). "Structural and frictional unemployment in an equilibrium search model with heterogeneous agents." *Journal of Applied Econometrics*.

Krueger, A. B. and Summers, L. H. (1988). "Efficiency wages and the inter-industry wage structure." *Econometrica*, 56 (2): 259–93.

Lancaster, T. and Chesher, A. (1983). "An econometric analysis of reservation wages." *Econometrica*, 51 (6): 1661–76.

Leth-Sorensen, S. (1995). "The IDA database: a longitudinal database of establishments and their employees." Mimeo, Danmarks Statistik.

Manning, A. (1993). "Endogenous labour market segmentation in a matching mode." Discussion Paper No. 126, Centre for Economic Performance.

Meyer, R. and Wise, D. (1983). "Discontinuous distributions and missing persons: the minimum wage and unemployed youth." *Econometrica*, 61: 1677–98.

Mincer, J. (1991). "Education and unemployment." NBER Working Paper.

Mortensen, D. T. (1986) "Job search and labor market analysis." In *Handbook of Labor Economics*. (eds.), Ashenfelter, O, and Layard, R. Amsterdam: North-Holland, pp. 849–920.

    (1990). "Equilibrium wage distributions: a synthesis." In *Panel Data and Labor Market Studies*. (eds.), Hartog, J., Ridder, G. and Theeuwes, J. Amsterdam: North-Holland, pp. 279–96.

Mortensen, D. T. and Neumann, G. R. (1988). "Estimating structural models of unemployment and job duration." Dynamic Econometric Modeling, Proceedings of the Third International Symposium in Economic Theory and Econometrics.

Mortensen, D. T. and Vishwanath, T. (1993). "Information sources and equilibrium wage outcomes." In *Panel data and labour market dynamics*. Bunzel, H., Jensen, P. and Westergard-Nielsen, N. Amsterdam: North-Holland, pp. 467–93.

    (1994). "Personal contacts and earnings: it is who you know!" *Labour Economics*, 1: 187–201.

Mortensen, D. T. and Wright, R. (1995). "Competitive pricing and efficiency in search equilibrium." Mimeo, Northwestern University.

Van Ours, J. C. and Ridder, G. (1992) "Vacancies and the recruitment of new employees." *Journal of Labor Economics*, 10: 138–55.

Pissarides, C. A. (1990). *Equilibrium Unemployment Theory*. Oxford: Basil Blackwell.

Pratt, J., Wise, D. and Zeckhauser, R. (1979). "Price differences in almost competitive markets." *Quarterly Journal of Economics*, 93: 189–212.

Ridder, G. (1984). "The duration of single-spell duration data." In *Studies in Labor Market Analysis*. (eds.), Neumann, G. R. and Westergard-Nielsen, N. Berlin: Springer.

Silverman, B. W. (1986). *Density Estimation for Statistics and Data Analysis*. London: Chapman and Hall.

Topel, R. H. (1991). "Specific capital, mobility, and wages: Wages rise with job seniority." *Journal of Political Economy*, 99: 145–76.

Van den Berg, G. J. (1990). "Search behavior, transitions to non-participation, and the duration of unemployment." *Economic Journal*, 100: 842–65.

Wolpin, K. I. (1994). "Empirical methods for the study of labor force dynamics." Manuscript, Department of Economics, New York University.

CHAPTER 5

Posterior simulators in econometrics

John Geweke

1   INTRODUCTION

Econometrics is the discipline of using data to revise beliefs about economic issues. In Bayesian econometrics the revision is conducted in accordance with the laws of probability, conditional on what has been observed. The normative appeal of Bayesian econometrics is the same as that of expected utility maximization and Bayesian learning, the dominant paradigms in economic theory. The questions that econometrics ultimately addresses are similar to those faced by economic agents in models, as well. Given the observed data, what decisions should be made? After bringing data to bear on two alternative models, how is their relative plausibility changed? Having updated a dataset how should decisions be changed? Any survey of the introductory and concluding sections of papers in the academic literature should provide more examples and illustrate the process of formally or informally updating beliefs.

Until quite recently applied Bayesian econometrics was undertaken largely by those primarily concerned with contributing to the theory, and the proportion of applied work that was formally Bayesian was rather small (Poirier (1989, 1992)). There are several reasons for this. First, Bayesian econometrics demands both a likelihood function and a prior distribution, whereas non-Bayesian methods do not. Second, the subjective prior distribution has to be defended, and if the reader (or worse, the editor) does not agree then, the work may be ignored. Third, most posterior moments cannot be obtained anyway because the requisite integrals cannot be evaluated.

The development of posterior simulators in the last decade has revised beliefs about the foregoing three propositions held by many econometricians who have followed these developments closely. The purpose of this chapter is to convey these innovations and their significance for applied econometrics to econometricians who have not followed the relevant mathematical and applied literature. There are four substantive sections. The next section sets up the notation and defines the key problem addressed by posterior simulators. Section 3 describes these simulators and provides the essential convergence results. Implications of these procedures for some selected econometric models are drawn in section 4. This is done to indicate the range of tasks to which posterior simulators are well suited, rather than to provide a representative survey of the recent Bayesian econometric literature. (The surveys of Chib and Greenberg (1994), Koop (1994), and Geweke (1995b) take up additional models.) Finally, the chapter turns to some implications for model comparison and for communication between those who do applied work and their audiences that are beginning to emerge from the use of posterior simulators in Bayesian econometrics.

2   BAYESIAN INFERENCE

This section describes the notation used throughout the chapter and introduces some basic terminology. It is assumed that the reader is familiar with the essentials of Bayesian inference. A short tutorial is provided in the expanded version of this chapter (Geweke (1995d)). Serious introductions include Berger (1985) and Bernardo and Smith (1994), perhaps supplemented by DeGroot (1970) and Berger and Wolpert (1988) on the distinction between Bayesian and non-Bayesian methods. On Bayesian econometrics in particular, see Zellner (1971) and Poirier (1995).

2.1   A single model

A model describes the behavior of a $p \times 1$ vector of observables y_t over a sequence of discrete time units $t = 1, 2, \ldots$. The history of the sequence $\{y_t\}$ at time t is given by $Y_t = \{y_s\}_{s=1}^t$. A *model* is a corresponding sequence of probability density functions

$$f_t(y_t \mid Y_{t-1}, \theta) \tag{1}$$

in which θ is a $k \times 1$ vector of unknown parameters, $\theta \in \Theta \subseteq R^k$. The function "$p(\cdot)$" will be used to denote a generic probability density function (p.d.f.). The p.d.f. of Y_T, conditional on the model and parameter vector θ, is

$$p(Y_T \mid \theta) = \Pi_{t=1}^T f_t(y_t \mid Y_{t-1}, \theta). \tag{2}$$

The *likelihood function* is any function $L(\theta; Y_T) \propto p(Y_T \mid \theta)$.

The objective of Bayesian inference can in general be expressed

$$E[g(\theta)|\mathbf{Y}_T],\tag{3}$$

in which $g(\theta)$ is a *function of interest*. There are several broad categories of functions of interest that together encompass most applied econometric work. Clearly the function of interest can be a parameter or a function of parameters. Another category is $g(\theta) = L(a_1, \theta) - L(a_2, \theta)$ in which $L(a, \theta)$ is the loss function pertaining to action a, parameter vector θ, and (implicitly, through (3)) the model itself. A third category is $g(\theta) = \chi_{\Theta_0}(\theta)$ which arises when a hypothesis restricts θ to a set Θ_0. (Here $\chi(\cdot)$ is the characteristic function $\chi_S(z) = 1$ if $z \in S$, $\chi_S(z) = 0$ if $z \notin S$.) Then $E[g(\theta)|\mathbf{Y}_T]$ $= P(\theta \in \Theta_0 | \mathbf{Y}_T)$. Yet another important category arises from predictive densities. Denote $\mathbf{y}^* = (y_{T+1}, \ldots, y_{T+f})'$. If $g(\theta) = E[h(\mathbf{y}^*)|\mathbf{Y}_T, \theta]$, then $E[g(\theta)|\mathbf{Y}_T] = E[h(\mathbf{y}^*)|\mathbf{Y}_T]$. Through the appropriate choice of $h(\mathbf{y}^*)$ this category includes point prediction, turning point probabilities, and predictive intervals.

The subject of this chapter is generic, numerical methods of evaluating (3). To the extent a method is generic, it can be applied to many models without requiring special adaptation, and most of the questions of applied econometrics can be addressed directly. This chapter concentrates on numerical methods because the combination of models and functions of interest for which (3) can be evaluated analytically are severely limited. It takes up posterior simulators in particular because this approach is quite general and is especially attractive when the parameter space is high dimensional (i.e., k is large) or the model involves latent variables.

The specification of the model (1) is completed with a *prior density* $p(\theta)$. It may be shown that given (1) and a density $p(\mathbf{Y}_T)$ (i.e., a density for the data *unconditional* on θ) a prior density must exist; see Bernardo and Smith (1994, section 4.2). It is more direct to place the specification of the prior density on the same logical footing as the specification of (1). Thus a *complete model* specifies

$$P(\theta \in \tilde{\Theta}) = \int_{\tilde{\Theta}} p(\theta)d\theta, P(\mathbf{Y}_T \in \tilde{Y} | \theta) = \int_{\tilde{Y}} \Pi_{t=1}^T f_t(\mathbf{y}_t | \mathbf{Y}_{t-1}, \theta)d\mathbf{Y}_T,\tag{4}$$

where $\tilde{\Theta}$ is any Lebesgue-measurable subset of Θ and $\tilde{Y}$ is any Lebesgue-measurable subset of R^{pT}. (To keep the notation simple, a strictly continuous prior probability distribution for θ is assumed.)

By Bayes' theorem the *posterior density* of θ is

$$p(\theta | \mathbf{Y}_T) = p(\mathbf{Y}_T | \theta)p(\theta)/p(\mathbf{Y}_T) \propto p(\mathbf{Y}_T | \theta)p(\theta) \propto L(\theta; \mathbf{Y}_T)p(\theta).$$

Thus

$$E[g(\theta)\,|\,\mathbf{Y}_T] = \int_\Theta g(\theta)p(\theta\,|\,\mathbf{Y}_T)d\theta = \frac{\int_\Theta g(\theta)L(\theta;\mathbf{Y}_T)p(\theta)d\theta}{\int_\Theta L(\theta;\mathbf{Y}_T)p(\theta)d\theta}. \tag{5}$$

In the representation (5), one may ·substitute for $p(\theta)$ any function $p^*(\theta) \propto p(\theta)$. The function $p^*(\theta)$ is a *kernel* of the prior density $p(\theta)$. Posterior moments in a given model are invariant to any arbitrary scaling of either the likelihood function or the prior density.

2.2 Model averaging

Typically one has under consideration several complete models of the form (4). For specificity suppose there are J models, and distinguish model M_j by the subscript "j":

$$P_j(\theta_j \in \tilde{\Theta}_j) = \int_{\tilde{\Theta}_j} p_j(\theta_j)d\theta_j,$$

$$P_j(\mathbf{Y}_T \in \tilde{Y}\,|\,\theta_j) = \int_{\tilde{Y}} \Pi_{t=1}^T f_{jt}(\mathbf{y}_t\,|\,\mathbf{Y}_{t-1},\theta_j)d\mathbf{Y}_T.$$

The J models are related by their description of a common set of observations $\mathbf{Y}_T$ and a common vector of interest ω. The number of parameters in the models may or may not be the same, and various models may or may not nest one another. The vector of interest ω – e.g., the outcome of a change in policy, or actual future values of $\mathbf{y}_t$ – is substantively the same in all models although its representation in terms of θ_j may vary greatly from one model to another. Each model specifies its conditional p.d.f. for ω, $p_j(\omega\,|\,\theta_j,\mathbf{Y}_T)$. The specification of the collection of J models is completed with the prior probabilities $p_j(j=1,\dots,J)$, $\Sigma_{j=1}^J p_j = 1$.

There are now three levels of conditioning. Given model j and θ_j, the p.d.f. of $\mathbf{Y}_T$ is $p_j(\mathbf{Y}_T\,|\,\theta_j)$. Given only model j, the p.d.f. of θ_j is $p_j(\theta_j)$. And given the collection of models $M_1,\dots,M_J$ the probability of model j is p_j. If the collection of models changes, then the p_j will change in accordance with the laws of conditional probability. There is no essential conceptual distinction between model and prior: one could just as well regard the entire collection as the model, with $\{p_j, p_j(\theta_j)\}_{j=1}^J$ as the characterization of the prior distribution. At an operational level the distinction is usually quite clear and useful: one may undertake the essential computations one model at a time.

Suppose that the posterior moment $E[h(\omega)|\mathbf{Y}_T]$ is ultimately of interest. (This expression is just as general as (3) and encompasses the particular cases discussed there.) The formal solution is

$$E[h(\omega)|\mathbf{Y}_T] = \sum_{j=1}^{J} E[h(\omega)|\mathbf{Y}_T, M_j]P(M_j|\mathbf{Y}_T). \qquad (6)$$

From (5)

$$E[h(\omega)|\mathbf{Y}_T, M_j] = \frac{\displaystyle\int_{\Theta_j} g(\theta_j)L_j(\theta_j; \mathbf{Y}_T)P_j(\theta_j)d\theta_j}{\displaystyle\int_{\Theta_j} L_j(\theta_j; \mathbf{Y}_T)p_j(\theta_j)d\theta_j} \qquad (7)$$

with $g(\theta_j) = \int_\omega h(\omega)p_j(\omega|\theta_j, \mathbf{Y}_T)d\omega$. There is nothing new in this part of (6). From Bayes' rule

$$P(M_j|\mathbf{Y}_T) = p(\mathbf{Y}_T|M_j)P(M_j)/p(\mathbf{Y}_T)$$

$$= p_j \int_{\Theta_j} p_j(\mathbf{Y}_T|\theta_j)p_j(\theta_j)d\theta_j/p(\mathbf{Y}_T)$$

$$\propto p_j \int_{\Theta_j} p_j(\mathbf{Y}_T|\theta_j)p_j(\theta_j)d\theta_j = p_j M_{jT}. \qquad (8)$$

The value M_{jT} is known as the *marginalized likelihood* of model j. The name reflects the fact that one can write

$$M_{jT} = \int_{\Theta_j} L_j(\theta_j; \mathbf{Y}_T)p_j(\theta_j)d\theta_j. \qquad (9)$$

Expression (9) must be treated with caution, because the likelihood function typically introduces convenient, model-specific proportionality constants: $\int_{\tilde{\mathbf{Y}}} p_j(\mathbf{Z}_T|\theta_j)d\mathbf{Z}_T = 1$ but $\int_{\tilde{\mathbf{Y}}} L_j(\theta_j; \mathbf{Z}_T)d\mathbf{Z}_T \neq 1$. Whereas (7), like (5), is invariant to arbitrary renormalizations of $p_j(\mathbf{Y}_T|\theta_j)$ and $p_j(\theta_j)$, (8) is valid only with the conditional p.d.f.'s themselves, not their kernels. As a simple corollary, model averaging cannot be undertaken using improper prior distributions, a point related to Lindley's paradox (Lindley (1957), Bernardo and Smith (1994, p. 394)).

Model averaging thus involves three steps. First, obtain the posterior moments (7) corresponding to each model. Second, obtain the marginalized likelihood M_{jT} from (8). Finally, obtain the posterior moment using (6) which now only involves simple arithmetic. Variation of the prior model probabilities p_j is a trivial step, as is the revision of the posterior moment following the introduction of a new model or deletion of an old one from the conditioning set of models, if (7) and (9) for those models are known.

3 SIMULATION[1]

Bayesian methods are operational only to the extent that posterior moments (5) can actually be computed. There are three ways in which this can be done. If the posterior distribution and the function of interest are sufficiently simple, the posterior moment may be obtained analytically. Most results in this category in econometrics may be found in Zellner (1971); few further analytical results for posterior moments in econometrics have been obtained since that work was published. If the required integration takes place in fewer than (say) six dimensions, then classical deterministic methods of numerical analysis, principally quadrature, are often practical. (A standard reference for these methods is Davis and Rabinowitz (1984).) In the remaining cases, which constitute the preponderance of applied econometrics, posterior simulators are the approach of choice.

Posterior simulators have a single characteristic principle: generate a sequence of vectors $\{\theta_m\}$ with the property that if $E[g(\theta)|\mathbf{Y}_T]$ exists, then there is a weighting function $w(\theta)$ such that

$$\bar{g}_M = \sum_{m=1}^{M} g(\theta_m)w(\theta_m)/\sum_{m=1}^{M} w(\theta_m) \to E[g(\theta)|\mathbf{Y}_T] = \bar{g}. \tag{10}$$

(Here and throughout this chapter, "$\to$" denotes almost sure convergence.) Many simulators produce $\{\theta_m\}$ that – at least asymptotically in M – all have the posterior distribution, and in this case $\bar{g}_M = M^{-1}\Sigma_{m=1}^{M}g(\theta_m)$.

Posterior simulators have several attractions. First and foremost, they are often straightforward to construct, even in quite elaborate models. This includes models sufficiently complex that non-Bayesian methods like maximum likelihood are impossible or impractical. Second, posterior simulators can take advantage of the structure of latent variable models, simulating parameters, and latent variables jointly. This often renders them operational even when the likelihood function cannot be evaluated. Third, posterior simulators are well suited to situations in which $g(\theta)$ cannot be evaluated in closed form, but unbiased simulators are available, because $g(\theta)$ may then be replaced by its simulator. Leading examples are forecasting and discrete-choice models. Finally, posterior simulators are practical: they can be executed in reasonable time using desktop equipment, and their very construction often provides further insight into the properties of the model.

All this comes at some cost. The proper use of posterior simulators requires analytical work on the part of the econometrician. First and foremost, the investigator must verify that the posterior distribution exists. A proper prior and a bounded likelihood function are sufficient for the existence of the posterior distribution, but if the prior is improper, then the existence of the posterior must be demonstrated. Simulators can appear well behaved over a finite number of iterations even though the product of the prior and the likelihood is not a probability density kernel in θ. Second, the investigator must verify analytically that the posterior moment of interest exists. In this section it is implicitly assumed that this has been done for the problem at hand; expectation operators used here all apply to moments that exist under the posterior. Third, the investigator must verify (10). This section provides conditions for the convergence in (10) for a variety of simulators.

3.1   Pseudorandom number generation

All pseudorandom number generators begin with a pseudorandom sequence $\{u_i\}$ in which the u_i are assumed to be independently and uniformly distributed on the unit interval $(0, 1)$. (An overview of the construction of these sequences, with references to the associated large literature, is given in Geweke (1995a).) Given $\{u_i\}$, one can in principle generate random variables from any univariate distribution whose inverse cumulative distribution function (c.d.f.) can be evaluated. Suppose x is continuous, and consequently the inverse c.d.f. $F^{-1}(p) = \{c: P(x \leq c) = p\}$ exists. Then x and $F^{-1}(u)$ have the same distribution: $P[F^{-1}(u) \leq d] = P[u \leq F(d)] = F(d)$. Hence pseudorandom drawings $\{x_i\}_{i=1}^{N}$ of x may be constructed as $F^{-1}(u_i)$, where $\{u_i\}_{i=1}^{N}$ is a sequence of pseudorandom uniform numbers. A simple example is provided by the exponential distribution with probability density $f(x) = \lambda\exp(-\lambda x)$, $x \geq 0$: $F(x) = 1 - \exp(-\lambda x)$, $F^{-1}(p) = -\log(1 - p)/\lambda$, and consequently, $x = -\log(u)/\lambda$.

Acceptance methods are widely used as a simpler and more efficient alternative to the inverse c.d.f. method. Suppose that x is continuous with p.d.f. $f(x)$ and support C. Let g be the p.d.f. of a different continuous random variable z with p.d.f. $g(z)$ which has a distribution from which it is possible to draw i.i.d. random variables and for which

$$\sup_{x \in C}[f(x)/g(x)] = a < \infty.$$

The function g is known as an *envelope* or *majorizing density* of f, and the distribution with p.d.f. g is known as the *source distribution*. To generate x_i,

(a) Generate u;
(b) Generate z;
(c) If $u > f(z)/[ag(z)]$, go to (a);
(d) $x_i = z$.

The unconditional probability of proceeding from step (c) to step (d) in any pass is

$$\int_{-\infty}^{\infty} \{f(z)/[ag(z)]\}g(z)dz = a^{-1},$$

and the unconditional probability of reaching step (d) with value at most c in any pass is

$$\int_{-\infty}^{c} \{f(z)/[ag(z)]\}g(z)dz = a^{-1}F(c).$$

Hence the probability that x_i is at most c at step (d) is $F(c)$.

A key advantage of acceptance methods is that they often can be tailored to idiosyncratic distributions that arise in the posterior distributions for specific econometric models. This frequently happens in conjunction with the Gibbs sampler (section 3.3); some examples are provided in Geweke and Keane (1995). In this use of acceptance sampling it is often useful to consider a family of source densities $g(\mathbf{x}; \alpha)$ indexed by a parameter vector α. It is then usually easy to choose α to maximize the probability of acceptance from the source density (Geweke (1995a, section 3.2)).

Acceptance and inverse c.d.f. methods have been used to construct efficient algorithms for the generation of pseudorandom numbers from all of the standard univariate and multivariate distributions. A few of the more important distributions for econometrics are reviewed in Geweke (1995a). Algorithms and code may be found in a number of sources, including Press et al. (1986), Brateley, Fox and Schrage (1987). (1986). However, use of these algorithms in the obvious way can be risky, because subtle interactions between software and hardware can arise; for an example, see Geweke (1995a, section 3.3). Furthermore, it is not necessary to program algorithms or even to use published portable code. The best software libraries use state-of-the-art algorithms and take care to avoid problems arising from interaction between software and hardware. An example is IMSL (1994).

3.2   Independence simulation

The simplest possible posterior simulator can be constructed if one can generate the i.i.d. sequence $\{\theta_m\}$ with common p.d.f. $p(\theta \mid \mathbf{Y}_T)$. Denoting

$\bar{g} = E[g(\theta)|\mathbf{Y}_T]$ and $\bar{g}_m = M^{-1}\Sigma_{m=1}^M g(\theta_m)$, we have by the strong law of large numbers

$$\bar{g}_m \to \bar{g}. \tag{11}$$

If the *posterior variance* of $g(\theta), \sigma_g^2 = \text{var}[g(\theta)|\mathbf{Y}_T] = E\{[g(\theta) - \bar{g}]^2 |\mathbf{Y}_T\} < \infty$, then by the Lindberg–Levy central limit theorem

$$M^{-1/2}(\bar{g}_M - \bar{g}) \Rightarrow N(0, \sigma_g^2). \tag{12}$$

(Here and in what follows "$\Rightarrow$" denotes convergence in distribution.)

The leading simple example of a posterior simulator based on independence sampling in econometrics is the normal linear model with conjugate prior distribution,

$$\underset{T \times 1}{\mathbf{y}} = \underset{T \times k}{\mathbf{X}} \underset{k \times 1}{\beta} + \underset{T \times 1}{\varepsilon}, \varepsilon|\mathbf{X} \sim N(0, \sigma^2 \mathbf{I}_T), \tag{13}$$

$$\underline{v}s^2/\sigma^2 \sim \chi^2(\underline{v}), \beta|\sigma^2 \sim N(\underline{\beta}, \sigma^2\underline{\mathbf{H}}_\beta^{-1}). \tag{14}$$

(The matrix $\sigma^{-2}\underline{\mathbf{H}}_\beta$ is the *precision* of the conditional prior distribution for β – i.e., the inverse of its variance matrix.) Straightforward manipulation shows

$$(\bar{v}\bar{s}^2/\sigma^2)|(\mathbf{y}, \mathbf{X}) \sim \chi^2(\bar{v}), \tag{15}$$

$$\beta|(\sigma^2, \mathbf{y}, \mathbf{X}) \sim N(\bar{\beta}, \sigma^2\bar{H}_\beta^{-1}), \tag{16}$$

where $\bar{v} = \underline{v} + T - k, \quad \bar{s}^2 = \bar{v}^{-1}[\underline{v}s^2 + (\mathbf{y} - \mathbf{X}b)'(\mathbf{y} - \mathbf{X}b)], \quad \bar{H}_\beta = \underline{H}_\beta + (\mathbf{X}'\mathbf{X})^{-1}, \bar{\beta} = \bar{H}_b^{-1}[\underline{H}_\beta\underline{\beta} + (\mathbf{X}'\mathbf{X})^{-1}b]$ with $b = (\mathbf{X}'\mathbf{X})^{-1}\mathbf{X}'\mathbf{y}$ (for derivations see Zellner (1971, section 3.2.3) or Poirier (1995, theorem 9.9.1)). Since the marginal posterior distribution of β is multivariate student-t, closed-form expressions for the moments of β exist. But many functions of interest are non-linear in β. For example, if the explanatory variables include lagged dependent variables, then conditional on the presample lagged dependent variables the posterior distribution is given by (15) and (16), but functions of interest like predictors of future values and spectral densities involve non-linear transformation of β and σ^2.

The generation of pseudorandom vectors following (15) and (16) in fact involves acceptance sampling, as explained in section 3.1, although this feature will be transparent to the user of a mathematical software library or a higher-level language. The acceptance sampling algorithm is quite general and can in principle be used to produce an independent sample from any posterior density $p(\theta|\mathbf{Y}_T)$. The essential requirement is that one be able to draw pseudorandom vectors from a distribution whose p.d.f. $r(\theta)$ is an envelope of $p(\theta|\mathbf{Y}_T)$. One then proceeds as in section 3.1. The advantages of the procedure are that it requires only specification of the kernels of the two p.d.f.'s and that it produces i.i.d. pseudorandom vectors from the posterior distribution. The disadvantages are that it is often difficult to find an envelope and determine $\sup_{\theta \in \Theta}[p(\theta \mid \mathbf{Y}_T)/r(\theta)]$ and that acceptance probabilities may be so low as to render the whole algorithm impractical. The potential for these difficulties generally increases with the dimension of θ, although the structure of the posterior density is also important. When acceptance sampling succeeds, however, (11) always applies, and (12) applies if the posterior variance exists.

A simulator closely related to acceptance sampling is importance sampling. Let $j(\theta)$ be a probability density kernel corresponding to a distribution from which an i.i.d. sequence $\{\theta_m\}$ can be drawn conveniently and whose support includes Θ. Define the corresponding weight function $w(\theta) = p(\theta \mid \mathbf{Y}_T)/j(\theta)$. (In this expression, $p(\theta \mid \mathbf{Y}_T)$ need only be the kernel of the posterior density.) Then

$$\bar{g}_M = \sum_{m=1}^{M} g(\theta_m) w(\theta_m) \bigg/ \sum_{m=1}^{M} w(\theta_m) \to \bar{g}. \tag{17}$$

If both

$$E[w(\theta)] = \int_{\Theta} [p(\theta \mid \mathbf{Y}_T)^2/j(\theta)]d\theta \tag{18}$$

and

$$E[g(\theta)^2 w(\theta) \mid \mathbf{Y}_T] = \int_{\Theta} [g(\theta)^2 p(\theta \mid \mathbf{Y}_T)^2/j(\theta)]d\theta$$

are absolutely convergent, then

$$M^{-1/2}(\bar{g}_M - \bar{g}) \Rightarrow N(0, \sigma^2) \tag{19}$$

and

$$s_M^2 = M \sum_{m=1}^{M} [g(\theta_m) - \bar{g}]^2 w(\theta_m) \bigg/ \left[\sum_{m=1}^{M} w(\theta_m) \right]^2 \to \sigma^2$$

where

$$\sigma^2 = E\{[g(\theta) - \bar{g}]^2 w(\theta)\}.$$

(For proofs see Geweke (1989b).)

In importance sampling the simulated θ_m are independent but the sample must be weighted to produce a simulation-consistent approximation of the posterior moment $\bar{g}$ from an "incorrectly drawn" sample. The intuition underlying (17) is that if θ_m is drawn from an area that is undersampled (oversampled), relative to the posterior distribution, then that drawing must receive a large (small) weight to compensate. Neither (17) or (19) requires that w(θ) be bounded, but as a practical matter if w(θ) is bounded and var[g(θ)|$\mathbf{Y}_T$].$< \infty$, then (18) is satisfied, and without this condition establishing (18) is usually tedious. Experience suggests that when w(θ) is unbounded convergence in (17) may be so slow as to make the method impractical.

In many circumstances one therefore can choose between acceptance and importance sampling. The choice depends on the computational demands of the problem. If evaluation of $g(\theta)$ is trivial relative to the generation of θ_m and computation of w(θ), then importance sampling is preferred; conversely, acceptance sampling is the method of choice. Geweke (1995a, section 4.4) provides elaborations on the comparison, as well as a mixture of acceptance and importance sampling that can be optimized for each problem.

3.3   The Gibbs sampler

The Gibbs sampler is a recently developed posterior simulator that has been especially useful in econometrics. The method may be traced to Geman and Geman (1984), who built on earlier Markov chain methods including Metropolis et al. (1953), Hastings (1970), and Peskun (1973). The work of Geman and Geman was shown to have great potential for Bayesian computation by Gelfand and Smith (1990). Their work, combined with data augmentation methods (Tanner and Wong (1987)), has proven very successful in the treatment of latent variables and other unobservables in econometric models. Since about 1990 application of Markov chain Monte Carlo methods has grown rapidly; new refinements, extensions, and applications appear almost continuously.

The Gibbs sampler begins with a partition, or *blocking*, of θ, $\theta' = (\theta'^{(1)}, \ldots, \theta'^{(B)})$. For $b = 1, \ldots, B$, $\theta'^{(b)} = (\theta_1^{(b)}, \ldots, \theta_{k(b)}^{(b)})$ where $k(b) \geq 1$; $\Sigma_{b=1}^B k(b) = k$; and the $\theta_i^{(b)}$ are the components of θ. Let $p(\theta^b | \theta^{(-b)}, \mathbf{Y}_T)$ denote the conditional p.d.f.'s induced by $p(\theta | \mathbf{Y}_T)$, where $\theta^{(-b)} = \{\theta^{(a)}, a \neq b\}$.

Suppose a single drawing $\theta_0, \theta'_0 = (\theta_0'^{(1)}, \ldots, \theta_0'^{(B)})$, from the posterior distribution is available. Consider successive drawings from the conditional distribution as follows:

$$\theta_1^{(1)} \sim p(\theta^{(1)} | \theta_0^{(-1)}, \mathbf{Y}_T)$$
$$\theta_1^{(2)} \sim p(\theta^{(2)} | \theta_1^{(1)}, \theta_0^{(3)}, \ldots, \theta_0^{(B)}, \mathbf{Y}_T)$$
$$\vdots$$
$$\theta_1^{(j)} \sim p(\theta^{(j)} | \theta_1^{(1)}, \ldots, \theta_1^{(j-1)}, \theta_0^{(j+1)}, \ldots, \theta_0^{(B)}, \mathbf{Y}_T)$$
$$\vdots$$
$$\theta_1^{(B)} \sim p(\theta^{(B)} | \theta_1^{(-B)}, \mathbf{Y}_T). \tag{20}$$

This defines a transition process from θ_0 to $\theta_1' = (\theta_1'^{(1)}, \ldots, \theta_1'^{(B)})$. The Gibbs sampler is defined by the choice of blocking and the forms of the conditional densities induced by $p(\theta \mid \mathbf{Y}_T)$ and the blocking. Since $\theta_0 \sim p(\theta \mid \mathbf{Y}_T), (\theta_1^{(1)}, \ldots, \theta_1^{(j-1)}, \theta_1^{(j)}, \theta_0^{(j+1)}, \ldots, \theta_0^{(B)}) \sim p(\theta \mid \mathbf{Y}_T)$ at each step in (20) by definition of the conditional density. In particular, $\theta_1 \sim p(\theta \mid \mathbf{Y}_T)$.

Iteration of the algorithm produces a sequence $\theta_1, \theta_2, \ldots, \theta_m, \ldots$, which is a realization of a Markov chain with the probability density function kernel for the transition from point θ_j to point θ_{j+1} given by

$$K_G(\theta_j, \theta_{j+1}) = \prod_{b=1}^{B} p[\theta_{j+1}^{(b)} \mid \theta_j^{(a)}(a > b), \theta_{j+1}^{(a)}(a < b), \mathbf{Y}_T]. \qquad (21)$$

Any single iterate θ_j retains the property that it is drawn from the distribution with p.d.f. $p(\theta \mid \mathbf{Y}_T)$.

For the Gibbs sampler to be practical, it is essential that the blocking be chosen in such a way that one can make the drawings (20) in an efficient manner. For many problems in economics, the blocking is natural and the conditional distributions are familiar; section 4 provides several examples.

The informal argument just given assumes that it is possible to make an initial draw from the posterior distribution. That is generally not possible; otherwise, one could use independence sampling. Even if it were, the argument potentially establishes only that given a collection of independent initial draws from the posterior distribution, one can generate a collection of independent final draws by iterating (20) on each initial draw. What is needed is a demonstration that one can consistently approximate a posterior moment with successive realizations of a single chain that begins with arbitrary $\theta_0 \in \Theta$. The stylized examples in figures 5.1 and 5.2 show that this need not be the case.

Conditions for this sort of convergence are based on the mathematics of continuous state-space Markov chains. Brief overviews for econometricians are presented in Chib and Greenberg (1994) and Geweke (1995a); from there the reader may turn to Tierney (1991) and to Tierney (1994) for a rigorous treatment based on Numelin (1984). There are two sets of convergence conditions emerging from this literature that are most directly useful in Bayesian econometric models. If either set holds, then $\bar{g}_M = M^{-1}\Sigma_{m=1}^{M} g(\theta_m) \to E[g(\theta) \mid \mathbf{Y}_T]$.

Gibbs sampler convergence condition 1 (after Tierney (1994)). For every point $\theta^* \in \Theta$ and every $\Theta_1 \subseteq \Theta$ with the property $P(\theta \in \Theta_1 \mid \mathbf{Y}_T) > 0$, it is the case that $P_G(\theta_{j+1} \in \Theta_1 \mid \theta_j = \theta^*, \mathbf{Y}_T) > 0$, where $P_G(\cdot)$ is the probability measure induced by the transition kernel (21).

Gibbs sampler convergence condition 2 (after Roberts and Smith (1994)). The density $p(\theta \mid \mathbf{Y}_T)$ is lower semi-continuous at 0, $\int_{\Theta^{(b)}} p(\theta \mid \mathbf{Y}_T) d\theta^{(b)}$ is

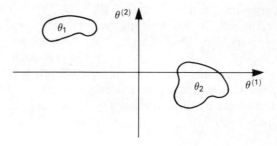

Figure 5.1 The disconnected support $\Theta = \Theta_1 \cup \Theta_2$ for the probability distribution implies that a Gibbs sampler with blocking $(\theta^{(1)}, \theta^{(2)})$ will not have the probability distribution as its invariant distribution, for any starting value.

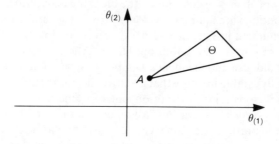

Figure 5.2 The probability density $p(\theta)$ is uniform on the closed set Θ and consequently is not lower semi-continuous at 0. The point A is absorbing for the Gibbs sampler with blocking $(\theta^{(1)}, \theta^{(2)})$, so if $\theta_0 = A$ convergence will not occur.

locally bounded ($b = 1, \ldots, B$), and Θ is connected. (A function h($\mathbf{x}$) is lower semi-continuous at 0 if, for all $\mathbf{x}$ with h($\mathbf{x}$) > 0, there exists an open neighborhood $N_{\mathbf{x}} \supset \mathbf{x}$ and $\varepsilon > 0$ such that for all $\mathbf{y} \in N_{\mathbf{x}}$, h($\mathbf{y}$) $\geq \varepsilon > 0$. This condition rules out situations like the one shown in figure 5.2.)

These conditions are by no means necessary for convergence of the Gibbs sampler; Tierney (1994) provides substantially weaker conditions. However, the conditions stated here are satisfied for a very wide range of posterior distributions in econometrics and are typically easier to verify than the weaker conditions. Furthermore, the appropriate blocking is usually inherent in the structure of the posterior density, as will be seen in several examples in section 4.

In practice one is concerned with the rate of convergence, not simply the fact, and also with assessment of numerical accuracy. A discussion of these topics to guide the practitioner is beyond the scope of this chapter. There is a substantial and growing literature on this topic, including Gelman and Rubin (1992), Geweke (1992), and Geyer (1992). Some of this work is reviewed in Geweke (1995a).

4   SOME MODELS

Recent innovations in posterior simulators have made possible routine and practical applications of Bayesian methods in statistics. This section reviews the implementation of posterior simulators in some common econometric models. The survey is selective. It concentrates on generic or "textbook" models to introduce approaches that can be applied in many specific settings. In so doing the interrelatedness of specific approaches is emphasized. All of the methods presented here can be combined, used in more elaborate models, and tailored to more specific models implied by the theory and data in a given application.

To keep the number of topics manageable the examples exclude time-series models, largely because of another survey (Geweke (1995b)) on that topic. The reader will note that many of the posterior simulators presented rely on the Gibbs sampler. This reflects the fact that more elaborate econometric models are typically constructed through the use of conditional distributions which can usually be undone by the Gibbs sampler to exploit the simpler conditionals. That is especially so in models involving latent variables.

4.1   Normal linear regression

The normal linear model with conjugate prior distribution was discussed in the context of independence simulation (section 3.2). This prior distribution links dispersion in prior beliefs about β and σ^2, since $\beta \sim t(\underline{\beta}, \underline{s}^2 \underline{\mathbf{H}}_\beta^{-1}; \underline{v})$. Suppose instead that prior beliefs about β are represented by $\beta \sim N(\underline{\beta}, \underline{\mathbf{H}}_\beta^{-1})$ independent of σ^2. Then the prior density kernel is

$$(\sigma^2)^{-(\underline{v}+2)/2} \exp(-\underline{v}\underline{s}^2/2\sigma^2) \exp[-\tfrac{1}{2}(\beta - \underline{\beta})'\underline{\mathbf{H}}_\beta(\beta - \underline{\beta})] \qquad (22)$$

and the likelihood function may be expressed as either

$$(\sigma^2)^{-T/2} \exp[-(\mathbf{y} - \mathbf{X}\beta)'(\mathbf{y} - \mathbf{X}\beta)/2\sigma^2] \qquad (23)$$

or

$$\exp(-vs^2/2\sigma^2) \exp[-(\beta - \mathbf{b})'\mathbf{X}'\mathbf{X}(\beta - \mathbf{b})/2\sigma^2], \qquad (24)$$

with $\mathbf{b} = (\mathbf{X'X})^{-1}\mathbf{X'y}, v = T - k, s^2 = v^{-1}(\mathbf{y} - \mathbf{Xb})'(\mathbf{y} - \mathbf{Xb})$. Form the posterior density kernel as the product of (22) and (23), and it is immediate that

$$\{[\underline{v}\underline{s}^2 + (\mathbf{y} - \mathbf{X}\beta)'(\mathbf{y} - \mathbf{X}\beta)]/2\sigma^2\} \,|\, (\beta, \mathbf{y}, \mathbf{X}) \sim \chi^2(T + \underline{v}). \tag{25}$$

Form the posterior density kernel as the product of (22) and (24) and complete the square:

$$\beta \,|\, (\sigma^2, \mathbf{y}, \mathbf{X}) \sim \mathrm{N}[(\underline{\mathbf{H}}_\beta + \sigma^{-2}\mathbf{X'X})^{-1}(\underline{\mathbf{H}}_\beta\underline{\beta} + \sigma^{-2}\mathbf{X'Xb}), (\underline{\mathbf{H}}_\beta + \sigma^{-2}\mathbf{X'X})^{-1}]. \tag{26}$$

In this model the prior for β is conjugate conditional on σ^2, and the prior for σ^2 is conjugate conditional on β. Hence the conditional posterior distribution of each is of the same family as its conditional prior distribution. Moreover, (25) and (26) indicate the obvious construction of a Gibbs sampler to draw from the posterior distribution. It is trivial to verify either Gibbs sampler convergence condition (section 3.3) in this model.

Several general principles are at work in this simple but important model.

(1) The decomposition of the posterior distribution into mutually conditional distributions can provide a convenient description of a non-standard distribution.

(2) Conditionally conjugate prior distributions are convenient representations of belief when their blocking coincides with that of the Gibbs sampler.

(3) Further blocking of the Gibbs sampler is clearly possible (by means of conditional normal posterior distributions for subvectors of β) but is counterproductive because it generally increases serial correlation in the Gibbs sampler thereby slowing the rate of convergence (Geweke (1992, section 3.6)).

To provide more flexibility in the representation of prior beliefs, suppose in lieu of $\beta \sim \mathrm{N}(\underline{\beta}, \underline{\mathbf{H}}_\beta^{-1})$ that $\beta \sim \mathrm{t}(\underline{\beta}, \underline{\mathbf{H}}_\beta^{-1}; \lambda)$. If the corresponding density kernel is substituted appropriately in (22) the resulting expressions are formidable. Instead, write the prior distribution in hierarchical form:

$$\lambda/w \sim \chi^2(\lambda), \beta \,|\, w \sim \mathrm{N}(\underline{\beta}, w\underline{\mathbf{H}}_\beta^{-1}). \tag{27}$$

Conditional on w the model has not changed: (22) remains true as does (26) once $\underline{\mathbf{H}}_\beta$ is replaced with $w^{-1}\underline{\mathbf{H}}_\beta$. It remains only to find the conditional posterior density kernel for w:

$$w^{-(\lambda+2)/2}\exp(-\lambda/2w) \,|\, w^{-1}\underline{\mathbf{H}}_\beta \,|^{1/2}\exp[-(\beta - \underline{\beta})'\underline{\mathbf{H}}_\beta(\beta - \underline{\beta})/2w] \tag{28}$$

which implies

$$[\lambda + (\beta - \underline{\beta})'\underline{\mathbf{H}}_\beta(\beta - \underline{\beta})]/w \,|\, (\sigma^2, \beta, \mathbf{y}, \mathbf{X}) \sim \chi^2(\lambda + k).$$

This modest extension of the model illustrates three further principles that hold more generally in using posterior simulators in econometrics.

(4) Decomposing a prior distribution into a hierarchy of simple distributions can simplify the model and help in constructing the posterior simulator.

(5) Correspondingly, conditional distributions are natural building blocks for more elaborate models and simulator design.

(6) While conditional posterior distributions may be obvious, there is no substitute for deliberately writing the entire posterior kernel in detail and then establishing kernels for conditionals.

The last point was honored in (22)–(24) but violated in the extension (27): it would have been easy to carelessly neglect the term $|w^{-1}\underline{\mathbf{H}}_\beta|$ in (28) because the corresponding term vanished in the kernel of the simpler model. While point (6) is essential to research practice, editorial constraints generally demand its violation in published scientific papers.

4.2 Normal linear regression with constraints

It is often the case that coefficients in the linear model are assumed to satisfy constraints that are not well represented by multivariate normal or student-t distributions, or there is a substantial prior probability that these constraints may be satisfied. Examples include the restriction of β to a subset of R^k and the event that some coefficients take on specified values, in particular, 0.

There is a long history of formal treatment of restrictions of this kind in linear models in econometrics including Judge and Takayama (1966), Lovell and Prescott (1970), Gourieroux, Holly, and Monfort (1982), and Wolak (1987). Analytical Bayesian treatments include Chamberlain and Leamer (1976), Leamer and Chamberlain (1976), and Davis (1978). Non-Bayesian approaches are technically awkward and lead to estimators with unappealing properties because of their *ex ante* conditioning (Poirier (1995, section 9.8)). Analytical Bayesian approaches produce useful results in one dimension but fail in higher dimensions.

The earliest treatment using a posterior simulator is Geweke (1986). That work considered the model (13) and (14) with $\underline{v} \to 0, \underline{\mathbf{H}}_\beta \to \mathbf{0}$, combined with the restriction $\beta \in Q \subseteq R^k$. A posterior independence simulator in this case generates a candidate using (15)–(16) and accepts it if and only if $\beta \in Q$. The advantage of the procedure is its simplicity and ability to handle constraints expressed implicitly as well as explicitly. Its disadvantage is that the rate of acceptance may be so low as to render it impractical. When k is large (exceeding 8), say computational efficiency can be quite poor even for restrictions that are reasonable when compared with the likelihood function. Nevertheless, the method works well for many problems, and no better method has been developed that applies to a general restriction set.

When the restrictions are linear inequalities, substantial improvements in efficiency are possible. Beginning with the model (13) and (22) suppose the constraints

$$\mathbf{a} \leq \underset{k \times k}{\mathbf{D}} \beta \leq \mathbf{w} \tag{29}$$

are added, where the elements of $\mathbf{a}$ and $\mathbf{w}$ are extended real numbers, and $\mathbf{D}$ is non-singular. Since this constraint has no effect if $a_i = -\infty$ and $w_i = +\infty$, fewer than k linear inequality restrictions may actually be involved. In particular, this model includes as specific cases sign restrictions on coefficients. Rewrite the model

$$\mathbf{y} = \mathbf{Z}\alpha + \varepsilon, \varepsilon \sim \mathrm{N}(\mathbf{0}, \sigma^2 \mathbf{I}_T),$$
$$\underline{v}s^2/\sigma^2 \sim \chi^2(\underline{v}), \alpha \sim \mathrm{N}(\underline{\alpha}, \underline{\mathbf{H}}_\alpha^{-1}),$$

where $\mathbf{Z} = \mathbf{X}\mathbf{D}^{-1}, \alpha = \mathbf{D}\beta, \underline{\alpha} = \mathbf{D}\underline{\beta}, \underline{\mathbf{H}}_\alpha = \mathbf{D}'^{-1}\underline{\mathbf{H}}_\beta \mathbf{D}^{-1}$. The Gibbs sampler may be applied to this model just as it was in (25) and (26) to (13) and (22), except that the conditional distribution of α is truncated normal

$$\alpha \,|\, (\sigma^2, \mathbf{y}, \mathbf{Z}) \sim \mathrm{N}[(\underline{\mathbf{H}}_\alpha + \sigma^{-2}\mathbf{Z}'\mathbf{Z})^{-1}(\underline{\mathbf{H}}_\alpha\underline{\alpha} + \sigma^{-2}\mathbf{Z}'\mathbf{Z}\mathbf{a}),$$
$$(\underline{\mathbf{H}}_\alpha + \sigma^{-2}\mathbf{X}'\mathbf{X})^{-1}], \mathbf{a} \leq \alpha \leq \mathbf{w},$$

with $\mathbf{a} = (\mathbf{Z}'\mathbf{Z})^{-1}\mathbf{Z}'\mathbf{y}$. The algorithm of Geweke (1991) for the truncated normal then applies directly to $\mathbf{a}$. Decompose α into k blocks of one parameter each, and draw each element successively conditional on the other. The conditional distributions involved are all truncated univariate normal, so this procedure is straightforward. Since no draw is ever rejected, the procedure does not suffer from the potential inefficiency of the more general acceptance algorithm.

In a variant on this method (Geweke (1995c)), $\beta_i = 0$ with prior probability $\underline{p}_i$; conditional on $\beta_i \neq 0$ the prior distribution of β_i is $\mathrm{N}(\underline{\beta}_i, \tau_i^2)$, possibly truncated to the interval (λ_i, v_i). These priors are independent across the k coefficients. This model characterizes the ubiquitous variable selection problem in regression. With a Bayesian treatment, problems of regression strategies and pretest estimators do not arise: the interpretation of the posterior distribution is unambiguous.

The posterior simulator for this model again has complete blocking, but now the conditional posterior distribution of each coefficient is mixed; the coefficient either is zero or is drawn from a possibly truncated normal distribution. The respective probabilities are proportional to the conditional marginalized likelihoods for each event. This amounts to evaluating the posterior distribution at $\beta_i = 0$ in the one case and integrating it over the permitted range of the coefficient in the other. The Gibbs sampler satisfies condition 1 for convergence, and the posterior probability of any configuration of regressors being in the model is the posterior expectation of the corresponding indicator function.

A closely related procedure is stochastic search variable selection (SVSS), introduced by George and McCulloch (1993, 1994). (A related work is Clyde and Parmigiani (1994).) The prior distribution in this model is

$$\beta_i = \gamma_i \delta_{i1} + (1 - \gamma_i)\delta_{i2},$$
$$\delta_{ij} \sim N(0, \tau_{ij}^2)(j = 1,2; \tau_{i2}^2 \gg \tau_{i1}^2),$$
$$P(\gamma_i = 0) = p_i, P(\gamma_i = 1) = 1 - p_i.$$

Here a regressor is selected if $\gamma_i = 1$ and not selected if $\gamma_i = 0$, but "not selected" means that the corresponding coefficient is small in absolute value, not 0. Posterior moments are obtained using a Gibbs sampler. Conditional on $(\gamma_1, \ldots, \gamma_k)$ the relevant conditional distributions are of the form (15) and (16), and the conditional posterior distribution of each γ_i is Bernoulli. Condition 1 for convergence of the Gibbs sampler again applies. But note that as $\tau_{i1}^2 \to 0$ the probability that γ_i will change from 0 to 1 in successive iterations also goes to 0.

Raftery, Madigan, and Hoeting (1993) take up the variable selection problem using a posterior simulator, but their approach is distinctly different. The "priors" employed are data dependent. The computational algorithm uses the Occam's window algorithm of Madigan and Raftery (1994) and therefore does not provide a simulation-consistent approximation of the posterior probability of all combinations of regressors.

These methods for normal linear models have much wider applicability than the normal linear model itself. The reason is principle (5) stipulated above: linear model posteriors appear as conditionals in many other models. In particular, the conditional posterior distribution of β as it appears in these models arises repeatedly in Bayesian econometrics.

4.3 Non-normality

Analytical approaches to Bayesian inference in econometrics rest heavily on normality assumptions: e.g., Zellner (1971) uses this distribution exclusively for continuously distributed disturbances. (The same is very nearly true of analytical non-Bayesian methods for which there exists a finite sample theory.) The combination of hierarchical models and posterior simulators has removed this constraint, so greatly expanding the scope for practical work that ideas about what the effective limitations of this approach might be are not yet well formed.

There are at least three compelling reasons why distributional assumptions are important in Bayesian econometrics.

(1) Distributional assumptions are central to Bayesian inference and its claim of exact finite sample results. Flexible representations of beliefs about the shapes of distributions are essential to reliable results.

(2) Many of the posterior moments of interest that motivate applied econometrics are sensitive to distributional assumptions. This is perhaps most evident in prediction of future events and the consequences of policy changes. (For a compelling example see Geweke and Keane (1995).)

(3) Utility functions typically assumed in general equilibrium models make equilibrium outcomes sensitive to the assumed distribution of shocks. Flexible assumptions about these distributions are therefore necessary in empirical work if the implications of these models for prices, welfare, and dynamics are to be evaluated.

The leading Bayesian approach to non-normality is the application of *normal mixture models*. The most general such model in the univariate case may be written

$$\varepsilon \mid (\mu, \sigma^2) \sim N(\mu, \sigma^2),$$
$$\mu \sim dP_\mu(\mu; \theta_\mu),$$

(30)

$$\sigma^2 \sim dP_{\sigma^2}(\sigma^2; \theta_{\sigma^2}).$$

(31)

Then

$$p(\varepsilon \mid \theta_\mu, \theta_{\sigma^2})$$
$$= (2\pi)^{-1/2} \int_{-\infty}^{\infty} \int_{0}^{\infty} \sigma^{-1} \exp[-(\varepsilon - \mu)^2/2\sigma^2] dP_{\sigma^2}(\sigma^2; \theta_{\sigma^2}) dP_\mu(\mu; \theta_\mu)$$

and the model is completed with prior distributions for the parameter vectors θ_μ and θ_{σ^2}. In practice the mixture may be either discrete or continuous. Continuous mixture models often mix only with respect to the scale parameter σ: if (30) degenerates to $\mu = \theta_\mu$ but (31) is non-degenerate, the mode is said to be a *scale mixture of normals*. Scale mixture normal models have a substantial history in the Bayesian hierarchical modeling literature, e.g., West (1984). In constructing such models one has available a rich set of results on the genesis of continuous distributions, which often involve scale mixtures of normals. (Two classic and quite useful references are Johnson and Kotz (1970, 1972).) For example, if $\theta_{\sigma^2} = (v, \sigma^{*2})$, $v\sigma^{*2}/\sigma^2 \sim \chi^2(v)$, then $\varepsilon \sim t(\mu, \sigma^{*2}; v)$. A convenient flexible completion of the model is provided by the independent prior distributions $\underline{v}\underline{s}^2/\sigma^{*2} \sim \chi^2(\underline{v})$, $v \sim \exp(\lambda)$. The implementation of this model is discussed fully in Geweke (1993) which finds $v < 10$ in autoregressive representations of a variety of US macroeconomic time series. Gamma mixing distributions yields a variety of other distributions for ε including the Erlang and LaPlace (Tsionas (1994, section 3.2)).

Another class of non-normal distributions with increasing application in Bayesian econometrics is the additive mixture model. The general formulation is $\eta_t = \zeta_t + \varepsilon_t$, where ζ_t and ε_t are mutually and serially independent, $\varepsilon_t \sim N(0, \sigma_2)$, and ζ_t has p.d.f. $p(\zeta_t \mid \theta_\zeta)$. Assume that η_t is observed. (In fact η_t may be the disturbance in a regression equation, or some similar unobservable, but in the context of a posterior simulator that applies the Gibbs sampler this assumption is typically innocuous.) Treating ζ_t as a latent variable, or equivalently a parameter in the first stage of a two-stage hierarchy, gives

$$p[\zeta_t \mid (\eta_t, \sigma^2)] \propto \exp[-(\eta_t - \zeta_t)^2/2\sigma^2] p(\zeta_t \mid \theta_\zeta),$$
$$p(\theta_\zeta \mid \zeta_1, \ldots, \zeta_T) \propto \prod_{t=1}^{T} p(\zeta_t \mid \theta_\zeta).$$

This procedure has found considerable application in stochastic frontier models in which distributions have constituents with sign constraints (van den Brock, Koop, Osiewalski, and Steel (1994), Koop, Steel, and Osiewalski (1995)). For an application to heterogeneity in panel data, see Geweke and Keane (1995).

The development of non-normal multivariate distributions along the same lines is clearly straightforward and should be practical, but there are as yet no published applications to the author's knowledge. A leading case is the multivariate student-t distribution in the context of the seemingly unrelated regressions model (section 4.5.1).

In implementing new non-normal distributions using normal or additive mixtures it is especially important to verify the existence of posterior distributions and moments of interest and to be cognizant of the role of prior distributions. If the likelihood function is bounded and prior distributions in all stages of the hierarchy are proper, the posterior distribution exists. If not, there may be no posterior distribution despite the existence of well-defined conditionals for each block of a Gibbs sampler. (In this case, no invariant distribution exists.) Verification of the existence of posterior expectations of unbounded functions of interest is typically more difficult and must proceed on a case-by-case basis. In any event, the econometrician will often find it enlightening to compare prior and posterior moments to assess, informally, the informativeness of the data.

4.4   Linear simultaneous equation models

The linear simultaneous equation model has a long and rich history in theoretical econometrics, approached from both Bayesian and non-Bayesian viewpoints. The canonical model

$$
\underset{1 \times L}{\mathbf{y}_t'} \; \underset{L \times L}{\Gamma} \; + \; \underset{1 \times k}{\mathbf{x}_t'} \; \underset{k \times L}{B} \; = \; \underset{1 \times L}{\varepsilon_t'} \;,\varepsilon_t \sim \mathrm{N}(\mathbf{0},\Sigma)
$$

consists of L equations with L endogenous variables $(\mathbf{y}_t)$ and k predetermined variables $(\mathbf{x}_t)$. The system is normalized by $\gamma_{jj} = -1$ $(j = 1,\ldots,L)$ and with this normalization one may write

$$
\mathbf{y}_t = \underset{L \times M}{A} \; \mathbf{z}_t + \varepsilon_t
$$

in which $M = K + L$, $\mathbf{z}_t' = (\mathbf{y}_t', \mathbf{x}_t')$, $a_{jj} = 0$ $(j = 1,\ldots,L)$, and for all $i = 1,\ldots,L$, $a_{ij} = \gamma_{ji}$ $(j \neq i, j = 1,\ldots,L)$ and $a_{i,L+j} = \beta_{ji}$ $(j = 1,\ldots,k)$. The corresponding reduced form is

$$
\mathbf{y}_t' = \mathbf{x}_t'\Pi + \mathbf{v}_t', \Pi = -B\Gamma^{-1}, \mathbf{v}_t \sim \mathrm{N}(\mathbf{0}, \Gamma'^{-1}\Sigma\Gamma^{-1}).
$$

The likelihood function is

$$
|\Gamma'^{-1}\Sigma\Gamma^{-1}|^{-T/2}\exp\left[-\tfrac{1}{2}\sum_{t=1}^{T}(\mathbf{y}_t + \Gamma'^{-1}B'\mathbf{x}_t)'\Gamma\Sigma^{-1}\Gamma'(\mathbf{y}_t + \Gamma'^{-1}B'\mathbf{x}_t)\right]
$$

$$
= |\Gamma|^{T}|\Sigma|^{-T/2}\exp\left[-\tfrac{1}{2}\sum_{t=1}^{T}(\Gamma'\mathbf{y}_t + B'\mathbf{x}_t)'\Sigma^{-1}(\Gamma'\mathbf{y}_t + B'\mathbf{x}_t)\right] \quad (32)
$$

$$
= |\Gamma|^{T}|\Sigma|^{-T/2}\exp\left[-\tfrac{1}{2}\sum_{t=1}^{T}(\mathbf{y}_t - A\mathbf{z}_t)'\Sigma^{-1}(\mathbf{y}_t - A\mathbf{z}_t)\right]. \quad (33)
$$

Even before we take up the completion of the model with the prior distribution for the parameters in Γ, B, and Σ, the essential technical difficulty with the posterior density is evident in the presence of the term $|\Gamma|^{T}$ in (33). The problems in using the posterior density that derive from any one of a variety of priors have been extensively studied. Richard (1973) and Rothenberg (1975) took up the general question, Drèze (1976) studied the analogous limited information problem, and Kloek and van Dijk (1978) approached the problem using importance sampling. A thorough survey of this work is Drèze and Richard (1983). In approaches using independence sampling poly-t densities have proven useful (Drèze (1977), Bauwens (1984),

Bauwens and Richard (1985)). Approaches using improper priors have proven especially troublesome, because of the ill-conditioned likelihood function (32); see Chao and Phillips (1994) and Kleibergen and van Dijk (1994) for recent work. No method emerging from this research has been used widely in applied work.

From (33) observe that if Γ is lower (or upper) triangular then $|\Gamma| = 1$ and the likelihood function is precisely that of the seemingly unrelated regressions model. If in addition Σ is diagonal, then the likelihood function factors equation-by-equation and if prior distributions are also independent across equations, then the methods of section 4.1 apply. This corresponds to the well-known fact that maximum likelihood is equivalent to least squares in a recursive simultaneous equation system. But the essential simplification requires *only* that $|\Gamma| = 1$. The significance of this point for applied work was first noted, to the author's knowledge, in Zellner, Min, and Dallaire (1994).

The leading instance of this case in applied econometrics is the incomplete simultaneous equation model that specifies only the first equation, leaving the rest of the system in reduced form

$$\Gamma = \begin{bmatrix} 1 & \mathbf{0}' \\ \gamma & \mathbf{I}_{L-1} \end{bmatrix}, \mathbf{B} = \begin{bmatrix} \beta & \Pi_{(1)} \\ & k \times (L-1) \end{bmatrix};$$

the variance matrix Σ is unrestricted. This is perhaps more commonly known as "the instrumental variables model" after the popular method of estimation. If the model is completed with a multivariate normal prior for β and $\Pi_{(1)}$ and (independently) a Wishart prior for Σ^{-1}, then the posterior simulator for the seemingly unrelated regressions model described in section 4.3 can be used with no change at all. The improper prior $p(\beta, \Pi_{(1)}, \Sigma) \propto |\Sigma|^{-(L+1)/2}$ is commonly employed.

While the difficulties surrounding the presence of $|\Gamma|^T$ in (32) have received most of the attention in the theoretical literature, most applications involve the incomplete (or instrumental variables) model in which $|\Gamma| = 1$. For these applications, the posterior simulator based on the Gibbs sampler provides a practical basis for Bayesian inference.

4.5   Other models

Posterior simulators for most of the canonical econometric models can be constructed by extension of these procedures or by their recombination in the Gibbs sampler. What follows provides outlines for the seemingly unrelated regressions model, the censored regression model, and the multi-nomial probit model. Fuller descriptions can be found in Geweke (1995d), and complete details are given in the indicated references.

4.5.1   Seemingly unrelated regressions model

The seemingly unrelated regressions (SUR) model of Zellner (1962) has been applied extensively in economics, especially in neoclassical models of production and consumption. It is described in every graduate-level econometrics textbook published in the past two decades. Zellner (1971) notes that Bayesian inference in the SUR model is straightforward conditional on the variance matrix of the disturbances in the different equations. This provides the key to the basic Gibbs sampling algorithm for this model, early descriptions of which are Blattberg and George (1991) and Percy (1992). Suppose the prior distribution for the coefficients is multivariate normal and that for the variance matrix is independently inverted Wishart; then given the variance matrix the coefficients are normally distributed, and conditional on the coefficients the variance matrix is inverted Wishart. Chib and Greenberg (1995) extend this approach to a hierarchical model for the coefficients, incorporating the pooling priors of Stein (1966) and Ghosh, Saleh, and Sen (1989). Further variants accommodate time-varying parameters (Gammerman and Migon (1993), Min and Zellner (1993), Chib and Greenberg (1995)). An alternative to hierarchical models is the recursive extended conjugate prior distribution of Richard and Steel (1988) in which some of the integrations can be performed analytically.

Since the conditional distribution of β is multivariate normal, the methods for coping with inequality constraints described in section 4.2 apply in the SUR model as well. Such constraints can be a fundamental part of the economics underlying the model. Perhaps the leading example is quasiconcavity constraints in neoclassical microeconomics, the imposition of which has spawned a substantial econometrics literature (e.g., Barnett and Lee (1985), Diewert and Wales (1987 and references therein)). Chalfant and Wallace (1993) and Terrell (1995) illustrate that simple acceptance sampling, in conjunction with a posterior simulator, can be a practical method for imposing these constraints.

4.5.2   Censored regression

The standard Tobit censored regression model (Tobin (1958)) is

$$y_t^* = \mathbf{x}_t'\beta + \varepsilon^t, \ \varepsilon_t \overset{i.i.d.}{\sim} N(0, \sigma^2), \ y_t = \max(y_t^*, 0).$$

The observed data are $\{\mathbf{x}_t, y_t\}_{t=1}^T$. The model may be completed with the independent prior distributions $\beta \sim N(\underline{\beta}, \underline{\mathbf{H}}_\beta^{-1}), \underline{vs}^2/\sigma^2 \sim \chi^2(\underline{v})$. This is one of the simplest latent variable models in econometrics and is also a simple example of a limited dependent variable model (Maddala (1983)). Censored regression models are widely applied; Amemiya (1984) provides a survey.

The only econometric novelty here is that y_t^* is unobserved. If it were observed, the model would revert to normal linear regression (section 4.1). On the other hand, conditional on β, σ^2, and the data, the distribution of the y_t^* is simple. These latent variables are conditionally independent: $y_t^* = y_t$ if $y_t > 0$, $y_t^* \sim N(\mathbf{x}_t'\beta, \sigma^2)$ s.t. $y_t^* \leq 0$ if $y_t = 0$. Bayesian inference proceeds by means of a posterior simulator employing the Gibbs sampler with three blocks: the coefficients, the variance parameter, and the latent variables. Condition 1 for convergence applies, although condition 2 does not. The earliest published implementations of this algorithm appear to be Chib (1992) and Geweke (1992), but see Wei and Tanner (1990) for a similar approach.

The step of drawing $\{y_t^*\}_{t=1}^T$ is known as *data augmentation* after Tanner and Wong (1987). The single step of drawing from the conditional distribution of the latent variables has been used in non-Bayesian approaches as well, and hence the distinction. (For a closely related procedure, see Rubin (1987).)

4.5.3 Probit models

The standard multinomial probit model is econometrically equivalent to the seemingly unrelated regressions model, except that the left-hand-side variables are unobserved utilities. Observed choices amount to inequality restrictions on the utilities. In the presence of a multivariate normal prior for the coefficients and an independent inverted Wishart prior for the variance matrix, one need only add additional blocks, to the seemingly unrelated regressions Gibbs sampling algorithm, that draw the utilities. This amounts to a draw from a multivariate normal distribution, subject to linear inequality restrictions, for each observation. This can be accomplished as described in section 4.2.

This procedure was developed contemporaneously by Geweke, Keane, and Runkle (1994a) and McCulloch and Rossi (1995a), and two developments handling normalizations somewhat differently. Yet another treatment of normalization is provided in McCulloch, Polson, and Rossi (1995). For extensions to panel data, see Geweke, Keane, and Runkle (1994b). A recent survey is McCulloch and Rossi (1995b).

5   MODEL COMPARISON AND COMMUNICATION

For a subjective Bayesian decisionmaker the computation of the posterior moment (5) for a suitable model, prior, and function of interest is the final objective of inference. For an investigator reporting results for other potential decisionmakers, however, the situation is quite different. In the language of Hildreth (1963) these decisionmakers are *remote clients*, who ideally have agreed to disagree in terms of the prior (Poirier (1988)). Clients may also have different uses for the model. In general, therefore, the investigator will not know either the priors or the functions of interest of her clients.

What should the investigator report? Traditionally, published articles report a few posterior moments, and more rarely some indication of the sensitivity to prior distributions and alternative data densities may be given. Such information is generally much too limited. At the other extreme, the investigator may simply report some likelihood functions, but this leaves most of the work to the client. Investigators almost never report marginalized likelihoods, thereby leaving unrealized the promise inherent in model averaging.

This section first takes up the model comparison question, which has been intensively studied in the past five years in the wake of the rapid innovations in posterior simulators. It surveys some of these developments and argues that one method in particular is most promising for the generic comparison of models to which posterior simulators apply. It then turns to the more general question of Bayesian communication. Here it appears that posterior simulators, coupled with current storage, communication, and computation capabilities (to say nothing of future developments in these areas), offer the potential to revolutionize applied econometrics.

5.1   Model comparison

Posterior odds ratios are the basis of model comparison, by which is meant both model averaging and model choice. The essential technical task in model comparison is obtaining the marginalized likelihood M_{jT} defined in (8). In describing how the marginalized likelihood can be obtained using a posterior simulator it is convenient to drop the subscript j denoting the model. For reasons discussed in section 2.2 it is essential to distinguish between probability distribution functions and their kernels in the marginalized likelihood. In what follows, $p(\theta)$ always denotes the properly normalized prior density and $p(Y_T \mid \theta)$ the properly normalized data density.

There are three conditions that a good approach to the computation of the marginalized likelihood M_T should satisfy.

(1) Given a large number of models it is much easier to summarize the comparative evidence through the marginalized likelihood than through pairwise Bayes factors. Therefore, the approach should provide a simulation-consistent approximation of M_T alone, rather than the Bayes factor comparing two models.

(2) The development of a posterior simulator, its execution, and the organization of simulator output all require real resources. Therefore, the numerical approximation of M_T should require only the original simulator output and not any additional, auxiliary simulations.

(3) Accurate approximations are always desirable. The accuracy of the approximation of M_T should be of the same order as the approximation of posterior moments in the model. Ideally, it should be convenient to assess numerical accuracy using a central limit theorem.

For posterior simulators based on independence sampling it is generally straightforward to satisfy all three criteria. In the case of importance sampling let $j(\theta)$ denote the p.d.f. of the importance sampling distribution, not merely the kernel. Since importance sampling distributions are chosen in part with regard to the convenience of generating draws from them, their normalizing constants are generally known. As long as the support of the importance sampling distribution includes the support of the posterior distribution

$$\hat{M}_T^{(M)} = M^{-1} \sum_{m=1}^{M} p(\theta_m)p(\mathbf{Y}_T \mid \theta_m)/j(\theta_m)$$

$$= M^{-1} \sum_{m=1}^{M} w(\theta_m) \rightarrow \int_{\Theta} p(\theta)p(\mathbf{Y}_T \mid \theta)d\theta = M_T. \qquad (34)$$

And if

$$\int_{\Theta} [p(\theta)^2 p(\mathbf{Y}_T \mid \theta)^2/j(\theta)]d\theta = \int_{\Theta} w(\theta)^2 j(\theta)d\theta < \infty \qquad (35)$$

then

$$M^{1/2}(\hat{M}_T^{(M)} - M_T) \Rightarrow N(0, \sigma^2)$$

where

$$\sigma^2 = \int_{\Theta} [p(\theta)p(\mathbf{Y}_T \mid \theta)/j(\theta) - M_T]^2 j(\theta)d\theta$$

and

$$\hat{\sigma}^2 = M^{-1} \sum_{m=1}^{M} [p(\theta_m)p(\mathbf{Y}_T \mid \theta_m)/j(\theta_m) - \hat{M}_T]^2 \to \sigma^2.$$

A sufficient condition for these results is that the weight function $w(\theta)$ be bounded above, the same condition that is most useful in establishing the simulation-consistency of importance sampling simulators.

This approximation to the marginalized likelihood was used in Geweke (1989a). More recently it has been proposed by Gelfand and Dey (1994); see also Raftery (1995). The practical considerations involved are the same as those in the approximation of posterior moments using importance sampling. For the sake of efficiency the importance sampling distribution should not be too diffuse relative to the posterior distribution. For example $j(\theta) = p(\theta)$ satisfies (35) and leads to the very simple approximation $\hat{M}_T^{(M)} = M^{-1} \Sigma_{m=1}^{M} p(\mathbf{Y}_T \mid \theta_m)$. But the prior distribution works well as an importance sampler only if sample size is quite small and θ is of very low dimension (Kloek and van Dijk (1978)). For an evaluation of the use of the prior in this way, see McCulloch and Rossi (1991).

Acceptance sampling from a source density $r(\theta)$ is so similar to importance sampling that exactly the same procedure can be used to produce $\hat{M}_T^{(M)}$. The ratio $p(\theta_m)p(\mathbf{Y}_T \mid \theta_m)/r(\theta_m)$ is needed for the acceptance probability in any event. The only additional work is to record $p(\theta_m)p(\mathbf{Y}_T \mid \theta_m)/r(\theta_m)$ whether the draw is accepted or not and then to set

$$\hat{M}_T^{(M)} = M^{-1} \Sigma_{m=1}^{M} p(\theta_m)p(\mathbf{Y}_T \mid \theta_m)/r(\theta_m),$$

the summation being taken over all candidate draws.

Simulation-consistent approximation of the marginalized likelihood from the output of a Markov chain Monte Carlo posterior simulator is a greater challenge and has spawned a substantial recent literature. No method will fully meet the three criteria stipulated above without more fundamental progress on the application of central limit theorems. Many methods are specialized to particular kinds of models and require at least two models for the computations because they provide Bayes factors rather than marginalized likelihoods. One example was presented in section 4.2: the prior distribution that places mass at zero on regression coefficients produces a posterior distribution which provides Bayes factors for models in which the regressors are subsets of the superset. Methods have been developed for approximation of Bayes factors when the dimension of the parameter vectors in the two models is the same (Meng and Wong (1993), Chen and Shao (1994), Gelman and Meng (1994)) or the models are nested (Chen and Shao (1995)). A more general procedure is due to Carlin and

Chib (1995), but this requires simultaneous simulation of two models. Methods that exploit the decomposition of the marginalized likelihood into predictive likelihoods (Kass and Raftery (1995, section 3.2)) in effect require the consideration of many models (Gelfand, Dey, and Chang (1992), Geweke (1994), Min (1995)).

Many straightforward approaches yield procedures with impractically slow convergence rates. A leading example is the "harmonic mean of the likelihood function" suggested by Newton and Raftery (1994): if $g(\theta) = [p(\theta)p(\mathbf{Y}_T \mid \theta)]^{-1}$, then $E[g(\theta)] = M_T^{-1}$. But $g(\theta)$ generally has no higher moments, and consequently numerical approximations are poor.

At this juncture the procedure for approximating the marginalized likelihood from the output of a Markov chain Monte Carlo posterior simulator that comes closest to satisfying all three criteria is a modification of the harmonic mean of the likelihood function, suggested by Gelfand and Dey (1994). They observed that

$$E[f(\theta)/p(\theta)p(\mathbf{Y}_T \mid \theta)] = M_T^{-1} \qquad (36)$$

for any p.d.f. $f(\theta)$ whose support is contained in Θ. One can approximate (36) from the output of any posterior simulator in the obvious way, but for this approximation to have a practical rate of convergence $f(\theta)/p(\theta)p(\mathbf{Y}_T \mid \theta)$ should be uniformly bounded. Gelfand and Dey (1994) and Raftery (1995) interpret this condition as requiring that $f(\theta)$ have "thin tails" relative to the likelihood function.

In the case of the Gibbs sampler there is an entirely different procedure due to Chib (1995) that provides quite accurate evaluations of the marginalized likelihood, at the cost of additional simulations. Suppose that the output from the blocking $\theta' = (\theta'^{(1)}, \ldots, \theta'^{(B)})$ is available and that the conditional p.d.f.'s $p(\theta^{(j)} \mid \theta^{(i)}(i \neq j), \mathbf{Y}_T)$ can be evaluated in closed form for all j. (This latter requirement is generally satisfied.) Suppose further that condition 1 or 2 for convergence of the Gibbs sampler is satisfied.

From the identity

$$p(\theta \mid \mathbf{Y}_T) = p(\theta)p(\mathbf{Y}_T \mid \theta)/M_T, \quad M_T = p(\theta^*)p(\mathbf{Y}_T \mid \theta^*)/p(\theta^* \mid \mathbf{Y}_T)$$

for any $\theta^* \in \Theta$. (In all cases, $p(\cdot)$ denotes a properly normalized density and not merely a kernel.) Typically $p(\mathbf{Y}_T \mid \theta^*)$ and $p(\theta^*)$ can be evaluated in closed form, but $p(\theta^* \mid \mathbf{Y}_T)$ cannot. A marginal/conditional decomposition of $p(\theta^* \mid \mathbf{Y}_t)$ is

$$p(\theta^* \mid \mathbf{Y}_T) = p(\theta^{*(1)} \mid \mathbf{Y}_T)p(\theta^{*(2)} \mid \theta^{*(1)}, \mathbf{Y}_T) \cdot \ldots \cdot p(\theta^{*(B)} \mid \theta^{*(1)}, \ldots,$$
$$\theta^{*(B-1)}, \mathbf{Y}_T).$$

The first term in the product of B terms can be approximated from the output of the posterior simulator because

$$M^{-1} \sum_{m=1}^{M} p(\theta^{*(1)} \mid \theta_m^{(2)}, \ldots, \theta_m^{(B)}, \mathbf{Y}_T) \to p(\theta^{*(1)} \mid \mathbf{Y}_T).$$

To approximate $p(\theta^{*(j)} \mid \theta^{*(1)}, \ldots, \theta^{*(j-1)}, \mathbf{Y}_T)$, first execute the Gibbs sampling algorithm with the parameters in the first j blocks fixed at the indicated values, thus producing a sequence $\{\theta_{jm}^{(j+1)}, \ldots, \theta_{jm}^{(B)}\}$ from the conditional posterior. Then

$$M^{-1} \sum_{m-1}^{M} p(\theta^{*(j)} \mid \theta^{*(1)}, \ldots, \theta^{*(j-1)}, \theta_{jm}^{(j+1)}, \ldots, \theta_{jm}^{(B)}, \mathbf{Y}_T)$$

$$\to p(\theta^{*(j)} \mid \theta^{*(1)}, \ldots, \theta^{*(j-1)}, \mathbf{Y}_T).$$

Chib (1995) describes an extension to include latent variables.

5.2   Bayesian communication

An investigator cannot anticipate the uses to which her work will be put or the variants on her model that may interest a client. Different uses will be reflected in different functions of interest. Variants will often revolve around changes in the prior distribution. Any investigator who has publicly reported results has confronted the constraint that only a few representative findings can be conveyed in written work.

Posterior simulators provide a clear answer to the question of what the investigator should report and in the process remove the constraint that only a few representative findings can be communicated. What should be reported is the $M \times (k + 2)$ *simulator output matrix*,

$$\begin{bmatrix} \theta_1' & w(\theta_1) & p(\theta_1) \\ \vdots & \vdots & \vdots \\ \theta_m' & w(\theta_m) & p(\theta_m) \end{bmatrix},$$

by making it publicly and electronically available. In a reasonably large problem ($M = 10{,}000$ and $k = 100$) the corresponding file occupies about 3.2 megabytes of storage (at a current capital cost of about US\$1.40) and can be moved over the Internet in under a minute.

Given the simulator matrix the client can immediately compute approximations to posterior moments not reported or even considered by the investigator. For example, a client reading a research report might be skeptical that the investigator's model, prior, and dataset provide much information about the effects of an interesting change in a policy variable on the outcome in question. If the simulator output matrix is available via FTP anonymous, the client can obtain the exact (up to numerical approximation error, which can also be evaluated) answer to his query without rising from his office chair in considerably less time than is required to read the research report.

With a small amount of additional effort the client can modify many of the investigator's assumptions. Suppose the client wishes to evaluate $E[g(\theta)|\mathbf{Y}_T]$ using his own prior density $p^*(\theta)$ rather than the investigator's prior density $p(\theta)$. Suppose further that the support of the investigator's prior distribution includes the support of the client's prior. Then the investigator's posterior distribution may be regarded as an importance sampling distribution for the client's posterior density. The client reweights the investigator's $\{\theta^m\}_{m-1}^M$ using the function

$$w^*(\theta) = \frac{p^*(\theta|\mathbf{Y}_t)}{p(\theta|\mathbf{Y}_t)} = \frac{p^*(\theta)L(\theta|\mathbf{Y}_t)}{p(\theta)L(\theta|\mathbf{Y}_t)} = \frac{p^*(\theta)}{p(\theta)},$$

where $p^*(\theta|\mathbf{Y}_t)$ denotes the client's posterior distribution. The client then approximates his posterior moment $E^*[g(\theta)|\mathbf{Y}_t]$ by

$$\bar{g}_M^* \equiv \sum_{m=1}^M w^*(\theta_m)w(\theta_m)g(\theta_m)/\sum_{m=1}^M w^*(\theta_m)w(\theta_m)$$

$$\rightarrow E^*[g(\theta)|\mathbf{Y}_t] \equiv \bar{g}^*.$$

(The result $\bar{g}_M^* \rightarrow \bar{g}^*$ follows almost at once from Tierney (1994).)

The efficiency of the reweighting scheme requires some similarity of $p^*(\theta)$ and $p(\theta)$. In particular, both reasonable convergence rates and the use of a central limit theorem to assess numerical accuracy essentially require that $p^*(\theta)/p(\theta)$ be bounded. Across a set of diverse clients this condition is more likely to be satisfied the more diffuse is $p(\theta)$ and is trivially satisfied for the improper prior $p(\theta) \propto$ constant if the client's prior is bounded. In the latter case the reweighting scheme will be efficient as long as the client's prior is uninformative relative to the likelihood function. This condition is stated precisely in theorem 2 of Geweke (1989b). Diagnostics described there will detect situations in which the reweighting scheme is inefficient, as will standard errors of numerical approximation as well. If the investigator chooses to use an improper prior for reporting, it is of course incumbent on her to verify the existence of the posterior distribution and convergence of her posterior simulator.

Including $p(\theta_m)$ in the standard simulator output file avoids the need for every client who wishes to impose his own priors to re-evaluate the investigator's prior. Of course, the $p^*(\theta)$s need not be the client's subjective priors: they may simply be devices by which clients explore the robustness of results with respect to alternative reasonable priors.

The potential for clients to alter investigators' priors, update their results, and examine alternative posterior moments exists given current technology.

All that is required is for Bayesian investigators to begin making their results available in a conventional format, in the same way that many now provide public access to text and data. Once this is done, colleagues, students, and policymakers may employ the results to their own ends much more flexibly than has heretofore been possible, with modest technical requirements.

6   CONCLUSION

The introduction set forth three propositions which, if believed, would keep most econometricians from using Bayesian methods in most applications. This chapter has presented some developments that, to the extent an econometrician was previously unaware of them, might well revise beliefs about these propositions. I conclude with a personal revision, taking the propositions in reverse order.

The statement that most posterior moments are unobtainable because of technical difficulties with integration was true for many models a decade ago, although steady inroads have been made (Zellner (1971), Richard (1973), Drèze (1977), Kloek and van Dijk (1978), Bauwens (1984)). With breakthroughs in importance sampling (Geweke (1988, 1989b)) and especially in Markov chain Monte Carlo (Gelfand and Smith (1990), Tierney (1994)) the statement is false. Econometric models in which any posterior moment of interest that exists cannot be obtained using a posterior simulator are now the exception, not the rule. In the past two years there have emerged important cases in which the posterior moments are more easily and reliably obtained than are non-Bayesian estimates. This is especially the case for models with latent variables.

The implications of posterior simulators for model comparison and the communication of results bear on the subjectivity of the prior distribution. It is now the case that the reader – or more generally the client, as described in section 5 – need not be passive and can conveniently take a role in the specification of econometric models and their application. The reader is free to explore posterior moments of his choice and examine the implications of revisions of the investigator's prior distribution for those moments. Indeed, the investigator can choose her prior to facilitate this process, as described in section 5.2.

If exploration of priors by readers becomes commonplace, then questions about the impact of subjective choices made by the econometrician shifts from the prior distribution to the functional form of the data distribution. This choice is made subjectively in Bayesian and many non-Bayesian procedures alike, and when it is not made explicitly in non-Bayesian procedures, then implicit restrictions on functional form exist in the assumed applicability of a central limit theorem. Alternative functional forms for data distributions can be compared using Bayes factors; no such general comparison is possible using non-Bayesian methods. Within the past two years reliable methods of approximation for the marginalized likelihoods that constitute Bayes factors have become available, and rapid further progress is currently being made.

None of the innovations in posterior simulators relieves the Bayesian econometrician of the burden of specifying a likelihood function and a prior distribution. On the contrary, there are three reasons for the econometrician to subject himself to this discipline, two of which have been made more compelling by developments in posterior simulators. First, specification of the likelihood function and prior distribution makes assumptions explicit, and this has clear benefits in interpreting what the econometrician has done. (For example, in non-Bayesian approaches an alternative to specifying a likelihood function is to assume the applicability of a central limit theorem or a particular non-parametric expansion, and an alternative to stipulating a prior distribution is to discard or discount results that do not look right.) Posterior simulators have no implications here. Second, if one specifies a likelihood function and prior distribution, then one can obtain useful results, not merely expressions. Posterior simulators have made this possible to the point that it is now increasingly easier to obtain posterior moments than to compute non-Bayesian estimates. Finally, and most important, economic theory that addresses decision making under uncertainty – which is to say, most economic theory – requires distributional assumptions, and results in theory are generally not robust to changes in these distributions. Decisions and policy recommendations depend on distributional assumptions. Econometricians cannot address these matters without being concerned with likelihood functions and prior distributions.

Notes

University of Minnesota and Federal Reserve Bank of Minneapolis. Paper prepared for invited symposium, Seventh World Congress of the Econometric Society, Tokyo, August 22–29, 1995. Partial financial support from NSF grant SES-9210070 is gratefully acknowledged. The views expressed in this paper are those of the author and not necessarily those of the Federal Reserve Bank of Minneapolis or the Federal Reserve System.

1 This section draws heavily on Geweke (1995a).

References

Amemiya, T. (1984). "Tobit models: a survey." *Journal of Econometrics*, 27: 3–61.
Barnett, W. A. and Lee, Y. W. (1985). "The global properties of the Minflex Laurent, Generalized Leontief, and Translog Functional forms." *Econometrica*, 53: 1421–37.

160   John Geweke

Bauwens, L. (1984). *Bayesian Full Information Analysis of Simultaneous Equation Models Using Integration by Monte Carlo.* Berlin: Springer-Verlag.
Bauwens, L. and Richard, J. F. (1985). "A 1-1 Poly-t random variable generator with applications to Monte Carlo integrations." *Journal of Econometrics*, 29: 19–46.
Berger, J. O. (1985). *Statistical Decision Theory and Bayesian Analysis*, 2nd edn. New York: Springer-Verlag.
Berger, J. O. and Wolpert, R. L. (1988). *The Likelihood Principle*, 2nd edn. Hayward: Institute of Mathematical Statistics.
Bernardo, J. M. and Smith, A. F. M. (1994). *Bayesian Theory.* New York: Wiley.
Blattberg, R. C. and George, E. I. (1991). "Shrinkage estimation of price and promotional elasticities: seemingly unrelated equations." *Journal of the American Statistical Association*, 86: 304–15.
Bratley, P., Fox, B. L., and Schrage, L. E. (1987). *A Guide to Simulation*, 2nd edn. New York: Springer-Verlag.
van den Broeck, J., Koop, G., Osiewalski, J., and Steel, M. F. J. (1994). "Stochastic frontier models: a Bayesian perspective." *Journal of Econometrics*, 61: 273–303.
Carlin, B. and Chib, S. (1995). "Bayesian model choice via Markov chain Monte Carlo." *Journal of the Royal Statistical Society, Series B*, 57: 473–84.
Chalfant, J. A. and Wallace, N. E. (1993). "Bayesian analysis and regularity conditions on flexible functional forms: application to the U.S. motor carrier industry." In Griffiths, W. E., Lütkepohl, H., and Bock, M. E. (eds.), *Readings in Econometric Theory and Practice.* Amsterdam: Elsevier–North-Holland.
Chamberlain, G. and Leamer, E. (1976). "Matrix weighted averages and posterior bounds." *Journal of the Royal Statistical Society, Series B*, 38: 73–84.
Chao, J. C. and Phillips, P. C. B. (1994). "Bayesian posterior distributions in limited information analysis of the simultaneous equations model." Yale University Cowles Foundation Working Paper.
Chen, M. and Shao, Q. (1994). "On Monte Carlo methods for estimating ratios of normalizing constants." National University of Singapore Department of Mathematics Research Report No. 627.
  (1995). "Estimating ratios of normalizing constants for densities with different dimensions." Worcester Polytechnical Institute Technical Report.
Chib, S. (1992). "Bayes inference in the Tobit censored regression model." *Journal of Econometrics*, 51: 79–99.
  (1995). "Marginal likelihood from the Gibbs output." *Journal of the American Statistical Association*, 90: 1313–21.
Chib, S. and Greenberg, E. (1994). "Markov chain simulation methods in econometrics." Washington University Olin School of Business Working Paper.
  (1995). "Hierarchical analysis of SUR models with extensions to correlated serial errors and time varying parameter models." *Journal of Econometrics*, 68: 339–60. Also Washington University Olin School of Business Working Paper.
Clyde, M. and Parmigiani, G. (1994). "Bayesian variable selection and prediction with mixtures." *Journal of Biopharmaceutical Statistics*, forthcoming. Also Duke University ISDS Discussion Paper.

Davis, P. J. and Rabinowitz, P. (1984). *Methods of Numerical Integration*, 2nd edn. Orlando: Academic Press.

Davis, W. W. (1978). "Bayesian analysis of the linear model subject to linear inequality constraints." *Journal of the American Statistical Association*, 73: 573–9.

DeGroot, M. (1970) *Optimal Statistical Decisions*. New York: McGraw-Hill.

Diewert, W. E. and Wales, T. J. (1987). "Flexible functional forms and global curvature conditions." *Econometrica*, 55: 43–88.

Drèze, J. H. (1976). "Bayesian limited information analysis of the simultaneous equation model." *Econometrica*, 46: 1045–75.

(1977). "Bayesian regression analysis using poly-*t* densities." *Journal of Econometrics*, 6: 329–54.

Drèze, J. H. and Richard, J. F. (1983). "Bayesian analysis of simultaneous equation systems." In Griliches, Z. and Intriligator, M. (eds.), *Handbook of Econometrics*, Vol. I. Amsterdam: North-Holland, pp. 517–98.

Gammerman, D. and Migon, H. S. (1993). "Dynamic hierarchical models." *Journal of the Royal Statistical Society, Series B*, 55: 629–42.

Gelfand, A. E. and Dey, D. K. (1994). "Bayesian model choice: asymptotics and exact calculations." *Journal of the Royal Statistical Society, Series B*, 56: 501–14.

Gelfand, A. E., Dey, D. K., and Chang, H. (1992). "Model determination using predictive distributions with implementation via sampling-based methods." In Bernardo, J. M., Berger, J. O., Dawid, A. P., and Smith, A. F. M. (eds.), *Bayesian Statistics*, Vol. IV. Oxford: Oxford University Press.

Gelfand, A. E. and Smith, A. F. M. (1990). "Sampling based approaches to calculating marginal densities." *Journal of the American Statistical Association*, 85: 398–409.

Gelman, A. and Rubin, D. B. (1992). "Inference from iterative simulation using multiple sequences." *Statistical Science*, 7: 457–72.

Gelman, A. and Meng, X. L. (1994). "Path sampling for computing normalizing constants: identities and theory." University of Chicago Department of Statistics Technical Report No. 377.

Geman, S. and Geman, D. (1984). "Stochastic relaxation, Gibbs distributions and the Bayesian restoration of images." *IEEE Transactions on Pattern Analysis and Machine Intelligence*, 6: 721–41.

George, E. I. and McCulloch, R. E. (1993). "Variable selection via Gibbs sampling." *Journal of the American Statistical Association*, 88: 881–9.

(1994). "Fast Bayes variable selection." University of Texas CSS Technical Report No. 94-01.

Geweke, J. (1986). "Exact inference in the inequality constrained normal linear regression model." *Journal of Applied Econometrics*, 1: 127–41.

(1988). "Antithetic acceleration of Monte Carlo integration in Bayesian inference." *Journal of Econometrics*, 38: 73–89.

(1989a). "Exact predictive densities in linear models with ARCH disturbances." *Journal of Econometrics*, 40: 63–86.

(1989b). "Bayesian inference in econometric models using Monte Carlo integration." *Econometrica*, 57: 1317–40.

(1991). "Efficient simulation from the multivariate normal and student-t distributions subject to linear constraints." In Keramidas, E. M. (ed.), *Computing Science and Statistics: Proceedings of the 23rd Symposium on the Interface*. Fairfax, VA: Interface Foundation of North America, pp. 571–8.

(1992). "Evaluating the accuracy of sampling-based approaches to the calculation of posterior moments." In Berger, J. O., Bernardo, J. M., Dawid, A. P., and Smith, A. F. M. (eds.), *Proceedings of the Fourth Valencia International Meeting on Bayesian Statistics*. Oxford: Oxford University Press, pp. 169–94.

(1993). "Bayesian treatment of the student-t linear model." *Journal of Applied Econometrics*, 8: S19–S40.

(1994). "Bayesian comparison of econometric models." Federal Reserve Bank of Minneapolis Research Department Working Paper No. 532.

(1995a). "Monte Carlo simulation and numerical integration." In Amman, H., Kendrick, D., and Rust, J. (eds.), *Handbook of Computational Economics*. Amsterdam: North-Holland. Also Federal Reserve Bank of Minneapolis Research Department Staff Report No. 192.

(1995b). "Simulation-based Bayesian inference for economic time series." In Mariano, R. S., Schuermann, T., and Weeks, M. (eds.), *Simulation-based Inference in Econometrics: Methods and Applications*. Cambridge: Cambridge University Press.

(1995c). "Bayesian inference for linear models subject to linear inequality constraints." In Johnson, W. O., Lee, J. C., and Zellner, A. (eds.), *Forecasting, Prediction and Modeling in Statistics and Econometrics: Bayesian and non-Bayesian Approaches*. New York: Springer-Verlag. Also Federal Reserve Bank of Minneapolis Research Department Working Paper No. 552.

(1995d). "Posterior simulators in econometrics." Federal Reserve Bank of Minneapolis Research Department Working Paper No. 555.

Geweke, J. and Keane, M. (1995). "An empirical analysis of the male income dynamics in the PSID: 1986–1989." University of Minnesota Department of Economics Working Paper.

Geweke, J., Keane, M., and Runkle, D. (1994a). "Alternative computational approaches to statistical inference in the multinomial probit model." *Review of Economics and Statistics*, 76: 609–32.

(1994b). "Statistical inference in multinomial multiperiod probit models." Federal Reserve Bank of Minneapolis Research Department Staff Report No. 177.

Geyer, C. J. (1992). "Practical Markov chain Monte Carlo." *Statistical Science*, 7: 473–81.

Ghosh, M., Saleh, A. K., and Sen, P. K. (1989). "Empirical Bayes subset information in regression models." *Statistics and Decisions*, 7: 15–36.

Gourieroux, C., Holly, A., and Monfort, A. (1982). "Likelihood ratio test, Wald test, and Kuhn–Tucker test in linear models with inequality constraints on the regression parameters." *Econometrica*, 50: 63–80.

Hastings, W. K. (1970). "Monte Carlo sampling methods using Markov chains and their applications." *Biometrika*, 57: 97–109.

Hildreth, C. (1963). "Bayesian statisticians and remote clients." *Econometrica*, 31: 422–38.

IMSL (1994). *IMSL Stat/Library*. Houston: Visual Numerics, Inc.

Johnson, N. L. and Kotz, S. (1970). *Distributions in Statistics: Continuous Univariate Distributions* (in two volumes). New York: Wiley.

———— (1972). *Distributions in Statistics: Continuous Multivariate Distributions*. New York: Wiley.

Judge, G. G. and Takayama, T. (1966). "Inequality restrictions in regression analysis." *Journal of the American Statistical Association*, 61: 166–81.

Kass, R. E. and Raftery, A. E. (1995). "Bayes factors." *Journal of the American Statistical Association*, 90: 773–95.

Kleibergen, F. and van Kijk, H. K. (1994). "Bayesian analysis of simultaneous equation models using non-informative priors." Tinbergen Institute Discussion Paper, 94-134.

Kloek, T. and van Kijk, H. K. (1978). "Bayesian estimates of equation system parameters: an application of integration by Monte Carlo." *Econometrica*, 46: 1–19.

Koop, G. (1994). "Recent progress in applied Bayesian econometrics." *Journal of Economic Surveys*, 8: 1–34.

Koop, G., Steel, M. F. J., and Osiewalski, J. (1995). "Posterior analysis of stochastic frontier models using Gibbs sampling." *Computational Statistics*, forthcoming.

Leamer, E., and Chamberlain, G. (1976). "A Bayesian interpretation of pretesting." *Journal of the Royal Statistical Society, Series B*, 38: 85–94.

Lindley, D. V. (1957). "A statistical paradox." *Biometrika*, 44: 187–92.

Lovell, M. C. and Prescott, E. (1970). "Multiple regression with inequality constraints: pretesting bias, hypothesis testing, and efficiency." *Journal of the American Statistical Association*, 65: 913–25.

Maddala, G. S. (1983). *Limited-dependent and Qualitative Variables in Econometrics*. Cambridge: Cambridge University Press.

Madigan, D. and Raftery, A. E. (1994). "Model selection and accounting for model uncertainty in graphical models using Occam's window." *Journal of the American Statistical Association*, 89: 1535–46.

McCulloch, R. E., Polson, N. G., and Rossi, P. E. (1995). "A Bayesian analysis of the multinomial probit model with fully identified parameters." University of Chicago Graduate School of Business Working Paper.

McCulloch, R. E. and Rossi, P. E. (1991). "A Bayesian approach to testing the arbitrage pricing theory." *Journal of Econometrics*, 49: 141–68.

———— (1995a). "An exact likelihood analysis of the multinomial probit model." *Journal of Econometrics*, 64: 207–40.

———— (1995b). "Bayesian analysis of the multinomial probit model." In Mariano, R. S., Weeks, M., and Schuermann, T. (eds.), *Simulation-Based Inference in Econometrics: Methods and Applications*. Cambridge: Cambridge University Press.

164   John Geweke

Meng, X. L. and Wong, W. H. (1993). "Simulating ratios of normalizing constants via a simple identity." University of Chicago Department of Statistics Technical Report No. 365.
Metropolis, N., Rosenbluth, A. W., Rosenbluth, M. N., Teller, A. H., and Teller, E. (1953). "Equation of state calculations by fast computing machines." *The Journal of Chemical Physics*, 21: 1087–92.
Min, C. (1995). "Forecasting the adoptions of new consumer durable products." George Mason University School of Business Administration Working Paper.
Min, C. and Zellner, A. (1993). "Bayesian and non-Bayesian methods for combining models and forecasts with applications to forecasting international growth rates." *Journal of Econometrics*, 56: 89–118.
Newton, M. A. and Raftery, A. E. (1994). "Approximate Bayesian inference by the weighted likelihood bootstrap" (with discussion). *Journal of the Royal Statistical Society, Series B*, 56: 3–48.
Numelin, E. (1984). *General Irreducible Markov Chains and Non-negative Operators*. Cambridge: Cambridge University Press.
Percy, D. F. (1992). "Prediction for seemingly unrelated regressions." *Journal of the Royal Statistical Society, Series B*, 54: 243–52.
Peskun, P. H. (1973). "Optimum Monte-Carlo sampling using Markov chains." *Biometrika*, 60: 607–12.
Poirier, D. J. (1988). "Frequentist and subjectivist perspectives on the problem of model building in economics" (with discussion). *Journal of Economic Perspectives*, 2: 120–70.
(1989). "A report from the battlefront." *Journal of Business and Economic Statistics*, 7: 137–9.
(1992). "A return to the battlefront." *Journal of Business and Economic Statistics*, 10: 473–4.
(1995). *Intermediate Statistics and Econometrics: A Comparative Approach*. Cambridge, MA: MIT Press.
Press, W. H., Flannery, B. P., Teukolsky, S. A., and Vetterling, W. T. (1986). *Numerical Recipes: The Art of Scientific Computing*. Cambridge: Cambridge University Press.
Raftery, A. E. (1995). "Hypothesis testing and model selection via posterior simulation." University of Washington Working Paper.
Raftery, A., Madigan, D., and Hoeting, J. (1993). "Model selection and acounting for model uncertainty in linear regression models." University of Washington Department of Statistics Technical Report No. 262.
Richard, J. F. (1973). *Posterior and Predictive Densities for Simultaneous Equation Models*. Berlin: Springer-Verlag.
Richard, J. F. and Steel, M. F. J. (1988). "Bayesian analysis of systems of seemingly unrelated regression equations under a recursive extended natural conjugate prior density." *Journal of Econometrics*, 38: 7–37.
Roberts, G. O. and Smith, A. F. M. (1994). "Simple conditions for the convergence of the Gibbs sampler and Metropolis–Hastings algorithms." *Stochastic Processes and Their Applications*, 49: 207–16.

Rothenberg, T. J. (1975). "Bayesian analysis of simultaneous equations models." In Fienberg, S. E. and Zellner, A. (eds.), *Studies in Bayesian Econometrics and Statistics*. Amsterdam: North-Holland.

Rubin, D. B. (1987). *Multiple Imputation for Nonresponse in Surveys*. New York: Wiley.

Stein, C. (1966). "An approach to the recovery of inter-block information in balanced incomplete block designs." In David, F. N. (ed.), *Festschrift for J. Neyman*. New York: Wiley, pp. 351–66.

Tanner, M. A. and Wong, W.-H. (1987). "The calculation of posterior distributions by data augmentation." *Journal of the American Statistical Association*, 82: 528–50.

Terrell, D. (1995). "Incorporating monotonicity and concavity conditions in flexible functional forms." *Journal of Applied Econometrics*, forthcoming. Also Kansas State University Department of Economics Working Paper.

Tierney, L. (1991). "Exploring posterior distributions using Markov chains." In Keramaidas, E. M. (ed.), *Computing Science and Statistics: Proceedings of the 23rd Symposium on the Interface*. Fairfax: Interface Foundation of North America, Inc., pp. 563–70.

(1994). "Markov chains for exploring posterior distributions" (with discussion and rejoinder). *Annals of Statistics*, 22: 1701–62. (Also Technical Report No. 560, University of Minnesota School of Statistics.)

Tobin, J. (1958). "Estimation of relationships for limited dependent variables." *Econometrica*, 26: 24–36.

Tsionas, E. G. (1994). "Asset returns in general equilibrium with scale-mixture-of-normals endowment processes." Unpublished Ph.D. Dissertation, University of Minnesota.

Wei, C. G. and Tanner, M. A. (1990). "Posterior computations for censored regression data." *Journal of the American Statistical Association*, 85: 829–39.

West, M. (1984). "Outlier models and prior distributions in Bayesian linear regression." *Journal of the Royal Statistical Society, Series B*, 46: 431–9.

Wolak, F. A. (1987). "An exact test for multiple inequality and equality constraints in the linear regression model." *Journal of the American Statistical Association*, 82: 782–93.

Zellner, A. (1962). "An efficient method of estimating seemingly unrelated regressions and test of aggregation bias." *Journal of the American Statistical Association*, 57: 500–9.

(1971). *Bayesian Inference in Econometrics*. New York: Wiley.

Zellner, A., Min, C., and Dallaire, D. (1994). "Bayesian analysis of simultaneous equation, asset-pricing and related models using Markov chain Monte Carlo techniques and convergence checks." University of Chicago Graduate School of Business Working Paper.

CHAPTER 6

Restricted least squares subject to monotonicity and concavity constraints

Paul A. Ruud

1   INTRODUCTION

Economists have devoted much research effort to the estimation of cost functions and profit functions. Since the popularization of the dual approach to such functions, econometricians have focused particularly on methods for fitting functions that satisfy the restrictions implied by optimizing behavior, minimizing costs, or maximizing profits. For the most part, researchers have sought simple parametric functional forms that are sufficiently flexible to approximate well all possible cost and profit functions. Given such parametric functions, much of the estimation has followed the method of least squares.

In this chapter, I will describe a computational approach to fitting cost and profit functions by the method of least squares subject only to the restrictions imposed by the theory of optimizing behavior. Instead of tightly parameterized functional forms, I will use as many parameters as required to cover all the permissible functions. The computational approach has a long history, but this chapter grows specifically out of previous, joint research with my colleague, Steven Goldman. I will illustrate the computation with two examples drawn from the empirical literature on the estimation of cost functions.

There are several reasons to pursue the least-squares fit of cost and conditional factor demands. First of all, researchers have worked for many years on appropriate functional forms for these functions.[1] Economists have proposed various parametric functional forms designed to exhibit their theoretical properties and to be amenable to conventional parametric statistical estimation methods.[2] This requirement explains the popularity of such parametric cost functions as the translog. In addition, researchers desire flexible functional forms so that their inferences are not misled by statistical artifacts of parametric misspecification. The approach presented here also yields a specification that accommodates factor and output levels of zero naturally.

Another motivation for our line of research is the desire to explore various ways to let the data determine the amount of smoothing in regression estimation. Non-parametric research has focused heavily on such techniques as kernel smoothing. In this chapter, we obtain smoothness through structural restrictions of monotonicity and concavity on the regression function. One can also view the fits we compute here as the best smooth function that satisfies these structural constraints. Anything else is a further restriction. Thus, one can learn what additional structure must be imposed to sharpen one's empirical inference.

This chapter focuses on computational problems. We do not consider the statistical properties of the least-squares estimator. Hanson and Pledger (1976) have demonstrated the consistency of the estimator for the univariate case. Approximate (asymptotic) distributions are non-normal and quite complicated for the simplest cases. See Yazhen (1992) for an analysis. Our purpose is to introduce the computational problem and its history, describe a solution method, and apply this method to estimating a cost function and its associated factor demand functions. See Matzkin (1992) for an alternative approach.

2 THE COMPUTATIONAL APPROACH

Computing the least-squares fit of a cost or profit function is a classic quadratic programming problem. Our computational approach is to compute the solution to a dual problem. The solution to the dual quadratic programming problem is computed by a combination of standard Gauss–Seidel and programming algorithms. However, the dimensions of "typical" problems in econometrics are too large for software engineered for a wide range of applications. We exploit the special structure of our particular problems to overcome this dimensionality.

2.1 Statement of the problem

2.1.1 Univariate concave regression

To introduce our discussion, consider a particular example of restricted least squares, fitting a univariate, concave regression function, as proposed by Hildreth (1954). Given observations $\{(x_n, y_n); n = 1, \ldots, N\}$, ordered so

168   **Paul A. Ruud**

that $x_1 < x_2 < \cdots < x_N$, find

$$\min_{z} \| \mathbf{y} - \mathbf{z} \|^2 \tag{1}$$

subject to

$$\frac{z_{n+2} - z_{n+1}}{x_{n+2} - x_{n+1}} \leq \frac{z_{n+1} - z_n}{x_{n+1} - x_n}, n = 1, \ldots, N - 2, \tag{2}$$

where $\mathbf{y} \equiv [y_n; n = 1, \ldots, N]$ and $\mathbf{z} \equiv [z_n; n = 1, \ldots, N]$. For exposition, we have specified that the x_n have distinct values.[3] A direct approach would be to optimize the elements of $\mathbf{z}$. But this is awkward because most z_n must satisfy several constraints simultaneously. Hildreth used an alternative approach.

Instead, Hildreth computed the solution to the dual problem. Let $\mathbf{Rz} \leq 0$ denote the inequality constraints (2) gathered into matrix form. The dual program is

$$\min_{\lambda \geq 0} \| \mathbf{y} - \mathbf{R'}\lambda \|^2 \tag{3}$$

which has an analytically simpler form for the constraints: Each element of λ must satisfy a single positivity constraint. These scalars are the Lagrange multipliers associated with each constraint. Given the optimal $\hat{\lambda}$, the optimum of the primal problem is calculated simply as

$$\hat{\mathbf{y}} = \mathbf{y} - \mathbf{R'}\hat{\lambda}. \tag{4}$$

Hildreth applied Gauss–Seidel to (3), optimizing iteratively over each element of λ in an (arbitrary) fixed sequence. Each optimization has a simple solution

$$\max\{0, b_r/c_r\} = \arg\min_{\lambda_r \geq 0} \| \mathbf{y} - \mathbf{R'}\lambda \|^2, \tag{5}$$

where b_r and c_r are taken from the expansion of the objective function in each element λ_r:

$$\| \mathbf{y} - \mathbf{R'}\lambda \|^2 \equiv a_r - b_r\lambda_r + \frac{1}{2}c_r\lambda_r^2.$$

In this way, he converted a relatively difficult problem into a series of very simple ones.

The basic duality is illustrated in figure 6.1. The vectors R_1 and R_2 are two rows in the constraint matrix $\mathbf{R}$. The constrained set is $K = \{\mathbf{z} \,|\, \mathbf{Rz} \leq 0\}$

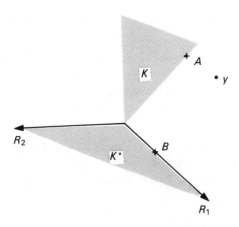

Figure 6.1 Quadratic program duality

and its dual is $K^* = \{\mathbf{w} \mid \mathbf{w}'\mathbf{z} \leq 0 \; \forall \mathbf{z} \in K\}$. The optima $\hat{\mathbf{y}}$ and $\mathbf{R}'\hat{\lambda}$ are denoted by the points A and B respectively. Note that these are orthogonal projections of $\mathbf{y}$ onto subspaces.

By updating each element of λ, λ_r, with (5) sequentially as $r = 1, \ldots, M$ over M constraints, one completes a cycle of Hildreth's algorithm. A convenient starting point is to set $\lambda = 0$. At every step within a cycle, say the ith from $\hat{\lambda}_i$ to $\hat{\lambda}_{i+1}$, one reduces the length of the implicit fit, $\hat{\mathbf{y}}_i \equiv \mathbf{y} - \mathbf{R}'\hat{\lambda}_i$.[4] Hildreth also proved that this Gauss–Seidel sequence converges to the optimum of (3). His proof is a classic demonstration of a contraction mapping, resting on the uniqueness of the optimal λ, the boundedness of λ, and the continuity of the objective function. See Goldman and Ruud (1993b) for a generalization of his theorem and proof that applies to the problems we consider below.

2.1.2 Cost functions

This univariate case is simpler than the general problem that we consider here: fitting a cost function for production with multiple inputs and outputs. The basic structure is the same, but the constraints are more complicated. Let q denote a vector of J output levels, y denote a vector of M input factor levels, and p denote a vector of M corresponding factor prices. The cost function is

$$c(p, q) = \min_{\substack{(\tilde{q}, y) \in Q \\ \tilde{q} \geq q}} p'y,$$

where $\mathbf{Q}$ is the production set.[5] Such functions are characterized by four properties:

1 $c(\cdot)$ is monotonically increasing in input prices and output levels;
2 $c(\cdot)$ is homogeneous of degree one in input prices;
3 $c(\cdot)$ is concave; and
4 $c(\cdot)$ is continuous.[6]

Associated with the cost function is a vector of M conditional factor demand correspondences that we denote by

$$z(p,q) \equiv [z_m(p,q); m = 1, \ldots, M].$$

These are characterized by

1 $z_m(\cdot)$ is monotonically decreasing in p_m,
2 $z(\cdot)$ is homogeneous of degree zero in p,
3 if $z(\cdot)$ is single-valued at (p_1, q_1), then $z(p_1, q_1) = \nabla_p c(p_1, q_1)$, and
4 if $z(\cdot)$ is differentiable at (p_1, q_1), then $\nabla_p(p_1, q_1)'$ is a symmetric, negative semi-definite matrix.[7]

Given a dataset of N observations $\{(p_n, q_n, y_n); n = 1, \ldots, N\}$ on the price vector, output vector, and input vector, we will seek

$$\hat{y} = \arg\min_{z \in C} \sum_{n=1}^{N} \| y_n - z(p_n, q_n) \|^2, \tag{6}$$

where $\mathbf{C}$ is the set of single-valued conditional factor demand functions that are consistent with the properties of cost minimization listed above.[8] This problem is a generalization of the parametric estimators econometricians typically employ. It can be motivated by assuming normally distributed error terms associated with the demand or by specifying that the conditional factor demand function is the conditional expectation of the observable factor levels. We will refer to $\hat{y}$ as the "non-parametric" fit, though we will actually work with a high-dimensional parameterization below.

First of all, consider the constraints that cost minimization imposes on this minimization problem. We will not impose differentiability of z. Clearly, only the points $\{z_n \equiv z(p_n, q_n); n = 1, \ldots, N\}$ are relevant to the least-squares problem. Therefore, we can restrict our parameterization, without loss of generality, to

$$\mathbf{C}_N = \{[z_{nm}] \in \mathbb{R}^N \times \mathbb{R}^M \mid z_n = z(p_n, q_n), z \in \mathbf{C}\}.$$

Similarly, the continuity of the cost function is not a binding restriction in this problem.

Imposing linear homogeneity as a restriction on z is straightforward: One simply chooses one input as numéraire and normalizes all prices by the price of the numeraire. Monotonicity and convexity restrictions result in a non-trivial computational problem. The monotonicity constraints on cost functions require simply that every z_{nm} be non-negative

$$z_{nm} \geq 0. \tag{7}$$

As Varian (1984) points out, the concavity constraints imply that[9]

$$p'_n z_n \leq p'_n z_i \qquad \forall n, i: q_n \leq q_i. \tag{8}$$

In words, the cost function $p'_n z_n$ is less than the cost at prices p_n of the conditional factor demands for producing at least the same output q_i at any other prices p_i.

Goldman and Ruud (1993b) observe that these constraints (7)–(8) together describe a closed convex polyhedral cone. It is an immediate consequence of the convexity of C_N (and the strict concavity of the objective function) that $\hat{y}$ is unique. This uniqueness is, of course, a highly desirable property for computation because it rules out the need to seek out multiple potential local optima.

It is also interesting to consider the estimation of the cost function without the factor input level data. Occasionally, input data are not available. In addition, comparisons of cost function estimates with and without input data may serve as a natural specification test. Given a data set of N observations $\{(p_n, q_n, c_n); n = 1, \ldots, N\}$ on the price vector, output vector, and total costs, the cost function estimation program solves

$$\min_{z \in C_N} \| c - z \|^2,$$

where $c \equiv [c_n]$ is the vector of observed costs and C_N is a subset of $\mathbb{R}^N$ where $z \in C_N$ if

$$z_n \leq z_i \qquad \forall n, i: p_n \leq p_i, q_n \leq q_i, \tag{9}$$

$$\exists \gamma_n \in \mathbb{R}_+^M: z_n = p'_n \gamma_n, z_i \leq p'_i \gamma_n \qquad \forall n, i: q_i \leq q_n. \tag{10}$$

We normalize prices and costs so that homogeneity is imposed. The restrictions in (9) describe monotonicity and the restrictions in (10) describe concavity. The latter is a convenient alternative in higher dimensions to explicit expressions like (2), which require extensive computation and work space to apply. Also, (10) is the natural analog to (8): the γ_n correspond to possible factor demands and the constraint states that the cost of the factor

172   **Paul A. Ruud**

demands at (p_n, q_n) valued at prices p_i must not undercut minimized costs at p_i and any output less than q_n.

Again, the parameter space C_N is a closed convex cone so that there is a unique fitted $\hat{c}$. Note, however, that the implicit conditional factor demands will be a correspondence, not a function. In general, the values of γ_n that satisfy (10) will not be unique. Instead, the conditional factor demands will be a closed set.

Although the parameterization of the cost or conditional factor demands can be restricted to a finite number of points, the points where prices and outputs are observed in the sample, there are implicit restrictions on the cost function and demands at other prices and outputs as well. These restrictions yield estimators for prices and quantities that are correspondences, in much the same way as for conditional factor demands above.[10] Thus, for conditional factor demands, $\hat{y}(p, q)$ is the set that satisfies constraints exactly analogous to (7)–(8)

$$z(p,q) \geq 0,$$

$$p'z(p,q) \leq \min_{i:q \leq q_i} p'\hat{y}_i$$

$$p_i'\hat{y}_i \leq p_i'z(p,q) \qquad \forall i: q_i \leq q.$$

For the cost function, $\hat{c}(p, q)$ is the set that satisfies

$$\hat{c}(p,q) \leq \hat{c}_i \qquad \forall i: p \leq p_i, q \leq q_i,$$
$$\hat{c}_i \leq \hat{c}(p,q) \qquad \forall i: p_i \leq p, q_i \leq q,$$
$$\exists \gamma \in \mathbb{R}^M: \hat{c}(p,q) = p'\gamma, \hat{c}_i \leq p_i'\gamma \qquad \forall i: q_i \leq q,$$
$$\exists \gamma_i \in \mathbb{R}^M: \hat{c}_i = p_i'\gamma_i, \hat{c}(p,q) \leq p'\gamma_i \qquad \forall i: q \leq q_i.$$

These constraints are analogous to (9)–(10). For any (p, q), either of these sets can be computed easily with linear programming software.[11]

The computational problem that we face is that the number and dimension of constraints in a dataset is often so enormous that general programs for solving quadratic programs cannot accommodate them. Varian (1985) has computed the solution to a problem similar to (6) for a relatively small dataset (18 observations, 3 factors, 1 output) using the MINOS package by Murtagh and Saunders (1967). In one of the examples below, there are over 200,000 restrictions on more than 2,500 parameters for a dataset with 630 observations.

Goldman and Ruud (1993a) fit factor demands for a somewhat larger problem using Hildreth's method. In their work, each Gauss–Seidel iteration corresponds to updating the fitted factor demands with

$$
\begin{pmatrix} z_i \\ z_n \end{pmatrix} = \begin{cases} \begin{pmatrix} w_i \\ w_n \end{pmatrix} & \text{if } \begin{Bmatrix} p_n' w_n \le p_n' w_i, \\ q_n \le q_i \end{Bmatrix} \\ \begin{pmatrix} w_i \\ w_n \end{pmatrix} - \alpha_{ni} \cdot \begin{pmatrix} p_n \\ -p_n \end{pmatrix} & \text{if } \begin{Bmatrix} p_n' w_n > p_n' w_i, \\ q_n \le q_i \end{Bmatrix} \end{cases}, \quad (11)
$$

$$
\alpha_{ni} = \frac{p_n'(w_i - w_n)}{2p_n' p_n}
$$

where the other components of z are set equal to the corresponding components of w. The projections for the inequalities (7) are even simpler

$$
z_{nm} = \max\{0, w_{nm}\}.
$$

These calculations can be done very rapidly, rendering large problems into many, workable subproblems. Goldman and Ruud (1993a) found that the convergence of such sequences was extremely slow in the problem they considered. This slowness is a well-studied characteristic of a general class of calculations called *alternating projections*.[12]

3   GENERALIZING HILDRETH'S PROCEDURE

The components of Hildreth's computational method have been generaliz-ed by Goldman and Ruud (1993a).[13] Their basic, and simple, insight is that one need not restrict the iterations of Gauss–Seidel to one element of λ at a time. More generally, one can optimize over subsets of the elements of λ simultaneously or alter the order in which the elements are taken. These two possibilities make the range of possible algorithms much bigger and their exploitation can substantially improve the speed of convergence. Goldman and Ruud (1993b) prove that the contraction property of such generalizations rests solely on the requirement that every constraint appears in at least one subproblem of an iteration.

For calculations like (11), one can understand the slow speed of convergence as a symptom of near multi-collinearity among the restric-tions. Each iteration of Gauss–Seidel corresponds to a projection on to a half space.[14] See figure 6.2 for an illustration. The solid line depicts the path of two iterations, through all constraints, of the Hildreth algorithm. In the second iteration, the circles depict the location of the fitted vector when $\lambda_r = 0$ and the dashed line represents a projection onto a half space as λ_r is set to its optimal positive value. Alternating projections between several highly collinear subspaces is illustrated in figure 6.3. Because the intermedi-ate projections are so close to one another, the algorithm makes small incremental steps toward the ultimate solution.

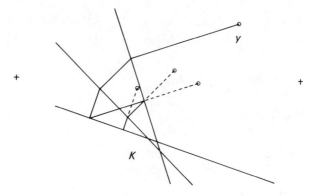

Figure 6.2 Alternating projections

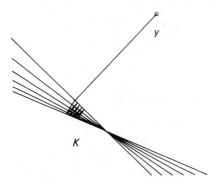

Figure 6.3 Nearly collinear subspaces

Goldman and Ruud (1993a) combine the elements of λ in two instances. First of all, for the estimation of cost functions without factor demand data, they construct a sequence of least-squares regressions that optimize with respect to the intersection of the concavity constraints (10) for fixed n. Secondly, when the iterations of Hildreth's procedure cycle over the same active constraints, they check whether the active constraints comprise a basis for the final solution. If so, they calculate the optimum (by direct linear calculation) and end the iterations. In this chapter, we extend the principle of optimizing over several elements in λ in two additional ways. Firstly, we replace the individual factor demand projections in (11) with a single projection onto the intersection of a set of concavity restrictions. This is analogous to the projection for costs used by Goldman and Ruud (1993a). Secondly, we reduce the active constraint set by removing as many constraints as possible through periodic optimization over all positive elements of λ. This procedure is a generalization of the attempt to solve for a final solution.

3.1 Projection onto concavity constraints

Our experience shows that the greater speed of such simple projections as (11) can be overcome by the greater improvements achieved by more complex projections onto higher dimensional cones. In our case, we make projections on to the sequence of cones

$$K_r \equiv \{p_r'z_r \le p_r'z_i \quad \forall i: q_r \le q_i\}, r = 1, \dots, S,$$

the intersections of subsets of the half spaces Goldman and Ruud (1993a) consider. The projection onto this cone is non-linear, but it can be accomplished efficiently using a conventional quadratic programming algorithm (see Gill, Murray, Saunders, and Writhgt (1982)).[15] This is possible because the special structure of these cones allows us to compute the search direction without numerical inversion of a large Hessian term. The constraints in K_r have a convenient tensor form by virtue of the common price vector p_r. The constraints can always be written in the form

$$(R_r \otimes p_r')\mathbf{z} = 0$$

by stacking the fitted factor demand vectors into a single vector. For notational convenience, suppose all the elements of $\mathbf{z}$ are actively constrained elements and suppose z_r is the last element of $\mathbf{z}$. Then

$$R_r = (-I \; \iota),$$

where I is an identity matrix and ι is a vector of ones. The search direction for an iteration of the quadratic programming algorithm is similar to (11)

$$\mathbf{z} = \mathbf{w} - \frac{1}{p_r'p_r}[p_rp_r'(w_i - \bar{w})],$$

where $\bar{w}$ is the simple average of the elements of w and w_i is the ith element of $\mathbf{w}$. Clearly, this direction can be computed easily for large numbers of active constraints. One simply computes an average of conditional demand vectors. One must iterate through a sequence of such search directions, but the cost of these iterations is overcome by the improvement in search efficiency.

The monotonicity constraints can also be conveniently combined. The projection joint simply replaces every negative entry with zero. The simplicity of this intersection arises from the mutual orthogonality of the constraints. This orthogonality also implies what is obvious here: that there is no gain in the efficiency of the algorithm derived from forming this "monotonicity" cone.

3.2   Optimal constraint elimination

There is a general pattern in the paths of the Gauss–Seidel iterations in the dual: The number of active constraints usually declines, especially over the initial iterations. The approach to the optimal solution is monotone in the length of the fitted vector. As one approaches the optimal solution, constraints that are satisfied at the solution are eliminated. Therefore, a general strategy to accelerate Hildreth's procedure seeks ways to eliminate constraints from the current basis.

We have found a rapid and convenient method for such elimination. When the set of active constraints remains unchanged for two successive iterations, we attempt to jump to a final solution by computing the constrained optimum that imposes all active constraints as equalities. Denoting the active constraints by $\mathbf{R}z = 0$, this point is

$$\begin{aligned}\mathbf{y}^* &= (I - \mathbf{R}^-\mathbf{R})\mathbf{y} \\ &= (I - \mathbf{R}'(\mathbf{R}^-)')\mathbf{y} \\ &= (I - \mathbf{R}'(\mathbf{R}')^-)\mathbf{y},\end{aligned}$$

where $\mathbf{R}^-$ is a generalized inverse of $\mathbf{R}$. The corresponding value for the Lagrange multiplier vector λ is, therefore, $\lambda^* = \mathbf{R}'^- y$. If the active constraints do not comprise the set of constraints binding at the optimum, but instead include extra constraints, then elements of λ^* will be negative. The optimal, constrained, point on the line segment between the current value of λ and λ^* will set one element of λ to zero, effectively eliminating one active constraint and improving the objective function. We repeat this process with the remaining constraints, until λ^* contains strictly positive values.

This procedure does not produce a projection onto the intersection of the active constraints. That would require the entry of inactive constraints into the active constraint set. We have not yet explored whether the computational effort would be worthwhile. Our current procedure is rapid and speeds convergence significantly.

3.3   Additional considerations

Finally, we remark that numerical round-off errors can play a significant role in preventing successful iteration. To summarize our experience, we find it critical to parameterize the computational problem in terms of the Lagrange multiplier vector λ. Dykstra (1983), for example, uses a theoretically equivalent parameterization in the primal parameter space that often failed us as we developed our algorithm and software. Dykstra writes the Gauss–Seidel sequence as

$$\hat{y}_i = P(\hat{y}_{i-1} - \hat{u}_{i-s} \mid K_r),$$
$$\hat{u}_i = \hat{y}_i - (\hat{y}_{i-1} - \hat{u}_{i-s}),$$

where S is the number of constraint sets K_r, $r = (i - 1 \text{ modulo } S) + 1$, and $P(z \mid K)$ denotes the orthogonal projection of z on to K.[16] This formulation has theoretical appeal for generalizations of Hildreth's approach to other optimization problems. However, in practice numerical round-off errors in the $\hat{u}$ may accumulate so that the fitted value $\hat{y}_i$ does not satisfy the constraints of the dual problem. Therefore, we retain the parameterization of the problem in terms of the dual, thereby ensuring that these constraints are respected at every step of the calculations.

We have written our programs in Matlab. Although Gauss is generally very similar, Matlab has an ability to handle sparse matrices that is particularly convenient for our algorithm. The constraint matrix **R** contains many zeros, because the constraints are pair-wise in the observations. Sparse matrix routines save a great deal of work space and computational time.

4 EXAMPLES

We give two examples as applications of the computation of restricted least squares. The first is based on the classic paper by Christensen and Greene (1976), one of the earliest applications of the translog cost function to cost function estimation. Goldman and Ruud (1993a) also used this example, but made some computational errors which are corrected here. The second example examines US trucking costs, one of the areas in which cost function estimation has been applied extensively.

4.1 Electric power generation

Christensen and Greene (1976) estimated a translog cost function for electricity generation as a function of three factor prices: prices for capital, labor, and fuel. Their primary interest was economies of scale. Using seemingly unrelated regressions, they tested the cost function for homogeneity and found convincing evidence against these restrictions. We use the 99 observations from the original Christensen–Greene data set that Berndt (1991) provides. The imposition of homogeneity makes no appreciable difference in the calculations of scale economies. If one checks for concavity at the data points, 12 observations are at points where the translog cost function is not concave. All monotonicity restrictions are satisfied. All in all, this is an application where the translog specification appears to be successful.

We fit the cost function with least squares applied to conditional factor demands. To account for differences in scale, the factor levels were scaled by their empirical standard deviations. We made no attempt to exploit cross-equation covariance in estimation. The quadratic programming problem has 4,862 constraints. Our algorithm converged in 11 iterations, which take less than five minutes on a 486-33 PC microcomputer. No monotonicity constraints are binding. Only 54 of the concavity constraints were binding. Out of the 99 observations, 22 have perfect fits. The sample standard deviations for the residuals in the translog share equations are 0.042, 0.051, and 0.064 for labor, capital, and fuel respectively. For the non-parametric fit, these standard deviations are 0.008, 0.010, and 0.108. As one might expect, the fit of the non-parametric model is much tighter. If we make a ball park adjustment for degrees of freedom, by treating the number of observations minus the active constraints (54) as the number of parameters, the non-parametric fit remains substantially tighter.

In figures 6.4 and 6.5, we graph the fitted average cost functions for the two specifications, computed at the sample average of the prices. The non-parametric fit has two lines, which are the upper and lower bounds of the fitted correspondence. The bulk of the output levels actually observed in the dataset are below 20 billion KWH (see figure 6.6) so that the second figure, graphing the logarithm of output, gives an expanded view of that region of the average cost function. Without statistical distribution theory, we cannot make a formal statement about the similarity of these functions but we think that there is substantial similarity. The estimated translog function does not appear to be misleading. This occurs in a dataset where the usual diagnostics suggest confidence in the translog parameterization is justifiable.

4.2   Transportation by truck

Our second illustration is somewhat more ambitious in scale. We re-examine the estimation of cost functions for US trucking firms. This industry has received repeated attention because it has been heavily regulated in the past, so that data describing its costs, outputs, and factor inputs are relatively easy to obtain. Also, recent deregulation gives economists an opportunity to assess its effects on costs. Our reference point is work by Ying (1990), who references many of the earlier studies.

Our dataset is a cross-section of trucking firms observed in 1976. This is the first year of a panel that we have been constructing for joint research with Goldman and Keeler on the effects of deregulation on this industry.

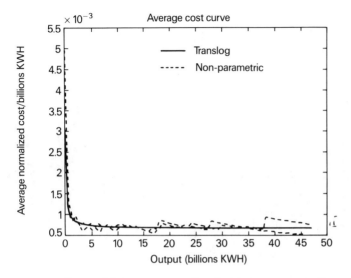

Figure 6.4 Average costs for electric power generation

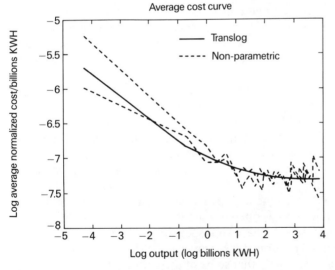

Figure 6.5 Average costs for electric power generation

There are 630 observations and we have followed Ying's methods to construct the dataset and to estimate a translog cost function. The data contain class I and II common carriers of general freight specializing in relatively small "less-than-truckload" shipments. The data are taken from

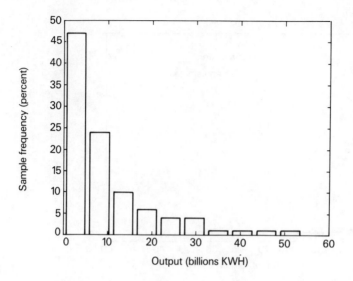

Figure 6.6 Size distribution of electric utilities

Trinc's Blue Book of the Trucking Industry. The factor inputs are fuel, purchased transportation, labor, and capital. Output is measured by revenue ton-miles, although the translog specification includes average length of haul, average shipment size, and average load as additional explanatory variables.

Translog estimates of the cost function suggest that this parametric specification is inappropriate. Although no monotonicity restrictions in output are violated in the sample, 67 percent of the observations are at points where the estimated cost function is not concave and 9 percent fail monotonicity in factor prices. The likelihood ratio test for cross-equation constraints on parameters rejects these restrictions at all conventional levels of significance.

One of the reasons for the failures in monotonicity is that one factor, purchased transportation, is often not used: 226 observations (36 percent) in the sample do not use purchased transportation. As a result, the translog is fitting a substantial portion of the sample in the vicinity of a factor share equal to zero. It is inevitable that some of these observations will predict negative shares, and thereby violate monotonicity in a factor price. The nonparametric fit has no such difficulty. Factor levels of zero can be a natural outcome of cost minimization and correspond to directions in which the cost function is flat.

Another cause of the failures to meet cost function restrictions may be the simplification that output is the scalar ton-miles. Researchers have routine-

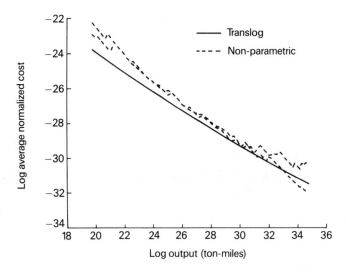

Figure 6.7 Average costs for 1976 trucking (output ton-miles)

ly added such variables as "average length of haul" to the translog specification to account for differences in shipping environment. These attribute variables also appear to measure such other characteristics of output as the number of trips. Therefore, we consider treating them as additional components of a multidimensional output vector.

We fit the non-parametric conditional factor demand functions using the original output of ton-miles and specifying output to be the vector tons, miles, and trips. The average cost functions, translog and non-parametric, for the scalar output measure ton-miles are shown in figure 6.7 and a histogram of firm sizes in figure 6.8. In this case there appears to be some disagreement between the two specifications. For most of the lower output levels, there is evidence that the translog is underestimating average costs and understating the potential economies of scale.

The programming problem had 198,135 concavity restrictions and 2,520 monotonicity constraints. The computer program took 44 iterations and approximately 30 hours on a Sun Sparc 10 to converge. We do not give precise timing because the workstation was not dedicated to this one task. If it were, the duration would be of this order of magnitude.

It is interesting to find that the non-parametric fit does not appear to over-fit in this case. There are only 13 observations that obtain perfect fits. There are 1,138 active constraints in the non-parametric fit, 98 of which are monotonicity constraints. The translog fit has smaller error sums of squares for the cost and share equations, while the non-parametric fit has smaller

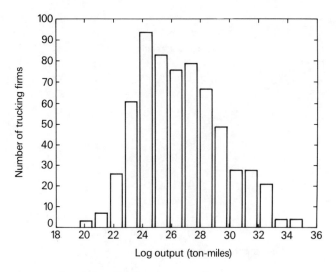

Figure 6.8 Size distribution of 1976 trucking

error sums of squares for the factor demand levels. The statistical evidence against the translog cost specification is consistent with a constrained non-parametric fit that is looser than we observe here.

The presence of binding monotonicity constraints is worth special note because Varian (1985) does not consider these constraints in his work. This reflects a difference in approach. Varian considers *testing* for cost minimization in the presence of observation error, where the observed factor demands are always positive. We are fitting a cost function with concavity constraints that can push the least squares fit into violations of monotonicity. Thus, the monotonicity constraints may constrain the fit.

We also fit the non-parametric conditional factor demand functions, specifying output to be three-dimensional: tons, miles, and trips. The scalar ton-mile specification has obvious appeal as a physical measure of work, but this is by no means definitive. As we have already noted, previous studies add additional explanatory variables that one can interpret as measures of other dimensions to output. The program had 127,838 concavity constraints and 2,520 monotonicity constraints. The generalization of the output specification reduces the number of constraints relative to the scalar specification. Convergence required 22 iterations and approximately ten hours. At convergence, only 359 concavity constraints and 92 monotonicity constraints were binding. One third (207 of 630) of the observations have a perfect fit.

In figure 6.9, we examine the possibility that the ton-miles specification

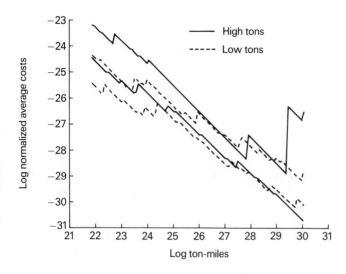

Figure 6.9 Average costs for 1976 trucking

may be too restrictive. We graph the average cost correspondences for two paths in output space, a "low ton" and a "high ton" path, with corresponding levels of ton-miles. The two paths are shown in figure 6.10, along with a scatter plot of the actual tons and miles data. Trips are fixed at the level of the sample average, as are prices. The evidence is much less clear here,

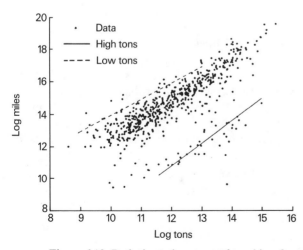

Figure 6.10 Path through output of trucking firms

relative to the comparison of the translog and non-parametric fits earlier. There is substantial agreement between these two average cost fits. Nevertheless, the fits indicate that at low ton-miles the higher tons are more costly than at higher miles. Given the relatively fixed costs of loading each truck, this is a sensible outcome.

5   CONCLUSION

The immediate econometric application of least-squares estimation subject only to monotonicity and concavity constraints is limited by the lack of a statistical theory. The consistency of such estimators has been established, but a general approximate distribution theory remains to be found. There are at least two directions in which this computational research may link with a distribution theory.

First of all, it seems fruitful to combine the local smoothing approaches of non-parametric estimation with restricted estimation. Local smoothing will surely provide convergence rates comparable with those for unrestricted estimators. There are several ways to combine smoothing with restricted estimation, all of which use the methods developed here. The simplest may be to apply the restricted least-squares program to the smoothed regression, rather than to the data as we do here. An attractive alternative is to change the least-squares objective function (6) to a smoothed version

$$\hat{y} = \arg\min_{z\in C} \sum_{n=1}^{N} \sum_{i=1}^{N} K_h(p_n - p_i, q_n - q_i) \| y_i - z(p_n, q_n) \|^2, \qquad (12)$$

where $K_h(\cdot)$ is a multivariate kernel density. This is equivalent to a weighted least-squares problem which is easily accommodated by our approach.

Secondly, the computation of Bayesian posterior moments (Geweke (1995)) may be enhanced by our methods. The least-squares fit may provide a good approximation to the mode of the posterior of a Bayesian non-parametric analysis of these estimation problems. In that case, the central tendency of the posterior can be located with our technique, providing a useful starting point for such posterior simulators as the Gibbs sampler. The latter is natural for restricted least-squares problems where the support of the posterior distribution is truncated by the restrictions. See Geweke (1995) for an introduction.

Notes

1 The econometric literature on parametric functional forms is extensive and so we point to some leading examples. Diewert (1973) initiated much of the analysis

of flexible functional forms. Lau (1978) proposed a transformation of parameters for imposing monotonicity and convexity in quadratic functions.

2 Diewert and Wales (1987) call the construction of restricted parametric functions "one of the most vexing problems applied economists have encountered" and comment that the compromises which strike have often proved unsatisfactory. They propose a family of semi-flexible functions with which one can impose convexity and choose the degree of flexibility.

3 If there were any n such that $x_n = x_{n+1}$, then one must insert equality constraints $z_n = z_{n+1}$. Hildreth allowed for these multiplicities. We avoid such additional detail.

4 One cycles through all the constraints repeatedly, in the sequence $\{1,\ldots,M,1,\ldots,M,\ldots\}$. Thus, the ith cycle will handle constraint $r = (i-1$ modulo $M) + 1$.

5 The production set is assumed to be non-empty and compact.

6 In mathematical terms, $z \in C$ if and only if z is continuous and

(a) $p_1 \geq p_2 \Rightarrow z(p_1, q) \geq z(p_2, q)$,
(b) $p \gg 0, \alpha \geq 0 \Rightarrow z(\alpha \cdot p, q) = \alpha \cdot z(p, q)$,
(c) $p_1, p_2 \Rightarrow 0, 0 \leq \alpha \leq 1 \Rightarrow z[\alpha \cdot p_1 + (1-\alpha) \cdot p_2] \leq \alpha \cdot z(p_1, q) + (1-\alpha) \cdot z(p_2, q)$.

7 These well-known properties of cost functions and conditional factor demand correspondences are explained in Varian (1992) and Mas-Colell et al. (1995). We use ∇_p to denote the vector of partial derivatives with respect to the elements of p.

8 It will be convenient to think of the norm $\|\cdot\|$ as the simple Euclidean norm, but one can generalize to generalized least-squares problems straightforwardly.

9 Varian (1984) calls these constraints the "Weak Axiom of Cost Minimization" (WACM). He restricts his analysis to a scalar output, but this is not necessary for our analysis.

10 Generally, we restrict attention within the convex hull of observed values of prices and quantities.

11 If we treat the fitted restricted least-squares values $\{\hat{y}_i; i = 1,\ldots,N\}$ as observed data, the boundaries of these cost functions correspond to the under- and overcost functions derived by Varian (1984, p. 593). The boundaries of the conditional factor demands correspond to Varian's $VI(q)$ and $VO(q)$ (p. 591).

12 Many authors cite von Neumann (1950) as the originator of the method of alternating projections.

13 See Goldman and Ruud (1993b) for a description of related research.

14 This interpretation is emphasized by Dykstra (1983).

15 Here is a brief description. Given a feasible starting point for an iteration, the quadratic programming algorithm computes the solution to the restricted least-squares (RLS) problem constructed from imposing the active constraints as equalities. If it satisfies all constraints, then this solution also solves the projection problem. If not, one computes the point on the line segment between the initial value and the RLS solution closest to the initial value where a

186   Paul A. Ruud

constraint changes status. The fit at this point becomes the starting value for the next iteration.
16 This equivalence requires that one begin with $\hat{y}_0 = y$, which corresponds to setting $\hat{u}_i = 0$ for $i = 1 - S, \ldots, 0$.

References

Berndt, E. R. (1991). "The practice of econometrics: classic and contemporary."
Christensen, L. R. and Greene, W. H. (1976). "Economies of scale in US electric power generation." *Journal of Political Economy*, 84(4): 655–76.
Diewert, W. E. (1973). "Functional forms for profit and transformation functions." *Journal of Economic Theory*, 6: 284–316.
Diewert, W. E. and Wales, T. J. (1987). "Flexible functional forms and global curvature conditions." *Econometrica*, 55(1): 43–68.
Dykstra, R. L. (1983). "An algorithm for restricted least squares." *Journal of the American Statistical Association*, 78(364): 837–42.
Geweke, J. (1995). "Posterior simulators in econometrics." Chapter 5 in this volume.
Gill, P. E., Murray, W., Saunders, M. A., and Writhgt, M. H. (1982). "The design and implementation of a quadratic programming algorithm." Technical Report SOL 8207, Department of Operations Research, Stanford University.
Goldman, S. M. and Ruud, P. A. (1993a). "Nonparametric multivariate regression subject to monotonicity and convexity constraints." Mimeo.
(1993b). "Nonparametric multivariate regression subject to constraint." Technical Report 93-213, Department of Economics, University of California, Berkeley.
Hanson, D. L. and Pledger, G. (1976). "Consistency in concave regression." *Annals of Statistics*, 4(6): 1038–50.
Hildreth, C. (1954). "Point estimates of ordinates of concave functions." *Journal of the American Statistical Association*, 49: 598–619.
Lau, L. J. (1978). *Production Economics: A Dual Approach to Theory and Applications*, Vol. II. Amsterdam: North-Holland (esp. chapter "Testing and imposing monotonicitey, convexity and quasi-convexity constraints").
Mas-Colell, A., Whinston, M. D., and Green, J. R. (1995). *Microeconomic Theory*. New York: Oxford University Press.
Matzkin, R. L. (1992). "Computation and operational properties of nonparametric concavity-restricted estimators." Technical Report, Northwestern University.
Murtagh, B. and Saunders, M. (1967). "MINOS: large scale nonlinear programming system (for problems with linear constraints)." Technical Report SOL 77-9, Department of Operations Research, Stanford University.
Varian, H. R. (1984). "The nonparametric approach to production analysis." *Econometrica*, 52(2): 579–97.
(1985). "Non-parametric analysis of optimizing behavior with measurement error." *Journal of Econometrics*, 30(1/2): 445–58.
(1992). *Microeconomic Analysis*, third edn. New York: Norton.
von Neumann, J. (1950). *Functional Operators*, Vol. II. Princeton, NJ: Princeton

University Press. This is a reprint of lecture notes first distributed in 1933.

Yazhen (1992). "Nonparametric estimation subject to shape restrictions." Ph.D. Thesis, Department of Statistics, University of California at Berkeley.

Ying, J. S. (1990). "The inefficiency of regulating a competitive industry: productivity gains in trucking following reform." *Review of Economics and Statistics*, 72(2): 191–201.

CHAPTER 7

Bootstrap methods in econometrics: theory and numerical performance

Joel L. Horowitz

1   INTRODUCTION

The bootstrap is a method for estimating the distribution of an estimator or test statistic by resampling the data. It amounts to treating the data as if they were the population for the purpose of evaluating the distribution of interest. Under mild regularity conditions, the bootstrap yields an approximation to the distribution of an estimator or test statistic that is at least as accurate as the approximation obtained from first-order asymptotic theory. Thus, the bootstrap provides a way to substitute computation for mathematical analysis if calculating the asymptotic distribution of an estimator or statistic is difficult. The maximum score estimator (Manski (1975, 1985)), the statistic developed by Härdle et al. (1991) for testing positive-definiteness of income-effect matrices, and certain functions of time-series data (Blanchard and Quah (1989), Runkle (1987), West (1990)) are examples in which evaluating the asymptotic distribution is difficult and bootstrapping has been used as an alternative.[1]

In fact, the bootstrap is often more accurate in finite samples than first-order asymptotic approximations but does not entail the algebraic complexity of higher-order expansions. Thus, it can provide a practical method for improving upon first-order approximations. First-order asymptotic theory often gives a poor approximation to the distributions of test statistics with the sample sizes available in applications. As a result, the nominal levels of tests based on asymptotic critical values can be very different from the true levels. The information matrix test of White (1982) is a well-known example of a test in which large finite-sample distortions of level can occur when asymptotic critical values are used (Horowitz (1994), Kennan and Neumann (1988), Orme (1990), Taylor (1987)). Other illustrations are given later in this chapter. The bootstrap often provides a tractable way to reduce or eliminate finite-sample distortions of the levels of statistical tests.

The bootstrap has been the object of much research in statistics since its introduction by Efron (1979). The results of this research are synthesized in the books by Beran and Ducharme (1991), Efron and Tibshirani (1993), Hall (1992), and Mammen (1992). Li and Maddala (1995), Maddala and Jeong (1993), and Vinod (1993) provide reviews with an econometric orientation. Nonetheless, the bootstrap's ability to improve upon the approximations of first-order asymptotic theory appears not to be widely appreciated or used in econometrics.

The purpose of this chapter is to explain and illustrate the usefulness and limitations of the bootstrap for improving upon first-order asymptotic approximations in contexts of interest in econometrics. The discussion is informal and expository. I hope it will give readers a feeling for the practical value of the bootstrap in econometrics. Mathematically rigorous treatments of the theory of the bootstrap are available in the books by Beran and Ducharme (1991) and Hall (1992) as well as in journal articles that are cited later in this chapter.

The discussion concentrates on the use of the bootstrap to obtain improved finite-sample critical values for test statistics. Particular emphasis is placed on the importance of applying the bootstrap to statistics whose asymptotic distributions are independent of unknown population parameters. Such statistics are called "asymptotically pivotal." Simple bootstrap procedures provide improved approximations to the distributions of asymptotically pivotal statistics but not to the distributions of statistics that lack this property.

The problem of obtaining critical values for test statistics is closely related to that of obtaining confidence intervals. As is discussed in more detail in section 2.3, many of the methods that are described here for obtaining critical values of test statistics can also be used to obtain confidence intervals with improved finite-sample coverage probabilities.

It is not possible in a single chapter to provide a thorough treatment of all aspects of the bootstrap that may be useful in econometrics. Accordingly, the discussion in this chapter is selective. It focuses on methods that I believe are especially likely to be useful to applied researchers. Topics that are not discussed but that may be useful in some settings include bootstrap iteration and prepivoting, bias-correction methods, and bootstrap methods for semi- and non-parametric estimators that converge at slower than root n rates. Discussion of the first two topics can be found in Beran and Ducharme (1991), Efron and Tibshirani (1993), and Hall (1992). Hall (1992) also discusses the theory of the bootstrap for kernel non-parametric density estimation and regression. The theory of the bootstrap for many semi-parametric estimators of interest in econometrics (e.g., single-index models, sample-selection models, partially linear models) is still largely undeveloped.

It should be borne in mind throughout this chapter that, although the bootstrap often provides better finite-sample critical values for test statistics than does first-order asymptotic theory, bootstrap critical values are still approximations and are not exact. Although the accuracy of bootstrap approximations is often very high, this is not always the case. Even when theory indicates that it provides asymptotic refinements, the bootstrap's numerical performance may be poor. In some cases, the numerical accuracy of bootstrap approximations may be even worse than the accuracy of first-order asymptotic approximations. This is particularly likely to happen with estimators whose asymptotic covariance matrices are "nearly singular," as in instrumental-variables estimation with poorly correlated instruments and regressors. Thus, the bootstrap should not be used blindly or uncritically.

However, in the many cases where the bootstrap works well, it essentially removes getting the level right as a factor in selecting a test statistic. Among other benefits, this enables one to direct attention to choosing a statistic that has high power against alternatives of interest. This chapter does not treat the problem of choosing statistics to maximize power in applications. It does, however, provide some numerical examples illustrating that achieving high power and getting the level right are different problems. Tests whose finite-sample distortions of level are small when asymptotic critical values are used may have lower power than tests whose level distortions with asymptotic critical values are large but removable by the bootstrap. Thus, in terms of power, one may do better by using a statistic with large finite-sample level distortions than one with small level distortions if the distortions of the former statistic can be made small through the use of bootstrap critical values.

The remainder of this chapter is divided into three sections. Section 2 presents the theory of the bootstrap, section 3 presents Monte Carlo evidence on the numerical performance of the bootstrap in a variety of settings that are relevant to econometrics, and section 4 presents concluding comments.

2   THE THEORY OF THE BOOTSTRAP

This section explains why the bootstrap provides an improved approximation to the distributions of asymptotically pivotal test statistics. It also discusses the performance of the bootstrap when the hypothesis being tested is false. In addition, several special problems are discussed. These include bootstrapping overidentified estimators derived from moment conditions and the use of the bootstrap with dependent data.

2.1   Why the bootstrap provides asymptotic refinements

This section gives a heuristic explanation of why the bootstrap provides an improved approximation to the finite-sample distributions of test statistics. Let the data be a random sample of size n from a probability distribution whose cumulative distribution function (CDF) is F. Denote the data by $\{X_i : i = 1, \ldots, n\}$. F may belong to a finite- or infinite-dimensional family of distribution functions. If F belongs to a finite-dimensional family indexed by the parameter θ whose population value is θ_0, write $F(x, \theta_0)$ for $P(X \leq x)$ and $F(x, \theta)$ for a general member of the parametric family. The empirical distribution function (EDF) based on the sample is denoted by F_n. F_n will also denote a generic estimator of F when this can be done without confusion.

Let $T_n = T_n(X_1, \ldots, X_n)$ be a statistic for testing a hypothesis H_0 about the distribution from which $\{X_i\}$ is drawn. Let $G_n(z, F) \equiv P(T_n \leq z)$ denote the exact, finite-sample CDF of T_n when H_0 is true. Consider a symmetrical, two-tailed test of H_0. With such a test, H_0 is rejected at the α level if $|T_n| > z_{n\alpha}$, where the critical value, $z_{n\alpha}$, satisfies $G_n(z_{n\alpha}, F) - G_n(-z_{n\alpha}, F) = 1 - \alpha$. Usually, $z_{n\alpha}$ cannot be evaluated in applications because F is unknown. An exception occurs if G_n does not depend on F, in which case T_n is said to be "pivotal." For example, the t-statistic for testing a hypothesis about the mean of a normal population is independent of unknown-population parameters and, therefore, pivotal. The same is true of the t-statistic for testing a hypothesis about a slope coefficient in a normal linear regression model. Pivotal statistics are not available in most econometric applications, however, especially without making strong distributional assumptions (e.g., the assumption that the random component of a linear regression model is normally distributed). Thus, it is usually necessary to find an approximation for $z_{n\alpha}$.

First-order asymptotic theory provides one approximation. Most test statistics used in econometrics are asymptotically pivotal; their asymptotic distributions do not depend on unknown population parameters. If n is sufficiently large, one can approximate $G_n(\cdot, F)$ by the asymptotic distribution of T_n. This does not depend on F if T_n is asymptotically pivotal. Therefore, approximate critical values for T_n can be obtained from the asymptotic distribution without having to know F.

Another possibility is to replace the unknown F in $G_n(\cdot, F)$ with a consistent estimator F_n. $G_n(\cdot, F)$ is then approximated by $G_n(\cdot, F_n)$. If F belongs to a known finite-dimensional parametric family $F(x, \theta)$, one can set

$F_n(x) = F(x, \theta_n)$, where θ_n is a consistent estimator of θ. Otherwise, one can use the EDF

$$F_n(x) = n^{-1} \sum_{i=1}^{n} I(X_i \leq x),$$

where $I(\cdot)$ is the indicator function. With the approximation $G_n(\cdot, F_n)$, the approximate α-level critical value for $|T_n|, z_{n\alpha}^*$, solves $G_n(z_{n\alpha}^*, F_n) - G_n(-z_{n\alpha}^*, F_n) = 1 - \alpha$.

The bootstrap consists of approximating $G_n(\cdot, F)$ with $G_n(\cdot, F_n)$. Usually, $G_n(\cdot, F_n)$ and $z_{n\alpha}^*$ cannot be evaluated analytically. They can, however, be estimated with arbitrary accuracy by carrying out a Monte Carlo simulation in which random samples are drawn from F_n. Thus, the bootstrap is usually implemented by Monte Carlo simulation. The essential characteristic of the bootstrap, though, is the use of F_n to approximate F in $G_n(\cdot, F)$, not the method that is used to evaluate $G_n(\cdot, F_n)$.

Under mild regularity conditions, $\sup_x |F_n(x) - F(x)|$ and $\sup_z |G_n(z, F_n) - G_n(z, F)|$ converge to 0 in probability or almost surely. This guarantees that the bootstrap provides good approximations to $G_n(z, F)$ and $z_{n\alpha}$ if n is sufficiently large. Of course, first-order asymptotic theory also provides good approximations to these quantities if n is sufficiently large. It turns out, however, that under conditions that are explained below, the bootstrap provides approximations that are more accurate than those of first-order asymptotic theory.

To see why, it is necessary to develop a higher-order approximation to $G_n(z, F)$. Under regularity conditions, $G_n(z, F)$ has an asymptotic expansion of the form

$$G_n(z, F) = G(z, F) + n^{-\frac{1}{2}}g_1(z, F) + n^{-1}g_2(z, F) + o(n^{-1}) \tag{1}$$

uniformly over z, where $G(z, F)$ is the asymptotic CDF of T_n, g_1, and g_2 are functionals of (z, F), $g_1(z, F)$ is an even function of z for each F, $g_2(z, F)$ is an odd function of z, and $g_2(z, F_n) \to g_2(z, F)$ almost surely or in probability as $n \to \infty$ uniformly over z. It follows from (1) and the symmetry of g_1 and g_2 that

$$P(|T_n| > z) = 1 - [G(z, F) - G(-z, F)]$$
$$- 2n^{-1}g_2(z, F) + o(n^{-1}) \tag{2}$$

uniformly over $z \geq 0$.

The bootstrap replaces F with F_n and samples F_n conditional on the original sample $\{X_i\}$. Let T_n^* be the bootstrap version of T_n and P^* be the probability measure induced by bootstrap sampling. Then under bootstrap sampling

$$P^*(|T_n^*| > z) = 1 - [G(z, F_n) - G(-z, F_n)]$$
$$- 2n^{-1}g_2(z, F_n) + o_p(n^{-1}), \tag{3}$$

uniformly over $z \geq 0$. It follows from (2) and (3) that if G is sufficiently smooth

$$P^*(|T_n^*| > z) - P(|T_n| > z) = O\{[G(z, F_n) - G(z, F)]$$
$$- [G(-z, F_n) - G(-z, F)]\}$$
$$= O[F_n(z) - F(z)] = O_p(n^{-1/2})$$

uniformly over $z \geq 0$. Thus, the bootstrap makes an error of size $O_p(n^{-1/2})$, which is the same as the size of the error made by first-order asymptotic approximations.

Now suppose that T_n is asymptotically pivotal. Then its asymptotic distribution is independent of F, and $G(z, F_n) = G(z, F)$ for all z. Equations (2) and (3) yield

$$P^*(|T_n^*| > z) - P(|T_n| > z) = 2n^{-1}[g_2(z, F) - g_2(z, F_n)]$$
$$+ o_p(n^{-1}) = o_p(n^{-1}) \tag{4}$$

uniformly over $z \geq 0$. Now the bootstrap is accurate through $O_p(n^{-1})$, which is more accurate than first-order asymptotic approximations. Thus, the bootstrap is more accurate than first-order asymptotic theory for estimating the distribution of a "smooth" asymptotically pivotal statistic.

It follows from (4) that

$$P(|T_n| > z_{n\alpha}^*) = \alpha + o(n^{-1}).$$

Thus, with the bootstrap critical value $z_{n\alpha}^*$, the level of a symmetrical, two-tailed, test based on an asymptotically pivotal statistic is correct through $O(n^{-1})$. In contrast, first-order asymptotic theory ignores all but the leading term in (1). Therefore, when a critical value based on first-order asymptotic theory is used, the error in the level of the test is $O(n^{-1})$.

In fact, symmetry arguments that are more refined than those given above show that with a bootstrap critical value, the error in the level of a symmetrical test based on an asymptotically pivotal statistic is usually of size $O(n^{-2})$. For a one-tailed test, the error with the bootstrap critical value is usually of size $O(n^{-1})$, and the error with the asymptotic critical value is of size $O(n^{-1/2})$. See Hall (1992) for details.

Singh (1981), who considered a one-tailed test of a hypothesis about a population mean, apparently was the first to show that the bootstrap provides a higher-order asymptotic approximation to the distribution of an asymptotically pivotal statistic. Singh's test was based on the standardized sample mean. Early papers giving results on higher-order approximations for studentized means and for more general hypotheses and test statistics include Babu and Singh (1983, 1984), Beran (1988), and Hall (1986, 1988).

2.2   The importance of asymptotically pivotal statistics

The arguments in section 2.1 show that the bootstrap provides higher-order asymptotic approximations to the distributions and critical values of "smooth" asymptotically pivotal statistics. These include test statistics whose asymptotic distributions are standard normal or chi-square. The ability of the bootstrap to provide asymptotic refinements for such statistics provides a powerful argument for using them in applications of the bootstrap.

The bootstrap may also be applied to statistics that are not asymptotically pivotal, such as regression coefficients, but it does not provide a higher-order approximation to their distributions. Bootstrap estimates of the distributions of statistics that are not asymptotically pivotal have the same accuracy as first-order asymptotic approximations.

Higher-order approximations to the distributions of statistics that are not asymptotically pivotal can be obtained through the use of prepivoting or bootstrap iteration (Beran (1987, 1988)) or bias-correction methods (Efron (1987)). Bootstrap iteration is highly computationally intensive, however, which makes it unattractive when an asymptotically pivotal statistic is available.

2.3   Confidence intervals

Let θ be a population parameter, θ_n be a $n^{1/2}$-consistent, asymptotically normal estimator of θ, and s_n be an estimate of the asymptotic standard deviation of $n^{1/2}(\theta_n - \theta)$. Then an asymptotic $1 - \alpha$ confidence interval for θ is $\theta_n - z_{\alpha/2}s_n \leq \theta \leq \theta_n + z_{\alpha/2}s_n$, where $z_{\alpha/2}$ is the $1 - \alpha/2$ quantile of the standard normal distribution. The error in the coverage probability of this confidence interval is $O(n^{-1})$. The bootstrap can be used to reduce the error in the coverage probability.

To do this, let θ_n^* and s_n^* be the bootstrap analogs of θ_n and s_n. That is, θ_n^* and s_n^* are the estimators that are obtained by sampling the distribution whose CDF is F_n, rather than the population distribution. Let T_n^* be the t-statistic for testing the hypothesis $H_0^*: \theta = \theta_n$ using the bootstrap sample, and let $z_{n\alpha}^*$ be the $1 - \alpha$ quantile of the bootstrap distribution of $|T_n^*|$. Then $\theta_n - z_{n\alpha}^*s_n \leq \theta \leq \theta_n + z_{n\alpha}^*s_n$ is a $1 - \alpha$ confidence interval for θ based on the bootstrap critical value. It follows from the arguments made in section 2.1

that the coverage probability of this confidence interval is correct through $O(n^{-1})$. Usually, the error in its coverage probability is $O(n^{-2})$. See Hall (1992) for details.

2.4   The parametric versus the non-parametric bootstrap

The size of the error in the bootstrap estimate of a distribution or critical value is determined by the size of $F_n - F$. Thus, F_n should be the most efficient available estimator. If F belongs to a known parametric family $F(\cdot, \theta)$, $F(\cdot, \theta_n)$ should be used to generate bootstrap samples, rather than the EDF. Although the bootstrap provides asymptotic refinements regardless of whether $F(\cdot, \theta_n)$ or the EDF is used, the results of Monte Carlo experiments have shown that the numerical accuracy of the bootstrap tends to be much higher with $F(\cdot, \theta_n)$ than with the EDF. If the objective is to test a hypothesis H_0 about θ, further gains in efficiency and performance can be obtained by imposing the constraints of H_0 when obtaining the estimate θ_n.

To illustrate, consider testing the hypothesis $H_0: \beta_1 = 0$ in the Box–Cox regression model

$$Y^{(\lambda)} = \beta_0 + \beta_1 X + U, \tag{5}$$

where $Y^{(\lambda)}$ is the Box–Cox (1964) transformation of Y. Suppose that $U \sim N(0, \sigma^2)$.[2] Then bootstrap sampling can be carried out in the following ways:

1 Sample (Y,X) pairs from the data randomly with replacement.
2 Estimate λ, β_0, and β_1 in (5) by maximum likelihood, and obtain residuals $\hat{U}$. Generate Y values from $Y = [\lambda_n(b_0 + b_1 X + U^*) + 1]^{1/\lambda_n}$, where λ_n, b_0, and b_1 are the estimates of λ, β_0, and β_1; and U^* is sampled randomly with replacement from the $\hat{U}$.
3 Same as method 2 except U^* is sampled randomly from the distribution $N(0, s_n^2)$, where s_n^2 is the maximum-likelihood estimate of σ^2.
4 Estimate λ, β_0, and σ^2 in (5) by maximum likelihood subject to the constraint $\beta_1 = 0$. Then proceed as in method 2.
5 Estimate λ, β_0, and σ^2 in (5) by maximum likelihood subject to the constraint $\beta_1 = 0$. Then proceed as in method 3.

In methods 2–5, the values of X may be fixed in repeated samples or sampled independently of $\hat{U}$ from the empirical distribution of X.

Method 1 provides the least efficient estimator of F_n and typically has the poorest numerical accuracy. Method 5 has the greatest numerical accuracy. Method 3 will usually have greater numerical accuracy than method 2. If the distribution of U is not assumed to belong to a known parametric family, then methods 3 and 5 are not available, and method 4 will usually have greater numerical accuracy than methods 1-2. Of course, parametric maximum likelihood cannot be used to estimate β_0, β_1, and λ if the distribution of U is not specified parametrically.

If the objective is to obtain a confidence interval for β_1 rather than to test a hypothesis, methods 4 and 5 are not available. Method 3 will usually provide the greatest numerical accuracy if the distribution of U is assumed to belong to a known parametric family, and method 2 if not.

One reason for the relatively poor performance of method 1 is that it does not impose the condition $E(U \mid X) = 0$. This problem is discussed further in section 3.2, where heteroskedastic regression models are considered.

2.5   Recentering

By replacing F with F_n in (1), it can be seen that the bootstrap will not obtain even the correct asymptotic distribution of a statistic T_n unless $G_n(\cdot, F_n)$ converges weakly in probability to $G(z, F)$. One important situation in which this does not necessarily happen is generalized method of moments (GMM) estimation of an overidentified parameter when F_n is the EDF of the sample.

To see why, suppose that θ is identified by the moment condition $Eh(X, \theta) = 0$, where $\dim(h) > \dim(\theta)$. If, as is often the case in applications, the distribution of X is not assumed to belong to a known parametric family, the EDF of X is the most obvious candidate for F_n. The sample analog of $Eh(X, \theta)$ is then

$$E^*h(X, \theta_n) = n^{-1} \sum_{i=1}^{n} h(X_i, \theta_n),$$

where E^* denotes the expectation relative to F_n, and θ_n is the GMM estimate of θ. In general, $E^*h(X, \theta_n) \neq 0$ in an overidentified model, so bootstrap estimation based on the EDF of X implements a moment condition that does not hold in the population that the bootstrap samples.

This problem can be solved by basing bootstrap estimation on the recentered moment condition $E^*h^*(X, \theta_n) = 0$, where

$$h^*(X, \theta_n) = h(X, \theta_n) - n^{-1} \sum_{i=1}^{n} h(X_i, \theta_n).$$

Freedman (1981) recognized the need for recentering residuals in regression models without intercepts. See, also, Efron (1979). Brown and Newey (1992) show that recentering also can be accomplished by replacing F_n with an empirical-likelihood estimate of F.

2.6   Dependent data

With dependent data, asymptotic refinements cannot be obtained by using independent bootstrap samples. Bootstrap sampling must be carried out in a way that suitably captures the dependence of the data-generation process.

This can be done relatively easily if one has a parametric model, such as an ARMA model, that reduces the data-generation process to a transformation of independent random variables. For example, suppose that the series $\{Y_t\}$ is generated by the ARMA model

$$A(L,\alpha)Y_t = B(L,\beta)U_t, \tag{6}$$

where A and B are known functions, L is the backshift operator, α and β are vectors of parameters, and $\{U_t\}$ is a sequence of independently and identically distributed random variables. Let α_n and β_n be $n^{1/2}$-consistent estimators of α and β, and let $\{\hat{U}_t\}$ be the centered residuals of the estimated model (6). Then a bootstrap sample $\{Y_t^*\}$ can be generated as

$$A(L,\alpha_n)Y_t^* = B(L,\beta_n)U_t^*,$$

where $\{U_t^*\}$ is a random sample from the empirical distribution of the residuals $\{\hat{U}_t\}$. If the distribution of U_t is assumed to belong to a known parametric family (e.g., the normal distribution), then $\{U_t^*\}$ can be generated by independent sampling from the estimated parametric distribution. Bose (1988) provides a rigorous discussion of the use of the bootstrap with autoregressions.

When there is no parametric model that reduces the data-generation process to independent sampling from some probability distribution, the bootstrap can be implemented by dividing the data into blocks and sampling the blocks randomly with replacement. This approach to bootstrap sampling is important in GMM estimation with dependent data, since the moment conditions on which GMM estimation is based usually do not specify the dependence structure of the GMM residuals. Lahiri (1992) gives conditions under which the block bootstrap provides asymptotic refinements through $O(n^{-1/2})$ for normalized sample moments and for a studentized sample moment with m-dependent data. Hall and Horowitz (1996) give conditions under which the block bootstrap provides asymptotic refinements through $O(n^{-1})$ for test statistics associated with GMM estimation. Hall and Horowitz (1996) do not assume that the data-generation process is m-dependent.

The blocks into which the data are divided for purposes of block-bootstrap sampling may be non-overlapping (Carlstein (1986)) or overlapping (Künsch (1989)). See, also, Hall (1985). Overlapping blocks provide somewhat higher bootstrap estimation efficiency than non-overlapping ones, but available evidence indicates that the efficiency gain from using overlapping blocks is quite small. Hall *et al.* (1995) report the results of an analytic comparison of the estimation efficiencies of overlapping and non-overlapping blocks for bootstrap estimation of the distribution of a sample mean. Let $\bar{X}$, μ, and s denote the sample mean, population mean, and sample standard deviation of $\bar{X}$, respectively. For estimating $P(|\bar{X} - \mu|/s \le z)$ the reduction in asymptotic root-mean-square error from using overlapping blocks instead of non-overlapping ones is less than 10 percent.

Regardless of whether overlapping or non-overlapping blocks are used, block bootstrap sampling does not exactly replicate the dependence structure of the original data-generation process. For example, if non-overlapping blocks are used, bootstrap observations that belong to the same block are deterministically related, whereas observations that belong to different blocks are independent. This dependence structure is unlikely to be present in the original data-generation process. As a result, the covariance matrices of the asymptotic forms of parameter estimators obtained from the original sample and from the bootstrap sample are not the same. The practical consequence of this difference is that asymptotic refinements cannot be obtained by applying the "usual" formulae for test statistics to the block-bootstrap sample. It is necessary to develop special formulae for the bootstrap versions of test statistics. These formulae contain factors that correct for the differences between the asymptotic covariances of the original-sample and bootstrap versions of test statistics without distorting the higher-order terms of asymptotic expansions that produce refinements.

Lahiri (1992) derives the bootstrap version of a studentized sample mean for m-dependent data. Hall and Horowitz (1996) derive formulae for the bootstrap versions of the GMM symmetrical, two-tailed t-statistic and the statistic for testing overidentifying restrictions. As an illustration of the form of the bootstrap statistics, consider the GMM t-statistic for testing a hypothesis about a component of a parameter θ that is identified by the moment condition $Eh(X, \theta) = 0$. Hall and Horowitz (1996) show that the correct formula for the bootstrap version of the GMM t-statistic is

$$T_n^* = (S_n/S_b)\tilde{T}_n,$$

where $\tilde{T}_n$ is the "usual" GMM t-statistic applied to the bootstrap sample, S_n is the "usual" GMM standard error of the estimate of the component of θ that is being tested, and S_b is the exact standard deviation of the asymptotic form of the bootstrap estimate of this component. S_n is computed from the original estimation sample, not the bootstrap sample. Hansen (1982) gives formulae for the "usual" GMM t-statistic and standard error. S_b can be calculated because the process generating bootstrap data is known exactly. An analogous formula is available for the bootstrap version of the statistic for testing overidentifying restrictions but is much more complicated algebraically than the formula for the t-statistic (see Hall and Horowitz (1996) for details).

At present, the block-bootstrap is known to provide asymptotic refinements in GMM estimation only if the residuals $\{h(X_i, \theta_0): i = 1, 2, \ldots\}$ at the true parameter point, θ_0, are uncorrelated after finitely many lags. That is

$$Eh(X_i, \theta_0)h(X_j, \theta_0) = 0 \text{ if } |i - j| > M \qquad (7)$$

for some $M < \infty$. This restriction is not equivalent to m-dependence since it does not preclude correlations among higher powers of components of h that persist at arbitrarily large lags (e.g., stochastic volatility). Although the restriction is satisfied in many econometric applications (see, e.g., Hansen (1982), Hansen and Singleton (1982)), there are others in which relaxing it would be useful. The main problem in doing so is that without (7), it is necessary to use a kernel-type estimator of the GMM covariance matrix (see, e.g., Newey and West (1987, 1994), Andrews (1991), Andrews and Monahan (1992)). Kernel-type estimators are not functions of sample moments and converge at rates that are slower than root n. However, present results on the existence of higher-order asymptotic expansions with dependent data (Götze and Hipp (1983)) apply only to functions of sample moments that have root n rates of convergence. Thus, it is necessary to extend existing theory of asymptotic expansions with dependent data before (7) can be relaxed.

2.7   Special problems

The discussion in section 2.1 shows that the bootstrap provides asymptotic refinements because it amounts to a one-term Edgeworth expansion. The bootstrap cannot be expected to perform well when an Edgeworth expansion provides a poor approximation to the distribution of interest. An important case of this is instrumental-variables estimation with poorly correlated instruments and regressors. It is well known that first-order asymptotic approximations are especially poor in this situation (Hillier (1985), Nelson and Startz (1990a and b), Phillips (1983)). The bootstrap does not offer a solution to this problem. With poorly correlated instruments and regressors, Edgeworth expansions of estimators and test statistics involve denominator terms that are close to zero. As a result, the higher-order terms of the expansions may dominate the lower-order ones for a given sample size, in which case the bootstrap may provide little improvement over first-order asymptotic approximations. Indeed, with small samples the numerical accuracy of the bootstrap may be even worse than that of first-order asymptotic approximations.

Other examples of bootstrap failure that are relevant to econometrics include estimating the distribution of the maximum of a sample from the uniform distribution (Bickel and Freedman (1981)), estimating the distribution of the mean of a sample from a population with infinite variance (Athreya (1987)), and unit-root models with certain resampling procedures (Basawa *et al.* (1991)). Politis and Romano (1994) describe an alternative to the·bootstrap that provides the correct asymptotic distribution in some of these cases.

2.8   The bootstrap when the null hypothesis is false

To understand the power of a test based on a bootstrap critical value, it is necessary to investigate the behavior of the bootstrap when the null hypothesis being tested, H_0, is false. Suppose that bootstrap samples are generated by a model that satisfies a false H_0 and, therefore, is misspecified relative to the true data-generation process. If H_0 is simple, meaning that it completely specifies the data-generation process, the bootstrap amounts to Monte Carlo estimation of the exact finite-sample critical value for testing H_0 against the true data-generation process. Indeed, the bootstrap provides the exact critical value, rather than a Monte Carlo estimate, if $G(\cdot, F_n)$ can be calculated analytically. Tests of simple hypotheses are rarely encountered in econometrics, however.

In most applications, H_0 is composite. That is, it does not specify the value of a finite- or infinite-dimensional "nuisance" parameter ψ. In the remainder of this section, it is shown that a test of a composite hypothesis using a bootstrap-based critical value is a higher-order approximation to a certain exact test. The power of the test with a bootstrap critical value is a higher-order approximation to the power of the exact test.

Except in the case of a test based on a pivotal statistic, the exact finite-sample distribution of the test statistic depends on ψ. Therefore, except in the pivotal case, it is necessary to specify the value of ψ to obtain exact finite-sample critical values. The higher-order approximation to power provided by the bootstrap applies to a value of ψ that will be called the "pseudo-true value." To define the pseudo-true value, let ψ_n be an estimator of ψ that is obtained under the incorrect assumption that H_0 is true. Under regularity conditions (see, e.g., Amemiya (1985) and White (1982)), ψ_n converges in probability to a limit ψ^*, and $n^{1/2}(\psi_n - \psi^*) = O_p(1)$. ψ^* is the pseudo-true value of ψ.

Now let T_n be a statistic that is asymptotically pivotal under H_0. Suppose that its exact CDF with an arbitrary value of ψ is $G_n(\cdot, \psi)$, and that under H_0

its asymptotic CDF is $G(\cdot)$. The bootstrap generates samples from a model whose parameter value is ψ_n, so the exact distribution of the bootstrap version of T_n is $G_n(\cdot, \psi_n)$. Under H_0 and subject to regularity conditions, $G_n(\cdot, \psi_n)$ has an asymptotic expansion of the form

$$G_n(z, \psi_n) = G(z) + n^{-j/2} g_j(z, \psi_n) + o_p(n^{-j/2}) \tag{8}$$

uniformly over z, where $j = 1$ or 2 depending on the symmetry of T_n. Usually $j = 1$ if T_n is the statistic for a one-tailed test and $j = 2$ if T_n is the statistic for a symmetrical, two-tailed test. It follows from (8) and the convergence of ψ_n to ψ^* that

$$G_n(z, \psi_n) = G_n(z, \psi^*) + o_p(n^{-j/2})$$

uniformly over z. Therefore, through $O_p(n^{-j/2})$, bootstrap sampling when H_0 is false is equivalent to generating data from a model that satisfies H_0 with pseudo-true values of the parameters not specified by H_0. It follows that when H_0 is false, bootstrap-based critical values are equivalent through $O_p(n^{-j/2})$ to the critical values that would be obtained if the model satisfying H_0 with pseudo-true parameter values were correct. Moreover, the power of a test of H_0 using a bootstrap-based critical value is equal through $O(n^{-j/2})$ to the power against the true data-generation process that would be obtained by using the exact finite-sample critical value for testing H_0 with pseudo-true parameter values.

3   MONTE CARLO EVIDENCE ON NUMERICAL PERFORMANCE

The bootstrap provides a higher-order asymptotic approximation to critical values for tests based on "smooth" asymptotically pivotal statistics. When a bootstrap-based critical value is used for such a test, the difference between the test's true and nominal levels decreases more rapidly with increasing sample size than it does when the critical value is obtained from first-order asymptotic theory. Given a sufficiently large sample, the nominal level of the test will be closer to the true level when a bootstrap critical value is used than when a critical value based on first-order asymptotic theory is used. However, nothing in the theory guarantees that the numerical difference between the true and nominal levels of a test using a bootstrap critical value will be small in a specific application with a fixed sample size.

This section provides Monte Carlo evidence on the numerical perform-ance of the bootstrap as a means of reducing differences between the true and nominal levels of tests. In the examples that are presented, the bootstrap often, though not always, essentially eliminates the distortions of level that occur when critical values are obtained from first-order asymptotic theory. In cases where the bootstrap does not remove distortions of level, it provides an indication that first-order asymptotic approximations are inaccurate.

3.1   The information-matrix test

White's (1982) information-matrix (IM) test is a specification test for parametric models estimated by maximum likelihood. It tests the hypothesis that the Hessian and outer-product forms of the information matrix are equal. Rejection implies that the model is misspecified. The test statistic is asymptotically chi-square distributed, but Monte Carlo experiments carried out by many investigators have shown that the asymptotic distribution is a very poor approximation to the true, finite-sample distribution. With sample sizes in the range found in applications, the true and nominal levels of the IM test with asymptotic critical values can differ by a factor of 10 or more (Horowitz (1994), Kennan and Neumann (1988), Orme (1990), and Taylor (1987)).

Horowitz (1994) reports the results of Monte Carlo experiments that investigate the ability of the bootstrap to provide improved finite-sample critical values for the IM test, thereby reducing the distortions of level that occur with asymptotic critical values. Three forms of the test were used: the Chesher (1983) and Lancaster (1984) form, White's (1982) original form, and Orme's (1990) ω_3. The Chesher–Lancaster form is relatively easy to compute because it does not require third derivatives of the log-density function or analytic expected values of derivatives of the log density. However, first-order asymptotic theory gives an especially poor approximation to its finite-sample distribution. Orme (1990) found through Monte Carlo experimentation that the level distortions of ω_3 are smaller than those of many other forms of the IM-test statistic. Orme's ω_3 uses expected values of third derivatives of the log density, however, so it is relatively difficult to compute.

Horowitz's (1994) experiments consisted of applying the three forms of the IM test to Tobit and binary probit models. Each model had either one or two explanatory variables X that were obtained by sampling either the $N(0, 1)$ or the $U[0, 1]$ distribution. The Monte Carlo procedure consisted of repeating the following steps 1,000 times for each form of the IM test:

1   Generate an estimation dataset of size $n = 50$ or 100 by random sampling from the model under consideration. X was fixed in repeated samples. Estimate the unknown parameters of the model by maximum likelihood and compute the IM-test statistic using the full vector of indicators. Call its value IM_0.

Table 7.1. *Empirical levels of nominal 0.05-level information-matrix tests of probit and Tobit models*

n	Distr. of X	Level using asymptotic critical values			Level using bootstrap-based crit. values		
		White	Chesher Lanc.	Orme	White	Chesher Lanc.	Orme
Binary probit models							
50	$N(0, 1)$	0.385	0.904	0.006	0.064	0.056	0.033
	$U(-2, 2)$	0.498	0.920	0.017	0.066	0.036	0.031
100	$N(0, 1)$	0.589	0.848	0.007	0.053	0.059	0.054
	$U(-2, 2)$	0.632	0.875	0.027	0.058	0.056	0.049
Tobit models							
50	$N(0, 1)$	0.112	0.575	0.038	0.083	0.047	0.045
	$U(-2, 2)$	0.128	0.737	0.174	0.051	0.059	0.054
100	$N(0, 1)$	0.065	0.470	0.167	0.038	0.039	0.047
	$U(-2, 2)$	0.090	0.501	0.163	0.046	0.052	0.039

2 Generate a bootstrap sample of size n by random sampling from the model under consideration but using the parameter values estimated in step 1 instead of the true values. Using this sample, re-estimate the model's parameters by maximum likelihood and compute the IM-test statistic. Call its value IM_B. Estimate the 0.05-level critical value of the IM test from the empirical distribution of IM_B that is obtained by repeating this step 100 times.[3] Let z_n^* denote the estimated critical value.

3 Reject the model being tested at the nominal 0.05 level based on the bootstrap critical value if $IM_0 > z_n^*$. Reject the model at the nominal 0.05 level based on the asymptotic critical value if IM_0 exceeds the 0.95 quantile of the chi-square distribution with degrees of freedom equal to the number of indicators.

Table 7.1 summarizes the results of the experiments. As expected, the differences between empirical and nominal levels are very large when asymptotic critical values are used. This is especially true for the Chesher–Lancaster form of the test. When bootstrap critical values are used, however, the differences between empirical and nominal levels are very small. The bootstrap essentially eliminates the level distortions of the three forms of the IM test.

Horowitz (1994) also carried out a Monte Carlo investigation of the power of the IM test with bootstrap critical values. This investigation, like the investigation of levels, was carried out using Tobit and binary probit models. However, the models used to generate data in step 1 above were different from those estimated in steps 1 and 2. Data were generated from models that either included interaction terms among the components of X or were heteroskedastic. The estimated models did not have either interactions or heteroskedasticity.

Table 7.2 summarizes the results of the power experiments. The powers of Chesher–Lancaster and original White forms of test are similar and larger than those of ω_3 when bootstrap critical values are used. Since the Chesher–Lancaster form has larger distortions of level with asymptotic critical values than do the other forms, these results show that getting the level of a test right and getting high power are different tasks. A test with severe distortions of level when asymptotic critical values are used may have higher power once the distortions are removed than a test whose true and nominal levels with asymptotic critical values are similar to one another. In the examples shown here, the bootstrap eliminates the problem of getting level right and permits concentration on choosing a form of the *IM* test with high power.

3.2   The *t*-test in a heteroskedastic regression model

In this section, the heteroskedasticity-consistent covariance matrix estimator (HCCME) of Eicker (1963, 1967) and White (1980) is used to carry out a *t*-test of a hypothesis about β in the model

$$Y = X\beta + U. \tag{9}$$

In this model, U is an unobserved random variable whose probability distribution is unknown and that may have heteroskedasticity of unknown form. It is assumed that $E(U \mid X = x) = 0$ and $\Omega(x) \equiv \mathrm{Var}(U \mid X = x) < \infty$ for all x in the support of X.

Let b_n be the ordinary least squares (OLS) estimator of β in (9), b_{ni} and β_i be the ith components of b_n and β, and s_{ni} be the square root of the (i, i) element of the HCCME. The *t*-statistic for testing $H_0 : \beta_i = \beta_{i0}$ is

$$T_n = (b_{ni} - \beta_{i0})/s_{ni}.$$

Under regularity conditions, T_n is asymptotically distributed as $N(0, 1)$. However, Chesher and Jewitt (1987) have shown that s_{ni}^2 can be seriously biased downward. Therefore, the true level of a test based on T_n is likely to exceed the nominal level. As is shown later in this section, the differences between the true and nominal levels can be very large when n is small.

The bootstrap can be implemented for model (9) by resampling observa-

Table 7.2. *Power of the information-matrix test with bootstrap critical values*

Form of misspec.	Power with boot. crit. values		
	White	Chesher–Lanc.	Orme
Probit models			
Interaction	0.652	0.667	0.311
Heterosked.	0.881	0.875	0.556
Tobit models			
Interaction	0.458	0.459	0.444
Heterosked.	0.506	0.401	0.028

tions of (Y, X) randomly with replacement. The resulting bootstrap sample is used to estimate β by OLS and compute T_n^*, the t-statistic for testing $H_0^*: \beta_i = b_{ni}$. The bootstrap empirical distribution of T_n^* is obtained by repeating this process many times, and the α-level bootstrap critical value for T_n^* is estimated from this distribution. Since U may be heteroskedastic, the bootstrap cannot be implemented by resampling OLS residuals, $\hat{U}$, independently of X. Similarly, one cannot implement the bootstrap by sampling U from a parametric model because (9) does not specify the distribution of U or the form of any heteroskedasticity.

Randomly resampling (Y, X) pairs does not impose the restriction $E(U \mid X = x) = 0$ on the bootstrap sample. As will be seen later in this section, the numerical performance of the bootstrap can be improved greatly through the use of an alternative resampling procedure, called the "wild bootstrap," that imposes this restriction. The wild bootstrap was introduced by Liu (1988) following a suggestion of Wu (1986). Mammen (1993) established the ability of the wild bootstrap to provide asymptotic refinements for the model (9). Cao-Abad (1991), Härdle and Mammen (1993), and Härdle and Marron (1991) use the wild bootstrap in non-parametric regression.

To describe the wild bootstrap, write the estimated form of (9) as

$$Y_i = X_i b_n + \hat{U}_i, \, i = 1, \dots, n \tag{10}$$

where Y_i and X_i are the ith observed values of Y and X, and $\hat{U}_i$ is the ith OLS residual. For each $i = 1, \dots, n$ let F_i be the unique two-point distribution that satisfies

$$E(Z \,|\, F_i) = 0$$
$$E(Z^2 \,|\, F_i) = \hat{U}_i^2$$
$$E(Z^3 \,|\, F_i) = \hat{U}_i^3,$$

where Z is a random variable with the CDF F_i. In this distribution, $Z = (1 - \sqrt{5})\hat{U}_i/2$ with probability $(1 + \sqrt{5})/(2\sqrt{5})$, and $Z = (1 + \sqrt{5})\hat{U}_i/2$ with probability $1 - (1 + \sqrt{5})/(2\sqrt{5})$. The wild bootstrap is implemented as follows:

1 For each $i = 1, \ldots, n$, sample U_i^* randomly from the distribution F_i. Set $Y_i^* = X_i b_n + U_i^*$.
2 Estimate (9) by OLS using the bootstrap sample $\{Y_i^*, X_i: i = 1, \ldots, n\}$. Compute the resulting t-statistic, T_n^*.
3 Obtain the empirical distribution of the wild-bootstrap version of $T_n{}^*$ by repeating steps 1 and 2 many times. Obtain the wild-bootstrap critical value of $T_n{}^*$ from the empirical distribution.

I have carried out a small Monte Carlo investigation of the ability of the bootstrap and wild bootstrap to reduce the distortions in the level of a symmetrical, two-tailed t-test that occur when asymptotic critical values are used. The bootstrap is implemented by resampling (Y, X) pairs, and the wild bootstrap is implemented as described above. The Monte Carlo experiments also investigate the level of the t-test when the HCCME is used with asymptotic critical values and when a jackknife version of the HCCME is used with asymptotic critical values (MacKinnon and White (1985)). MacKinnon and White found through Monte Carlo experimentation that with the jackknife HCCME and asymptotic critical values, the t-test had smaller distortions of level than it did with several other versions of the HCCME.

In the experiments reported here, $n = 25$. X is fixed in repeated samples and consists of an intercept and either one or two explanatory variables. In experiments in which X has an intercept and one explanatory variable, $\beta = (1, 0)'$. In experiments in which X has an intercept and two explanatory variables, $\beta = (1, 0, 1)'$. The hypothesis tested in all experiments is $H_0: \beta_2 = 0$. The components of X were obtained by independent sampling from a mixture of normal distributions in which $N(0, 1)$ was sampled with probability 0.9 and $N(2, 9)$ was sampled with probability 0.1. The resulting distribution of X is skewed and leptokurtotic. Experiments were carried out using homoskedastic and heteroskedastic Us. When U was homoskedastic, it was sampled randomly from $N(0, 1)$. When U was heteroskedastic, the U value corresponding to $X = x$ was sampled from $N(0, \Omega_x)$, where $\Omega_x = 1 + x^2$ or $\Omega_x = 1 + x_1^2 + x_2^2$, depending on whether X consists of one or two components in addition to an intercept. Ω_x is the covariance matrix of U corresponding to the random-coefficients model

$$Y = X\beta + X\delta + V, \tag{11}$$

where V and the components of δ are independently distributed as $N(0, 1)$.

There were 1,000 Monte Carlo replications in each experiment. In the experiments with the HCCME, each replication consisted of the following steps:

1 Generate an estimation dataset of size n by random sampling from model (9) or (11). Estimate β by OLS and compute the t-statistic, T_n, for testing H_0. Also estimate β by OLS subject to the constraint that H_0 is true.

2 Generate a bootstrap sample of size n. This is done by either resampling (Y, X) pairs randomly with replacement or by using $Y_i^* = X_i b_n + U_i^*$ with b_n the constrained OLS estimate of β and U_i^* generated by the wild bootstrap. Using the bootstrap or wild bootstrap sample, re-estimate β by unconstrained OLS and compute the t-statistic for testing $H_0^*: \beta_2 = b_{n2}$ if (Y, X) pairs are resampled or $H_0^*: \beta_2 = 0$ if the wild bootstrap is used. Call the value of the bootstrap or wild bootstrap t-statistic T_n^*. Estimate the 0.05-level critical value of the t-test from the empirical distribution of T_n^* that is obtained by repeating this step 100 times. Let $z_{0.05}^*$ denote the estimated critical value. Increasing the number of repetitions of this step beyond 100 has little effect on the results of the experiments.

3 Reject H_0 at the nominal 0.05 level based on the bootstrap critical value if $|T_n| > z_{0.05}^*$. Reject H_0 at the nominal 0.05 level based on the asymptotic critical value if $|T_n| > 1.96$, which is the asymptotic 0.05-level critical value for the symmetrical, two-tailed t-test.

The experiments with the jackknife version of the HCCME did not include bootstrapping or constrained OLS estimation but were identical in other respects.

Table 7.3 shows the empirical levels of the nominal 0.05-level t-tests of H_0. The differences between the empirical and nominal levels using the HCCME and asymptotic critical values are very large. Using the jackknife version of the HCCME or critical values obtained from the bootstrap greatly reduces the differences between the empirical and nominal levels, but the empirical levels are still two to three times the nominal levels. With critical values obtained from the wild bootstrap, the differences between the

Table 7.3. *Empirical levels of t-tests using heteroskedasticity-consistent covariance matrix estimators* ($n = 25$)
Empirical level at nominal 0.05 level

Form of test	1-variable homoskedastic model	1-variable random coeff. model	2-variable homoskedastic model	2-variable random coeff. model
Asymptotic	0.156	0.306	0.192	0.441
Jackknife	0.096	0.140	0.081	0.186
Bootstrap (Y, X) pair	0.100	0.103	0.114	0.124
Wild bootstrap	0.050	0.034	0.062	0.057

empirical and nominal levels are very small. In these experiments, the wild bootstrap essentially removes the distortions of level that occur with asymptotic critical values.

3.3   Non-invariance of the Wald test

The Wald statistic is not invariant to the specification of the null hypothesis being tested, H_0. The statistic is a different function of the data for different but algebraically equivalent specifications of H_0, and its numerical value can vary greatly according to the specification that is used. As a result the finite-sample level of the Wald test based on the asymptotic critical value depends on the specification of H_0 and can differ greatly from the nominal level. Gregory and Veall (1985), Lafontaine and White (1986), Breusch and Schmidt (1988), and Dagenais and Dufour (1991) discuss this problem.

A related problem concerns the t-statistic for testing a hypothesis about a slope coefficient in a linear regression model with a Box–Cox (1964) transformed dependent variable. The t-statistic is a Wald statistic and is not invariant to changes in the measurement units, or scale, of the dependent variable (Spitzer (1984)). Thus, the numerical value of the t-statistic and the finite-sample levels of the t-test with asymptotic critical values vary according to the measurement units or scale that is used. As a result, the finite-sample levels of the t-test with asymptotic critical values can be far from the nominal levels.

The distortions of level that occur when asymptotic critical values are used indicate that first-order asymptotic theory does not provide a good approximation to the finite-sample distribution of the Wald statistic. The bootstrap provides a better approximation to the finite-sample distribution and, therefore, better finite-sample critical values. This section reports the results of a Monte Carlo investigation of the ability of the bootstrap to provide improved finite-sample critical values for the Wald statistic and, thereby, to reduce the sensitivity of the finite-sample level of the Wald test to reparameterizations and rescalings.

Reparameterizations of the null hypothesis

This section reports the results of a Monte Carlo investigation of the finite-sample levels of Wald tests of algebraically equivalent specifications of H_0 when bootstrap critical values are used. See Horowitz and Savin (1992) for a more extensive investigation.

The model that generates the data is

$$Y = \beta_0 + \beta_1 X_1 + \beta_2 X_2 + U; U \sim N(0, \sigma^2), \tag{12}$$

where X_1 and X_2 are fixed in repeated samples. This is a slightly modified version of the model investigated by Gregory and Veall (1985). Two algebraically equivalent null hypotheses are tested. These are $H_0^A: \beta_1 - 1/\beta_2 = 0$, and $H_0^B: \beta_1\beta_2 - 1 = 0$. X_1 and X_2 are generated by independent random sampling from the $N(0,1)$ distribution, and $\beta_0 = \sigma^2 = 1$ in all of the experiments. The values of β_1 and β_2 vary according to the experiment. Formulae for the Wald statistics for testing H_0^A and H_0^B are given by Gregory and Veall (1985).

The sample size in all of the Monte Carlo experiments is $n = 20$. Each experiment consisted of repeating the following sequence of steps 500 times:

1 Generate an estimation data set of size n by random sampling from model (12). Estimate the βs and σ^2 by maximum likelihood, and compute the Wald statistic, W_n, for testing the specified form of H_0. Also estimate the βs and σ^2 by maximum likelihood subject to the constraint that H_0 is true.

2 Generate a bootstrap sample of size n by random sampling from (12) but using the constrained maximum-likelihood estimates of the parameters instead of the true values. Using this sample, re-estimate β and σ^2 by unconstrained maximum likelihood and compute the Wald statistic. Call its value W_n^*. Estimate the 0.05-level critical value of the Wald test from the empirical distribution of W_n^* that is obtained by repeating this step 100 times. Let $z_{0.05}^*$ denote the estimated critical value. Increasing the number of repetitions of this step beyond 100 has little effect on the results of the experiments.

3 Reject H_0 at the nominal 0.05 level based on the bootstrap critical value if $W_n > z_{0.05}^*$. Reject H_0 at the nominal 0.05 level based on the asymptotic critical value if $W_n > 3.84$, which is the 0.95 quantile of the chi-square distribution with one degree of freedom.

The results are shown in table 7.4. As in Gregory and Veall (1985), the empirical levels of the Wald tests based on the asymptotic critical value are larger than the nominal level, especially with H_0^A and $\beta_1 = 10$ or 5. The reason for this is clear from the table: the empirical critical values of the various forms of the Wald statistic are larger than the asymptotic critical value of 3.84. With H_0^A and $\beta_1 = 10$, the empirical critical value exceeds the asymptotic critical value by more than a factor of 25. In contrast, the mean bootstrap critical values are close to the empirical ones, and the differences between the nominal and empirical levels of the Wald tests with bootstrap critical values are small.

Rescaling the dependent variable in a Box–Cox regression model

This section reports the results of a Monte Carlo investigation of the finite-sample level of a symmetrical, two-tailed t-test of a hypothesis about a slope coefficient in a linear regression model with a Box–Cox transformed dependent variable. The model generating the data is given by equation (5) with $U \sim N(0, \sigma^2)$, $\beta_0 = 2$, $\beta_1 = 0$ and $\sigma^2 = 0.0625$. X was sampled from $N(4, 4)$ and was fixed in repeated samples. The hypothesis being tested is $H_0: \beta_1 = 0$. The value of λ is either 0.01 or 1, depending on the experiment, and the scale of Y is either 0.2, 1, or 5. The sample sizes were $n = 50$ and 100.

Each experiment consisted of repeating the following sequence of steps 1,000 times.

1 Generate an estimation dataset of size n by random sampling from model (5) and multiplying Y by 0.2, 1, or 5. Estimate the βs, λ, and σ^2 by maximum likelihood, and compute the t-statistic, T_n, for testing H_0. Also estimate β_0, λ, and σ^2 by maximum likelihood subject to the constraint that $\beta_1 = 0$.

2 Generate a bootstrap sample of size n by random sampling from (5) but using the constrained maximum-likelihood estimates of the parameters instead of the true values. Using this sample, re-estimate the βs, λ, and σ^2 by unconstrained maximum likelihood and compute the t-statistic. Call its value T_n^*. Estimate the 0.05-level critical value of the t-test from the empirical distribution of T_n^* that is obtained by repeating this step 100 times. Let $z_{0.05}^*$ denote the estimated critical value.

Table 7.4. *Empirical levels of Wald tests of H_0^A and H_0^B ($n = 20$; nominal level = 0.05)*

β_1, β_2	Null hyp.	Level with crit. val. from		Empirical critical value	Mean bootstrap crit. val.
		Asymp.	Boot.		
10, 0.1	H_0^A	0.378	0.066	101.69	87.70
	H_0^B	0.082	0.074	4.12	3.69
5, 0.2	H_0^A	0.254	0.074	29.17	25.58
	H_0^B	0.092	0.074	4.01	3.68
2, 0.5	H_0^A	0.092	0.048	7.32	6.62
	H_0^B	0.074	0.074	4.31	3.75
1, 1	H_0^A	0.050	0.042	4.21	4.12
	H_0^B	0.104	0.080	5.04	4.71

Increasing the number of repetitions of this step beyond 100 has little effect on the results of the experiments.

3 Reject H_0 at the nominal 0.05 level based on the bootstrap critical value if $|T_n| > z_{0.05}^*$. Reject H_0 at the nominal 0.05 level based on the asymptotic critical value if $|T_n| > 1.96$.

The results are shown in table 7.5. The empirical critical value of the t-test tends to be much smaller than the asymptotic value of 1.96, especially in the experiments with a scale factor of 5. As a result, the empirical level of the t-test is usually much smaller than its nominal level. The mean bootstrap critical values, however, are very close to the empirical critical values, and the levels based on bootstrap critical values are very close to the nominal level.

3.4   A t-test in a trend model with AR(1) errors

This section reports the results of a Monte Carlo investigation of the finite-sample level of a symmetrical, two-tailed t-test of a hypothesis about the parameter β in the following time-series model

$$Y_t = \alpha_0 + \alpha_1 t + U_t; t = 1, 2, \ldots$$
$$U_t = \beta U_{t-1} + V_t; V_t \sim \text{i.i.d.}$$

This model has been investigated in detail by Nankervis and Savin (1996). The results presented here are taken from their paper.

The test is based on the t-statistic that is obtained from OLS estimation of the reduced-form model

$$Y_t = \gamma + \delta t + \beta Y_{t-1} + V_t; t = 1, 2, \ldots \tag{13}$$

Table 7.5. *Empirical levels of t-tests for a Box–Cox regression model* (*nominal level* = 0.05)

n	λ	Scale fac.	Level using crit. val. from		Empirical crit. val.	Mean bootstrap crit. val.
			Asymp.	Boot.		
50	0.01	0.2	0.048	0.066	1.930	1.860
		1.0	0.000	0.044	0.911	0.909
		5.0	0.000	0.055	0.587	0.571
100	0.01	0.2	0.047	0.053	1.913	1.894
		1.0	0.000	0.070	1.201	1.165
		5.0	0.000	0.056	0.767	0.759
50	1.0	0.2	0.000	0.057	1.132	1.103
		1.0	0.000	0.037	0.625	0.633
		5.0	0.000	0.036	0.289	0.287
100	1.0	0.2	0.000	0.051	1.364	1.357
		1.0	0.000	0.044	0.836	0.835
		5.0	0.000	0.039	0.401	0.391

where $\gamma = [\alpha_0(1 - \beta) + \alpha_1\beta]$ and $\delta = \alpha_1(1 - \beta)$. Two versions of the model were investigated. In one version, called the stationary model, δ is known to be zero and Y_0 is random. Thus, only γ, β and the variance of V are estimated. In the second version, called the trend model, δ is estimated by OLS along with the other parameters, and Y_0 is a constant equal to the first observed value of Y.

In all of the experiments, data were generated using $\gamma = \delta = 0$. In experiments with the trend model, $Y_0 = 0$. The value of β varies according to the experiment. The hypothesis being tested is $H_0: \beta = \beta_0$, where β_0 is the value of β used to generate the data. Three different distributions of V were used: $N(0, 1)$, the lognormal with $\log V \sim N(0, 1)$, and a mixture of normals in which V is sampled from $N(0, 1)$ with probability 0.8 and from $N(0, 16)$ with probability 0.2. The sample sizes were 10 or 20 in experiments with the stationary model and 100 with the trend model, where larger samples were needed to obtain satisfactory numerical accuracy with the bootstrap.

For purposes of bootstrap sampling, it was assumed that the distribution of V is unknown. Bootstrap realizations of V were generated by sampling the residuals of the stationary or trend model that was estimated subject to the constraint that H_0 holds (that is, β was constrained to equal β_0). In experiments with the stationary model, the initial value of Y in the bootstrap sample was

$$Y_0^* = [\hat{\gamma}/(1 - \beta_0)] + \sum_{j=0}^{m} \beta_0^j V_{-j}^*,$$

where $\hat{\gamma}$ is the constrained estimate of γ, and the V_{-j}^* are sampled randomly from the empirical distribution of constrained least squares residuals. The values of m are 1, 50, 100, 150, 200 for $\beta_0 = 0.0, 0.5, 0.9, 0.95$, and 0.99, respectively.

Each experiment consisted of carrying out the following steps 15,000 times:

1. Generate a sample of size n from (13) with the chosen parameter values and distribution of V. Estimate the parameters by OLS and compute the t-statistic for testing $H_0: \beta = \beta_0$. Call this value of the t-statistic T_n. Also estimate the parameters by OLS subject to the constraint $\beta = \beta_0$.
2. Generate a bootstrap sample of size n from the constrained estimate of (13). Bootstrap values of V are sampled from the empirical distribution of the residuals of the constrained estimated model. Using this sample, re-estimate γ, β, and, in the trend model, δ. Compute the t-statistic for testing H_0. Call its value T_n^*. Estimate the 0.05-level critical value of the t-test from the empirical distribution of T_n^* that is obtained by repeating this step 1,000 times. Let $z_{0.05}^*$ denote the estimated critical value.
3. Reject H_0 at the nominal 0.05 level based on the bootstrap critical value if $|T_n| > z_{0.05}^*$. Reject H_0 at the nominal 0.05 level based on the asymptotic critical value if $|T_n| > 1.96$.

The results are shown in table 7.6. The empirical level of the t-test using the asymptotic critical value is much larger than the nominal level when $\beta_0 > 0.5$. The error in the level increases as β_0 approaches 1. This is not surprising since the t-statistic is not asymptotically normal when $\beta_0 = 1$. In contrast, the empirical level of the t-test using bootstrap critical values is close to the nominal level in all of the experiments.

3.5 The bootstrap as an indicator of the accuracy of asymptotic critical values

In section 2.7 it was noted that the bootstrap cannot be expected to perform well when an Edgeworth expansion provides a poor approximation to the distribution of interest. Phillips and Park (1988) have argued that, even when an Edgeworth expansion does not improve the numerical quality of asymptotic approximations, it may provide information on whether

Table 7.6. *Empirical levels of t-tests for an AR(1) model (nominal level = 0.05)*

β	Empirical level with asymptotic critical value Distribution of V			Empirical level with bootstrap critical value Distribution of V		
	Normal	Lognorm.	Mixture	Normal	Lognorm.	Mixture
Stationary model, n = 10 or 20						
0.0	0.032	0.017	0.024	0.050	0.035	0.050
0.50	0.054	0.023	0.038	0.052	0.035	0.052
0.90	0.129	0.097	0.103	0.055	0.040	0.059
0.95	0.159	0.138	0.145	0.057	0.042	0.063
0.99	0.182	0.193	0.198	0.056	0.048	0.073
Trend model, n = 100						
0.0	0.051	0.031	0.049	0.051	0.042	0.053
0.50	0.066	0.034	0.054	0.053	0.041	0.052
0.90	0.164	0.129	0.148	0.054	0.050	0.054
0.95	0.255	0.225	0.240	0.054	0.050	0.054
0.99	0.479	0.461	0.465	0.056	0.055	0.059

first-order approximations are accurate. Specifically, first-order approximations are likely to be inaccurate if higher-order terms through $O(n^{-1})$ in the expansion of the distribution of a statistic are large compared with the first-order term.

Since the bootstrap amounts to a one-term Edgeworth expansion, it can provide an indication of the accuracy of first-order approximations to the distributions of test statistics without the tedious algebra associated with analytic Edgeworth expansions. In particular, large differences between bootstrap and asymptotic critical values may indicate that first-order approximations are inaccurate. This idea will now be illustrated with some Monte Carlo experiments.

The experiments consist of testing $H_0: \beta = 0$ in the following linear model with an endogenous right-hand side variable, X, and two instruments, Z_1 and Z_2

$$Y = \beta X + U, \tag{14}$$

$$X = \gamma Z_1 + \gamma Z_2 + V, \tag{15}$$

$$\begin{bmatrix} U \\ V \end{bmatrix} = N(0, \Sigma); \ \Sigma = \begin{bmatrix} 1 & r_{uv} \\ r_{uv} & 1 \end{bmatrix}. \tag{16}$$

X and the Zs are scalars, and the true value of β is 0. X is endogenous if $r_{uv} \neq 0$. Z_1 and Z_2 are generated independently of one another and of U by Gaussian AR(1) processes with means of 0, variances of 1, and first-order serial correlation coefficients of r_z. Experiments were carried out with $\gamma = 0.25$ and 1.0, $r_z = 0$ and 0.75, and $r_{uv} = 0.75$. With $\gamma = 0.25$, the correlation between the instruments Z and the endogenous regressor X is relatively low; the asymptotic value of R^2 from the regression of X on Z_1 and Z_2 is 0.11. With $\gamma = 1$, the value of R^2 is 0.67. The sample sizes used in the experiments are $n = 50$ and $n = 100$.

The value of β is estimated by GMM using the moment conditions $E[Z_1(Y - \beta X)] = 0$ and $E[Z_2(Y - \beta X)] = 0$. GMM estimation is carried out in two stages. The first stage is two-stage least squares using the instruments Z_1 and Z_2, and the second stage uses an estimate of the asymptotically optimal GMM weight matrix. This yields an asymptotically efficient estimator of β. H_0 is tested with a symmetrical, two-tailed t-test based on the second-stage estimation results.

In experiments with $r_z = 0$, bootstrap samples are obtained by resampling the quadruplets (Y, X, Z_1, Z_2) randomly with replacement. In experiments with $r_z = 0.75$, (Y, X, Z_1, Z_2) is resampled in non-overlapping blocks. Experiments were carried out using block lengths of $n/5$ and $n/10$. The block bootstrap procedure is summarized in section 2.6 of this chapter and discussed in detail in Hall and Horowitz (1996). Recentering and correction of block bootstrap t-statistics were carried out using the methods described in sections 2.5 and 2.6.

Each experiment consisted of carrying out the following steps 1,000 times:

1 Generate an estimation sample of size n from (14)–(16) with $\beta = 0$. Estimate β by two-stage GMM. Call the estimate b_n and compute the t-statistic, T_n, for testing $H_0: \beta = 0$.

2 Generate a bootstrap sample by sampling the quadruplet (Y, X, Z_1, Z_2) from the estimation data randomly with replacement or in non-overlapping blocks. Estimate β from the bootstrap sample by using GMM after recentering, and compute the bootstrap t-statistic, T_n^*, for testing $H_0^*: \beta = b_n$. Estimate the 0.05-level critical value of the t-test from the empirical distribution of T_n^* that is obtained by repeating this step 100 times. Let $z_{0.05}^*$ denote the estimated critical value.

3 Reject H_0 at the nominal 0.05 level based on the bootstrap critical value if $|T_n| > z_{0.05}^*$. Reject H_0 at the nominal 0.05 level based on the asymptotic critical value if $|T_n| > 1.96$.

Table 7.7. *Empirical levels of t-tests for linear model with an endogenous regressor (nominal level = 0.05)*

				Empirical level	
				Asymp. crit. value	Boot. crit. value
n	γ	r_z	Blks		
50	0.25	0.0	50	0.128	0.124
	0.25	0.75	5	0.098	0.085
			10		0.079
100	0.25	0.0	100	0.082	0.085
	0.25	0.75	10	0.080	0.072
			20		0.076
50	1.0	0.0	50	0.077	0.058
	1.0	0.75	5	0.084	0.061
			10		0.049
100	1.0	0.0	100	0.063	0.056
	1.0	0.75	10	0.065	0.063
			20		0.060

The results of the experiments are shown in table 7.7. In most cases the bootstrap reduces but does not remove the distortions of the level of the t-test that occur with asymptotic critical values.

The bootstrap does, however, provide a warning that first-order asymptotic approximations are inaccurate. In figure 7.1, the 25th, 50th, and 75th percentiles of the empirical distributions of the nominal 0.05-level bootstrap critical values in the experiments are plotted against the empirical levels of the tests based on the asymptotic critical value. The figure also contains a horizontal line indicating the asymptotic critical value. The figure shows that the difference between the bootstrap and asymptotic critical values is an increasing function of the distortion of the level of the asymptotic test. Thus, the bootstrap is informative about the accuracy of first-order asymptotic approximations despite its inability to correct fully the distortions of levels caused by these approximations. In particular, the 25th percentile of the bootstrap critical value of the t-test exceeds the asymptotic critical value whenever the level of the asymptotic test exceeds roughly 0.08. Further research might usefully investigate ways to decide in applications whether an observed difference between asymptotic and bootstrap critical values is evidence that first-order approximations are inaccurate or is simply an artifact of random sampling errors.

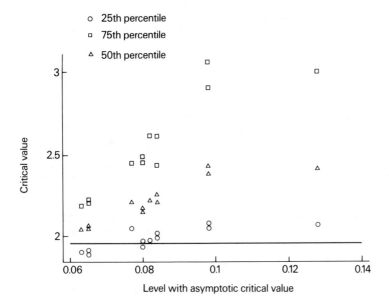

Figure 7.1 Bootstrap critical values for t in linear model.

4 CONCLUSIONS

In applied econometrics, the bootstrap is often used as a substitute for analytical asymptotic formulae when the statistics of interest have complicated asymptotic distributions. This chapter has focussed on another important use of the bootstrap: it often provides a better approximation to the finite-sample distribution of an asymptotically pivotal statistic than does first-order asymptotic theory.

First-order asymptotic theory often gives a poor approximation to the finite-sample distributions of test statistics. As a result, the true and nominal levels of hypothesis tests can be greatly different. The examples presented in section 3 show that the use of bootstrap-based critical values instead of asymptotic ones can provide dramatic reductions in the differences between the true and nominal levels of tests based on asymptotically pivotal statistics. In many cases of practical importance, the bootstrap essentially eliminates finite-sample errors in levels. Even when the bootstrap is not numerically accurate, it can provide a warning that first-order asymptotic approximations are inaccurate.

Although the discussion here has concentrated on reducing distortions in the levels of hypothesis tests, similar conclusions can be drawn concerning

218   Joel L. Horowitz

confidence intervals. The use of bootstrap-based critical values instead of asymptotic ones often greatly reduces the difference between true and nominal coverage probabilities.

Of course, the bootstrap should not be used blindly. It does not always eliminate distortions of levels and sometimes makes them worse. Proper attention must be given to matters such as recentering, correction of test statistics in the block bootstrap for dependent data, and choosing the distribution from which bootstrap samples are drawn. In other words, the bootstrap like any other statistical method, is not foolproof and works best in the hands of a careful, informed user.

Notes

Prepared for presentation to the Invited Symposium on Bootstrap Methods in Econometrics, 7th World Congress of the Econometric Society, Tokyo, August 1995. I thank Narayana Kocherlakota, Charles F. Manski, John Nankervis, N. E. Savin, and Kenneth D. West for helpful comments and suggestions. Research supported in part by NSF grant SBR-9307677.

1 Härdle and Hart (1992) proved consistency of a modified version of the bootstrap estimator used by Härdle, et al. (1991). "Consistency" in this setting means that the bootstrap estimator of the distribution function of the test statistic converges weakly to the correct asymptotic distribution function. Proving that the bootstrap is consistent for the maximum score estimator is a difficult problem that has not yet been solved.

2 Strictly speaking, U cannot be normally distributed unless $\lambda = 0$ or 1, but the error made by assuming normality is negligibly small if the right-hand side of the model has a negligibly small probability of being negative.

3 Horowitz (1994) also considered the 0.01-level critical value, but these results are not reported here.

References

Amemiya, T. (1985). *Advanced Econometrics*. Cambridge, MA: Harvard University Press.
Andrews, D. W. K. (1991). "Heteroskedasticity and autocorrelation consistent covariance matrix estimation." *Econometrica*, 59: 817–58.
Andrews, D. W. K. and Monahan, J. C. (1992). "An improved heteroskedasticity and autocorrelation consistent covariance matrix." *Econometrica*, 59: 817–58.
Athreya, K. (1987). "Bootstrap of the mean in the infinite variance case." *Annals of Statistics*, 15: 724–31.
Babu, G. J. and Singh, K. (1983). "Inference on means using the bootstrap." *Annals of Statistics*, 11: 999–1003.
(1984). "On one term correction by Efron's bootstrap." *Sankhya, Series A*, 46: 219–32.
Basawa, I. V., Mallik, A. K., McCormick, W. P., Reeves, J. H., and Taylor, R. L.

(1991). "Bootstrapping unstable first-order autoregressive processes." *Annals of Statistics*, 19: 1098–101.

Beran, R. (1987). "Prepivoting to reduce level error of confidence sets." *Biometrika*, 74: 457–68.

(1988). "Prepivoting test statistics: a bootstrap view of asymptotic refinements." *Journal of the American Statistical Association*, 83: 687–97.

Beran, R. and Ducharme, G. R. (1991). *Asymptotic Theory for Bootstrap Methods in Statistics*. Les Publications CRM, Centre de recherches mathématiques, University of Montreal, Montreal, Canada.

Bickel, P. and Freedman, D. A. (1981). "Some asymptotic theory for the bootstrap." *Annals of Statistics*, 9: 1196–217.

Blanchard, O. J. and Quah, D. (1989). "The dynamic effects of aggregate demand and supply disturbances." *American Economic Review*, 79: 655–73.

Bose, A. (1988). "Edgeworth correction by bootstrap in autoregressions." *Annals of Statistics*, 16: 1709–22.

Box, G. E. P. and Cox, D. R. (1964). "An analysis of transformations." *Journal of the Royal Statistical Society, Series B*, 26: 211–43.

Breusch, T. and Schmidt, P. (1988). "Alternative forms of the Wald test: how long is a piece of string?" *Communications in Statistics A, Theory and Methods*, 17: 2789–95.

Brown, B. and Newey, W. K. (1992). "Bootstrapping for GMM." Seminar notes, Department of Economics, Massachusetts Institute of Technology.

Cao-Abad, R. (1991). "Rate of convergence for the wild bootstrap in nonparametric regression." *Annals of Statistics*, 19: 2226–31.

Carlstein, E. (1986). "The use of subseries methods for estimating the variance of a general statistic from a stationary time series." *Annals of Statistics*, 14: 1171–9.

Chesher, A. (1983). "The information matrix test." *Economics Letters*, 13: 45–8.

Chesher, A. and Jewitt, I. (1987). "The bias of a heteroskedasticity consistent covariance matrix estimator." *Econometrica*, 55: 1217–22.

Dagenais, M. G. and Dufour, J.-M. (1991). "Invariance, nonlinear models, and asymptotic tests." *Econometrica*, 59: 1601–15.

Efron, B. (1979). "Bootstrap methods: another look at the jackknife." *Annals of Statistics*, 7: 1–26.

(1987). "Better bootstrap confidence intervals." *Journal of the American Statistical Association*, 82: 171–85.

Efron, B. and Tibshirani, R. J. (1993). *An Introduction to the Bootstrap*. New York: Chapman & Hall.

Eicker, F. (1963). "Asymptotic normality and consistency of the least squares estimators for families of linear regressions." *Annals of Mathematical Statistics*, 34: 447–56.

(1967) "Limit theorems for regression with unequal and dependent errors." In LeCam, L. and Neyman, J. (eds.), *Proceedings of the 5th Berkeley Symposium on Mathematical Statistics and Probability*. Berkeley, CA: University of California Press, pp. 59–82.

Freedman, D. A. (1981). "Bootstrapping regression models." *Annals of Statistics*, 9:

1218–28.

Götze, F. and Hipp, C. (1983). "Asymptotic expansions for sums of weakly dependent random vectors." *Zeitschrift für Warscheinlichkeitstheorie und verwandte Gebiete*, 64: 211–39.

Gregory, A. W. and Veall, M. R. (1985). "Formulating Wald tests of nonlinear restrictions." *Econometrica*, 53: 1465–8.

Hall, P. (1985). "Resampling a coverage process." *Stochastic Process Applications*, 19: 259–69.

—— (1986). "On the bootstrap and confidence intervals." *Annals of Statistics*, 14: 1431–52.

—— (1988). "Theoretical comparison of bootstrap confidence intervals." *Annals of Statistics*, 16: 927–53.

—— (1992). *The Bootstrap and Edgeworth Expansion*. New York: Springer-Verlag.

Hall, P. and Horowitz, J. L. (1996). "Bootstrap critical values for tests based on generalized-method-of-moments estimators." *Econometrica*, 64: 891–916.

Hall, P., Horowitz, J. L., and Jing, B.-Y. (1995). "On blocking rules for the bootstrap with dependent data." *Biometrika*, 82: 561–74.

Hansen, L. P. (1982). "Large sample properties of generalized method of moments estimators." *Econometrica*, 50: 1029–54.

Hansen, L. P. and Singleton, K. (1982). "Generalized instrumental variables estimation of nonlinear rational expectations models." *Econometrica*, 50: 1269–86.

Härdle, W. and Hart, J. D. (1992). "A bootstrap test for positive definiteness of income effect matrices." *Econometric Theory*, 8: 276–90.

Härdle, W., Hildenbrand, W., and Jerison, M. (1991). "Empirical evidence on the law of demand." *Econometrica*, 59: 1525–50.

Härdle, W. and Mammen, E. (1993). "Comparing nonparametric versus parametric regression fits." *Annals of Statistics*, 21: 1926–47.

Härdle, W. and Marron, J. S. (1991). "Bootstrap simultaneous error bars for nonparametric regression." *Annals of Statistics*, 19: 778–96.

Hillier, G. H. (1985). "On the joint and marginal densities of instrumental variables estimators in a general structural equation." *Econometric Theory*, 1: 53–72.

Horowitz, J. L. (1994). "Bootstrap-based critical values for the information-matrix test." *Journal of Econometrics*, 61: 395–411.

Horowitz, J. L. and Savin, N. E. (1992). "Noninvariance of the Wald test: the boostrap to the rescue." Working Paper No. 92-04, Department of Economics, University of Iowa.

Kennan, J. and Neumann, G. R. (1988). "Why does the information matrix test reject so often?" Working Paper No. 88-4, Department of Economics, University of Iowa.

Künsch, H. R. (1989). "The jackknife and the bootstrap for general stationary observations." *Annals of Statistics*, 17: 1217–41.

Lafontaine, F. and White, K. J. (1986). "Obtaining any Wald statistic you want." *Economics Letters*, 21: 35–48.

Lahiri, S. N. (1992). "Edgeworth correction by 'moving block' bootstrap for stationary and nonstationary data." In LePage, R. and Billard, L. (eds.), *Exploring the Limits of Bootstrap*. New York: Wiley, pp. 183–214.

Lancaster, T. (1984). "The covariance matrix of the information matrix test." *Econometrica*, 52: 1051–3.

Li, H. and Maddala, G. S. (1995). "Bootstrapping time series models." *Econometric Reviews*, forthcoming.

Liu, R. Y. (1988). "Bootstrap procedures under some non-i.i.d. models." *Annals of Statistics*, 16: 1696–708.

MacKinnon, J. G. and White, H. (1985). "Some heteroskedasticity-consistent covariance matrix estimators with improved finite sample properties." *Journal of Econometrics*, 29: 305–25.

Maddala, G. S. and Jeong, J. (1993). "A perspective on application of bootstrap methods in econometrics." In Maddala, G. S., Rao, C. R., and Vinod, H. D. (eds.), *Handbook of Statistics*, Vol. XI. Amsterdam: North-Holland, pp. 573–610.

Mammen, E. (1992). *When Does Bootstrap Work? Asymptotic Results and Simulations*. New York: Springer-Verlag.

(1993). "Bootstrap and wild bootstrap for high dimensional linear models." *Annals of Statistics*, 21: 255–85.

Manski, Charles F. (1975). "Maximum score estimation of the stochastic utility model of choice." *Journal of Econometrics*, 3: 205–28.

(1985). "Semiparametric analysis of discrete reesponse: asymptotic properties of the maximum score estimator." *Journal of Econometrics*, 27: 313–34.

Nankervis, J. C. and Savin, N. E. (1996). "The level and power of the bootstrap *t*-test in the trend model with AR(1) errors." *Journal of Business and Economic Statistics*, 14: 161–8.

Nelson, C.R. and Startz, R. (1990a). "The distribution of the instrumental variable estimator and its *t* ratio when the instrument is a poor one." *Journal of Business*, 63: S125–S140.

(1990b). "Some further results on the exact small sample properties of the instrumental variable estimator." *Econometrica*, 58: 967–76.

Newey, W. K. and West, K. D. (1987). "A simple, positive semi-definite, heteroskedasticity and autocorrelation consistent covariance matrix." *Econometrica*, 55: 703–8.

(1994). "Automatic lag selection in covariance matrix estimation." *Review of Economic Studies*, 61: 631–53.

Orme, C. (1990). "The small-sample performance of the information-matrix test." *Journal of Econometrics*, 46: 309–31.

Phillips, P. C. B. (1983). "Exact small sample theory in the simultaneous equations model." In Griliches, Z. and Intriligator, M. D. (eds.), *Handbook of Econometrics*, Vol. I. Amsterdam: North-Holland, chapter 8.

Phillips, P. C. B. and Park, J. Y. (1988). "On the formulation of Wald tests of nonlinear restrictions." *Econometrica*, 56: 1065–83.

Politis, D. N. and Romano, J. P. (1994). "Large sample confidence regions based on subsample under minimal assumptions." *Annals of Statistics*, 22: 2031–50.

Runkle, D. E. (1987). "Vector autoregressions and reality." *Journal of Business and Economic Statistics*, 5: 437–42.

Singh, K. (1981). "On the asymptotic accuracy of Efron's bootstrap." *Annals of Statistics*, 9: 1187–95.

Spitzer, J. J. (1984). "Variance estimates in models with the Box–Cox transformation: implications for estimation and hypothesis testing." *Review of Economics and Statistics*, 66: 645–52.

Taylor, L. W. (1987). "The size bias of White's information matrix test." *Economics Letters*, 24: 63–7.

Vinod, H. D. (1993)."Bootstrap methods: applications in econometrics." In Maddala, G. S., Rao, C. R., and Vinod, H. D. (eds.), *Handbook of Statistics*, Vol. XI. Amsterdam: North-Holland, pp. 629–61.

West, K. D. (1990). "The sources of fluctuations in aggregate inventories and GNP." *Quarterly Journal of Economics*, 105: 939–71.

White, H. (1980). "A heteroscedasticity-consistent covariance matrix estimator and a direct test for heteroscedasticity." *Econometrica*, 48: 817–38.

 (1982). "Maximum likelihood estimation of misspecified models." *Econometrica*, 50: 1–26.

Wu, C. F. J. (1986). "Jackknife, bootstrap and other resampling methods in regression analysis." *Annals of Statistics*, 14: 1261–95.

CHAPTER 8

Econometric models of option pricing errors

Eric Renault

1 INTRODUCTION

On prefacing his excellent textbook on dynamic asset pricing theory, Duffie (1992) distinguishes two decades to characterize the progress in this field:

> First, the "golden decade" (1969–79): "Robert Merton started continuous-time financial modeling with his explicit dynamic programming solution for optimal portfolio and consumption policies. ... His next major contribution was his continual development of the option pricing formula introduced by Fisher Black and Myron Scholes in 1973."

> Second, the decade after 1979 described by Duffie as a "mopping-up operation": "the various problems have become much more unified under the umbrella of the Harrison–Kreps model."

Amazingly the end of this second decade (namely the year 1990) was marked by two events:

> First, Merton has provided in a single volume his gigantic contribution to "continuous-time finance" through a collection of fourteen previously published papers and five new essays.

> Second, Angelo Melino gave at the World Congress of the Econometric Society (WCES) a very stimulating invited lecture on "Estimation of continuous-time models in finance."

Among the array of influences that, over the five years between two WCES, led me to the conceptions set forth in the present chapter, I want first to stress my debt with respect to Merton and Melino:

On one hand, R. Merton's 1990 book was so seminal that I felt the need to base by conclusion on it. Moreover, it is worth noting that as long ago as 1976, R. Merton was perhaps the first to place "The Impact on Option Pricing of Specification Error" as the central issue of a research paper (unfortunately not reprinted in the 1990 book. See Merton (1976b)).

On the other hand, it is for me an honor to focus this chapter on the line of Melino's lecture when he claimed that "Statistically speaking, we need to model the source of the prediction errors in option pricing and to relate the distribution of these errors to the stock price process."

Indeed, A. Melino was entirely conscious on the fact that, when one wants "to speculate on the reasons for the widespread adoption of continuous-time models in asset pricing," one could "argue that they have been widely adopted not because of their empirical properties but in spite of them." In other words, continuous-time models and associated arbitrage-free pricing techniques are a convenient "black box" approach to derivative asset pricing (see Duffie (1992), "Equivalent Martingales Measures in a Black Box") which is often used under implausibly restrictive statistical specifications. Therefore, Melino focused on *estimation of primitive* asset price processes but, simultaneously, announced a more ambitious research agenda:

(i) To address "the more interesting and challenging questions of *model specification* and *testing*."
(ii) To combine two sources of information (both *primitive* and *derivative* asset prices data) since "information about the stochastic properties of an asset's price is contained both in the history of the price series as well as the price of any options written on it."

The objective of this chapter is to present some versatile and productive tools for this research agenda. The presentation is organized as follows.

Section 2 provides a brief introduction to the specification strategies I will be interested in through systematic reference to the concept of residual, i.e., "measures of differences between observed values and fitted values" (of option prices) as generally defined by F. J. Anscombe (1990). I shall *first* argue that the best-known extensions of the Black and Scholes (1973) option pricing model like the Merton (1976a) jump-diffusion model or the Hull and White (1987) stochastic volatility model are nothing but that the introduction of an *error term* (eventually interpreted as an unobserved heterogeneity factor) into a theoretical model as is always done in standard econometrics. This error term may provide a satisfactory statistical model if we observe at each date *only one* option price written on a given asset. My *second* claim will be about the *panel* structure of option prices data: several option prices written on a same asset at each date (with various exercise prices and maturity dates). In this case, the above error structure is not rich enough and we shall need to introduce new tools to get a panel structure of error terms. *Finally*, I will recall the usual modeling strategy in econometrics when observed residual plots are not satisfactory as they may detect non-zero correlation with the independent variables or entail some unexplained serial correlation. In this case, it is usual to *extend* the basic model by introducing some additional explanatory variables or by changing the functional form. The remainder of the chapter focuses on various ways to adapt to option pricing issues these three sequential stages of modeling strategy already well known for the linear regression model.

In a preliminary stage, I first build in section 3 a large class of stochastic processes which may provide convenient statistical models of the time-series properties of the underlying asset price. More precisely, I propose a desirable homogeneity property, that alternatives to the Black–Scholes option pricing model should obey for both pricing and hedging purposes. This homogeneity property can be characterized in terms of non-causality in the Granger sense (which gives precise statistical meaning to the useful concept of state variables in finance) and I stress its implication for hedging in relation to the so-called "smile phenomenon" (the U-shaped pattern of implicit volatilities across different strike prices).[1] This volatility smile is often called a *bias* in Black–Scholes option pricing.

We will bear out this terminology in section 4 by showing that extensions of the Black and Scholes option pricing model in the spirit of section 2 (introduction of an error term corresponding to unobserved heterogeneity) do imply the smile phenomenon as an heterogeneity bias. As a matter of fact, these extensions lead to a class of econometric models, named "empirical martingale models" by B. J. Christensen (1992) which share a similar statistical structure: the econometrician observes at time t a derivative asset price c_t depending on an unobservable state process ω_t and on the probability distribution of this process (taken into account in the option pricing formula).

Moreover, this shared structure leads to common statistical methologies. Various convenient strategies of inference are then discussed and we will show in particular that the use of implicit volatilities time series, widespread among practitioners, may have nice statistical properties. To conclude section 4, we discuss some statistical properties of implicit volatilities and suggest some extensions of the Hull and White model, to capture well-documented evidence like skewness and persistence in the smile.

A common feature of the models studied in section 4 is the introduction of a finite set of, say, *n* unobservable errors terms, according to usual practice in econometrics. But, while markets are incomplete with these *n* additional sources of error, it should be noted that observing *n* synchronous option prices should be sufficient to complete the markets. This has the unpleasant consequence that these option pricing models should fail if a lot of option prices are simultaneously observed:

> It suffices to back parameter values out of a limited set of option prices, and to find an additional option price which does not exactly match the corresponding theoretical price at these parameter values. This deficiency is caused by a crucial assumption of traditional models, namely that the option price path *can be duplicated perfectly*. This allowed pricing *by arbitrage*, an analytically attractive concept, but at the same time generated empirically untenable results. (Quoted from Bossaerts and Hillion (1993))

This criticism is relevant, even in the setting of section 4, since, when the market is completed by *n*-quoted options, other derivative assets can be duplicated perfectly.

Faced with this criticism, we have the choice between at least three strategies: the first and the third ones remain "under the umbrella of the Harrison–Kreps [1979] model" while the second does not maintain the assumption of perfect frictionless markets:

(i) If we want to remain true to the *parametric* empirical martingale approach, we may be forced to increase the number of state variables when the cross section of observed option prices is increased.[2] But one would probably not want to go beyond two or three factors, or have the numbers of factors dictated by the number of cross-sectional observations. All remaining deviations between model prices and the observed option prices would then still require an *ad hoc* econometric error term which would be generally inconsistent with the no arbitrage opportunity condition.

(ii) One way to avoid this inconsistency is to put forward some transaction costs, execution price uncertainty, impossibility of continuous-time trading strategies, to explain why we do not observe degenerate distributions. Such an approach could provide some kind of *semi-parametric* structure to a set of option pricing errors through conditional moment restrictions. For instance, to take into account execution price uncertainty, Bossaerts and Hillion (1993) have shown that the pricing error divided by the return on the market has to be zero mean and uncorrelated with a set of instruments representing any information of the representative investor at the time of order submission. On the other hand, to take into account the impact of transaction costs on option replication and thus on option prices, Boyle and Vorst (1992) have presented a simple Black–Scholes type approximation and demonstrated numerically that it is quite accurate for plausible parameter values. In the present chapter, however, we do not question here the assumption of perfect frictionless markets.

(iii) Finally, a really *non-parametric* way of modeling random fluctuations in option pricing has been recently pioneered by Clément, Gouriéroux, and Monfort (1993). Their basic idea is indeed very natural: since we have to randomize the equivalent martingale measure, let us consider it as a latent random variable. In other words, instead of randomizing some parameters involved in the definition of this pricing measure (as in the approaches described in section 4 and in point (*i*) above), which looks like a Bayesian approach, Clément, Gouriéroux, and Monfort propose to adopt a rather non-parametric Bayesian methodology and to define a latent statistical model whose sample space is itself the set of possible values of the pricing probability measure. In order to specify this latent model, an usual and tractable distribution of a set of probability distributions is the so-called Dirichlet process.[3]

Finally, section 5 concludes by attempting to extend the research agendas suggested earlier by Merton (1990) and Melino (1994). The main issue for future research is clearly to propose models for the *econometrics of option mispricing* taking into account the precise operational modalities of the market organization: transaction costs, timing, orders, traders identities.[4]

2   RESIDUALS AND GOODNESS OF FIT FOR ASSET PRICING MODELS

Before describing model errors, we have first to recall what is well-specified structural modeling and the related steps of any inferential approach in statistics.

2.1   Estimation, tests, and pricing models

Lo (1986) was one of the first to try to rigorously connect option pricing and statistical inference. We are nevertheless going to show that to go further in the *specification analysis* of option pricing models, it is necessary to be more precise about the distinction between (i) estimation, (ii) pricing, and (iii) tests of fit. Indeed, Lo (1986) relates option pricing errors to *errors in the estimation* of the parameters of the model: "since parameter estimates are ultimately employed in the pricing formulas in place of the true but unknown parameters, *the sampling variations of parameter estimates* will of course induce sampling variation in *the estimated* contingent claims about their true values." He introduces his methodology in the context of the Black–Scholes (BS) European call-option pricing model; for a value S of the price of the underlying asset and a strike price K the call option price at time t for a given maturity T is written as

$$BS(S, K, \sigma) = S\Delta_1 - KB(t, T)\Delta_2 \tag{1}$$

with

$$\Delta_1 = \Phi\left[\frac{\log\dfrac{S}{KB(t, T)} + \dfrac{1}{2}\sigma^2(T - t)}{\sigma\sqrt{T - t}}\right], \tag{2}$$

$$\Delta_2 = \Phi\left[\frac{\log\dfrac{S}{KB(t, T)} - \dfrac{1}{2}\sigma^2(T - t)}{\sigma\sqrt{T - t}}\right]. \tag{3}$$

Φ is the cumulative normal distribution function, $B(t, T)$ is the price at time t of a zero-coupon bond which pays 1\$ at time T, and σ is the so-called volatility parameter. Moreover, let us recall that the BS analysis takes as its starting point the assumption that the stock price process S_t is the usual geometric Brownian motion so that consecutive regularly sampled log-returns

$$Z_{t_i} = \log\frac{S_{t_i}}{S_{t_{i-1}}}, \ i = 1, 2, \ldots, n, t_i - t_{i-1} = \Delta t$$

are independent, identically normally distributed with variance $\sigma^2\Delta t$. In this framework, it is well founded to say that

$$\hat{\sigma}^2_{ML} = \frac{1}{n\Delta t}\sum_{i=1}^{n}\left[Z_{t_i} - \frac{1}{n}\sum_{i=1}^{n}Z_{t_i}\right]^2$$

provides the maximum-likelihood estimator of σ^2, which has the following asymptotic distribution

$$\sqrt{n}(\hat{\sigma}^2_{ML} - \sigma^2) \xrightarrow{L} \mathcal{N}(0, 2\sigma^4). \tag{4}$$

But, to go further, it is important to keep in mind the role of pricing with respect to classical statistical issues: estimation, test, and prediction.

1 *Estimation versus pricing* From the classical statement, "the ML estimator of any well-behaved non-linear function of a given parameter is simply the non-linear function of the ML estimator of that parameter." Lo (1988) deduces a second statement which could be misleading: "the ML estimator $\widehat{BS}_{ML}$ of the option price BS may be obtained by evaluating BS at $\hat{\sigma}^2_{ML}$." Indeed, it is important to keep in mind that we are not estimating a particular option price but a *prediction function* $BS(\cdot, K, \sigma)$; an option price is not a *parameter* of the statistical model (which could be estimated) but a *statistical variate* (which has to be predicted). This distinction is not a statistical purism of language but is important for instance to properly use asymptotic distribution theory deduced from (4) using the delta method; Lo (1986) writes

$$\sqrt{n}(\widehat{BS}_{ML} - BS) \xrightarrow{L} \mathcal{N}(0, V_{BS}(\sigma^2)) \tag{5}$$

with

$$V_{BS}(\sigma^2) = 2\sigma^4 \left[\frac{\partial BS(\sigma^2)}{\partial \sigma^2} \right]^2 = \frac{1}{2} S^2 \sigma^2 \tau \phi^2(d_1)(T - t),$$

where ϕ is the standard normal density function. But it is not correct to say that the prediction interval

$$\widehat{BS}_{ML} \pm 2 \sqrt{\frac{V_{BS}(\hat{\sigma}^2_{ML})}{n}}$$

contains (for large n) the true option price C_t with a probability of about 95 percent. Indeed this interval contains the *predictor* $BS(S_t, K, \sigma)$ with a probability about 95 percent. For instance, if the theory was able to state that this predictor is optimal in the mean-squared error sense among all functions of S_t, it would coincide with $E[C_t | S_t]$ but definitely not with C_t itself![5]

If C_t was always equal to $E[C_t | S_t]$, C_t would be a deterministic function of S_t, which is stated by the Black–Scholes model but is clearly inconsistent with any statistics: *either* we trust the Black–Scholes model *stricto sensu*, and, in this case, maximum-likelihood theory is *irrelevant* (only *one* observed option price is sufficient to *compute exactly* σ and not to estimate it!) *or* we are led to admit that

$$C_t = E[C_t | S_t] + u_t, \tag{6}$$

where u_t is a zero-mean (but not degenerated!) *error term*.

230   **Eric Renault**

2 *Test of fit versus pricing* The above-described contradiction between perfect Black–Scholes pricing and statistical inference is even clearer for testing. Lo (1988) suggests that the BS option-pricing model may be tested by checking if the intervals $\widehat{BS}_{ML} \pm 2\sqrt{\dfrac{V_{BS}(\hat{\sigma}_{ML}^2)}{n}}$ contain the observed option prices C_t. But, once more

> *Either*, we want to check the BS model *stricto sensu*, and in this case we do not need a statistical apparatus but only to check the *existence of* σ fulfilling the deterministic restrictions: $C_t = BS[S_t, K, \sigma]$.
> *Or*, we admit that the bivariate probability distribution of (S_t, C_t) is not degenerated, and, in this latter case, this joint probability distribution must be used for maximum-likelihood inference according to Melino's research agenda: "information about the stochastic properties of an asset's price is contained both in the history of the asset's price and the price of any options written on it."

Since an option pricing model must be viewed as a prediction model which provides a predictor $\hat{C}_t = F(S_t)$ of the option price *given* the stock price, it is equivalent to specifying the joint probability distribution of (S_t, C_t) or (given the option pricing formula) the joint probability distribution of (S_t, u_t) where u_t is a *pricing error* which characterizes the discrepancy between the actual option price C_t and the theoretical one $\hat{C}_t$. For instance, if $\hat{C}_t = E(C_t/S_t)$, u_t is defined by (6). But "such residuals are, however, often not just simple differences between observed values and fitted values" (Anscombe (1990)) and the convenient way to introduce error terms in the model must be conceived in harmony with the model structure.

2.2   How to introduce model errors

Of course, we do not pretend to be exhaustive about sources of pricing errors for any contingent claim. Following a classification recently suggested by Jacquier and Jarrow (1995), we have only in mind "model errors" (no model can perfectly explain prices) and not "market errors," that is mispricing which could be the basis of an arbitrage strategy whereas a model error could not.

In other words, we stay "under the umbrella of the Harrison–Kreps model" by assuming that both the theoretical price $\hat{C}_t$ and the actual price C_t can be computed as expected values of the discounted terminal payoff with respect to an equivalent martingale measure (whose existence is ensured by a no arbitrage argument as in Harrison and Kreps (1979)). On the one hand, the pricing model $\hat{C}_t = m(x_t, \theta)$ for the equilibrium (arbitrage free) contingent price at time t depends on the observable vector process x_t and fixed (eventually unknown) parameters θ through an expectation operator $\tilde{E}$ with respect to an equivalent martingale measure $\tilde{Q}$. More precisely if we denote by $r(t)$ the short-term interest rate and I_t the available information at time $t (x_t \in I_t)$, the European call option (model) price on the underlying asset (say a stock) of price S_t is given (with the notations of the previous subsection)[6] by

$$m(x_t, \theta) = \tilde{E}\left[\exp\left[-\int_t^T r(u)du\right]\max[0, S_T - K]\,|\,I_t, \theta\right]. \qquad (7)$$

On the other hand, since we know that no model can perfectly explain prices, we have then to specify an econometric model for another equivalent martingale measure, that is for option pricing errors u_t such that the actual option price C_t at a time t can be written

$$C_t = m(x_t, \theta) + u_t. \qquad (8)$$

For this purpose, the well-known extensions of the BS option pricing formula ($m(x_t, \theta)$ defined by (1)) provide us with helpful guidance. We are going first to summarize briefly Merton's (1976a and b) and Hull and White's (1987) proposals for this issue before trying to state a general methodology.

1 Merton (1976a) generalized the basic BS model by questioning the continuity of sample paths of price processes. The idea is to allow for *jump processes*, i.e., for a positive probability of a stock-price change of extraordinary magnitude, no matter how small the time interval between successive observations. In the simplest model, the stock-price returns are then viewed as a mixture of a usual geometric Brownian motion and a Poisson driven process; with usual notations

$$\frac{dS_t}{S_t} = (\mu - \lambda k)dt + \sigma dW_t \qquad (9a)$$

if the Poisson event does not occur, and

$$\frac{dS_t}{S_t} = (\mu - \lambda k)dt + \sigma dW_t + (Y_t - 1) \qquad (9b)$$

if the Poisson event occurs.

In this setting: μ is the instantaneous expected return on the stock, σ^2 is the instantaneous variance of the return, conditional on no arrivals of important new information (i.e., the Poisson event does not occur), dW_t is a standard Gauss–Wiener process, $k = E(Y_t - 1)$, where $Y_t - 1$ is the random percentage change in the stock price if the Poisson event occurs. The Poisson process, the Wiener process W, and the random amplitude process Y are assumed to be mutually independent: λ denotes the mean number of arrivals of events per unit of time in the Poisson process.

To obtain tractable option pricing formulas, Merton (1976a) considers an example where:

First, the variables $\log Y_t, t \in \mathbb{R}^+$, are independent, identically distributed with normal probability distribution of variance δ^2. Second, the short-term interest rate is time invariant ($r(t) = r, \forall t$) and deterministic, so that

$$B(t, T) = \exp[-r(T - t)].$$

With a slight change of notation, the Black–Scholes price (1) will then be written $BS(S, K, \sigma, r)$.

Moreover since (9b) produces some incompleteness of the market by introducing new sources of risk due to the Poisson driven process (as soon as $\lambda \neq 0$) the use of the "black box" approach to derivative asset pricing through equivalent martingale measures implies an assumption about risk premia related to this "jump risk." Merton (1976a) suggests considering that this risk is diversifiable and therefore not compensated for. Subsequent work (Jones (1984), and Naik and Lee (1990)) shows that Merton's option pricing formulae are still relevant under non-diversifiable jump risk and more general distributional assumptions provided we modify some parameters.

Therefore, the general methodology can be presented here through a particular example in the simplest case. Merton (1976a) states for instance that the option price at time t can be written as (see (9.19) in Merton (1990, p. 321))

$$\sum_{n=0}^{\infty} \frac{\exp(-\lambda'\tau)(\lambda'\tau)^n}{n!} BS(S_t, K, \sigma_n, r) \tag{10a}$$

$$\tau = T - t, \lambda' = \lambda(1 + k) \tag{10b}$$

$$\sigma_n^2 = \sigma^2 + \frac{n\delta^2}{\tau} \tag{10c}$$

$$r_n = r - \lambda k + \frac{n\gamma}{\tau}, \gamma = \log(1 + k). \tag{10d}$$

In other words, the option price is the following expectation of the BS price

$$\underset{N}{E} BS(S_t, K, \sigma_N, r_N), \tag{11}$$

where $\underset{N}{E}$ is the expectation operator over the probability distribution of a

Poisson variable N of parameter $\lambda' = \lambda(1 + k)$. Thus the heterogeneity factor is introduced *via* a randomization of the "interest rate" r and the "volatility parameter" σ.

At first sight, this extension of the BS option pricing model does not fall into the category (8); the Merton's option price is a deterministic function of the underlying asset price and we have not succeeded in introducing a non-degenerated error term u_t.[7]

Nevertheless, Merton (1979b) suggests a way to interpret his model as the addition of a random error term to a Black–Scholes price. He explains that "many practitioners who use the Black–Scholes option formula estimate the variance by using a relatively short length of past history (e.g., six months) and a short time between observations (e.g., daily) because they believe that the variance parameter does not remain constant over long periods of time." Indeed, they thus obtain a consistent[8] estimator of:

$$\sigma_n^2 \tau = \sigma^2 \tau + n\delta^2$$
$$= V^2 \tau + (n - \lambda\tau)\delta^2,$$

where $V^2 = \lambda\delta^2 + p^2$ is the total instantaneous variance of the returns and n is the number of jumps having occurred during the observation period.[9] Merton (1976b) is then correct to conclude that "if investors believe that the underlying process for the stock does not have jumps, then they may be led to the inference that the parameters of the process are not constant when indeed they are." In other words, the stochastic feature of the number n of jumps does *play the role* of a random error term: an investor who prices options by using the BS formula with σ_n as volatility parameter (where n fluctuates randomly among periods of observations) may consider the randomness due to n as an unobservable error term "around" a theoretical BS price.

It is important to keep in mind that this randomization does not necessarily admit a straightforward interpretation with respect to the data generating process. For instance, Merton (1976a) provides two other pricing formulae (see (9.16) p. 320 and (9.29) p. 326 in Merton (1990)) which show, in some cases, that *the same option pricing model* can be presented within the general framework (9) with *randomization of S_t* (for (9.16)) or *randomization of τ* (for (9.29)). Hence, the randomization may be purely conventional (a tool for modeling) and does not necessarily mimic a random feature of the real world. As far as we are concerned by the option pricing formula (11), σ_N *plays the role of a stochastic volatility process*, while for small k (indeed, Merton (1976a) stresses the particular case $k = 0$) the "implicit" stochastic interest rate r_N remains quite near to the constant true one r.

2 Hull and White (1987) was one of the first papers to propose an option pricing formula for a European call on a stock that has genuine stochastic volatility. Their paper focuses specifically on the case in which the stochastic volatility is dependent[10] of the stock price while more recent Fourier inversion techniques proposed by Heston (1993a) and Scott (1994) allow European option pricing even when there are non-zero volatility shock correlations with underlying asset and interest rate shocks. Since we focus here on the introduction of a latent state variable as an *heterogeneity factor*, no matter how it is interpreted, we do not care about such correlations, often attributed to the so-called "leverage effect" (see Black (1976)). Moreover, while the leverage effect is often used to explain some well-documented *skewness* in the *smile*, we suggest in section 4 below an easier way to capture this skewness effect.

A Hull–White type model is then defined by a stock price process whose *conditional* probability distribution, *given* a path (σ_t) of the volatility process, is the usual goemetric Brownian Motion

$$\frac{dS_t}{S_t} = \mu_t dt + \sigma_t dW_t$$

(with $\mu_t = r$ for an equivalent martingale measure), but where (σ_t) is itself a stochastic process independent from W.

Note that, thanks to that independence, the conditioning by a sample path of σ is fully taken into account by fixing σ_t at its deterministic value, without modifying the other probability distributions. This explains the Hull–White lemma (Hull and White (1987 p. 284)) stating that: "In a risk neutral world . . . let V_t^T be the mean variance over some time interval $[t, T]$ defined by

$$V_t^T = \frac{1}{T-t} \int_t^T \sigma^2(u)du$$

. . . the distribution of $\log \frac{S_T}{S_t}$ conditional upon V_t^T is normal with mean $r(T-t) - \frac{\bar{V}(T-t)}{2}$ and variance $\bar{V}(T-t)$." Following (7) with a two-stage computation of the expected value as $E[E(\,|\,V_t^T)]$, we are then able to conclude that the Hull–White (HW) option price is given by

$$\tilde{E}[BS(S_t, K, V_t^T)\,|\,I_t, \theta], \tag{12}$$

where expectation is taken over a risk–neutral probability distribution of V_t^T given I_t and some parameters θ which characterize this probability distribution. It should be noted that we always say "a" risk-neutral probability, since, due to the exogenous volatility risk, markets are incomplete and unicity of the equivalent martingale measure is not guaranteed. Nevertheless, if we assume that the volatility risk is not compensated, (12) is an expectation with respect to the true data generating process (DGP). Moreover, it is also worth noting that, if we are not ready to assume that the volatility risk is diversifiable (see Hull and White (1987) for some tentative justifications), one only has to specify a parametric model of risk premia to rewrite (12) as an expectation with respect to the DGP which may involve some other unknown parameters (required to characterize the risk premia).

Such risk premia may be characterized either via equilibrium models (Renault (1996, section 6)) or through price dynamics of another asset which completes the markets (see Eisenberg and Jarrow (1994)). The first approach may introduce some characteritistics of individual preferences while, in the second approach, these characteristics are "hidden" in market dynamics (see Heston (1993b)). In any case, inference methodologies, which are described in section 4 in the simplest case of a diversifiable volatility risk, can easily be extended to take into account well-specified risk premia. Inference is typically founded on the assumption that the bivariate continuous-time process (S_t, σ_t) is a diffusion process with a continuous sample path. In this case, the option price (12) is, for given K, t and T, as well-defined function $HW(S_t, \sigma_t, \theta)$ where θ is the vector of unknown parameters which characterizes the volatility dynamics. It depends on the actual value σ_t of the instantaneous volatility process since the expectation operator in (12) is defined by a risk-neutral conditional probability distribution of V_t^T given σ_t. Moreover, it is possible to show (see Bajeux and Rochet (1992), Renault and Touzi (1992)) that

$$\frac{\partial HW(S_t, \sigma_t, \theta)}{\partial \sigma_t} > 0. \tag{13}$$

Hence, the markets are completed as soon as one option is traded since the option price is a one-to-one function of the underlying volatility process. In this case the volatility process plays exactly the required role of *unobserved state variable*: unlike the BS model, the HW model is consistent with statistical inference as long as we observe only one option price at each date since $HW(S_t, \sigma_t, \theta)$ is no longer a deterministic function of the underlying asset price S_t.

3 To summarize, we want to stress here the following lesson of the two above extensions of the basic BS option pricing model: in such a non-linear statistic framework, a good way to specify errors terms is not to simply add mutually independent, zero mean, homoskedastic error terms to the basic

model $\hat{C}_t = m(x_t, \theta)$. On the other hand, Jacquier and Jarrow (1995) suggest a multiplicative error specifications

$$C_t = m(x_t, \theta)e^{u_t} \tag{14}$$

with $E(u_t \mid I_t, \theta) = 1$ for unbiasedness; the underlying idea is that homoskedasticity is more likely in relative terms rather than in absolute ones.

But the two above examples prove that *even unbiasedness is not a convenient restriction*.

Let us assume more generally that our model choice has neglected some heterogeneity factory that is some unobserved stochastic process λ_t, whose probability distribution should have been taken into account in the ·expectation operator (7). This factor of heterogeneity is hidden in seemingly constant parameters θ, so that if heterogeneity was observed the equilibrium price would be $m^*(x_t, \theta, \lambda_t)$. Thus, when unobserved heterogeneity is taken into account in the pricing formula (7), we obtain option prices

$$\begin{aligned}\tilde{E}\{\tilde{E}[e^{-r(T-t)}\max[0, S_T - K] \mid \lambda_t, I_t, \theta] \mid I_t, \theta\} \\= \tilde{E}[m^*(x_t, \theta, \lambda_t) \mid I_t, \theta].\end{aligned} \tag{15}$$

On the other hand, the approximate option pricing model provides option prices from the form

$$m(x_t, \theta) = m^*(x_t, \theta, \bar{\lambda}_t(x_t, \theta)), \tag{16}$$

where λ_t is replaced by a deterministic function for x_t, for instance[11]

$$\bar{\lambda}_t(x_t, \theta) = E[\lambda_t \mid I_t, \theta]. \tag{17}$$

So, even if the heterogeneity risk is not compensated so that it has the same probability distribution for the data generating process (DGP) and the equivalent martingale measure

$$E[\lambda_t \mid I_t, \theta] = \tilde{E}[\lambda_t \mid I_t, \theta]$$

the approximate model will be biased in general if the complete pricing formula $m^*(x_t, \theta, \lambda_t)$ *does not depend linearly* on the heterogeneity factor. Merton (1976a and b) and Hull and White (1987) are excellent examples of such an approach, since they introduce the heterogeneity factor (namely the volatility risk) upstream in the risk-neutral model of the dynamics of the underlying asset price. Even though they were not presented in such a way in the finance literature, they belong to a long tradition in econometrics, that is the introduction of *neglected heterogeneity*, through the existence of an unobservable random characteristic. For instance, Hausman, Hall, and Griliches (1984) interpret the Poisson model for count data as an approximation of a more sophisticated model which could account for the unobserved individual heterogeneity. This approximation is not able to capture the well-documented "overdispersion" of count data; this high-lights once more that the introduction of neglected heterogeneity into a non-linear econometric model does not lead in general to an "unbiased" model (see, e.g., Fourgeaud, Gouriéroux, and Pradel (1990) about hetero-geneity biases). Such heterogeneity biases are well-documented empirical evidence when observing cross-sectional sets of option prices written on the same asset; as will be proved in section 4 this is nothing but the so-called smile effect.

2.3 Panel structure of option pricing errors and extended models

2.3.1 Transversal versus longitudinal modeling

Following Rubinstein (1985), a useful approach to examining the cross-sectional pricing errors of the BS model is to compute, for a cross-section $\Pi_{jt}, j = 1, 2, \ldots, J$ of option prices (at time t) written on the same asset, BS implicit volatilities σ_{jt}^{imp} defined by

$$\Pi_{jt} = BS(S_t, K_{jt}, \sigma_{jt}^{imp}) \tag{18}$$

and to look for typical patterns of these implicit volatilities across different strike prices and maturities (corresponding to the J possible values of index j). Let us first notice that stochastic volatility models of the type studied above, that postulates $\Pi_{jt} = \tilde{E}[BS(S_t, K_{jt}, \tilde{\sigma}) \mid I_t, \theta]$ may explain how σ_{jt}^{imp} depends on a stochastic process σ_t. For instance, the HW model which implies that $\Pi_{jt} = HW(S_t, \sigma_t, \theta)$ is a one-to-one function of the underlying volatility process σ_t, leads to a parametric specification for BS implicit volatilities

$$\sigma_{jt}^{imp} = f(S_t, \sigma_t, \theta).$$

Once more, in order to be consistent with any statistical approach with transversal data ($J > 1$) such a specification must be completed by an error term

$$\sigma_{jt}^{imp} = f(S_t, \sigma_t, \theta) + \eta_{jt}. \tag{19}$$

As far as econometric methodology is concerned, this suggests some panel data techniques in order to identify individual/temporal effects on biases, heteroskedasticity, and autocorrelation of error terms. This panel data methodology is implicit in the current practices to aggregate the information from different options into a single volatility assessment. Indeed, most methods involve weighting schemes that ought to be rationalized through a prediction strategy: when we have to choose a prediction function $BS(\cdot, K, \sigma)$ (see section 2.1), it might be convenient to "calibrate" the volatility parameter σ as a weighted average of observed implicit volatilities

$$\sum_{j=1}^{J} a_{jt}\sigma_{jt}^{imp} = f(S_t, \sigma_t, \theta) + \sum_{j=1}^{J} a_{jt}\eta_{jt}. \qquad (20)$$

Such weighting schemes are well summarized in a recent very comprehensive survey by Bates (1995a):

"Most ... assign equal weight to in- and out-of-the-money options, and most give heavier weight to near-the-money options." "Engle and Mustafa (1992) and Bates (1995b) propose a non-linear generalized least squares methodology that allows the appropriate weights to be determined endogenously by the data."

But these empirical strategies suffer from two main shortcomings:

First, as noticed by Melino (1994) among others, "taken literally, the implicit estimation strategy is fraught with internal inconsistencies." To complete Melino's statement, "there should be considerable unease about a procedure that uses the assumption that volatility is constant" to derive a prediction function $BS(\cdot, K, \sigma)$ and to produce estimates of volatility that often change significantly in both transversal (index j) and temporal (index t) dimensions. We may nevertheless admit that a prediction function BS-shaped provides a quick-pricing strategy in so far as σ is suitably calibrated. Even though there are no genuine theoretical foundations for such a practice (see however a discussion in 2.3.2. below), some recent works about non-parametric fitting of BS implicit volatilities (see Renault (1996 subsection 6.2)) would tend to confirm that $BS(\cdot, K, \sigma)$ may be a relatively accurate prediction function when σ is estimated as a non-parametric function of a given set of state variables. But it is important to keep in mind that this is only "*objective driven inference*": in so far as we know that the BS option pricing model is misspecified, the best calibrated σ for pricing does not coincide either with the best calibrated σ for hedging or with any pseudo-true value in a statistical sense (quasi-likelihood for instance). Moreover, this non-parametric objective driven inference provides *no underpinning for linear aggregation schemes* like (20).

Second, if we look for theoretical foundations for a linear aggregation scheme like (2), we may find it in the Clément, Gouriéroux, and Monfort (1993) approach of randomization of the pricing probability measure (see also Renault (1996)). Indeed, if we consider that this pricing measure is a latent random variable whose generating process is well specified by a statistical model "around" the BS pricing measure, we should obtain a set of pricing errors u_{jt} or equivalently, in a volatility terms η_{jt}, whose variances and mutual covariances depend in a well-defined (non-linear) way on strike prices, maturities. But, in this case, the weights a_{jt} used for prediction have to be chosen in an optimal way: a_{jt} inversely related to the variance of η_{jt} (in the simplest case of zero covariances) and more generally several alternative forecasting procedures (defined by several choices of weights a_{jt}) must be compared by their expected costs (and the best one chosen), *according to our model* of option pricing errors. In this respect, there is no rationale to consider the wide range of procedures suggested in the empirical literature and summarized by Bates (1995a).

2.3.2   Extended models

The fact that the Black–Scholes formula is preference-free is often perceived as its main advantage. In reality, the argument is hard to understand if one considers that practitioners habitually infer implicit parameters from option prices, whatever their theoretical interpretation. As stressed above, implicit volatilities serve as a useful unit of measure on option markets even though internal consistency prohibits one from interpreting it as a *BS* volatility parameter. As far as we are concerned with units of measure, irrespective of any economic interpretation, it is not forbidden to consider some risk-aversion index or an intertemporal elasticity of substitution as useful parameters for option pricing.

This last remark leaves the door open to make an equilibrium-based approach for option pricing attractive to practitioners as no-arbitrage valuation models. Moreover the pricing of options in an equilibrium setting is important in at least two respects.

First, there is evidence that the volatility of stock prices is not only stochastic but also highly correlated with the volatility of the market as a whole. This makes highly debatable the usual no-arbitrage approach for option pricing that leads us to assume, for sake of tractability, that the volatility risk (see Hull and White (1987)) or the interest-rate risk (see Turnbull and Milne (1991)) has either a zero price (because it is non-systematic) or an *ad hoc* functional form of risk premium.

Second, the no-arbitrage models make strong assumptions about market completeness in two respects. On the one hand, as Kallsen and Taqqu (1994) among others have remarked, "for a discrete time market consisting of only two securities (stock and bond) to be complete, it is necessary, roughly speaking, that over any single time period the stock price has at most two possible values to move to," which prevents one from using GARCH-type models, which are, however, the most popular statistical tools to filter stochastic volatility in discrete time. On the other hand, as already reported from Bates (1995a), "even minuscule transaction costs vitiate the continuous-time no-arbitrage argument."

This is the reason why, following Naik and Lee (1990), Amin and Ng (1993), and Garcia and Renault (1995), we propose in Renault (1996) an equilibrium model of option pricing which provides appropriate pricing of systematic volatility and interest risk. The statistical setting for this equilibrium model is presented like a stochastic volatility model in discrete time but it could be easily associated with a stochastic volatility model in continuous time (see, e.g., Ghysels, Harvey, and Renault (1995 section 4.1)). Indeed, we provide that the asset price dynamics we derive in this general equilibrium setting are something like a necessary and sufficient condition for the desirable homogeneity property of option pricing formulae set forth in section 3.

The qualifying *"Extended models"* is then justified because we are able to show that the derived option pricing formula entails as special cases the formula derived by Amin and Ng (1993) and *a fortiori* all the other pricing formulae that were nested in the latter. When the stochastic processes associated with consumption growth and dividend growth are predictable, the pricing formula is independent of the preference parameters, but this property is lost when the processes are unpredictable. In the Amin and Ng (1993) terminology, predictability is akin to the opposite of the leverage effect documented in Black (1976). There are then two cases to distinguish:

> Either, predictability (that is no leverage effect) is a maintained assumption, and then we are allowed to use the preference-free option pricing formulae of the BS or HW type.
> Or, it is not the case (according to a well-documented evidence for stock prices) and these option pricing models have to be *extended* to involve some preference parameters like risk aversion, intertemporal elasticity of substitution, and some new state variables, like consumption growth or market return. Moreover, it is worthwhile to notice that these extended option pricing models provide some economic foundations to option pricing formulae that have a shape globally similar to the BS formula, but with some well-

defined differences through new parameters and new state variables. This is the reason why it might be argued that these models provide some underpinnings to the more descriptive approach like non-parametric fitting of BS implicit volatility against some state variables, as recently proposed by Gouriéroux, Monfort, and Tenreiro (1994, 1995), Ait-Sahalia, Bickel, and Stoker (1995) and Bossaerts and Hillion (1994). Indeed, insofar as, roughly speaking, a BS-shaped prediction function $BS(\cdot, K, \sigma)$ appears to be derived from more general option pricing models, a natural attempt to extend the BS model is to look for variables which have a good predictive content of the biases inherent in the BS procedures for pricing and/or hedging. We are then led to consider (see Renault (1996)) *"functional residual plots"* (Gouriéroux, Monfort, and Tenreiro) and *"Goodness-of-Fit Tests for Regression Using Kernel Methods"* (Ait-Sahalia, Bickel, and Stoker) to fit the observed smile against natural explanatory variables. Once more, an usual econometric practice is well suited for the analysis of option pricing errors.

3 THE IMPACT ON OPTION PRICING OF VARIOUS SPECIFICATIONS OF THE UNDERLYING ASSET PRICE DYNAMICS

In this section, we will propose a desirable homogeneity property that alternatives to the Black–Scholes option pricing model should obey both for pricing and hedging purposes. This homogeneity property can be characterized in terms of causality in the Granger sense. This characterization will be used in the remainder of the chapter.

3.1 A desirable homogeneity property for alternatives to the Black–Scholes option pricing model

The dominance of the BS model is reflected in the fact that the *implicit volatility* becomes the standard method of quoting option prices. Similarly to yields on the bond market, implicit volatilies serve as a useful units of measure on option markets. The usefulness of this unit of measure comes from the fact that it does not depend on the stock price level, in other words, that the implicit volatility function is homogenous of degree zero with respect to the pair (S, K) where S is the price of the underlying asset and K is the strike price. It should be emphasized, however, that this homogeneity property holds if and only if the market option pricing formula[12] itself is homogeneous of degree one with respect to the same pair (S, K). This is the case of course of the Black–Scholes formula itself. Therefore, any option pricing formula that features this homogeneity property should be of interest to practitioners, be it based on preferences or not. Let us first notice the equivalence between the homogeneity of degree zero of the implicit volatility function and the homogeneity of degree one of the option pricing formula. To show this, let us note that any observed European call option price π_t, for a given maturity T, can be written as

$$\pi_t = BS(S_t, K, \sigma_t(S_t, K)), \tag{21}$$

where $\sigma_t(S_t, K)$ is the BS implicit volatility parameter.

Let us consider now an option pricing model whereby the option price is an homogeneous function of degree one (*ceteris paribus*) of the pair (S_t, K). Then, for every positive scalar λ

$$\lambda\pi_t = BS(\lambda S_t, \lambda K, \sigma_t(\lambda S_t, \lambda K)).$$

But, since the Black–Scholes option pricing formula itself is a homogeneous function of degree one with respect to (S_t, K), we also have

$$BS(\lambda S_t, \lambda K, \sigma_t(S_t, K)) = \lambda BS(S_t, K, \sigma(S_t, K)) = \lambda\pi_t.$$

By identification of these two expressions of $\lambda\pi_t$, we have, thanks to the unicity of the BS, implicit volatility

$$\sigma_t(\lambda S_t, \lambda K) = \sigma_t(S_t, K)$$

which establishes the announced results. This homogeneity property is important in several respects.

(i) First, it helps to interpret option quotations since practitioners are interested primarily in the percentage $x_t = \log\dfrac{S_t}{KB(t,T)}$ of the in-the-moneyness or out-of-the-moneyness of the options.[13] Indeed, the homogeneity property ensures that BS implicit volatility depends on (S_t, K) only through x_t.

(ii) Secondly, for hedging purposes, we are interested in the so-called Δ ratio

$$\Delta_t = \frac{\partial\pi_t}{\partial S_t} = \frac{\partial BS}{\partial S}(S_t, K, \sigma_t(S_t, K))$$

$$+ \frac{\partial BS}{\partial\sigma}(S_t, K, \sigma_t(S_t, K))\frac{\partial\sigma_t}{\partial S}(S_t, K) \tag{22}$$

By the Euler characterization of the homogeneity property, we also have

$$S_t \frac{\partial \sigma_t}{\partial S}(S_t, K) + K \frac{\partial \sigma_t}{\partial K}(S_t, K) = 0 \qquad (23)$$

so that

$$\Delta_t = \frac{\partial \pi_t}{\partial S_t} = \frac{\partial BS}{\partial S}(.) - \frac{\partial BS}{\partial \sigma}(.) \frac{K}{S_t} \frac{\partial \sigma_t}{\partial K}(.). \qquad (24)$$

Since $\frac{\partial BS}{\partial \sigma}(.) > 0$, equation (24) shows that the two expressions $\Delta_t - \frac{\partial BS}{\partial S}(S_t, K, \sigma_t(S_t, K))$ and $\frac{\partial \sigma_t}{\partial K}(.)$ are of opposite signs. This provides a useful relationship since the first expression measures the hedging error due to the misspecification of the BS option pricing model used to infer the implicit volatility and the second expression is the so-called "smile effect" which characterizes the variations of BS implicit volatility σ_t as a function of the strike price K.

(iii) Thirdly, Merton (1973) has stressed that the above homogeneity property ensures that the option price is *convex* with respect to the underlying asset price (since it is obviously always convex w.r.t the strike price). Merton (1973) noticed that "although convexity is usually assumed to be a property which always holds for warrants," "*perverse local concavity*" may occur if we do not ensure homogeneity (see section 3.2 below for a characterization of the homogeneity property which extends Merton's sufficient condition). Indeed, convexity w.r.t S is not only "natural" (as opposed to "perverse") but corresponds to the nowadays empirical evidence of the destabilizing effect of portfolio insurance strategies (since the Δ ratio is an increasing function of the underlying asset price).

3.2   A characterization of homogeneity in terms of causality

According to the "black box" approach to derivative asset pricing, we consider a pricing probability measure Q_t under which the price π_t at time t of any contingent claim is the discounted expectation of its terminal payoff. In the case of a European call option, it is given by the following dynamic version of (7).

$$\pi_t = B(t, T)\tilde{E}_t(S_T - K)^+,$$

where $\tilde{E}_t$ denotes the expectation operator with respect to Q_t. Of course, Q_t

is generally different from the data generating process P_t of S_T given I_t, the available information at time t.

We will first call a well-known proposition (see, e.g., Huang and Litzenberger (1988, p. 140)) that establishes a fundamental bijective relationship between an option pricing function $\pi_t(.)$ as a function of the strike price K and the pricing probability measure $Q_t(.)$.

Proposition 1: The pricing function $\pi_t(.)$ and the pricing probability measure $Q_t(.)$ are linked by the following bijective relationship (for a given S_t)

$$Q_t(.) \rightarrow \pi_t(K) = B(t, T)\tilde{E}_t[(S_T - K)^+]$$

$$\pi_t(.) \rightarrow Q_t\left[\frac{S_T}{S_t} \geq k\right] = -\frac{1}{B(t, T)}\frac{\partial \pi_t}{\partial K}(S_t, K) \text{ where } k = \frac{K}{S_t}.$$

Of course, S_t is known at time t and the pricing probability measure Q_t describes equivalently the probability distribution of the future asset price S_T or of the return $\frac{S_T}{S_t}$. Proposition 1 shows how this probability measure, as the probability distribution of the return, is characterized by its cumulative distribution function. This characterization appears all the more useful when one realizes that the previous homogeneity property can be expressed as a simple condition about the pricing probability measure.

Proposition 2: The option pricing function $\pi_t(.)$ is homogeneous of degree one with respect to (S_t, K) if and only if the pricing probability measure Q_t does not depend on S_t.

A proof is provided in Garcia and Renault (1995). To understand proposition 2, it may help to see Q_t as the conditional probability distribution of a process of interest defined on a probability space (Ω, a, Q) given the available information I_t at time t. Whereas Merton (1973) showed that serial independence of asset returns is a sufficient condition for homogeneity, proposition 2 establishes that a necessary and sufficient condition for homogeneity is the conditional independence (under Q) between future returns and the current price, given the currently available information (other than the history of the underlying asset price).[14]

$$\frac{S_T}{S_t} \perp^Q S_t \mid I_t - S. \tag{25}$$

It should be stressed that conditional independence neither implies nor is implied by marginal independence. Roughly speaking, the property (25) must be understood as a non-causality relationship in the Granger sense between the current price and future returns (for a given informational setting) and not as independence property.

To see the full generality of condition (25), we will illustrate it in the modern finance framework where asset prices evolve as diffusion processes:

$$\frac{dS_t}{S_t} = r(t)dt + \sigma(t)dW^s(t), \tag{26}$$

where $W^s(t)$ is a standard Wiener process under Q, and $r(t)$ and $\sigma(t)$ are the two state variables of interest: $\sigma(t)$ is the instantaneous volatility process and $r(t)$ can be seen as an instantaneous interest rate process, since, under Q, the risk is not compensated.[15] In this framework, we can assume without loss of generality that available information at time t is described by the σ-field

$$I_t = \sigma[r(\tau), \sigma(\tau), W^s(\tau), \tau \le t]. \tag{27}$$

In this framework, we will make specific which assumptions are needed to ensure property (25) of Granger non-causality. This will help us later on to define our structural statistical model of price options in an equilibrium setting.

We therefore prove in Garcia and Renault (1995) the following proposition.

Proposition 3: A sufficient condition for Granger non-causality from S_t to future returns $\frac{S_T}{S_t} T > t$ (relation 25) is ensured by the conjunction of the following assumptions.

A1: $(\sigma(\tau), r(\tau))_{\tau > t} \perp^Q (S_\tau)_{\tau \le t} \mid r(\tau), \sigma(\tau), \tau \le t$

A2: $(dW^s(\tau))_{\tau > t} \perp^Q (S_\tau)_{\tau \le t} \mid r(.), \sigma(.)$

where $r(.)$ and $\sigma(.)$ refer to the whole sample path of the processes r and σ.

Assumption A1 states that the price process S does not "*strongly globally cause*" the state variables process (r, σ) (see Comte and Renault (1996) and Florens and Fougère (1996) for a review of non-causality properties in continuous time). Assumption A1 is quite natural in the context of state variables which are usually seen as being exogenous. This exogeneity assumption is however less restrictive than independence, that is r and σ are not necessarily independent of W^s, in order to allow the presence of leverage effects. As a matter of fact, if r and σ were independent of W^s, A2 would be automatically satisfied by the recursive property of conditional independence

$$X \perp (Y, Z) \Rightarrow X \perp Y \mid Z$$

which could be applied in this case to: $X = ((dW^s(\tau))_{\tau > t};$ $Y = (S_\tau)_{\tau \le t}; Z = r(.), \sigma(.).$

On the contrary, in the general case where (r, σ) and W^s are correlated, the conditional independence A2 is not implied by the well-known marginal independence

$$(dW^s(\tau))_{\tau > t} \perp (S_\tau)_{\tau \le t}.$$

To illustrate the empirical content of assumptions A1 and A2, we can characterize them in the framework of a Markovian process (S, r, σ) defined by the diffusion equations[16]

$$\frac{dS_t}{S_t} = r(t)dt + \sigma(t)dW^s(t)$$

$$dr(t) = \alpha(t)dt + \beta(t)dW^r(t)$$
$$d\sigma(t) = \gamma(t)dt + \delta(t)dW^\sigma(t)$$

$$\mathrm{Var}\begin{bmatrix} dW^s(t) \\ dW^r(t) \\ dW^\sigma(t) \end{bmatrix} = \begin{bmatrix} 1 & \rho_{sr}(t) & \rho_{s\sigma}(t) \\ \rho_{sr}(t) & 1 & \rho_{r\sigma}(t) \\ \rho_{s\sigma}(t) & \rho_{r\sigma}(t) & 1 \end{bmatrix} dt, \tag{28}$$

where $\alpha(t)$, $\beta(t)$, $\gamma(t)$, $\delta(t)$, $\rho_{sr}(t)$, $\rho_{s\sigma}(t)$, $\rho_{r\sigma}(t)$ are I_t – adapted stochastic processes.[17]

We can then establish the following proposition.

Proposition 4:

    (i) *Assumption (A1) is implied by the following assumption (A1)'.*
    (A1)' *The processes α, β, γ, δ, and $\rho_{r\sigma}$ are deterministic functions of the processes r and σ*

$$\alpha(t) = \alpha[r(t), \sigma(t)]$$
$$\beta(t) = \beta[r(t), \sigma(t)]$$
$$\gamma(t) = \gamma[r(t), \sigma(t)]$$
$$\delta(t) = \delta[r(t), \sigma(t)]$$
$$\rho_{r\sigma}(t) = \rho_{r\sigma}[r(t), \sigma(t)].$$

    (ii) *If assumption (A1)' holds, Assumption (A2) is implied by the following assumption (A2)':*
    (A2)' *The processes ρ_{sr} and $\rho_{s\sigma}$ are deterministic functions of the processes r and σ.*

$$\rho_{sr}(t) = \rho_{sr}[r(t), \sigma(t)]$$
$$\rho_{s\sigma}(t) = \rho_{s\sigma}[r(t), \sigma(t)].$$

In other words, leverage effects $(\rho_{s\rho} \ne 0)$ and cross-correlations between the stock price and the interest rate $(\rho_{sr} \ne 0)$ are allowed provided that they do not depend on the level of the stock price. More generally, propositions 2, 3, and 4 prove that a sufficient (and almost necessary)[18] condition for the fundamental homogeneity property of option prices is that the underlying asset price process is of the "stochastic volatility" type, i.e., it obeys the assumed non-causality relationship from the price process S to the state variables σ and r.

At first sight, this framework seems to differ fundamentally from the endogenous volatility paradigm where the volatility process $\sigma(t)$ is viewed as a deterministic function of S_t. However these endogenous volatility models, also called "implied tree models" by Duffie (1992), have regained some popularity recently (See Dupire (1994), Hobson and Rogers (1994), and Rubinstein (1994)); moreover they seem to be more conformable to usual discrete-time statistical models like ARCH-type models. This is the ostensible conflict between two paradigms but the truth is quite different for several reasons.

Firstly, Nelson (1990) has shown that the distinction between "stochastic volatility" (where the source of randomness in the underlying asset volatility is exogenous) and endogenous volatility is not robust to temporal aggregation. ARCH-type discrete-time models may converge towards stochastic volatility models in continuous time as the time interval goes to zero. Therefore, ARCH-type models and SV models are not competitors (as it was commonly believed) but rather complements, since the ARCH model offers a useful discrete-time filter for SV models, Secondly, as explained by Rubinstein (1994), implied tree models are usually good for pricing options but not for hedging. Among the four categories of violations to the constant volatility Black–Scholes model that he refers to, only the less serious one, whereby the local volatility of the underlying asset is a function of the concurrent underlying asset price, allows for a computationally effective way to price as well as to hedge options. More serious violations, like the dependence on past asset prices and *a fortiori* on exogenous state variables, invalidate the methodology for hedging purposes. Thirdly, it is worthwhile noticing that, strictly speaking, the endogenous volatility paradigm is not excluded by the proposition 4: a correlation process $\rho_{s\sigma}(t)$ always equal to 1 is not inconsistent with (A2)'. But this case is indeed a degenerate limit one: there is a one-to-one mapping between the two filtrations $[\sigma(\tau), \tau \le t]$ and $[S(\tau), \tau \le t]$ so that:

First, the non-causality assumption (A1) is fulfilled in a degenerate way.
Secondly, as noticed by Kallsen and Taqqu (1994) in the context of Δ-hedging with a GARCH underlying asset price, there is in this case an ambiguity about the extent to which the option price

is a function of the underlying asset price (depending on whether volatility is considered an independent variable or not). Therefore, the homogeneity property itself becomes ambiguous. However, as a result of Kallsen and Taqqu's (1994) analysis, the correct way to compute the Δ ratio in this case is to consider that the option price depends on the level of the underlying asset price *including* through volatility, so that the homogeneity property is lost (see Garcia and Renault (1996) for more details). Moreover, the counter-example provided by Merton (1973) "where the distribution of future returns in the common stock is sufficiently dependent on the level of the stock price to cause perverse local concavity" and thus non-homogeneity is precisely of the ARCH type. This is the reason why the exogenous volatility paradigm will be preferred hereafter.

4   SMILE, SKEWNESS AND APPROXIMATE LIKELIHOOD INFERENCE USING OPTION PRICES DATA

4.1   The smile as an heterogeneity bias

Equations (11) and (12) have proposed an interpretation of respectively Merton (1976a and b) and Hull and White (1987) as models for *parameter heterogeneity* in the Black and Scholes model: The option price Π_t at time t is the conditional expectation, given I_t, of the Black–Scholes price $BS(S_t, K, \tilde{\sigma})$ where the expectation operator is considered with respect to a *fictitious probability distribution* whose only function is to characterize the unobserved *heterogeneity* distribution of the volatility parameter σ; this probability distribution does not necessarily coincide either with the data generating process or with the equivalent martingale measure as it can be seen in some of Merton's examples.[19] This hypothesis, according to which *observed* option prices are well-specified expectation of Black–Scholes prices over an heterogeneity distribution of the volatility parameter, is maintained throughout section 4. It offers two types of advantages:

First, it preserves some fundamental properties of the Black–Scholes formula, namely the *homogeneity* property already stressed in section 3 and also a useful *symmetry* property.

On the other hand, it allows to use a Jensen's convexity inequality in order to characterize the shape of the smile. Its relaxation is considered in Renault (1996, section 6).

4.1.1 Homogeneity and symmetry

The maintained hypothesis

$$\Pi_t(S_t, K) = \tilde{E}_t[BS(S_t, K, \tilde{\sigma})] \tag{29}$$

implies of course that the option price is, as for the Black–Scholes option pricing formula itself, an homogeneous function of degree one (*ceteris paribus*) of the pair (S_t, K). Therefore, the associated BS implicit volatility $\sigma_t(S_t, K)$ is an homogeneous function of degree zero which depends on (S_t, K) only through the moneyness x_t of the option.

Thus with a slight change of notation the BS implicit volatility parameter $\sigma_t(x_t)$ is defined as the solution of

$$BS(x_t, \sigma_t(x_t)) = \tilde{E}_t[BS(x_t, \tilde{\sigma})] \text{ with } x_t = \log \frac{S_t}{KB(t, T)}. \tag{30}$$

Moreover, we know from (24) that the sign of the Δ-hedging error due to the misspecification of the BS option pricing model is determined by the sign of the derivative of the BS implicit volatility as a function of K (or of x_t, for fixed S_t)

$$\frac{\partial \sigma_t}{\partial x_t}(x_t) \text{ has the same sign as } \Delta_t(x_t) - \Delta_t^{BS}(\sigma_t(x_t)), \tag{31}$$

where $\Delta_t(x_t) = \dfrac{\partial \Pi_t}{\partial S_t}(S_t, K)$ is the correct Δ ratio, while

$$\Delta^{BS}(\sigma_t(x_t)) = \frac{\partial BS}{\partial S_t}(S_t, K, \sigma_t(x_t))$$

is the misspecified one.[20] As far as the sign of $\dfrac{\partial \sigma_t}{\partial x_t}(x_t)$ is concerned, one just has to characterize it for negative x_t since we can show that for any x_t

$$\sigma_t(x_t) = \sigma_t(-x_t). \tag{32}$$

Equation (32) is a fundamental symmetry property of a smile which makes equal the BS implicit volatilities[21] of two call options *whose strikes are chosen so that their geometric mean is the current forward price*.[22] It was already derived by Renault and Touzi (1992) in an Hull and White (1987) setting by an argument easy to generalize in the general setting (29) since it mainly uses the symmetry of the Gaussian probability distribution

$$(\Phi(u) = 1 - \Phi(-u)).$$

4.1.2   Convexity

The well-known formula to compute the hedge ratio Δ^{BS} in the Black and Scholes setting

$$\Delta^{BS}(x_t, \sigma_t(x_t)) = \frac{\partial BS}{\partial S_t}(S_t, K, \sigma_t(x_t)) = \Phi\left(\frac{x_t}{\sigma\sqrt{\tau}} + \frac{\sigma\sqrt{\tau}}{2}\right) \qquad (33)$$

can be easily extended to the general option pricing (29) by a simple differentiation under the expectation operator (assuming usual regularity conditions for application of Lebesgue's theorem)

$$\Delta_t(x_t) = \frac{\partial \pi_t}{\partial S_t}(S_t, K) = \tilde{E}_t \frac{\partial BS}{\partial S_t}(S_t, K, \tilde{\sigma})$$

$$= \tilde{E}_t \Phi\left(\frac{x_t}{\tilde{\sigma}\sqrt{\tau}} + \frac{\tilde{\sigma}\sqrt{\tau}}{2}\right)$$

$$= \tilde{E}_t \Delta^{BS}(x_t, \tilde{\sigma}). \qquad (34)$$

The hedging error issue, i.e., the issue of the difference between $\Delta_t(x_t) = \tilde{E}_t \Delta^{BS}(x_t, \tilde{\sigma})$ and $\Delta^{BS}(x_t, \sigma_t(x_t))$, where

$$BS(x_t, \sigma_t(x_t)) = \tilde{E}_t BS(x_t, \tilde{\sigma})$$

is then clearly a convexity issue about the parametrized curve

$$\sigma \rightarrow \begin{cases} BS(x, \sigma) \\ \Delta^{BS}(x, \sigma) \end{cases} \qquad (35)$$

for given x. Let us note that this parametric representation is well defined for given $x \leq 0$ since

$$\sigma \rightarrow BS(x, \sigma) \text{ is strictly increasing for any } x,$$
$$\sigma \rightarrow \Delta^{BS}(x, \sigma) \text{ is strictly increasing for any } x \leq 0.$$

Indeed

$$\frac{\partial BS}{\partial \sigma}(x_t, \sigma) = S_t \phi(d_1(x_t, \sigma))\sqrt{\tau}$$

$$\frac{\partial \Delta^{BS}}{\partial \sigma}(x_t, \sigma) = \phi(d_1(x_t, \sigma))\frac{\partial d_1(x_t, \sigma)}{\partial \sigma},$$

where

$$d_1(x_t, \sigma) = \frac{x_t}{\sigma\sqrt{\tau}} + \frac{\sigma\sqrt{\tau}}{2} \text{ and } \phi = \Phi'$$

is the density function of the standard normal probability distribution.

Hence, for $x_t < 0$ (resp. $x_t 0$), $\frac{\partial d_1}{\partial \sigma}(x_t, \sigma)$ is a positive decreasing (resp.

constant) function of σ. In other words, the parametric curve (35) is strictly concave for $x_t < 0$ (resp. affine for $x_t = 0$), which implies, thanks to the Jensen's inequality

$$\tilde{E}_t[\Delta^{BS}(BS)] \leq \Delta^{BS}[\tilde{E}_t(BS)]$$

that is

$$\Delta_t(x_t) \leq \Delta^{BS}(x_t, \sigma_t(x_t))$$

for $x_t \leq 0$, with a strict inequality if $x_t < 0$ and the probability distribution of $\tilde{\sigma}$ (the heterogeneity distribution) is not degenerated. We are then able to conclude from (31) and (32):

Proposition 5:[23]
If call prices are given by (29), the BS implicit volatility, as function of the strike is increasing (resp. decreasing) for out-of-the money (resp. in-the-money) options:

$$\frac{\partial \sigma_t(x_t)}{\partial K} > 0 \text{ if } x_t < 0,$$

$$\frac{\partial \sigma_t(x_t)}{\partial K} < 0 \text{ if } x_t > 0,$$

$$\frac{\partial \sigma_t(x_t)}{\partial K} = 0 \text{ if } x_t = 0.$$

Moreover, this U-shaped pattern (the so-called smile phenomenon) is symmetric as a function of the log-strike price K.

In terms of hedging, the above proposition claims that:

(i) For an *in-the-money* option, the use of the BS implicit volatility leads to an *underhedged position* in the sense that:

$$\Delta^{BS}(x_t, \sigma_t(x_t)) < \Delta_t) \text{ if } x_t > 0.$$

(ii) For an *out-of-the-money* option, the use of the BS implicit volatility leads to an *overhedged* position.

(iii) For an *at-the-money* option, the use of the BS implicit volatility leads to a correct Δ-ratio.

These errors of hedging (and the related smile) can be interpreted as *heterogeneity biases.*

By neglecting the heterogeneity distribution of the volatility parameter, non-linear aggregates as hedge ratios are biased. Some convenient statistical procedures which take into account this heterogeneity distribution are described in the following subsection.

4.2   A general class of estimation problems

4.2.1   The smile revisited: a statistical point of view

In practice, the smile is usually defined as the plot of $\sigma_t(x)$ against x. Such a definition implicitly assumes the existence of a proper function $x \to \sigma_t(x) = \sigma_t(x)$ which would be deterministic and time-invariant. However this assumption is inconsistent with any statistical approach. For instance using a dataset of option prices, one gets, for a same degree of moneyness at various dates, different values of the Black–Scholes implicit volatility. This is the so-called term structure of implicit volatilities (see, e.g., Bates (1995a), Heynen, Kemna, and Vorst (1994)). If we do not want to question the stationarity of the returns, the only way to capture the time variability of the function $\sigma_t(\cdot)$ is to introduce one or several sources of heterogeneity. The random (eventually stationary) variations of one heterogeneity process ω_t are sufficient to explain one term structure. As an example, the Hull and White stochastic volatility model (see section 2) is often used to explain the term structure of at-the-money $(x = 0)$ BS implicit volatilities by considering $\omega_t = \sigma_t$ the instantaneous stochastic volatility process. More generally, if we introduce a vector ζ_t of J sources of randomness, provided that at each date we do not observe more than J option prices (written on the same asset), we shall avoid any logical inconsistency between observed term structures and our option pricing model. Since the pricing model will generally provide the relation between state variables and observed prices through a known function indexed by d unknown parameters $\theta \in \Theta \subset \mathbb{R}^d$, (30) may be rewritten as[24]

$$\pi(x_{jt}, \zeta_t, \theta^\circ) = \widetilde{BS}\,(x_{jt}, \sigma_I(x_{jt}, \zeta_t, \theta^\circ)), j = 1, 2, \ldots, J, \tag{36}$$

where J is the dimension of the unobservable state process $(\zeta_t)_{t \geq 0}$ (J coincides with the number of observed synchronous option prices which we assume to be time invariant), π and σ_I are deterministic time-invariant functions and θ° is the true unknown value of the parameters. Then model (36) leads to the so-called *empirical martingale model* introduced by Christensen (1992) but, while Christensen has introduced it in terms of option prices, we prefer here to characterize it in terms of BS implicit volatilities which are more familiar for using options in practice.

Therefore, in our framework, a convenient statistical methodology has to perform inference about $\pi(\cdot, \cdot, \theta^0)$ (more precisely about θ^0) using a "data set" $(S_{t_i}, (\sigma_{I,t_i}(x_{jt_i}))_{1 \leq j \leq J})$, $i = 1, 2, \ldots, n$ associated with the observation times $t_1 < t_2 < \ldots < t_n$. Indeed, taking into account the dynamic feature of the model, we will always consider a conditional distribution of $(S_{t_i}, (\sigma_{I,t_i}(x_{jt_i}))_{1 \leq j \leq J})$, $i = 1, 2, \ldots, n$ given an initial value observed at time $t_0 < t_1$.

4.2.2   The empirical martingale model

Following Christensen (1992) we build a non-linear state-space model as a statistical rewriting of the option pricing model (36) based on the underlying dynamics of the state process (ζ_t, z_t), where ζ_t is unobserved and z_t is observed. The equations of our model are:

(i) The measurement equation is the option pricing equation in terms of implicit volatilities

$$\sigma_{I,t}(x_{jt}) = \sigma_I(x_{jt}, \zeta_t, \theta), \tag{37}$$

where $\sigma_{I,t}(x_{jt})$ is the observed BS implicit volatility, i.e., $\widetilde{BS}(x_{jt}, \sigma_{I,t}(x_{jt})) = \pi_t$, where $S_t \pi_t$ is observed option price corresponding to x_{jt}.

(ii) The transition equation which specifies the dynamic of the state process $\eta_t = (\zeta_t, z_t)$ by the transition probability density $l(\eta_t \mid \eta_{t-1}, \theta)$, itself indexed by θ.

A benchmark example of such an approach is the Hull and White (1987) stochastic volatility model. In that model the two state variables are, on the one hand, the underlying asset price $z_t = S_t$ (which is observed) and, on the other hand, the instantaneous volatility $\zeta_t = \sigma_t$ (which is unobserved). The transition equation is then the discrete time dynamics associated with a continuous time model of the form

$$\frac{dS_t}{S_t} = \mu dt + \sigma_t dW_t^S$$

$$d(\log \sigma_t) = k(c - \log \sigma_t)dt + \gamma dW_t^\sigma; \tag{38}$$

where $(W_t^S, W_t^\sigma)'$ is a two-dimensional standard Brownian motion. The measurement equation of the Hull and White model is given by the so-called Hull and White option pricing formula (for $J = 1$ observed option price at each date)

$$\sigma_{I,t}(x_t) = \sigma_I(x_t, \sigma_t, \theta),$$

where $\theta = (\mu, k, c, \gamma)'$ and $\sigma_I(\cdot, \cdot, \cdot)$ is defined from (with a straightforward adaptation of the notations of section 2)

$$\pi(x_t, \sigma_t, \theta) = HW(x_t, \sigma_t, \theta).$$

Moreover, we know in this case that $\pi_t(x_t, \cdot, \theta)$, and consequently $\sigma_I(x_t, \cdot, \theta)$, are one-to-one functions of the underlying stochastic process σ_t. In other words

$$\sigma_{I,t}(x_t) = \sigma_I(x_t, \sigma_t, \theta)$$
$$\Leftrightarrow \sigma_t = \sigma_I^{-1}(x_t, \sigma_{I,t}(x_t), \theta). \tag{39}$$

More generally (see Christensen (1992)), we may argue that a well-specified empirical martingale model should provide a one-to-one relationship linking, at any time t, the unobservable state process (of dimension J) and J observed synchronous option prices or, equivalently, the unobservable state process and the "observed" BS implicit volatilities. Starting from (37) let us define $\bar{\sigma}_I(\cdot, \cdot, \theta): R^J \times R^J \to R^J$ by

$$\bar{\sigma}_I(x_t, \zeta_t, \theta) = (\sigma_I(x_{1t}, \zeta_t, \theta), \ldots, \sigma_I(x_{Jt}, \zeta_t, \theta)),$$

where $x_t = (x_{1t}, \ldots, x_{Jt})$ and ζ belong to R^J. In this case, at any time t, we may write the one-to-one relationship between the unobservable state process and the "observed" BS implicit volatilities as

$$(\sigma_{I,t}(x_{jt}))_{1 \leq j \leq J} = \bar{\sigma}_I(x_t, \zeta_t, \theta) \tag{40}$$

or, equivalently, as

$$\zeta_t = \bar{\sigma}_I^{-1}[(x_t, (\sigma_{I,t}(x_{jt}))_{1 \leq j \leq J}, \theta]. \tag{41}$$

Now, under some regularity conditions, we are able to write the conditional-likelihood function associated with a sample of observations $(z_{t_i}, (\sigma_{I,t_i}(x_{jt_i}))_{1 \leq j \leq J})$, $i = 1, 2, \ldots, n$ given $(z_{t_0}, (\sigma_{I,t_0}(x_{jt_0})))_{1 \leq j \leq J}$

$$\prod_{i=1}^{n} l^*[\bar{\sigma}_I^{-1}[x_{t_i}, (\sigma_{I,t_i}(x_{jt_i}))_{1 \leq j \leq J}, \theta], z_{t_i}|$$

$$\bar{\sigma}_I^{-1}[x_{t_{i-1}}, (\sigma_{I,t_i}(x_{jt_{i-1}}))_{1 \leq j \leq J}, \theta], z_{t_{i-1}}, \theta]$$

$$|\nabla_\zeta \bar{\sigma}_I^{-1}[x_{t_i}, (\sigma_{I,t_i}(x_{jt_i}))_{1 \leq j \leq J}, \theta], |, \tag{42}$$

where $|\nabla_\zeta \bar{\sigma}_I^{-1}[x_t, \cdot, \theta]|$ is the absolute value of the Jacobian of $\bar{\sigma}_I^{-1}[x_t, \cdot, \theta]$ considered as a function of ζ.

The likelihood written (42) is the so-called full structural likelihood introduced by Christensen (1992) (see also Duan (1994)). Even if the inverse $\bar{\sigma}_I^{-1}$ of the implicit volatility function w.r.t the unobserved state variables could be derived without too much difficulty, the full structural likelihood (42) is likely to be too cumbersome to maximize.

Indeed, this is a fairly general issue in econometric modeling through latent variables: these latent variables are generally chosen to have a law of motion well described by a simple model. For cross-sectional data, non-linear models like Probit, Tobit, etc. are built by reference to a simple latent linear regression model. For the same reason, we may hope that the latent likelihood

$$\prod_{i=1}^{n} l^*(\zeta_{t_i}, z_{t_i} \mid \zeta_{t_{i-1}}, z_{t_{i-1}}, \theta)$$

associated to the state process would be a tractable function of θ (based, e.g., on autoregressive Gaussian processes). However, in (42) one may observe another occurrences of θ (via the inverse $\bar{\sigma}_I^{-1}$ and its corresponding Jacobian) which may be awkward.

In the same way that the tractability of the latent model may be exploited for inference in Probit, Tobit type models (see, e.g., Gouriéroux, Monfort, Renault, and Trogon (1987a and b)), we suggest in the following subsections two approximate likelihood strategies which may be more realistic for an application to options markets precisely because they fully exploit the simplicity of the latent volatility model. However, in our approximate strategies we want to preserve, as much as possible, the attractive feature of the full structural likelihood strategy, namely to take into account the informational content of option prices with respect to θ. We propose two competitive strategies: the first one is based on a numerical computation of the inverse $\bar{\sigma}_I^{-1}$ while the second one uses a simpler proxy (namely the BS implicit volatilities) and corrects the resulting misspecification bias thanks to a simulation-based methodology. For reasons which will become clearer in the following, the first strategy will be called "direct" while the second is an "indirect" one.

4.2.3   A direct strategy for approximate maximum-likelihood inference

Since we want to stress here the use of option prices data, we simplify the presentation by neglecting the information about parameters which may be carried by the dynamics of observable state variables z_t (typically under-lying asset prices, interest rates, etc.). The rationale for this simplified presentation might be the following decomposition of the likelihood

$$(\zeta_{t_i}, z_{t_i} \mid \zeta_{t_{i-1}}, z_{t_{i-1}}, \theta)$$
$$= l^*(\zeta_{t_i} \mid \zeta_{t_{i-1}}, z_{t_{i-1}}, \theta) l(z_{t_i} \mid \zeta_{t_i}, \zeta_{t_{i-1}}, z_{t_{i-1}}, \theta). \tag{43}$$

In this decomposition we may assume:

First that the unobservable state variables ζ are not Granger-caused by primitive asset prices z according to the principles set forth in section 3

$$l^*(\zeta_{t_i} \mid \zeta_{t_{i-1}}, z_{t_{i-1}}, \theta) = l^*(\zeta_{t_i} \mid \zeta_{t_{i-1}}, \theta).$$

Secondly that the parameter θ can be written as $\theta = (\theta_*, \theta_{**})$ and the likelihood of the unobservable state variables depends on θ only through θ_*. That is we have

$$l^*(\zeta_{t_i} \mid \zeta_{t_{i-1}}, \theta) = l^*(\zeta_{t_i} \mid \zeta_{t_{i-1}}, \theta_*).$$

Moreover it is assumed that θ_* is identifiable from $l^*(\zeta_{t_i} \mid \zeta_{t_{i-1}}, \theta_*)$.[25]
Finally that the market option pricing formula (42) depends on θ only through θ_*.

We remark that a typical case where these conditions are fulfilled is the Hull and White framework, if the volatility risk is not compensated and $\theta_* = (k, c, \gamma)'$ defines the volatility dynamics. More generally the first two conditions mean that the unobservable state variables are strongly exogenous for θ_{**} while only θ_* is relevant for option pricing. In this case, we may hope to be able to perform inference about θ_* by using *only option prices data*. Of course, in order to do this, we have to drop z from (42), which will generally imply a lack of efficiency due to the eventual occurrence of θ_* in the second term $l(z_{t_i} \mid \zeta_{t_i}, \zeta_{t_{i-1}}, z_{t_{i-1}}, \theta)$ of the likelihood decomposition (43). However, we may hope that this lack of efficiency is not so important (see Patilea, Ravoteur, and Renault (1995) for a more complete discussion). Moreover, we may prefer to neglect this information in order to have an inference procedure robust with respect to a possible misspecification of the drift of the underlying asset price.

To summarize the likelihood-based methodology that we suggest here, let us consider as a starting point the likelihood (42) where z is dropped and θ is replaced by θ_*. Since θ_* defines the only parameters of interest, we decide to change hereafter our notations: θ_* becomes θ and the likelihood of interest is

$$\prod_{i=1}^{n} l^* [\bar{\sigma}_I^{-1}[x_{t_i}, (\sigma_{I,t_i}(x_{jt_i}))_{1 \le j \le J}, \theta] \mid$$

$$\bar{\sigma}_I^{-1}[(x_{t_{i-1}}, (\sigma_{I,t_i}(x_{jt_{i-1}}))_{1 \le j \le J}, \theta], \theta]$$

$$\mid \nabla_\zeta \bar{\sigma}_I^{-1}[x_{t_i}, (\sigma_{I,t_i}(x_{jt_i}))_{1 \le j \le J}, \theta] \mid. \tag{44}$$

The approximate likelihood strategy proposed here is a generalization of an inference method studied by Renault and Touzi (1992) and Pastorello, Renault, and Touzi (1993) in a pure Hull-White setting. Basically, the idea is to simplify the maximization of (44) with respect to θ in order to avoid the difficulties produced by the awkward occurrences of θ in the Jacobian $\nabla_\zeta \bar\sigma_I^{-1}$ and in the inverse $\bar\sigma_I^{-1}$. For this, firstly, we drop the Jacobian $\nabla_\zeta \bar\sigma_I^{-1}$ and, secondly, we define an iterative algorithm such that at each step $p + 1$ the awkward occurrences of θ are replaced by value $\theta^{(p)}$ obtained from the previous step of this algorithm. In other words, we suggest, at any step $p + 1$, to maximize with respect to θ the following objective function

$$\prod_{i=1}^{n} l^* [\bar\sigma_I^{-1}[x_{t_i}, (\sigma_{I,t_i}(x_{j t_i}))_{1 \le j \le J}, \theta^{(p)}]]$$

$$\bar\sigma_I^{-1}[x_{t_{i-1}}, (\sigma_{I,t_i}(x_{j t_{i-1}}))_{1 \le j \le J}, \theta^{(p)}], \theta]. \tag{45}$$

Let us denote by $\theta^{(p+1)}$ a maximizer of the objective function (45). If, for a well-chosen value $\theta^{(1)}$, such an algorithm converges, its limit

$\theta^\infty = \lim_{p = +\infty} \theta^{(p)}$ provides an estimator that is intuitively appealing for at least two reasons:

First, if $\theta^{(p)}$ is not too far from the true unknown value of θ°, (45) is a proxy of the latent likelihood.

Second, in order to make easier the computations, the maximization is performed only with respect to the natural occurrence of the parameter θ. For instance, in the Hull and White (1987) setting as considered by Renault and Touzi (1992), the criterion (45) is defined by the likelihood of a Gaussian AR (1) model. The maximization is then very easy to perform. However, at each step p, it remains to compute the inverse $\bar\sigma_I^{-1}[(x_{t_i}, (\sigma_{I,t}(x_{j t_i}))_1 \overset{\le}{} _{j \le J}, \theta^{(p)}]$ for all i, for instance to invert the HW option pricing formula for the Renault and Touzi (1992) application.

4.2.4 Identifiability, consistency, and indirect strategies

For a more general study of the statistical issue, let us first simplify the notations. We consider a time series[26] $(y_i)_{0 \le i \le n}$ of observable variables obtained from the latent variables $(y_i^*)_{0 \le i \le n}$ via a transformation which has the form

$$y_i = g(y_i^*, x_i, \theta), \tag{46}$$

where (46) is nothing but rewriting of (39). Indeed, x_i, y_i^*, and y_i replace respectively, (x_{t_i}), ζ_{t_i}, and $(\sigma_{I,t_i}(x_{t_i}))$. The unknown parameters $\theta \in \Theta \subset R^d$

characterize the conditional probability distribution P_θ of y_i^* given y_{i-1}^* for the stationary Markov process y_i^*. The function g has a known form, indexed by θ. Moreover, it is assumed that for all possible values of $(x_i, \theta,$ the function $g(\cdot, x_i, \theta)$ is one-to-one. Therefore we may write (46) in the equivalent form (see also (41) and (42))

$$y_i^* = g^{-1}(y_i, x_i, \theta).\tag{47}$$

Since, for the applications we have in mind, x_i may often be considered as deterministic and time invariant, we drop it hereafter for the sake of notational simplicity. At the step $(p+1)$ of our iterative algorithm, we define

$$\theta^{(p+1)} = \arg\max_{\theta\in\Theta} \sum_{i=1}^n \log l^*[g^{-1}(y_i, \theta^{(p)}) \mid g^{-1}(y_{i-1}, \theta^{(p)}), \theta].\tag{48}$$

In general, in order to ensure the consistency of an estimator obtained using such an algorithm, the initial value $\theta^{(1)}$ should not be taken too "far" from the true unknown value θ°. $\theta^{(1)}$ may be obtained, for instance, as a first step estimator of θ, deduced from a crude proxy of the latent log-likelihood. For example, in the Hull and White setting, Renault and Touzi (1992) suggest choosing

$$\theta^{(1)} = \arg\max_{\theta\in\Theta} \sum_{i=1}^n \log l^*(\tilde y_i^* \mid \tilde y_{i-1}^*, \theta),\tag{49}$$

where $\tilde y_i^*$ is a crude proxy of y_i^*. For instance, $\tilde y_i^*$ could be a BS implicit volatility for near-the-money options.

Even though a detailed discussion of regularity conditions (compacity, equicontinuity, ergodicity,) is beyond the scope of this chapter (see Patilea, Ravoteur, and Renault (1995) for complements), we can give a flavor of the asymptotic properties of the suggested algorithm by the five following arguments:

1 Let us first assume that the process y_i is Markovian, stationary, and ergodic and such that a uniform law of large numbers holds

$$\frac{1}{n}\sum_{i=1}^n \log l^*[g^{-1}(y_i, \gamma) \mid g^{-1}(y_{i-1}, \gamma), \theta]$$

converges uniformly with respect to $(\gamma, \theta)\in\Theta\times\Theta$ towards

$$E_{\theta^0}\log l^*[g^{-1}(y_1, \gamma) \mid g^{-1}(y_0\gamma), \theta].\tag{50}$$

Let us notice that the expectation operator in (50) is indexed by the true unknown value θ^0 of the parameters which characterizes the conditional probability distribution of y_1^* given y_0^* and a fortiori of $y_1 = g(y_1^*, \theta^0)$ given $y_0 = g(y_0^*, \theta^0)$.

2 Let us now assume that, for every $\tilde{\theta}, \gamma$ in Θ, there exists a non-empty set $\bar{\theta}(\tilde{\theta}, \gamma)$ of values of θ solution of

$$\max_{\theta \in \Theta} E_{\tilde{\theta}} \log l^*[g^{-1}(y_1, \gamma) | g^{-1}(y_0, \gamma), \theta]. \tag{51}$$

Moreover, if we notice that for $\tilde{\theta} = \gamma = \theta^0$, the objective function in (51) becomes $E_{\theta^0} \log l^*[y_1^* | y_0^*, \theta]$, we know (see, for instance, Newey and McFadden (1994), p. 2124) that a necessary and sufficient condition for identifiability of θ from the latent likelihood $l^*[y_i^* | y_{i-1}^*, \theta]$ is

$$\bar{\theta}(\theta, \theta) = \{\theta\} \text{ for any } \theta \in \Theta. \tag{52}$$

3 It is important to keep in mind that, although the observable variables y_i are one-to-one functions of the latent ones y_i^*, this one-to-one relationship depends on the unknown parameters θ so that identifiability of θ from the observations y_i is not implied by the identifiability property stated in the latent model. The following proposition characterizes clearly what additional requirement might be met to ensure identifiability from the observables:

Proposition 6: A sufficient condition for identifiability of θ from the conditional probability distribution of y_i given y_{i-1} is that, for each $\theta \in \Theta$: θ is the only fixed point of the correspondence $\bar{\theta}(\theta, \cdot)$.

To see that such an assumption ensures identifiability from the observables, let us consider $\tilde{\theta}$ such that, with obvious notations

$$P_{\theta^0}^{Y^1 | Y^0} = P_{\tilde{\theta}}^{Y^1 | Y^0}.$$

Then, for all $\theta \in \Theta$

$$E_{\tilde{\theta}} \log l^*[g^{-1}(y_1, \theta^0) | g^{-1}(y_0, \theta^0), \theta]$$
$$= E_{\theta^0} \log l^*[g^{-1}(y_1, \theta^0) | g^{-1}(y_0, \theta^0), \theta]$$

and, by maximizing over θ we conclude that

$$\bar{\theta}(\tilde{\theta}, \theta^0) = \bar{\theta}(\theta^0, \theta^0) = \{\theta^0\}.$$

Thus we can conclude that $\tilde{\theta} = \theta^0$ as only the fixed point of $\bar{\theta}(\tilde{\theta}, \cdot)$, which proves identifiability.
Thus, the only fixed point property implies identifiability in the observable model.
The regularity conditions needed to ensure that this condition is indeed necessary are beyond the scope of this paper.

But a pleasant feature of the sufficient condition provided by proposition 6 is that it is very close to what we need to get consistency of the iterative procedure (48).

4 An important class of correspondences that admit an only fixed point is provided by the so-called *strong contraction* property. In other words, let us assume that, for each $\theta \in \Theta$, there exists a scalar $k(\theta)$ such that

$$0 < k(\theta) < 1$$

and

$$\| \tilde{\alpha} - \tilde{\beta} \| \leq k(\theta) \| \alpha - \beta \|$$

for all $\alpha, \beta \in \Theta$ and

$$\tilde{\alpha} \in \bar{\theta}(\theta, \alpha), \tilde{\beta} \in \bar{\theta}(\theta, \beta).$$

We are then able to prove (see Patilea, Ravoteur, and Renault (1995) for more details) that:

First, $\bar{\theta}(\theta, \cdot)$ admits θ as the only fixed point for each $\theta \in \Theta$. In particular, for any initial value $\theta^{(1)} \in \Theta$, any algorithm defined by

$$\theta^{(p+1)} \in \bar{\theta}(\theta^0, \theta^{(p)})$$

will converge toward θ^0.

Secondly, a convenient stopping rule may be defined for the iterative procedure (48) in order to obtain a terminal value θ_n^∞ of the algorithm that is a consistent estimator of θ^0 as n goes to infinity.

A first application of this estimation strategy was proposed by Renault and Touzi (1992) in the Hull and White framework and they proved in this particular case, for plausible values of θ^0, that the strong contraction property is already fulfilled at the level of the finite sample criterion (48) for all sufficiently large sample sizes n and a fortiori for the limit criterion (51). Thus, they were able to state that the iterative procedure (48) converges, as p goes to infinity, and that its limit is a consistent estimator of θ^0. It is worthwhile to notice, however, that in this context Renault and Touzi (1992) have been able to check the strong contraction property by using a double asymptotic point of view: Δt sufficiently small (high frequency data) and n sufficiently large (a sufficiently long period of observation).

More recently this fixed point approach was used by Florens and Richard (1996) in the quite different setting of auction markets; y_i may represent for instance the bid formed by individual i and related (via an optimal strategy of the auction game) to his private value y_i^* for the object that is auctioned. Therefore the estimation strategy set forth here may be of general interest for other fields of application. As far as we are concerned with auction markets, it is likely to be more accurate than the so-called "simulated least squares" proposed by Laffont, Ossard, and Vuong (1995).

5 With regard to the asymptotic accuracy of the suggested estimator, Renault and Touzi (1992) have shown that the central issue is the contracting feature of the correspondence $\bar{\theta}(\theta^0, \cdot)$. More this correspondence is contracting, more accurate the resulting estimator is. Indeed (see Renault and Touzi (1992, theorem 4.2), the lack of efficiency of the suggested stimator with respect to the (infeasible) maximum-latent-likelihood estimator – which could be obtained by maximizing the latent likelihood (if we had observed $y_i^*, i = 1, 2, \ldots, n$) – is inversely related (in a very direct way) to the Lipschitz constant $k(\theta^0)$.

Indeed, in the Hull and White framework, Renault and Touzi (1992) found that, for plausible values of the parameters, this lack of efficiency is very limited. In other words, option prices data $\Pi_{t_i}, i = 0, 1, \ldots, n$ (and a well-specified option pricing model) allow us to estimate a continuous-time stochastic volatility model almost just as well a if a synchronous sample $\sigma_{t_i}, i = 0, 1, \ldots, n$ of stochastic volatilities was observed! Therefore, we can guess that the suggested estimator will be much more accurate than a traditional estimator of stochastic volatility models based on underlying asset prices data (see Ghysels, Harvey, and Renault (1995) for a survey). The only drawback of the methodology suggested above is that one needs at each step of the algorithm to *invert the option pricing formula* to recover latent state variables. If one has in mind for instance the HW option pricing formula, one can imagine how cumbersome such a *direct* strategy might be!

It is all the more a pity, that for a lot of applications, a natural representation of the structural model (46) allows one to guess that the function g is not so far from the identity:

> In the case of option pricing with stochastic volatility, a BS implicit volatility y_i (especially for near-the-money options) is often fairly well correlated to the stochastic volatility y_i^*.
>
> In the case of auction theory with the private value paradigm, the bid y_i formed by individual i should be close to his private value y_i^*.
> This remark leads one to conceive an *indirect* strategy, via the following three steps:

1st step We start by maximizing the latent log-likelihood (49) where the proxy $\tilde{y}_i^*$ of y_i^* is exactly y_i. By doing this, we generally get a consistent estimator $\hat{\beta}_n$ not of θ^0 but of a pseudo-true value $\beta(\theta^0)$. For instance, Pastorello, Renault, and Touzi (1993) show by a set of Monte-Carlo experiments that, while one obtains a quite asymptotically unbiased estimator of the mean value c of the volatility process (with the notation of (38)), one dramatically underestimates the diffusion coefficient γ. This is conformable with the intuition that the BS implicit volatility is a temporal average that smooths the random variations of the stochastic volatility process.

2nd step For a given value θ of the structural parameters, we draw randomly, according to the structural model, a sample path $\tilde{y}_i^*(\theta), i = 0, 1, 2, \ldots, n$ such that P_ζ is the conditional probability distribution of $\tilde{y}_i^*(\theta)$ given $\tilde{y}_{i-1}^*(\theta)$. We then compute $\tilde{y}_i(\theta) = g(\tilde{y}_i^*(\theta), \theta)$ and the estimator $\tilde{\beta}_n(\theta)$ that maximizes the pseudo-log likelihood (49) with $\tilde{y}_i^* = \tilde{y}_i^*(\theta)$. A possible refinement is to simulate H sample paths $(\tilde{y}_i^*(\theta))_{0 \le i \le n}^{(h)}, h = 1, 2, \ldots, H$, to compute the associated estimators $\tilde{\beta}_n^{(h)}(\theta)$ and

$$\tilde{\beta}_n(\theta) = \frac{1}{H} \sum_{h=1}^{H} \tilde{\beta}_n^{(h)}(\theta).$$

3rd step We look for θ solution of

$$\tilde{\beta}_n(\theta) = \hat{\beta}_n.$$

A solution $\hat{\theta}_n$ of this equation is, under suitable regularity conditions, a consistent estimator of θ^0. It is *indirect estimation*, according to a terminology first introduced in the simultaneous equations literature and extended by Gouriéroux, Monfort, and Renault (1993): the estimators of *structural* parameters θ are recovered indirectly from estimators of *reduced* form parameters β. Gallant and Tauchen (1994) have independently introduced a similar methodology in a paper entitled "Which Moments to Match?" But, while Gallant and Tauchen suggest characterizing these moments (via the auxiliary parameters β) thanks to a large (eventually semi-non-parametric) description of the dynamics of the underlying asset prices (conditional heteroskedasticity, skewness, kurtosis – see also Bansal, Gallant, Hussey, and Tauchen (1994) and Tauchen's (1995) invited lecture in the same volume), Gouriéroux, Monfort, and Renault (1993) for the general setting and Pastorello, Renault, and Touzi (1993) for an application to option pricing argue that it might be better to use a convenient proxy of the structural model. Typically, we guess that option prices data (or equivalently associated BS implicit volatilities) convey the best information about the volatility process so that *the moments to match* are provided by the *pseudo-true values* of the structural parameters corresponding to BS implicit volatilities.

This intuition is confirmed by the set of Monte-Carlo experiments performed by Pastorello, Renault, and Touzi (1993). For instance, they compare this option prices based indirect estimation with an indirect inference strategy involving GARCH (1,1) estimates obtained from the underlying asset (also independently suggested by Engle and Lee (1994)). This last strategy produces asymptotically unbiased but rather inefficient estimates while the indirect procedures involving options prices is far more efficient. Indeed, for a number H of simulated sample paths sufficiently large (in order to make negligible a factor $1 + \dfrac{1}{H}$ in the asymptotic covariance matrix), this indirect strategy is almost as efficient as the direct one described above. Moreover it involves only at each step a computation of the HW option pricing formula and not of its inversion. Another advantage of the indirect strategy is to perform automatically a correction for small sample bias that may be sensible for the autoregressive coefficient of the volatility process.[27]

4.3   Persistence and skewness of the smile

The small sample bias correction for the autoregressive coefficient of the volatility process is all the more needed because, generally speaking, volatility is highly persistent. Particularly for high frequency data one finds evidence of near unit root behavior of the conditional variance process, and this is the very case where maximum-likelihood estimation underestimates the autoregressive coefficient.

Indeed there is debate regarding modeling persistence in the conditional variance process via a unit root or a long memory process. The idea to introduce long memory in the ARCH setting was recently suggested by Baillie, Bollerslev, and Mikkelsen (1993) who stress:

> One the one hand, that the "striking empirical regularity that emerges from numerous studies of high frequency, say daily, asset pricing data with ARCH type models, concerns the apparent widespread finding of integrated GARCH behavior."
>
> On the other hand, the "extreme behavior of the IGARCH process" ("the occurrence of a shock to the IGARCH volatility process will persist for an infinite prediction horizon") "may reduce its attractiveness for asset pricing."

This is the reason why Baillie, Bollerslev, and Mikkelsen (1993) propose a way of extending the GARCH class to account for persistence without introducing the extreme behavior of unit roots (as in IGARCH); the key feature of their FIGARCH extension (Fractionally Integrated GARCH) is the inclusion of the factional difference operator $(1 - L)^d$, where L is the lag operator, in the lag structure of the conditional variance equation. In a later paper, Bollerslev and Mikkelsen (1995) consider a generalization of the EGARCH model of Nelson (1991) in which $\log \sigma_t^2$ is modeled as a distributed lag of past innovations involving the fractional difference operator. This FIEGARCH model is stationary and invertible of $|d| < 0.5$.

Independently, Comte and Renault (1995) have proposed a continuous-time stochastic volatility version of such models by introducing a fractional Brownian motion in (38). This allows them to exploit at the same time the advantages of two methodologies:

> On the one hand, the fractional differencing approach allows one to capture persistence without introducing non-stationarity.
> On the other hand, the stochastic volatility modeling in continuous time is well-suited for option pricing, as emphasized in section 3, especially when considering BS implicit volatilities. Moreover, it is worth noticing that, while the fractional Brownian motion is not a semi-martingale (and thus no change of probability of the Girsanov type could transform it into a martingale, see Maheswaran and Sims (1993) and Rogers (1995)), Comte and Renault (1995) stay "under the umbrella of the Harrison–Kreps model," since the non-standard fractional properties are set on σ_t and not directly on S_t. Indeed, as for usual HW option pricing, the volatility process appears in the option price only through the conditional probability distribution of $V_t^T = \dfrac{1}{T-t}\displaystyle\int_t^T \sigma^2(u)du.$

Comte and Renault (1995) are then able to show that:

> First, the persistence of volatility shocks introduced by fractional differencing yields leptokurtic features for return which vanish with temporal aggregation at a slow hyperbolic rate of decay instead of the usual exponential rate for short-memory GARCH or SV models (see Drost and Nijman (1993) and Drost and Werker (1994) for these issues in the short memory case). In other words, the *temporally aggregated volatility process* V_t^T is still genuinely random for long time to maturity $(T - t)$. This is well suited to capturing a first stylized fact about the *persistence of the smile*, that is the *slowly* decreasing amplitude of the smile being a function of time to maturity. Indeed, if we trust the usual short-memory models, temporal aggregation of volatilities erases

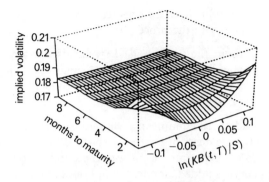

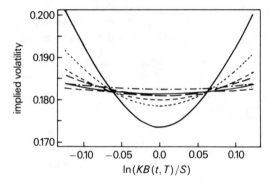

Figure 8.1

$$\tilde{S}_t = S_t$$

Volatility smiles associated to an HW option pricing model:

$$\log \sigma_t = \alpha + \delta \log \sigma_{t-1} + \gamma \varepsilon_t \qquad \varepsilon_t \, iid \, \mathcal{N}(0,1)$$
$$\alpha = -0.38, \, \delta = 0.9, \, \gamma = 0.4, \text{ time unit: 1 week.}$$

quickly conditional heteroskedasticity, which decreases the smile phenomenom, leading to flat smiles for relatively short time to maturity (around six months for plausible values of the parameters – see figure 8.1).

A second phenomenon of persistence of the smile is the persistent feature of the BS implicit volatility process for given time to maturity. It is well-captured by Comte and Renault (1995) who prove that $E_t V_t^{t+1}$ (that is the linear approximation of the squared

BS implicit volatility) is itself a long-memory process as soon as there is long-memory in the process σ_t.

Another recent debate about the smile is its skewness: is it more or less lopsided, which could change the smile into a smirk? Roughly speaking, one can observe somewhat of a consensus to define a stylized fact but a large variety of theoretical explanations:

1 On the one-hand, a widespread finding of asymmetric smiles seems to be conformable to the following description: the skewness effect can often be described as the addition of a monotonic curve to the standard symmetric smile. If a decreasing curve is added, implicit volatilities tend to rise more for decreasing than for increasing strike prices and the implicit volatility curve has its minimum out of the money (see figure 8.2). In the reverse case (addition of an increasing curve), implicit volatilities tend to rise more with increasing strike prices and their minimum is in the money (see figure 8.3).

2 On the other hand, if (almost) everybody agrees to think that this skewness is related to the discrepancy between the speeds at which stock and option prices adjust to new information and to the resulting causality relationships between the two markets, they often disagree about the main causal effect:

> According to Black (1976), "perhaps the most obvious causal relation runs from changes in the value of the firm to stock returns and volatility changes. A drop in the value of the firm will cause a negative return on its stock, and will usually increase the leverage of the stock . . .. That rise in the debt–equity ratio will surely mean a rise in the volatility of the stock." This is the so-called leverage effect which is usually captured by a negative correlation coefficient ($\rho_{s\sigma} < 0$ in (28) between the innovations of the two (stock and option) prices).
> Independently, there is a widespread belief that the most expensive options (the upper parts of the smile curve) are also the least liquid; skewness may therefore be attributed to specific configurations of liquidity in the two markets, as in a microstructure model recently proposed by Platten and Schweizer (1995).
> Other authors, like Manaster and Rendleman (1982) argue that "just as stock prices may differ, in the short run, from one exchange to another . . ., the stock prices implicit in option premia may also differ from the prices observed in the various markets for stock. In the long run, the trading vehicle that provides the greatest liquidity, the lowest trading costs, and the least restrictions is likely to play the predominant role in the market's determination of the

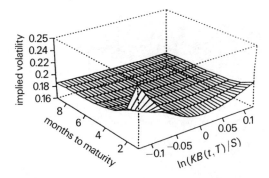

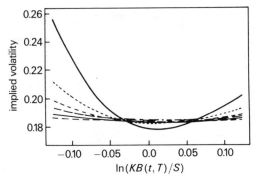

Figure 8.2

$$\frac{\tilde{S}_t - S_t}{S_t} = + 0.001$$

Volatility smiles associated to an HW option pricing model:

$$\log \sigma_t = \alpha + \delta \log \sigma_{t-1} + \gamma \varepsilon_t \qquad \varepsilon_t \, iid \, \mathcal{N}(0, 1)$$
$$\alpha = -0.38, \, \delta = 0.9, \, \gamma = 0.4, \text{ time unit: 1 week.}$$

$$HW\left(\frac{\tilde{S}_t}{K}, \sigma_t\right) = BS\left(\frac{S_t}{K}, \sigma_t^{imp}(x_t)\right)$$

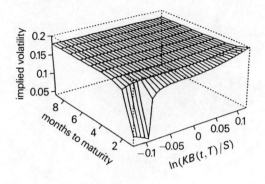

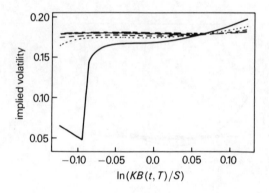

Figure 8.3

$$\frac{\tilde{S}_t - S_t}{S_t} = -0.001$$

equilibrium values of underlying stocks." Moreover, "investors may regard options as a superior vehicle" for several reasons like trading costs, short sales, margin requirements, etc. Thus, following these authors, option prices involve "*implicit stock prices*" that are "the option market's assessment of equilibrium stock values" and may induce a reverse causality relationship from option market to stock market.

Patilea, Ravoteur, and Renault (1995) propose an econometric approach which is also based on the concept of stock prices implicit in option prices but without choosing between the above theoretical explanations. Indeed, following the state variables methodology set forth above one may argue that if we observe (as it is often the case) mainly two liquid option contracts at each data, one near the money and another one more speculative (in or out) we need to introduce two unobserved state variables: the first one is stochastic volatility (to apply HW option pricing) and the second one is an "implicit" stock price which is taken into account when applying the HW option pricing formula. In other words, we assume that the market option price is $HW(\tilde{S}_t, \sigma_t, \theta)$ where $\tilde{S}_t$ may differ fro actual S_t for any of the reasons quoted above. Once more, state variables are a tool for modeling unobserved heterogeneity whatever the interpretation we have in mind. Moreover it is worth noting that $\tilde{S}_t$ is a HW implicit stock price and not a BS implicit stock price as in Manaster and Rendleman (1982). As far as we are concerned with BS implicit volatilities, it is important to know that a very small discrepancy between $\tilde{S}_t$ and S_t in the solution of the equation

$$HW\left(\frac{\tilde{S}_t}{K}, \sigma_t\right) = BS\left(\frac{S_t}{K}, \sigma_t^{imp}\left(\frac{S_t}{K}\right)\right) \tag{53}$$

which defines the BS implicit volatility as a function of three states variables: one observed S_t/K and two unobserved σ_t and $\tilde{S}_t/K$ – may capture a sensible skewness in the smile. For instance, figures 2 and 3 have been built according to (53) by choosing respectively

$$\frac{\tilde{S}_t - S_t}{S_t} = +0.001 \text{ and } \frac{\tilde{S}_t - S_t}{S_t} = -0.001. \tag{54}$$

This casts some doubt on the statistical identifiability of the testing problem one has to deal with to choose from among the various explanations quoted above, since (54) proves that even a very small lack of synchronism between the two markets (stock and option), that introduces some uncertainty in the choice of a quotation S_t to associate with the option price quoted at time t, may explain a sensible skewness. Of course, the well-known put/call parity relation allows one to know exactly the implicit stock price in option prices but:

First, there is a widespread finding of violations of the put/call parity, especially if we have in mind American options.
Second, it is clear that when we observe one more derivative asset price (namely a put price) we are able to identify one more unobserved state variable but this does not modify the general issue since one is always faced with option pricing errors!

5   CONCLUSION

We have summarized in this chapter some recent statistical methodologies "to formally incorporate model error in the analysis and implementation of contingent claim models" (Jacquier and Jarrow (1995)). As announced in the introduction, we hope that this compendium provides at the same time an useful preliminary step for a comprehensive theory of *option mispricing*. Indeed, according to the classification recently suggested by Jacquier and Jarrow (1995), we have only proposed in this chapter an "analysis of model error" (no model can perfectly explain prices) and not of a "market error," that is of a mispricing, which could be the basis of an arbitrage strategy whereas a model error is not. Of course, *econometrics of option mispricing* could be an exciting development of financial econometrics if it were possible to compare the execution costs against the apparent profit (mispricing) opportunities. This would need careful construction of "Trading strategy tests of Option Market Efficiency" (Bates (1995a)) such that we can be sure that "one can actually transact at the option price/asset price combinations identified as 'overvalued' or 'undervalued'."

Such a research agenda is very promising thanks to the recent great strides in both data collection of finance (not only high frequency datasets about asset prices but also about volumes, timing, orders, traders' identities . . .) and market microstructure theory, which now takes more and more into account the precise operational modalities of the market organization.

However, as far as we are concerned with the black box of continuous-time models and associated arbitrage-free pricing techniques, R. Merton taught us in a new contribution to his "Continuous-Time Finance" book (Merton (1990, p. 471)) a lesson on modesty and patience in the following terms:

> It is a dictum that financial markets will not long let stand prices that violate arbitrage. However, unlike with true arbitrage, the derived price relations in the continuous-time model are delicately conditional on the assumed stochastic process for the underlying securities and on the opportunity to trade continuously. Hence, with only conditional arbitrage, there are no assurances in the real world of an inexorable and swift convergence of actual prices to their theoretical model values. Thus, the simple but powerful argument of no violation of true arbitrage cannot be invoked to, *a priori*, validate the model.
>
> Validation must therefore rely on traditional a posteriori assessments. Empirical study of the model is still very much in an evolving stage. Hence, I simply note that at the moment the cumulative statistical evidence appears encouraging but also contains anomalies. The clinical evaluations from more than a decade of widespread and ongoing applications of the

continuous-time model by practitioners seem to provide inferentially favorable evidence of a different sort. But those who see the last decade of innovations as a fad are also likely to interpret this evidence as an instance of a self-fulfilling prophecy, serving only to confirm their hypothesis. Even without accepting this polar view, we must surely concede that practitioners, like academics, are not immune from following the *paths of error*.

But, I will go so far as to say that, for statistician academics, the *paths of error* lead to *the path of glory* since their job is precisely to identify and to quantify these *errors* between actual prices and their theoretical model values.

Finally, as already quoted by Melino (1994), Merton (1990) completed his scepticism by the following sentence: "Thus, although the prognosis may be good, the continuous-time model as an empirical hypothesis, strictly speaking, remains unproved." As a matter of fact, the continuous-time paradigm was never questioned in the present survey, even though we have sometimes used discrete-time representations for sake of simplicity. Although this issue was perhaps not exactly in Merton's mind in the above quoted sentence, I do find it strange that the most fundamental question of *embeddability* of our *discrete-time data* by some specified classes of *continuous-time models* is almost never addressed. Florens, Renault, and Touzi (1995), suggest a first specification test based on the simple idea that univariate diffusion models imply positive serial correlation.

Notes

I am grateful to the Institut universitaire de France for financial support. For the main ideas set forth in this chapter, I am of course largely indebted to both previously published papers and conversations with colleagues and students. While this chapter borrows from research papers jointly written with colleagues or students: Comte and Renault (1995), Garcia and Renault (1995), Pastorello, Renault, and Touzi (1993), Patilea, Ravoteur, and Renault (1995), Patilea and Renault (1995), Renault and Touzi (1992), the most elegant *proofs about the smile* are due to private communication with J. C. Rochet.

Indeed, I have many people to thank, in addition to those mentioned above as authors of papers. My understanding of recent developments of the Econometrics of option pricing and stochastic volatility has benefited from conversations with several colleagues: P. Bossaerts, E. Ghysels, E. Jacquier, C. Rogers, and Ph.D. students M. El Babsiri, M. Kouki, A. Lazrak, and N. Meddahi.

I have also benefited from very useful comments on a first draft of this chapter: P. Schotman's discussion at the 7th WCES, Tokyo, 1995, was very helpful for me in improving my arguments and I would like to thank too seminar participants at the University of Chicago, York university at Toronto and Laval University at Québec, especially Y. Ait-Sahalia, M. Gendron, L. P. Hansen, and J. Jasiak.

Above all, the general philosophy of this chapter, which could be called "How to live with misspecification if you must" (to paraphrase E. Maasoumi (1990)) is largely influenced by fifteen years of research collaboration with French econometricians (at INSEE Paris and Toulouse University), particularly J.-P.Florens, C. Gouriéroux, A. Monfort, and A. Trognon:

(i) They have introduced me to econometrics of misspecified models (pseudo-maximum-likelihood theory, encompassing etc.) See Monfort (1995).

(ii) Earlier joint work about residuals in non-linear models (Gouriéroux, Monfort, Renault, and Trognon, (1987a and b)) is related to the question of errors in option pricing which is addressed here.

(iii) I have benefited from the ideas of the "Indirect Inference" recently developed by Gouriéroux, Monfort, and myself and "Objective Driven Inference" strategy developed by Gouriéroux, Monfort, and Tenreiro (1995).

(iv) Some discussions with J. P. Florens have drawn my attention to the similarity of statistical issues implied by both the theory of *option pricing* and a class of game theory models like auction models. Finally, typographical assistance by E. Coutant and M. F. Durroux was more than essential to be close to meet the deadlines.

1 We follow here the Bates (1995a) terminology who defines the *implicit volatility* as "the value for the annualized standard deviation of log-differenced asset prices that equates the theoretical option pricing formula premised on geometric Brownian motion with the observed option price," by noticing that "it is also commonly if ungrammatically called the 'implied' volatility."

2 This issue was cleverly raised by P. Schotman in his discussion of a first version of this chapter during the Tokyo WCES. This is the reason why I try to be more precise here about both his main concerns (part (*i*)) and my main responses to them (part (ii) and (iii)).

3 Discussion of this last approach, and of extensions to the basic Black–Scholes model to account for well-documented departures from empirical stylized facts, is included in an extended version of this chapter (Renault (1996)).

4 Since we focus on a general econometric methodology, we do not address in this chapter the issue of adjustments required to take into account effect of dividends, early exercise premium (American options), and changing exercise prices (Asiatic options). American and Asiatic option pricing models may imply computer intensive methods which are time consuming. This may be another source of error (perhaps wrongly interpreted as mispricing by the econometrician) since a model can be implemented by traders with only timely and low-cost methods.

5 It is symptomatic that, writing (5), Lo (1986) is very vague about the choice of notations: "mute S" versus "observed S_t."

6 (7) is consistent with the BS pricing formula (1) at least in the particular case of a log-normal stock price and a deterministic interest rate

$$B(t, T) = \exp\left[- \int_t^T r(u)du \right] \text{ is known at time } t$$

7 As opposed to the HW stochastic volatility model that we shall present later, this drawback is due to the lack of memory of the Poisson process.

8 Consistency is obtained when the time interval between two consecutive observations goes to zero, for a fixed total time period of observation.

9 Of course, $\sigma_n^2 \tau$ is the variance *conditional on n jumps having occurred* and the expectation of this variance is $V^2 \tau$. We have here an example where the approximated heterogeneity factor $\tilde{\lambda}_t(x_t, \theta)$ defined by (16) is not necessarily the expectation of the true one.

10 "Independence" means here *conditional* independence: the volatility process is assumed to be independent from price innovations. See section 3 below for interpretations in terms of non-causality.

11 As a matter of fact, the specification of $\tilde{\lambda}_t(x_t, \theta)$ may depend on the context of application. See the wide range of conventional randomization in Merton's example above.

12 A maintained hypothesis hereafter is that the rational behavior of options traders leads to option prices which are a well-defined function of (S, K) among other characteristics. This function is the so-called market option pricing formula.

13 We use here a slightly modified terminology with respect to the usual one. Indeed, it is more common to call at-the-money/in-the-money/out-of-the-money options, when $S_t = K/S_t > K/S_t < K$ respectively. From an economic point of view, it is more appealing to compare S_t with the present value of the strike price K and to define moneyness by the sign of x_t.

14 The concept of conditional independence (and its mathematical formulation (25)) is rather vague as long as the stochastic framework and in particular filtrations of information sets have not been specified precisely. Such a specification is provided by (26) and (27).

15 The variables $r(t)$ and $\sigma(t)$ are called "state variables" in a loose sense since we are not assuming here that the (r, σ) process is Markovian. It may depend on a higher dimensional Markovian process.

16 We implicitly assume that the considered system of stochastic differential equations satisfy the usual regularity conditions (Lipschitz, growth, etc.) which ensure existence and unicity of a solution.

17 All these functions could be made dependent upon other state variables. In this case (S, r, σ) would no longer be Markovian and should be embedded in a higher dimensional Markovian process of state variables. This generalization would not present any added difficulty.

18 It is clear that, under convenient regularity conditions, propositions 3 and 4 could be reinforced to become necessary and sufficient conditions.

19 The possible randomization of the interest rate parameter implied by (11) is neglected here to encompass Merton's model with small k. Moreover, it is known (see e.g., Bates (1995a Section 4.1)) that randomness of interest rates has little effect on the smile.

20 Of course, the hedging ratios Δ are concerned only with the risk directly associated with stock price variations and not with the heterogeneity risk. For

instance, in the case of a Markov process (S, σ), a complete hedging would imply a delta-sigma hedging strategy as studied by Scott (1991). In any case, one must compute some Δ-ratios to compare optimal hedging strategies.

21 Thanks to the put call parity relation, BS implicit volatilities of European calls and puts coincide for a given strike price. In a different framework, P. Carr (1994) has recently derived a "put call symmetry" relation where he precisely states that "a European call scaled by the square root of its strike has the same value as a European put scaled by the square root of its strike" when the two strikes are *chosen so that their geometric mean is the current forward price.*

22 This analogy is all the more amazing because the fundamental assumption which allows P. Carr (1994) to derive his put-call symmetry relation is precisely an assumption of *symmetry of the true volatility process* which is similar to (32), even though (32) is *proved to hold* for the BS implicit volatility process. In other words, P. Carr's (1994) results and applications (zero-cost collars, Barrier options . . .) can be reinterpreted in a world where our BS implicit volatility process is considered by traders as the true volatility process.

23 To the best of our knowledge, the first complete proof of this result is due to Renault and Touzi (1992). But the elegant proof presented here is essentially due to private communication of J. C. Rochet.

24 Due to the homogeneity property, the market option pricing formula is now given by a unit of underlying asset price. In other words, the market price is $S_t \Pi_t(x_t, \zeta_t)$.

25 This last assumption, joint with the first one, amounts to a strong exogeneity assumption of ζ for θ_{**}.

26 The values y_i are observed at time $t_i, i = 0, 1, \ldots, n$. We prefer to write y_i instead of y_{t_i} because this allows us to consider sampling intervals $\Delta t_i = t_i - t_{i-1}$ of different lengths.

27 This "small sample bias correction" property of indirect inference was studied more systematically by Gouriéroux, Renault, and Touzi (1994) by comparison with more traditional bootstrap or median unbiased estimation suggested by Andrews (1993).

References

Ait-Sahalia, Y., Bickel, P. J., and Stoker, T. M. (1995). "Goodness-of-fit tests for regression using kernel methods." Discussion Paper, University of Chicago.

Amin, K. I. and Ng, V. K. (1993). "Option valuation with systematic stochastic volatility." *Journal of Finance*, 48(3): 881–909.

Andrews, D. W. K. (1993). "Exactly median-unbiased estimation of first order autoregressive unit root models." *Econometrica*, 61: 139–65.

Anscombe, F. J. (1990). "Residuals." In the *New Palgrave, Time Series and Statistics*, pp. 244–50.

Baillie, R. T., Bollerslev, T. and Mikkelsen, H. O. (1996). "Fractionally integrated generalized autoregressive conditional heteroskedasticity." *Journal of Econometrics*, 74: 3–30.

Bajeux, I. and Rochet, J. C. (1996). "Dynamic spanning: are options an appropriate instrument?" *Mathematical Finance*, 6: 1–16.

Bansal, R., Gallant, A. R., Hussey, R. and Tauchen, G. (1995). "Non-parametric estimation of structural models for high-frequency currency market data." *Journal of Econometrics*, 66: 251–87.

Bates, D. (1995b). "Jumps and stochastic volatility: exchange rate processes implicit in Deutschemark options." forthcoming, *Review of Financial Studies*.

Black, F. (1976). "Studies in stock price volatility changes." Proceedings of the 1976 Business Meeting of the Business and Economic Statistics Section, American Statistical Association, pp. 177–81.

Black, F. and Scholes, M. (1973). "The pricing of options and corporate liabilities." *Journal of Political Economy*, 81: 637–59.

Bollerslev, T. and Mikkelsen, H. O. (1996). "Modeling and pricing long-memory in stock market volatility." *Journal of Econometrics*, 73: 151–84.

Bossaerts, P. and Hillion, P. (1993). "A test of a general equilibrium stock option pricing model." *Mathematical Finance*, 3: 311–47.

(1994). "Local parametric analysis of hedging in discrete time." Discussion Paper, CENTER, Tilburg University.

Boyle, P. and Vorst T. (1992). "Option replication in discrete time with transaction costs." *The Journal of Finance*, 47(1).

Broadie, M., Detemple, J., Ghysels, E. and Torrès, O. (1995). "American options with stochastic volatility: A nonparametric approach." Discussion Paper, CIRANO, University of Montreal.

Carr, P. (1994). "European put-call symmetry with smiles." Working Paper, Johnson Graduate School of Management, Cornell University, Ithaca.

Christensen B. J. (1992). "Asset prices and the empirical martingale model." Working Paper, New York University.

Clément, E., Gouriéroux, C. and Monfort, A. (1993). "Prediction of contingent price measures." Presented at ESEM, Uppsala, 1993.

Comte, F. and Renault, E. (1995). "Long memory in continuous-time stochastic volatility models." 1st Conference HFDF, Zurich.

(1996). "Non causality in continuous time VARMA models." *Econometric Theory*, 12 (2).

Drost, F. C. and Nijman, T. E. (1993). "Temporal aggregation of GARCH processes." *Econometrica*, 61: 909–27.

Drost, F. C. and Werker, B. J. M. (1996). "Closing the GARCH gap: continuous time GARCH modeling." *Journal of Econometrics*, 74: 31–58.

Duan, J. C. (1994). "Maximum likelihood estimation using price data of the derivative contract." *Mathematical Finance*, 4 (2): 155–67.

Duffie, D. (1992). Dynamic Asset Pricing Theory. Princeton, NJ: Princeton University Press.

Dupire, B. (1994). "Pricing with a smile." *Risk*, 7: 18–20.

Eisenberg, L. and Jarrow, R. (1994). "Option pricing with random volatilities in complete markets." *Journal of Financial and Quantitative Analysis*, 4: 5–17.

Engle, R. F. and Lee, D. G. J. (1994). "Estimating diffusion models of stochastic volatility." Discussion Paper, University of California at San Diego.

Engle, R. F. and Mustafa, C. (1992). "Implied ARCH models from option prices." *Journal of Econometrics*, 52: 289–311.

Florens, J. P. and Fougère, D. (1996). "Noncausality in continuous time." *Econometrica*, 64: 1195–212.

Florens, J. P., Renault, E., and Touzi, N. (1995). "Testing for embedability by stationary reversible continuous-time Markov processes." Presented at the WCES, Tokyo, 1995.

Florens, J. P. and Richard, J. F. (1995). "Inference in a class of game theoretic models." Working Paper, GREMAQ.

Fourgeaud, C., Gouriéroux, C., and Pradel, J. (1990). "Hétérogénéité et hasard dans les modèles de durée." *Annales d'Economie et de Statistique*, 18: 1–24.

Gallant, A. R. and Tauchen, G. (1993). "Which moments to match?" Duke University Discussion Paper, forthcoming in *Econometric Theory*.

Garcia, R. and Renault, E. (1995). "Risk aversion, intertemporal substitution and option pricing." Working Paper, CIRANO, Montreal.

—— (1996). "A note on hedging in ARCH-type option pricing models." Discussion Paper, CIRANO, University of Montreal.

Ghysels, E., Harvey, A. and Renault, E. (1995). "Stochastic volatility." In G. S. Maddala (ed.), *Handbook of Statistics*, Vol. XIV, Statistical Methods in Finance. Amsterdam, North Holland.

Gouriéroux C., Monfort, A., and Renault, E. (1993). "Indirect inference." *Journal of Applied Econometrics*, 34: 5–32.

Gouriéroux, C., Monfort, A., Renault, E., and Trognon, A. (1987a). "Generalized residuals." *Journal of Econometrics*, 34: 5–32.

—— (1987b). "Simulated residuals." *Journal of Econometrics*, 34: 201–52.

Gouriéroux, C., Monfort, A., and Tenreiro, C. (1994). "Kernel M-estimators: nonparametric diagnostics for structural models." Discussion Paper, CEPREMAP.

—— (1995), "Kernel M-estimators and functional residual plots." Discussion Paper CREST-ENSAE, Paris.

Gouriéroux, C., Renault, E. and Touzi, N. (1994). "Calibration by simulation for small sample bias correction." Working Paper CREST-ENSAE Paris. Forthcoming in "Simulation-Based Inference in Econometrics: Methods and Applications", R. Mariano (ed).

Harrison J.-M. and Kreps, D. (1979). "Martingale and arbitrage in multiperiods securities markets." *Journal of Economic Theory*, 20: 381–408.

Hausman, J., Hall, B. H., and Griliches, Z. (1984). "Econometric models for count data with an application to the patents R&D relationship." *Econometrica*, 52(4): 909–38.

Heston, S. L. (1993a). "A closed-form solution for options with stochastic volatility with applications to bond and currency options." *Review of Financial Studies*, 6: 327–44.

—— (1993b). "Invisible parameters in option prices." *Journal of Finance* 48: 933–48.

Heynen, R., Kemna, A., and Vorst, T. (1994). "Analysis of the term structure of implied volatility." *Journal of Financial and Quantitative Analysis*, 39: 31–56.

Hobson, D. G. and Rogers, L. C. G. (1994). "Models of endogenous stochastic volatility." Working Paper, University of Bath.

Hang, C. F. and Litzenberger, R. (1988). *Foundations for Financial Economics.* Amsterdam: North-Holland.

Hull, J. and White, A. (1987). "The pricing of options on assets with stochastic volatilities." *Journal of Finance*, 42: 281–300.

Jacquier, E. and Jarrow, R. (1995). "Dynamic evaluation of contingent claim models." Working Paper, Cornell University, Ithaca.

Jones, E. P. (1984). "Option arbitrage and strategy with large price changes." *Journal of Financial Economics*, 13: 91–113.

Kallsen, J. and Taqqu, M. S. (1994). "Option pricing in ARCH-type models." Mimeo, Boston University.

Kreps, D. and Porteus, E. L. (1978). "Temporal resolution of uncertainty and dynamic choice theory." *Econometrica*, 46: 185–200.

Laffont, J. J., Ossard, H., and Vuong, Q. (1995). "Econometrics of first-price auctions." *Econometrica*, 63(4): 953–80.

Lo, A. (1986). "Statistical tests of contingent claims asset-pricing models." *Journal of Financial Economics*, 17: 143–73.

Maasoumi, E. (1990). "How to live with misspecification if you must?" *Journal of Econometrics*, 44: 67–86.

Maheswaran, S. and Sims, C. A. (1993). "Empirical implications of arbitrage-free asset markets." In Phillips, P. C. B. (ed.), *Models Methods and Applications of Econometrics*. Oxford: Blackwell.

Melino, A. (1994). "Estimation of continuous-time models in finance." In Sims, C. A. (eds.) *Advances in Econometrics*, Cambridge University Press.

Merton, R. C. (1973). "Theory of rational option pricing." *Bell Journal of Economics and Management Science*, 4: 141–83.

(1976a). "Option pricing when underlying stock returns are discontinuous." *Journal of Financial Economics*, 3: 125–44.

(1976b). "The impact an option pricing of specification error in the underlying stock price returns." *Journal of Finance*, 333–50.

(1990). *Continuous time finance.* Oxford: Blackwell.

Monfort, A. (1995). "A reappraisal of misspecified econometric models." Test of the 1994 Tjalling Koopmans Lecture of the Cowles Foundation, Working Paper CREST-INSEE No. 9545.

Naik, V. and Lee, M. H. (1990). "General equilibrium pricing of option on the market portfolio with discontinuous returns." *Review of Financial Studies*, 3: 493–522.

Nelson, D. (1990). "ARCH models as diffusion approximations." *Journal of Econometrics*, 45: 7–39.

(1991). "Conditional heteroskedasticity in asset returns: a new approach." *Econometrica*, 59: 347–70.

Newey, W. and McFadden, D. (1994). "Large sample estimation and hypothesis testing." In Engle, R. F. and MacFadden, D. L. (eds.) *Handbook of Econometrics*, Vol. IV.

Pastorello, S., Renault, E. and Touzi, N. (1993). "Statistical inference for random variance option pricing." Southern European Economics Discussion Series.

Patilea, V., Ravoteur, M P. and Renault, E. (1995). "Multivariate time series analysis of option prices." Working Paper GREMAQ, Toulouse.

Patilea, V. and Renault, E. (1995). "Random probabilities for option pricing." Discussion Paper GREMAQ, Toulouse.

Platten, E. and Schweizer, M. (1995). "On smile and skewness." Discussion Paper, Australian National University, Canberra.

Renault, E. (1996). "Econometric models of option pricing errors." Cahier No. 96.04.407, GREMAQ, Universite des Sciences Sociales de Toulouse.

Renault, E. and Touzi, N. (1996). "Option hedging and implied volatilities in a stochastic volatility model." Mathematical Finance, 6: 259–302.

Rogers, L. C. G. (1995). "Arbitrate with fractional Brownian motion." University of Bath. Discussion Paper.

Rubinstein, M. (1985). "Nonparametric tests of alternative option pricing models using all reported trades and quotes on the 30 most active CBOE option classes from august 23, 1976 through August 31, 1978." Journal of Finance, 40: 455–80.

(1994). "Implied binomial trees." Journal of Finance, 49(3): 771–818.

Scott, L. O. (1991). "Random-variance option pricing: empirical tests of the model and delta-sigma hedging." Advances in Futures and Options Research, 5: 113–35.

(1994). "Pricing stock options in a jump-diffusion model with stochastic volatility and interest rates: applications of fourier inversion methods." Working Paper, University of Georgia.

Sims, C. A. (1984). "Martingale-like behavior or prices." Working Paper, University of Minnesota.

Tauchen, G. (1995). "New minimum chi-square methods in empirical finance." Invited Paper presented at the 7th WCES, Tokyo.

Turnbull, S. and Milne, F. (1991). "A simple approach to interest-rate option pricing." Review of Financial Studies, 4: 87 121.

CHAPTER 9

New minimum chi-square methods in empirical finance

George Tauchen

1 INTRODUCTION

1.1 Background

A structural financial model typically defines a stochastic data generator. Using the data generator, it is relatively easy to compute expectations of non-linear functions, normally by simulation, but the likelihood function itself is intractable. This is the setup for Simulated Method of Moments (SMM), as set forth in Ingram and Lee (1991) and Duffie and Singleton (1993). SMM is the extension to the time-series context of the simulation estimators of McFadden (1989) and Pakes and Pollard (1989).

This estimation context arises across a broad range of areas in finance, including estimation of models of market microstructure (Foster and Viswanathan (1995)), estimation of equilibrium asset-pricing models (Gennotte and Marsh (1993)), and estimation of continuous-time models of interest rates and stock prices, as proposed by Melino (1994) in his address for the Sixth World Congress in 1990. The essential feature of each of these applications is the presence of unobserved stochastic processes that enter the structural model non-linearly. In the microstructure application, the latent processes comprise the random information flow to informed traders and the stochastic behavior of noise traders. For asset pricing, the latent processes are endowment processes along with taste and technology shocks. In continuous-time work, the latent processes are the underlying continuous-factor processes which may be only partially observed at discrete-time intervals.

Recent research develops a new class of minimum chi-square estimators that provide a systematic way of developing moment conditions for estimation by simulation. One approach, developed in Bansal, Gallant, Hussey, and Tauchen (1993, 1995), and Gallant and Tauchen (1996), and termed Efficient Method of Moments (EMM), uses the score function of an auxiliary model, called the score generator, to define a criterion function for GMM estimation (Hansen (1982)). The other, developed by Smith (1990, 1993) and extended by Gouriéroux, Monfort, and Renault (1993), and termed Indirect Inference, uses the parameters of the auxiliary model itself to define the GMM criterion. In either approach, so long as the underlying structural model is correctly specified, the auxiliary model need not nest the structural model and in fact may be misspecified. Subject only to minimal regularity and identifiability conditions, the estimators are still consistent and asymptotically normal. The score-based approach has some computational advantages, as it circumvents the need to refit the auxiliary model (evaluated the binding function) for each candidate value of the parameter vector, and it eliminates the need to estimate the Hessian matrix of the auxiliary model.

Using an auxiliary model to define the GMM criterion brings to bear on the task of estimation the accumulated body of knowledge regarding the statistical characteristics of the relevant data. This knowledge is acquired from the years of experience of many investigators using statistical models to describe the data. The statistical modeling effort typically provides a family of statistical models that are known to fit the data quite well. A case in point pertains to models in the ARCH/GARCH class (Engle (1982), Bollerslev, Chou, and Kroner (1992)) which provide excellent first approximations to the conditional distributions of financial returns. Another is the evidence from Hamilton (1989) and the follow-up literature that Markov-switching models provide excellent descriptions of the non-linear dynamics of macroaggregate series. ARCH/GARCH models and switching-regime models are candidate auxiliary models for any of the three classes of estimation mentioned above. ARCH-GARCH or switching models provide readily available statistical descriptions of the observed data in empirical microstructure research, in asset-pricing contexts, and in estimation of diffusion models as well.

Applications of these estimators include Smith (1993), who uses a VAR auxiliary model for estimation of a structural macroeconomic model. Engle and Lee (1994) use a GARCH model with Gaussian errors as an auxiliary model for fitting a volatility diffusion to daily stock returns data. Pagan, Hall, and Martin (1995) likewise use a GARCH model with Gaussian errors as the auxiliary model to estimate a diffusion model for monthly interest rates. Andersen and Lund (1996) employ non-parametric E-GARCH-SNP models as auxiliary models in order to estimate continuous-time stochastic volatility models for weekly interest rates. Gouriéroux and Monfort (1994, pp. 153–4) use an autoregressive model with a heteroskedastic error structure to estimate a model of geometric Brownian motion for monthly interest rate data. Buraschi (1994) uses an autoregressive model for fitting a model of the monthly term structure. Ghysels and Jasiak (1994) use a flexible, non-parametric auxiliary model to estimate a time deformation model for stock returns and volume. Hsu and Kugler (1995) and Bansal, Gallant, Hussey, and Tauchen (1995) also use more flexible auxiliary models to estimate term structure models and exchange rate models, while Gallant, Hsieh, and Tauchen (1995) do so for stochastic volatility models.

This chapter reviews these minimum chi-square estimators with a particular focus on the selection of the auxiliary model. Section 4 below examines several issues, including statistical efficiency, specification testing, behavior under misspecification, and numerical stability. The investigation indicates that appropriate choice of the auxiliary model must be based on non-parametric considerations, with particular care taken to ensure that the internal dynamics of the selected model are stable. Previous experience and prior knowledge can, of course, provide an indication of a preliminary candidate model. But one must go beyond such a candidate and actually find an auxiliary model that fully describes the data at hand. Only by using a flexible, non-parametric auxiliary model can one ensure that parameter estimates are fully efficient when the underlying structural model is true and that misspecification will be detected when the structural model is false.

The remainder of this chapter proceeds as follows. Section 2 sets up the notation and estimation context. Section 3 reviews the minimum chi-square estimators. Section 4 examines in detail the various considerations entailed in selecting the auxiliary model. Section 5 is the empirical application.

2   STOCHASTIC DATA GENERATORS

We set some basic notation where a structural model defines a data generator. Throughout, $\{w_t\}$ denotes a vector process of exogenous forcing variables. The process $\{w_t\}$ is assumed to be strictly stationary and Markovian with transition density $q(w_t \mid w_{t-L_w}, \ldots, w_{t-1}, \gamma)$, where γ is a parameter vector of length l_γ and L_w is the lag length. In many circumstances, w_t is unobserved, though the treatment here is sufficiently general to handle the case when some elements of w_t are observed and others are latent. Let v_t denote a vector outcome process, which is given by the *Solution Function*

$$v_t = h(v_{t-L_1}, \ldots, v_{t-1}, w_{t-L_2}, \ldots, w_{t-1}, w_t, \psi),\tag{1}$$

where L_1 and L_2 are the longest lags of v_t and w_t appearing in h and ψ is a parameter vector of length l_ψ.

The conditional density q and the solution function h jointly define a data generation process. Set $\rho = (\gamma'\psi')'$, where ρ is of length $l_\rho = l_\gamma + l_\psi$ and contains all of the parameters. For a candidate value ρ of the parameter, one simulates artificial realizations as follows: given initial values $\hat{w}_{-L_w+1}, \ldots, \hat{w}_0$, generate a realization on the forcing process $\{\hat{w}_\tau\}$ by drawing $\hat{w}_1$ from $q(w_1 | \hat{w}_{-L_w+1}, \ldots, \hat{w}_0)$, $\hat{w}_2$ from $q(w_2 | \hat{w}_{-L_w+2}, \ldots, \hat{w}_1)$, and so forth. Given initial values $\hat{v}_{L_1+1}, \ldots, \hat{v}_0$ and having let $\{\hat{w}_\tau\}$ run long enough so there are least L_2 values available, then vs can be generated iteratively through the solution function (1) above.

It is assumed that $\{q(\cdot | \gamma), h(\cdot | \psi)\}_{\rho \in \mathscr{R}}$, $\mathscr{R} \subset \mathfrak{R}^{l\rho}$, defines a strictly stationary Markov data generator. For each $\rho \in \mathscr{R}$, the simulated process $\{\hat{s}_\tau\}_{\tau=1}^N$ (given that ρ) is asymptotically stationary and ergodic with unconditional densities

$$\{p_J(s_{t-J}, s_{t-J+1}, \ldots, s_t | \rho)\}_{J=0}^\infty$$

of stretches of length $J + 1$, $J = 0, 1, 2, \ldots$.

The upshot is simply that Monte Carlo numerical integration works: for a function $e(s_{t-J}, s_{t-J+1}, \ldots, s_t)$ such that the expectation exists, then

$$\frac{1}{N} \sum_{\tau=J+1}^N e(\hat{s}_{\tau-J}, \hat{s}_{\tau-J+1}, \ldots, \hat{s}_\tau) \xrightarrow{as} \mathscr{E}_\rho[e(s_{t-J}, s_{t-J+1}, \ldots, s_t)],$$

where

$$\mathscr{E}_\rho[e(s_{t-J}, s_{t-J+1}, \ldots, s_t)] =$$

$$\int e(s_{t-J}, s_{t-J+1}, \ldots, s_t) p(s_{t-J}, s_{t-J+1}, \ldots, s_t | \rho)$$

$$d(s_{t-J}, s_{t-J+1}, \ldots, s_t), \tag{2}$$

and $\{\hat{s}_\tau\}_{\tau=1}^N$ is a simulated realization. Duffie and Singleton (1993) give more rigorous conditions for the data generator $\{q(\cdot | \gamma), h(\cdot | \psi)\}_{\rho \in \mathscr{R}}$, $\mathscr{R} \subset \mathfrak{R}^{l\rho}$ to be asymptotically stationary and ergodic.

In many applications, the elements of the process s_t are not completely observed. Let

$$y_t = \phi(s_t) \tag{3}$$

be an $M \times 1$ function of s_t that is observed by the econometrician. If any elements of the forcing process enter the observed vector y_t, then the mapping from these elements of w_t to y_t is just the identity map.

Since y_t is a function of s_t, y_t is also stationary and ergodic, though not necessarily Markovian. Let

$$p_J(y_t \mid y_{t-J}, \dots, y_{t-1}, \rho) = \frac{p_J(y_{t-J}, \dots, y_t \mid \rho)}{p_{J-1}(y_{t-J}, \dots, y_{t-1} \mid \rho)} \tag{4}$$

denote the implied transition densities, $J = 1, 2, \dots$. A common presumption in much of time-series econometrics is that the observed process is either Markovian, or nearly so, in the sense that $p_J(y_t \mid y_{t-J}, \dots, y_{t-1}) \approx p_L(y_t \mid y_{t-L}, \dots, y_{t-1}), J \geq L$, for some sufficiently large L.

Throughout, it is presumed the user has access to a good method to compute the solution function (1). Little attention is paid to that particular issue here, though it bears emphasizing that this is a very active research topic. Early work is discussed in Taylor and Uhlig (1990) and Tauchen and Hussey (1991); more recent work is reviewed in Judd (1994). The search for accurate and fast algorithms is well motivated, because experience suggests that most of the computer time in implementing simulation estimators is associated with generating the v_t, not with the calculations directly associated with the optimization.

3   ESTIMATORS

The notational convention in what follows is this: y_t is a subvector of a strictly stationary Markov process s_t generated by a stochastic model $\{q(\cdot \mid \gamma), h(\cdot \mid \psi)\}_{\rho \in \mathscr{R}}, \rho = (\gamma' \psi)'$, as considered in section 2. $p_J(y_{t-J}, \dots, y_t \mid \rho)$ denotes the implied joint density given ρ of a stretch of length $J + 1, J = 0, 1, 2, \dots$, and $\{\tilde{y}_t\}_{t=1}^n$ denotes the realization observed by the econometrician. The stochastic model is assumed to be correctly specified, meaning that the joint density of $\{\tilde{y}_t\}_{t=1}^n$ is $p_{n-1}(y_1, \dots, y_n \mid \rho_0)$ for all $n \geq 1$, where $\rho_0 \in \mathscr{R}$ is the true value. Below, we often refer to this stochastic model as simply the p-model.

The econometrician's task is to estimate ρ_0. The sample likelihood function $\mathscr{L}(\rho) = p_{n-1}(\tilde{y}_1, \dots, \tilde{y}_n \mid \rho)$ is presumed intractable, rendering maximum-likelihood estimation infeasible and motivating consideration of minimum chi-square estimation. The econometrician generates simulated realizations on $\{y_t\}$ given $\rho \in \mathscr{R}$. For a candidate value ρ, $\{\hat{y}_\tau(\rho)\}_{\tau=1}^N$ denotes a simulated realization of length N, i.e., a random draw from $p_{N-1}(y_1, \dots, y_N \mid \rho)$.

3.1   The auxiliary model

Suppose the conditional density $f(y_t \mid y_{t-L}, \dots, y_{t-1}, \theta)$ $\theta \in \Theta \subset R^{l_\theta}$ is found to provide a good statistical description of the data. This conditional density is called the f-model. The f-model providing a good fit means that it is selected on the basis of some model selection criterion such as the Schwarz criterion (BIC) and that it does well on a battery of specification tests. The score function of the f-model

$$s_f(y_{t-L}, \ldots, y_t, \theta) = \frac{\partial}{\partial \theta} \log[f(y_t \mid y_{t-L}, \ldots, y_{t-1}, \theta)] \tag{5}$$

is of central importance in what follows.

The quasi-maximum-likelihood estimator obtained by fitting the f-model to the realization $\{\tilde{y}_t\}_{t=1}^n$ is

$$\tilde{\theta} = \arg\max_{\theta} \mathcal{L}_n(\theta, \{\tilde{y}_t\}_{t=1}^n) \tag{6}$$

where

$$\mathcal{L}_n(\theta, \{y_t\}_{t=1}^n) = \frac{1}{n} \sum_{t=L+1}^{n} \log[f(\tilde{y}_t \mid \tilde{y}_{t-L}, \ldots, \tilde{y}_{t-1}, \theta)] \tag{7}$$

is the sample mean likelihood function. The first-order condition is

$$\frac{\partial}{\partial \theta} \mathcal{L}_n(\tilde{\theta}, \{y_t\}_{t=1}^n) = 0, \tag{8}$$

or, equivalently

$$\frac{1}{n} \sum_{t=L+1}^{n} s_f(\tilde{y}_{t-L}, \ldots, \tilde{y}_t, \theta) = 0. \tag{9}$$

It is to be emphasized that, although the dimension of the f-model needs to be at least as large as the p-model, i.e., $l_\theta \geq l_\rho$, the f-model need not nest the p-model. Indeed, the internal structure of the f-model might have little to do directly with the internal structure of the p-model.

3.1.1   Theory of misspecified models

The f-model is possibly misspecified, in the sense that there is no value of $\theta \in \Theta$ such that $f(y_t \mid y_{t-L}, \ldots, y_{t-1}, \theta) = p_L(y_t \mid y_{t-L}, \ldots, y_{t-1} \mid \rho_0)$ for all $y_{t-L}, \ldots, y_{t-1}$ in the support of $p_L(y_{t-L}, \ldots, y_t \mid \rho_0)$. It is well understood what happens if one fits an f-model when the truth is the p-model. From White (1994) and the references therein, it is well known that under reasonable regularity conditions $\tilde{\theta} \xrightarrow{as} \bar{\theta}$ where $\bar{\theta}$ is the *pseudo-true* value given by

$$\bar{\theta} = \mathcal{T}(\rho_0),$$

and $\mathcal{T}: \mathcal{R} \to \Theta$ denotes the *binding function* (Gouriéroux, Monfort, and Renault (1993)) given by

$$\mathcal{T}(\rho) = \arg\max_{\theta} \int \log[f(y_t \mid y_{t-L}, \dots, y_{t-1}, \theta)]$$

$$p_L(y_{t-L}, \dots, y_t \mid \rho) d(y_{t-L}, \dots, y_t). \tag{10}$$

The corresponding first-order condition is

$$\int \frac{\partial}{\partial \theta} \log[f(y_t \mid y_{t-L}, \dots, y_{t-1}, \mathcal{T}(\rho))]$$

$$p_L(y_{t-L}, \dots, y_t \mid \rho) d(y_{t-L}, \dots, y_t) = 0 \tag{11}$$

identically in $\rho \in \mathcal{R}$, and, in particular

$$\int \frac{\partial}{\partial \theta} \log[f(y_t \mid y_{t-L}, \dots, y_{t-1}, \bar{\theta})] p_L(y_{t-L}, \dots, y_t \mid \rho_0)$$

$$d(y_{t-L}, \dots, y_t) = 0. \tag{12}$$

The asymptotic distribution of $\tilde{\theta}$ about $\bar{\theta}$ is given by the usual three-term expression

$$\sqrt{n}(\tilde{\theta} - \bar{\theta}) \xrightarrow{\mathcal{D}} N(0, \mathcal{H}^{-1} \mathcal{I} \mathcal{H}^{-1}),$$

where

$$\mathcal{I} = \lim_{n \to \infty} \mathrm{Var} \left\{ \frac{1}{\sqrt{n}} \sum_{t=L+1}^{n} \frac{\partial}{\partial \theta} \log[f(y_t \mid y_{t-L}, \dots, y_{t-1}, \bar{\theta})] \right\} \tag{13}$$

is the *pseudo-information matrix*, and

$$\mathcal{H} = \int \frac{\partial^2}{\partial \theta \partial \theta'} \log[f(y_t \mid y_{t-L}, \dots, y_{t-1}, \bar{\theta})].$$

$$p_L(y_{t-L}, \dots, y_t \mid \rho_0) d(y_{t-L}, \dots, y_t) \tag{14}$$

is the hessian matrix. We note the characterization

$$\sqrt{n}(\tilde{\theta} - \bar{\theta}) \stackrel{LD}{=} \mathcal{H}^{-1} v, v \sim N(0, \mathcal{I}), \tag{15}$$

$$\stackrel{LD}{=} \mathcal{H}^{-1} \mathcal{I}^{1/2} z, z \sim N(0, I), \mathcal{I}^{1/2} \mathcal{I}^{1/2\prime} = \mathcal{I}, \tag{16}$$

where $\stackrel{LD}{=}$ means the left and right-hand sides have the same distribution asymptotically.

3.2   The score-based criterion (EMM)

One strategy for minimum chi-square estimation is to mimic the first-order condition (9) induced by QML estimation (6) of the f-model. This estimation is introduced in Bansal, Gallant, Hussey, and Tauchen (1993, 1995) and developed further in Gallant and Tauchen (1996).

The idea is this: since

$$\frac{1}{n} \sum_{t=L+1}^{n} s_f(\tilde{y}_{t-L}, \ldots, \tilde{y}_t, \tilde{\theta}) = 0,$$

where the left side is averaged over the observed realization $\{\tilde{y}_t\}_{t=1}^{n}$, then a good estimator for ρ would be one that makes

$$\frac{1}{N} \sum_{\tau=L+1}^{N} s_f(\hat{y}_{\tau-L}(\rho), \ldots, \tilde{y}_\tau(\rho), \tilde{\theta}) \approx 0, \qquad (17)$$

with the average taken over the simulated realization. If $l_\theta = l_\rho$, then (17) can hold with equality, but, if as is typical, $l_\theta > l_\rho$, then (17) cannot in general hold with equality, which motivates GMM of Hansen (1982). Put

$$\hat{m}_N(\rho, \theta) = \frac{1}{N} \sum_{\tau=L+1}^{N} s_f(\hat{y}_{t-L}(\rho), \ldots, \hat{y}_t(\rho), \theta). \qquad (18)$$

The estimator is

$$\hat{\rho} = \arg \min_{\rho} \{\hat{m}_N(\rho, \tilde{\theta})' \tilde{\mathscr{I}}^{-1} \hat{m}_N(\rho, \tilde{\theta})\}, \qquad (19)$$

where $\tilde{\mathscr{I}}^{-1}$ is a weighting matrix and $\tilde{\mathscr{I}} \xrightarrow{as} \mathscr{I}$ as $n \to \infty$.

In (18), the criterion $\hat{m}_N(\rho, \theta)$ is the mean score of the f-model averaged with respect to the simulation $\{\hat{y}_\tau(\rho)\}_{\tau=1}^{N}$. The estimator in (19) minimizes with respect to ρ the length of $\hat{m}_N(\rho, \tilde{\theta})$ relative to $\tilde{\mathscr{I}}^{-1}$, with θ left fixed at the QML estimator $\tilde{\theta}$ defined in (6) and (7) above.

With modern computing equipment one uses very long simulations, and so we consider letting simulated sample size N go to infinity. By assumption, the p-model defines a stationary data generator so, as discussed in section 2, $\hat{m}_N(\rho, \theta) \xrightarrow{as} m(\rho, \theta)$ as $N \to \infty$, where

$$m(\rho, \theta) = \int s_f(y_{t-L}, \ldots, y_t, \theta) p_L(y_{t-L}, \ldots, y_t \mid \rho) d(y_{t-L}, \ldots, y_t). \qquad (20)$$

The "almost surely" is with respect to the random number generator; the dataset $\{\tilde{y}_t\}_{t=1}^n$ is fixed. Here $m(\rho, \theta)$ is the mean score of the f-model with respect to the p-model. Apart from the small numerical error due to Monte Carlo integration, the estimator is the solution to the problem

$$\min_{\rho} m(\rho, \tilde{\theta})' \tilde{\mathscr{I}}^{-1} m(\rho, \tilde{\theta}). \tag{21}$$

A sketch of the asymptotics follows. Throughout, $\tilde{\rho}$ denotes the solution to either (19) or (21), since in practice the Monte Carlo integration should be accurate enough to reduce the numerical error to the point where the two problems are essentially equivalent.

Consistency
A standard result of $\sqrt{n}$ − asymptotics is that almost surely a solution to the problem (21) gets arbitrarily close to the set of solutions of the limiting problem

$$\min_{\rho} m(\rho, \bar{\theta})' \mathscr{I}^{-1} m(\rho, \bar{\theta}), \tag{22}$$

since $\tilde{\mathscr{I}} \overset{as}{\to} \mathscr{I}$ and $\tilde{\theta} \overset{as}{\to} \bar{\theta}$. Now, $m(\rho_0, \bar{\theta}) = 0$ by the first-order condition (12) of the optimization problem defining the binding function. Hence, ρ_0 is a solution to the problem (22)

$$0 = m(\rho_0, \bar{\theta})' \mathscr{I}^{-1} m(\rho_0, \bar{\theta}) = \min_{\rho} m(\rho, \bar{\theta})' \mathscr{I}^{-1} m(\rho, \bar{\theta}).$$

The only issue is uniqueness, which pertains to identification. We assume ρ_0 is the only solution of

$$m(\rho, \bar{\theta}) = \int s_f(y_{t-L}, \dots, y_t, \bar{\theta}) p_L(y_{t-L}, \dots, y_t \mid \rho) d(y_{t-L}, \dots, y_t) = 0. \tag{23}$$

Hence $\hat{\rho} \overset{as}{\to} \rho_0$.

Asymptotic normality
Asymptotic normality starts with the first-order condition of (21):

$$\frac{\partial m(\hat{\rho}, \tilde{\theta})'}{\partial \rho} \tilde{\mathscr{I}}^{-1} m(\hat{\rho}, \tilde{\theta}) = 0.$$

Taking a mean value expansion of $m(\hat{\rho}, \tilde{\theta})$ about $m(\rho_0, \bar{\theta})$, and noting that $m(\rho_0, \bar{\theta}) = 0$ by (12), gives

$$\frac{\partial m(\dot{\rho}, \tilde{\theta})'}{\partial \rho} \mathscr{\tilde{I}}^{-1} \left[\frac{\partial m(\dot{\rho}, \tilde{\theta})}{\partial \rho'} (\hat{\rho} - \rho_0) + \frac{\partial m(\dot{\rho}, \dot{\theta})}{\partial \theta'} (\tilde{\theta} - \bar{\theta}) \right] = 0,$$

where $\dot{\rho}$ and $\dot{\theta}$ mean that the rows of the derivative matrices are evaluated at intermediate points. This last expression gives

$$\sqrt{n}(\hat{\rho} - \rho_0) = - \left[\frac{\partial m(\dot{\rho}, \tilde{\theta})'}{\partial \rho} \mathscr{\tilde{I}}^{-1} \frac{\partial m(\dot{\rho}, \tilde{\theta})}{\partial \rho'} \right]^{-1}$$

$$\frac{\partial m(\dot{\rho}, \tilde{\theta})'}{\partial \rho} \mathscr{\tilde{I}}^{-1} \frac{\partial m(\dot{\rho}, \dot{\theta})}{\partial \rho'} \sqrt{n}(\tilde{\theta} - \bar{\theta}),$$

which highlights the fact that all of the randomness of the estimator is due solely to the fluctuations in $\tilde{\theta}$ about $\bar{\theta}$. Since $\mathscr{\tilde{I}} \overset{as}{\to} \mathscr{I}, \tilde{\theta} \overset{as}{\to} \bar{\theta}$, and $\hat{\rho} \overset{as}{\to} \rho_0$, then

$$\sqrt{n}(\hat{\rho} - \rho_0) \overset{LD}{=} - (D_\rho' \mathscr{I}^{-1} D_\rho)^{-1} D_\rho' \mathscr{I}^{-1} D_\theta \sqrt{n}(\tilde{\theta} - \bar{\theta}), \qquad (24)$$

where $D_\theta = \partial m(\rho_0, \bar{\theta})/\partial \theta'$ and $D_\rho = \partial m(\rho_0, \bar{\theta})/\partial \rho'$. A key fact is that $D_\theta = \mathscr{H}$ where the hessian $\mathscr{H}$ is given in (14); the verification is

$$D_\theta = \frac{\partial m(\rho_0, \bar{\theta})}{\partial \theta'}$$

$$= \int \frac{\partial}{\partial \theta'} s_f(y_{t-L}, \ldots, y_t, \bar{\theta}) p_L(y_{t-L}, \ldots, y_t \mid \rho_0) d(y_{t-L}, \ldots, y_t)$$

$$= \int \frac{\partial^2}{\partial \theta \partial \theta'} \log[f(y_t \mid y_{t-L}, \ldots, y_t, \bar{\theta})]$$
$$p_L(y_{t-L}, \ldots, y_t \mid \rho_0) d(y_{t-L}, \ldots, y_t)$$

$$= \mathscr{H}.$$

Using this fact together with (24) and the characterization (15) yields

$$\sqrt{n}(\hat{\rho} - \rho_0) \overset{\mathscr{D}}{\to} N[0, (D_\rho' \mathscr{I}^{-1} D_\rho)^{-1}]. \qquad (25)$$

In addition, the limiting value of the normalized objective function is asymptotically chi-square

$$n m(\hat{\rho}, \tilde{\theta})' \mathscr{\tilde{I}}^{-1} m(\hat{\rho}, \tilde{\theta}) \overset{\mathscr{D}}{\to} \chi^2(l_\theta - l_\rho). \qquad (26)$$

To justify (26), a mean-value approximation gives

$$m(\hat{\rho}, \tilde{\theta}) = \frac{\partial m(\dot{\rho}, \dot{\theta})}{\partial \rho'}(\hat{\rho} - \rho_0) + \frac{\partial m(\dot{\rho}, \dot{\theta})}{\partial \theta'}(\tilde{\theta} - \theta_0),$$

and so

$$\sqrt{n}m(\hat{\rho}, \tilde{\theta}) \overset{LD}{=} D_\rho \sqrt{n}(\hat{\rho} - \rho_0) + D_\theta \sqrt{n}(\tilde{\theta} - \theta_0).$$

Using (24) gives

$$\sqrt{n}m(\hat{\rho}, \tilde{\theta}) \overset{LD}{=} [I - D_\rho(D'_\rho \mathscr{I}^{-1}D_\rho)^{-1}D'_\rho \mathscr{I}^{-1}]D_\theta \sqrt{n}(\tilde{\theta} - \theta_0).$$

From (15) $\sqrt{n}(\tilde{\theta} - \theta_0) \overset{LD}{=} \mathscr{H}^{-1}\mathscr{I}^{1/2}z$, where $z \sim N(0, I)$. Thus, remembering that $D_\theta = \mathscr{H}$,

$$\sqrt{n}m(\hat{\rho}, \tilde{\theta}) \overset{LD}{=} -[I - D_\rho(D'_\rho \mathscr{I}^{-1}D_\rho)^{-1}D'_\rho \mathscr{I}^{-1}]\mathscr{I}^{1/2}z. \qquad (27)$$

Putting everything together gives

$$nm(\tilde{\rho}, \tilde{\theta})'\tilde{\mathscr{I}}^{-1}m(\tilde{\rho}, \tilde{\theta}) \overset{LD}{=} nm(\hat{\rho}, \tilde{\theta})'\mathscr{I}^{-1}m(\hat{\rho}, \tilde{\theta}) \qquad (28)$$

$$\overset{LD}{=} \{[I - D_\rho(D'_\rho \mathscr{I}^{-1}D_\rho)^{-1}\mathscr{I}^{-1}]\mathscr{I}^{1/2}z\}'\mathscr{I}^{-1} \qquad (29)$$

$$\{[I - D_\rho(D'_\rho \mathscr{I}^{-1}D_\rho)^{-1}\mathscr{I}^{-1}]\mathscr{I}^{1/2}z\} \qquad (30)$$

$$\overset{LD}{=} z'[I - H(H'H)^{-1}H']z, \qquad (31)$$

where $H = \mathscr{I}^{-1/2}D_\rho$. Note that H is $l_\theta \times l_\rho$ so rank$[I - H(H'H)^{-1}H']$ $= l_\theta - l_\rho$, and hence $nm(\hat{\rho}, \tilde{\theta})'\tilde{\mathscr{I}}^{-1}m(\hat{\rho}, \tilde{\theta}) \overset{LD}{=} \chi^2(l_\theta - l_\rho)$, as to be shown.

Gallant and Tauchen (1996) suggest using the estimate of $\mathscr{I}$ based on the mean outer-product-of-the-gradient

$$\tilde{\mathscr{I}} = \frac{1}{n}\sum_{t=L+1}^{n} s_f(\tilde{y}_{t-L}, \ldots, \tilde{y}_t, \tilde{\theta})s_f(\tilde{y}_{t-L}, \ldots, \tilde{y}_t, \tilde{\theta})', \qquad (32)$$

whenever the f-model is chosen so that $f(y_t \mid y_{t-L}, \ldots, y_{t-1}, \tilde{\theta})$ is a very good representation of the data. Then, the scores of the f-model are nearly serially uncorrelated as they are essentially martingale differences. If the scores of the f-model are not serially uncorrelated, the estimator is still consistent and asymptotically normal, though a weighted covariance matrix estimate would be needed

$$\tilde{\mathscr{J}} = \sum_{t=L+1}^{n} \sum_{r=L+1}^{n} \omega_n(t-r)s_f(\tilde{y}_{t-L}, \ldots, \tilde{y}_t, \tilde{\theta})s_f(\tilde{y}_{r-L}, \ldots, \tilde{y}_r, \tilde{\theta})',$$

where $\{\omega_n(k)\}_{k=-(n-L)+1}^{n-L-1}$ are weights ensuring that $\tilde{\mathscr{J}}$ is positive definite and consistently estimates $\mathscr{J}$. There is an extensive literature on HAC estimation including Gallant (1987, p. 446), Newey and West (1987), and Andrews (1991).

3.3   The indirect inference estimator

Smith (1990, 1993) develops a different strategy which is extended to very rich estimation environments by Gouriéroux, Monfort, and Renault (1993). This strategy, now termed "Indirect Inference," mimics directly the optimization underlying the QMLE (6) instead of the first-order conditions. Define

$$\mathscr{T}_N(\rho) = \arg\max_{\theta} \mathscr{L}_N(\theta, \{\hat{y}_\tau(\rho)\}_{\tau=1}^N), \tag{33}$$

where

$$\mathscr{L}_N(\theta, \{\hat{y}_\tau(\rho)\}_{\tau=1}^N) = \frac{1}{N}\sum_{\tau=L+1}^{N} \log[f(\hat{y}_\tau(\rho)\,|\,\hat{y}_{\tau-L}(\rho), \ldots, \hat{y}_{\tau-1}(\rho), \theta)] \tag{34}$$

The indirect inference estimator is

$$\hat{\rho}_{II} = \arg\min_{\rho}[\mathscr{T}_N(\rho) - \tilde{\theta}]'[\tilde{\mathscr{H}}^{-1}\tilde{\mathscr{J}}\tilde{\mathscr{H}}^{-1}]^{-1}[\mathscr{T}_N(\rho) - \tilde{\theta}], \tag{35}$$

where $\tilde{\mathscr{H}} \overset{as}{\to} \mathscr{H}$ and $\tilde{\mathscr{J}} \overset{as}{\to} \mathscr{J}$. The considerations raised at the end of Subsection 3.2 in regard to the estimator $\tilde{\mathscr{J}}$ apply to indirect inference as well. The natural estimator of $\mathscr{H}$ is

$$\tilde{\mathscr{H}} = \frac{1}{n}\sum_{t=L+1}^{n} \frac{\partial^2}{\partial\theta\partial\theta'} \log[f(\tilde{y}_t\,|\,\tilde{y}_{t-L}, \ldots, \tilde{y}_{t-1}, \tilde{\theta})]. \tag{36}$$

As before, we let $N \to \infty$ (use sufficiently long realizations), and observe that the indirect inference estimator solves

$$\arg\min_{\rho}[\mathscr{T}(\rho) - \tilde{\theta}]'[\mathscr{H}^{-1}\mathscr{I}\mathscr{H}^{-1}]^{-1}[\mathscr{T}(\rho) - \tilde{\theta}], \tag{37}$$

where $\mathscr{T}$ is the binding function given in (10).

To establish consistency, one observes that ρ_0 is a solution to the limiting problem

$$\arg\min_{\rho}[\mathscr{T}(\rho) - \tilde{\theta}]'[\mathscr{H}^{-1}\mathscr{I}\mathscr{H}^{-1}]^{-1}[\mathscr{T}(\rho) - \tilde{\theta}], \tag{38}$$

and the identification condition is that ρ_0 is the only solution to this optimization problem. The asymptotic distribution theory for this case (Smith (1990, 1993)) proceeds much as in subsection 3.2.

4   SELECTION OF THE AUXILIARY MODEL

We now examine in some detail four major considerations for selection of the auxiliary model: efficiency, diagnostics, behavior under misspecification, and dynamic stability. The discussion follows the score-based approach described in subsection 3.2, and so the auxiliary model is termed the score generator.

4.1   Efficiency

For any fixed score generator, the minimum chi-square estimator defined in (19) is not as efficient asymptotically as maximum likelihood. As will be seen, though, by following a suitable strategy for selecting the score generator, the efficiencies can be made arbitrarily close. This motivates the terminology efficient method of moments, as method of moments becomes asymptotically as efficient as maximum likelihood.

In what follows, $\mathscr{V}_f$ denotes the asymptotic variance from (25) for the estimator when the score generator is f, and $\mathscr{V}_0$ denotes the asymptotic variance of maximum likelihood. From standard efficiency theory, $\mathscr{V}_f \geq \mathscr{V}_0$, and we are interested in how close $\mathscr{V}_f$ comes to the lower bound.

To see the main idea, we start with the i.i.d. case. Suppose for all $J, p_J(y_t | y_{t-J}, \ldots, y_{t-1}, \rho_0) = p(y_t | \rho_0)$. Drop the time subscript and write the random variables $s_p = (\partial/\partial\rho)\log[f(Y | \rho_0)]$ and $s_f = (\partial/\partial\theta)\log[f(Y | \bar{\theta})]$, where $Y \sim p(y | \rho_0)$. As before, ρ_0 is the true value of ρ and $\bar{\theta}$ is the pseudo-true value of θ given by

$$\bar{\theta} = \arg\max_{\theta} \int \log[f(y | \theta)]p(y | \rho_0)dy.$$

From maximum-likelihood theory, $\mathscr{V}_0 = [\mathscr{E}(s_p s_p')]^{-1}$, while, from (25), $\mathscr{V}_f = (D_\rho' \mathscr{I}^{-1} D_\rho)^{-1}$. In this case, $\mathscr{I} = \operatorname{Var}(s_f) = \mathscr{E}(s_f s_f')$. Furthermore

$$D_\rho = \frac{\partial m(\rho_0, \bar\theta)}{\partial \rho'}$$

$$= \left[\frac{\partial}{\partial \rho'} \left(\int \frac{\partial}{\partial \theta} \log[f(y\,|\,\bar\theta)] p(y\,|\,\rho)\,dy \right) \right]_{\rho=\rho^0}$$

$$= \int \frac{\partial}{\partial \theta} \log[f(y\,|\,\bar\theta)] \left\{ \frac{\partial}{\partial \rho'} \log[p(y\,|\,\rho_0)] \right\} p(y\,|\,\rho_0)\,dy$$

$$= \mathscr{E}(s_f s_p').$$

Now consider the population regression of s_p on to s_f

$$s_p = B s_f + u, \operatorname{Var}(u) = \Omega,$$

where $B = \mathscr{E}(s_p s_f')[\mathscr{E}(s_f s_f')]^{-1}$ is $l_\rho \times l_\theta$ and by construction $\operatorname{Cov}(u, s_f) = 0$. Hence $\mathscr{E}(s_p s_p') = B\mathscr{E}(s_f s_f')B' + \Omega = D_\rho' \mathscr{I}^{-1} D_\rho + \Omega$, and so

$$\mathscr{V}_0 = (\mathscr{V}_f^{-1} + \Omega)^{-1}, \tag{39}$$

or, equivalently

$$\mathscr{V}_f = (\mathscr{V}_0^{-1} - \Omega)^{-1}. \tag{40}$$

The asymptotic variance–covariance matrix of the EMM estimator exceeds that of maximum likelihood by an amount that depends on the variance–covariance matrix of the error from a linear projection of s_p on to s_f. The closer s_p comes to lying in the linear span of s_f, then the closer is the EMM estimator to achieving the efficiency of maximum likelihood.

Recent work by Gallant and Long (1995) indicates that full efficiency can be achieved and in the dependent case as well. We first illustrate the ideas when $\{y_t\}$ is Markovian. Suppose there is an L such that

$$p_J(y_t\,|\,y_{t-J}, \ldots, y_{t-1}, \rho_0) = p_L(y_t\,|\,y_{t-L}, \ldots, y_{t-1}, \rho_0)]$$

for all $J \geq L$. The dynamic maximum-likelihood estimator

$$\hat\rho_{MLE} = \arg\max_\rho \frac{1}{n} \sum_{t=L+1}^n \log[p_L(y_t\,|\,y_{t-L}, \ldots, y_{t-1}, \rho_0)]$$

is asymptotically normal with variance–covariance matrix $\mathscr{V}_0 = [\mathscr{E}(s_{pt} s_{pt}')]^{-1}$, where

$$s_{pt} = \frac{\partial}{\partial \rho} \log[p_L(y_t\,|\,y_{t-1}, \ldots, y_{t-1}, \rho_0)].$$

Now consider using an SNP model for a score generator. The SNP family of conditional densities is an increasing nested hierarchy of finite dimensional models

$$\{f_K(y_t \mid y_{t-L}, \ldots, y_{t-1}, \theta_K)\}_{K=0}^{\infty},$$

where $\theta_K \in \Theta_K$ and $\Theta_K \subset \Theta_{K+1}$ is a nested sequence of Euclidean spaces. The relevant feature is that the SNP family is dense under a Sobelov norm $\|\cdot\|$

$$\lim_{K \to \infty} \inf_{\theta_K \in \Theta_K} \|f_K(\cdot \mid \cdot, \theta_K) - p_L(\cdot \mid \cdot, \rho_0)\| = 0.$$

The asymptotic variance of $\hat{\rho}$ with $f_K(y_t \mid y_{t-L}, \ldots, y_{t-1}, \theta_K)$ used as the score generator is

$$\mathcal{V}_{f_K} = [\mathscr{E}(s_{pt}s'_{f_K,t})(\mathscr{I}_K)^{-1}\mathscr{E}(s_{f_K,t}s'_{pt})]^{-1},$$

where

$$s_{f_K,t} = \frac{\partial}{\partial \theta} \log[f_K(y_t \mid y_{t-L}, \ldots, y_{t-1}, \bar{\theta}_K)],$$

with

$$\bar{\theta} = \arg\max_{\theta_K} \mathscr{E}\{\log[f_K(y_t \mid y_{t-L}, \ldots, y_{t-1}, \bar{\theta}_K)]\},$$

and

$$\mathscr{I}_K = \sum_{i=-\infty}^{\infty} \mathscr{E}(s_{f_K,t}s'_{f_K,t+j}).$$

One can check that $D_\rho = \mathscr{E}(s_{f_K,t}s'_{pt})$ in the dynamic case. Here, $\mathscr{E}(\cdot)$ means an expectation computed with respect to the joint p.d.f. $p_J(y_{t-J}, \ldots, y_t \mid \rho_0)$.

Suppose that for some finite and possibly large K, the p-model lies in the SNP hierarchy, though possibly with a reparameterization. Then $s_{pt} = Bs_{f_K,t}$ for some non-singular matrix of constants B. Evidently, then $\mathcal{V}_{f_K} = \mathcal{V}_0$, and full efficiency obtains. Of course, in general, no such K exists, though Gallant and Long show that

$$\lim_{k \to \infty} \mathcal{V}_{f_K} = \mathcal{V}_0.$$

Interestingly, analogous results remain true even when $\{y_t\}$ is not Markovian, with another limit being taken as $L \to \infty$.

294   George Tauchen

4.2   Diagnostics

The criterion

$$m(\rho, \theta) = \int s_f(y_{t-L}, \ldots, y_t, \theta) p_L(y_{t-L}, \ldots, y_t, \rho) d(y_{y-L}, \ldots, y_t)$$

is the mean score of the f-model under the p-model. By the definition of θ, $m(\rho_0, \theta) = 0$, and the EMM estimator $\hat{\rho}$ minimizes $m(\rho, \theta)' \mathscr{I}^{-1} m(\rho, \theta)$. The elements of $m(\hat{\rho}, \theta)$ contain diagnostic information on how well the p-model accounts for the scores of the f-model. Smaller elements indicate those scores that the p-model explains relatively well, while large elements indicate those scores that it has trouble accounting for. Of course small and large need to be judged relative to the statistical variability of the scores. For this assessment, note that from (27)

$$\sqrt{n}m(\hat{\rho}, \theta) \xrightarrow{\mathscr{D}} N(0, [\mathscr{I} - D_\rho (D_\rho' \mathscr{I}^{-1} D_\rho)^{-1} D_\rho']). \tag{41}$$

Thus, each element of the vector of t-statistics

$$T_n = \{ \text{diag}[\hat{\mathscr{I}} - \hat{D}_\rho (\hat{D}_\rho' \hat{\mathscr{I}}^{-1} \hat{D}_\rho)^{-1} \hat{D}_\rho'] \}^{-1/2} \sqrt{n}m(\hat{\rho}, \theta) \tag{42}$$

is asymptotically $N(0, 1)$, where $\hat{D}_\rho = (\partial/\partial \rho') m(\hat{\rho}, \theta)$ is a consistent estimate of D_ρ. The individual elements of T_n convey diagnostic information about how well the p-model fits the corresponding score of the f-model. If a closed-form expression for $(\partial/\partial \rho) m(\hat{\rho}, \theta)$ is not readily available, then a numerical estimate of D_ρ might be formed by taking difference quotients around the optimum.

For a quick and easy assessment not involving numerical derivatives, one can examine the quasi-t-ratios

$$\tilde{T}_n = \{ \text{diag}[\hat{\mathscr{I}}] \}^{-1/2} \sqrt{n}m(\hat{\rho}, \theta). \tag{43}$$

The quasi-t-ratios are readily computable and can provide useful diagnostic information. The quasi-t-ratios satisfy $\tilde{T}_n \xrightarrow{\mathscr{D}} N(0, \mathscr{V}^*)$, where

$$\mathscr{V}^* = [\text{diag}(\mathscr{I})]^{-1/2} [\mathscr{I} - D_\rho (D_\rho' \mathscr{I}^{-1} D_\rho)^{-1} D_\rho'] [\text{diag}(\mathscr{I})]^{-1/2}$$
$$\text{diag}(\mathscr{V}^*) \le I.$$

For the same reasons as in Durbin's (1970) classic paper, the quasi-t-ratios are downward biased relative to 2.0. Large magnitudes of the quasi-t-ratios indicate how a p-model goes wrong, but small magnitudes are not necessarily confirmation of the validity of the model.

4.3   Misspecification

The treatment of misspecification of the p-model is along the lines of Newey (1985a, 1985b) and Tauchen (1985), who consider the effects on the asymptotic chi-square non-centrality parameter of small deviations in the maintained model from the true model.

Suppose the process $\{y_t\}$ is strictly stationary and ergodic, but the true joint density of the stretch $(y_{t-J}, \ldots, y_t)$ is $h_J(y_{t-L}, \ldots, y_t)$, for $J = 0, 1, 2, \ldots$. Suppose also that the maintained density under the model is Markovian of lag length L with conditional density $p_L(y_t \mid y_{t-L}, \ldots, y_{t-1}, \rho)$ and joint density $p_L(y_{t-L}, \ldots, y_t \mid \rho)$. For notational ease we put $\xi_t = (y'_{t-L}, \ldots, y'_t)$ and drop the t and L subscripts where unneeded, so $h(\xi)$ represents the true density while $\{p(\xi, \rho)\}_{\rho \in \mathscr{R}}$ represents the maintained parametric family. The p-model is misspecified when there is no value of ρ in $\mathscr{R}$ such that $p(\xi, \rho) = h(\xi)$ h-almost everywhere. $\mathscr{E}[g(y_{t-J}, \ldots, y_t)]$ means the expectation computed under the true DGP

$$\int g(y_{t-J}, \ldots, y_t) h_J(y_{t-J}, \ldots, y_t) d(y_{t-J}, \ldots, y_t).$$

Suppose $f(y_t \mid y_{t-L}, \ldots, y_{t-1}, \theta)$ is the score generator. Let

$$s_f(\xi_t, \theta) = \frac{\partial}{\partial \theta} \log[f(y_t \mid y_{t-L}, \ldots, y_{t-1}, \theta)].$$

Then $\tilde{\theta} \overset{as}{\to} \bar{\theta}$, where the pseudo-true value $\bar{\theta}$ satisfies

$$\int s_f(\xi, \bar{\theta}) h(\xi) d\xi = 0.$$

Also, $\hat{\rho} \overset{as}{\to} \bar{\rho}$ where the pseudo-true value $\bar{\rho}$ satisfies

$$\bar{\rho} = \arg \min_{\rho} m(\rho, \bar{\theta})' \mathscr{I}^{-1} m(\rho, \bar{\theta}),$$

with

$$m(\rho, \bar{\theta}) = \int s_\xi(\xi, \bar{\theta}) p(\xi, \rho) d\xi,$$

and

$$\mathscr{I} = \sum_{i=-\infty}^{\infty} \mathscr{E}[s_f(\xi_t) s_f(\xi_{t-i})'].$$

By (26), under the maintained assumption of correct specification, the scaled value of the objective function, $c_n^2 = nm(\hat{\rho}, \bar{\theta})'\mathscr{J}^{-1}m(\hat{\rho}, \bar{\theta})$, satisfies $c_n^2 \xrightarrow{\mathscr{D}} \chi^2(l_\theta - l_\rho)$. Under misspecification, however

$$\frac{c_n^2}{n} \xrightarrow{as} \bar{c}^2 = m(\bar{\rho}, \bar{\theta})'\mathscr{J}^{-1}m(\bar{\rho}, \bar{\theta}).$$

Put $\bar{m} = m(\bar{\rho}, \bar{\theta})$ so $\bar{c}^2 = \bar{m}'\mathscr{J}^{-1}\bar{m}$. The value $\bar{c}^2$ is the approximate slope (Geweke (1983)) of the specification test. If, for a particular h, $\bar{c}^2$ is zero, then the test has no power against that alternative; if $\bar{c}^2 > 0$, then the test will ultimately reject the maintained model.

Write $p(\xi, \bar{\rho}) = [1 + \eta(\xi)]h(\xi)$, which defines $\eta(\xi)$, under the reasonable presumption that the supports of p and h are the same. The function η reflects the deviance of the maintained p-model from the true model. The value of $\bar{c}^2$ depends upon the maintained model only through $\bar{m}$. Observe that

$$\bar{m} = \int s_f(\xi, \bar{\theta})[1 + \eta(\xi)]h(\xi)d\xi = \int s_f(\xi, \bar{\theta})\eta(\xi)h(\xi)d\xi.$$

Consequently $\bar{m} = \mathrm{Cov}(s_f, \eta)$ under $h(\xi)$. With $\bar{c}^2 = \mathrm{Cov}(\eta, s_f)\mathscr{J}^{-1}$ $\mathrm{Cov}(s_f, \eta)$, then the test of the overidentifying restrictions ultimately detects any misspecification such that $\mathrm{Cov}(s_f, \eta) \neq 0$, and it will fail to detect misspecification such that $\mathrm{Cov}(s_f, \eta) = 0$.

We can thus have a situation where, for a particular score generator, f, and true DGP h, $\mathrm{Cov}(f, \eta) = 0$, so the test of the overidentifying restrictions is expected to be passed, but the model is misspecified. The test of the overidentifying restrictions will be fooled whenever the truth lies in a direction such that $\mathrm{Cov}(s_f, \eta) = 0$. Without very strong a priori knowledge, the only way to avoid this situation is to take a flexible, more nonparametric approach to specification of the score generator.

4.4   Dynamic stability

Tauchen (1995) examines the issue of dynamic stability of the p- and f-models. The upshot is that one really need not worry about imposing dynamic stability on the structural model itself. Dynamic stability is self-enforcing. If the optimizer wanders into the region of the parameter space where the underlying structural model is unstable, then the data simulator generates a wildly explosive simulated realization that induces a large value of the objective function. The time-series properties of this explosive realization are very much unlike the time-series properties of the observed dataset to which the auxiliary model has been fitted, so the objective function attains an exceedingly high value. The situation is actually a bit more subtle, because automatic stability is ensured only if the auxiliary model itself is dynamically stable. The use of a dynamically unstable auxiliary model can be expected to define a GMM to objective function with very poor numerical properties in both the stable and unstable regions of the parameter space.

Stability is of practical importance. It plays a role in the selection of the auxiliary model in the application below. Likewise, Andersen and Lund (1996) carefully examine a class of generalized GARCH and E-GARCH auxiliary models for the short-term interest rate. They find the former typically unstable, and therefore unusable as auxiliary models, while the latter are stable.

5   APPLICATION: AN INTEREST RATE DIFFUSION

5.1   The SDE

We now consider estimation of the continuous-time stochastic differential equation (SDE)

$$dV = \mu(V, \alpha)dt + \sigma(V, \beta)dW, \tag{44}$$

where V is a short-term interest rate, and $\mu(V, \alpha)$ and $\sigma(V, \beta)$ are the local drift and diffusion functions with parameters α and β, respectively. We let $\{V_t\}_{t\in[0,T]}$ denote a realization from the SDE and $\{v_t\}_{t=1}^{n}$ denote a discrete-time equispaced selection from the continuous realization, $v_t = V_{th}, t = 1, 2, \ldots, n, nh \le T$, for some $h > 0$. For a single-factor model of the term structure, with the factor being a short-term interest rate, one would need to estimate α and β in order to compute the bond prices and interest rates at various horizons.

To implement the SDE as a stochastic data generator, we employ the Platen Strong Order 1 Scheme (Kloeden and Platen (1992, pp. 374–5)). This scheme modifies the elementary Euler method to include a second-order correction to take account of curvature in the diffusion function. The scheme generates discrete-time data $\{v_t\}$ as

$$v_{t+1} = h(v_t, z_t^*, \alpha, \beta), \tag{45}$$

where $z^* = (z_{t1}, \ldots, z_{tS})$ is a vector of S i.i.d. $N(0, 1)$ deviates and where S is the number of subintervals that $[t, t + h)$ is divided into. The scheme generates a strong solution, and hence a weak solution. As $S \to \infty$, the joint density of N iterations on (45) starting from v_0 converges to $p_{N-1}(v_1, \ldots, v_N \mid v_0, \alpha, \beta)$ as implied by (44).

This scheme maps into the setup of section 2 as

$$y_t = v_t, \qquad \rho = (\alpha' \beta')',$$

and $w_t = z_t^*$ is the forcing process. By taking S very large and letting the iterations run for a long time to let transients die away, we can generate a simulated realization $\{\hat{y}_t\}_{t=1}^N$ from $p_{N-1}(y_1, \ldots, y_N \mid \rho)$, the joint density of $y_1, \ldots, y_N$ implied by the SDE.

In special cases, the functional form of the transition probability density $p(y_{t+1} \mid y_t, \rho)$ is known. For instance, with a linear drift and constant diffusion function, this scheme defines an AR(1) process for y_t. If the drift is linear and the diffusion function is proportional to $V^{1/2}$, i.e., the square root model of Cox, Ingersoll, and Ross (1985), $p(y_{t+1} \mid y_t, \rho)$ is a non-central chi-square. In this case, one can estimate ρ directly from an observed realization $\{\tilde{y}_t\}_{t=1}^n$ by dynamic maximum likelihood

$$\tilde{\rho}_{ML} = \arg\max_{\rho} \frac{1}{n} \sum_{t=2}^{n} \log[p(\tilde{y}_t \mid \tilde{y}_{t-1}, \rho)].$$

This approach is taken by Duffie and Singleton (1994) for the square-root model.

In general, however, the conditional density $p(y_{t+1} \mid y_t, \rho)$ does not have a tractable form, which motivates the use of alternative estimators. This point is well understood in the literature and highlighted in Melino's (1994) survey of continuous-time methods in finance.

Ait-Sahalia (1996a) observes that the unconditional density $p(y \mid \rho)$ of the discrete-time process $\{y_t\}$ implied by (44) has a closed-form expression in terms of the drift function μ and diffusion function σ. He develops and implements the estimator

$$\tilde{\rho}_{NP} = \arg\max_{\rho} \sum_{t=1}^{n} [p(\tilde{y}_t \mid \rho) - \tilde{p}_{NP}(\tilde{y}_t)]^2$$

where $\tilde{p}_{NP}(\tilde{y}_t)$ is a kernel estimate of the unconditional density of y_t. This method thus uses the unconditional density of y_t as the standard of fit. Ait-Sahalia (1996a) develops a second method that uses a kernel estimate of the discrete-time transition density $p(y_{t+1} \mid y_t)$. The criterion of fit is developed from two equivalent expressions for the evolution of the continuous-time transition probability as implied by the forward and backward Kolmogorov equations under stationarity. Both of these two methods, as well as the others discussed further below, work directly from parametric specifications for μ and σ. In contrast, Ait-Sahalia (1996b) considers another approach that entails inverting the expression for unconditional density to generate a non-parametric estimate of σ from a non-parametric estimate of the unconditional density. When both μ and σ are parameterized this approach is unneeded, though a comparison of the parametric and non-parametric estimates of σ can be the basis of a specification test.

Conley *et al.* (1995) adopt the methods of Hansen and Scheinkman (1995). They show how to compute tractable closed-form expressions for

$$\mu_\varphi(\rho) = \int \int \phi(y_{t-1}, y_t) p_1(y_{t-1}, y_t \mid \rho) dy_{t-1} dy_t$$

for test functions $\phi(y_{t-1}, y_t)$. Letting

$$m(y_{t-1}, y_t, \rho) = [\phi_1(y_{t-1}, y_t) - \mu_{\varphi_1(\rho)}, \cdots, \phi_J(y_{t-1}, y_t) - \mu_{\varphi_J}(\rho)],$$

for a batch of J-test functions, then a GMM estimator of ρ is given by

$$\tilde{\rho}_{GMM} = \arg\min_\rho \left[\frac{1}{n} \sum_{t=2}^{n} m(y_{t-1}, y_t, \rho) \right]' \tilde{\mathscr{B}}^{-1}$$

$$\left[\frac{1}{n} \sum_{t=2}^{n} m(y_{t-1}, y_t, \rho) \right],$$

where $\tilde{\mathscr{B}}$ is a weighted covariance matrix estimator of

$$\lim_{n \to \infty} \text{Var} \left[\frac{1}{\sqrt{n}} \sum_{t=2}^{n} m(y_{t-1}, y_t, \rho_0) \right].$$

Weighted covariance estimation is needed because $m(y_{t-1}, y_t, \rho_0)$ is not in general a serially uncorrelated vector process.

The EMM method provides an alternative to these procedures. A possible advantage of EMM in this context is that it provides a direct check on whether the time-series properties of discrete-time realizations $\{y_t\}$ generated via (44) are consistent with those implied by an independent estimate of the discrete-time conditional density $f(y_t \mid y_{t-L}, \ldots, y_{t-1})$. Another is that since the auxiliary model fits the data well, then the score should be nearly serially uncorrelated, thus eliminating the need for weighted covariance estimation. A disadvantage is that it entails the added complexity of a simulation-based method for a model with a single observed factor, whereas the other approaches do not need simulation. Plots of simulations are useful for assessing the predicted time-series properties though, as in figure 9.5 discussed below. All told, the procedures seem complementary. We now turn to implementation of EMM.

5.2   Data

The data are weekly (Friday) observations on the 30-day Eurodollar interest rate, January 1, 1975–October 28, 1994, for 1,035 observations. The top panel of figure 9.1 is a plot of $\{\tilde{y}_t\}_{t=1}^{1035}$. Data on the seven-day Eurodollar rate were also collected but not used. As is typical of interest rates quoted for very short maturity intervals, the seven-day rate shows occasional extraordinarily large movements, presumably due to short-term liquidity or microstructure effects. My view is that such effects are not characteristic of the dynamics of the fundamental factor for equilibrium asset pricing, though the EMM method could certainly be used to fit (44) to the seven-day rate.

5.3   Estimation of the score generator

The first step is to fit the auxiliary model for the conditional density of the interest rate process. Gallant and Tauchen (1989, 1992, 1995a) develop a very flexible approach, termed the semi-non-parametric (SNP) approach, to estimation of the conditional density of a discrete-time stationary process. The SNP approach is based on a truncated Hermite series expansion. For the interest rate process y_t, the SNP specification is

$$f_K(y_t \mid y_{t-L}, \ldots, y_{t-1}, \theta) = f_K(y_t \mid x_{t-1}, \theta) = \frac{[\mathscr{P}_t(z_t)]^2 n(z_t)}{\int [\mathscr{P}_t(u)]^2 n(u) du} \frac{1}{R_t}, \quad (46)$$

where $n(\cdot)$ is the standard normal density,

$$z_t = \frac{(y_t - \mu_t)}{R_t}, \quad (47)$$

$$x_{t-1} = (y_{t-L}, \ldots, y_{t-1}), \quad (48)$$

$$\mu_t = \theta_{10} + \sum_{j=1}^{L_u} \theta_{1j} y_{t-j}, \quad (49)$$

$$R_t = \theta_{20} + \sum_{j=1}^{L_r} \theta_{2j} \mathrm{abs}(z_{t-j}), \quad (50)$$

$$\mathscr{P}_t(z) = \sum_{\lambda \le K_z} a_{\lambda,t} z^\lambda, \quad (51)$$

$$a_{\lambda,t} = \sum_{|\eta| \le K_x} \theta_{3\lambda\eta} \Pi_{j=1}^{L_p} y_{t-j}^{\eta_j}, \quad (52)$$

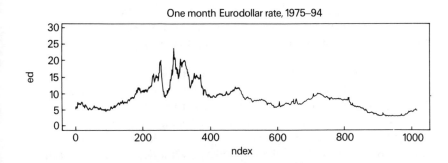

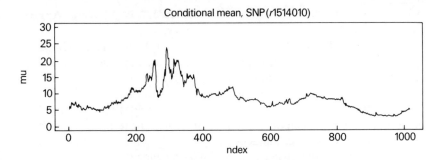

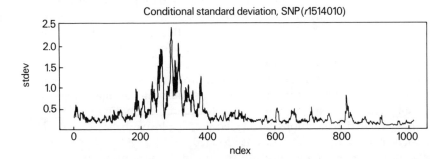

Figure 9.1 The top panel is a time series plot of weekly observations $\{\tilde{y}_t\}_{t=1}^{1035}$ on the 30-day Eurodollar interest rate, January 3, 1985–October 28, 1994. The middle and bottom panels are plots of the SNP one-step conditional mean, $\{\mathscr{E}(\tilde{y}_t \mid \tilde{y}_{t-5}, \ldots, \tilde{y}_{t-1})\}_{t=6}^{1035}$, and conditional standard deviation $\{\sqrt{\mathrm{Var}(\tilde{y}_t \mid \tilde{y}_{t-5}, \ldots, \tilde{y}_{t-1})}\}_{t=6}^{1035}$ from the fitted SNP model termed the "non-linear non-parametric," where $L_u = 1$, $L_r = 5$, $K_z = 4$, $L_p = 1$, $K_x = 1$

$\eta = \eta_1 + \cdots + \eta_{L_p}, |\eta| = \Sigma_{j=1}^{L} \eta_j, K = (K_z, K_x), L = \max\{L_u, L_r, L_p\}, \theta_{300}$ $= 1$ is a normalization to achieve identification, abs($\cdot$) is the absolute value function with the corner smoothed out, and by convention $L_p = 1$ when $K_x = 0$.

The SNP model takes the form of a truncated Hermite series expansion modified to make the polynomial non-negative and to integrate to unity. The leading term of the expansion, obtained by setting $K_z = K_x = 0$ an AR(L_u)-ARCH(L_r) model: a linear autoregression of lag length L_u with an ARCH error structure of lag length L_r. Higher-order terms accommodate deviations from this model. Letting $K_z > 0$, while $K_x = 0$, induces a time homogeneous non-Gaussian error structure, while $K_z > 0$ and $K_x > 0$ permits non-Gaussianity and conditional heterogeneity beyond ARCH. Because of the extreme persistence of the interest rate, we do not use the logistic transformation of x_{t-1} described in Gallant and Tauchen (1995a).

We need to determine the degrees K_z, K_x, of the polynomial defined in (51) and (52) and the lag lengths L_u, L_r, L_p in (49), (50), (51), (52). A selection strategy that has worked well across several financial market applications is to use the BIC, i.e., the Schwarz (1978) criterion, to guide first determination of the appropriate lag lengths, L_u and L_r, for the leading term and then go on to determine the appropriate degrees of the polynomials along with L_p.

Table 9.1 shows the objective function surface for the SNP estimation. Throughout, the first 15 observations are reserved for forming lags, leaving 1,020 observations, net. From the table, it is seen that $L_u = 1$ and $L_r = 5$ are appropriate under BIC. Expanding from this point to $K_z = 4$ does substantially better under BIC, which reflects a non-Gaussian error density typical of financial data. Fits with $K_z = 6$ and $K_z = 8$ did slightly better on BIC, though there were some numerical problems with convergence and with the parameter estimates locating in the non-stationary region of parameter space. (Non-stationarity is checked by examining plots of very long simulated realizations for evidence of explosive behavior, which is always readily apparent.) It was decided to leave $K_z = 4$, since it is imperative for the score generator to remain in the stationary region, so EMM is not trying to fit to an unstable model. Inspection of plots of error densities revealed only minor differences across the fits with $K_z = 4, 6,$ or 8; the densities all assumed the typical shape with high concentration of mass near the origin, thick tails, and thin shoulders relative to the Gaussian. In previous experience with financial applications, $K_z = 4$ has typically been found adequate.

The SNP specification with $L_u = 1, L_r = 5, L_z = 4,$ and $K_x = 0$ is a linear autoregression with an ARCH error structure and a homogeneous non-parametric error density. It is analogous to the semi-parametric GARCH model of Engle and Gonzales-Rivera (1991). The score from this specifica-

Table 9.1. *SNP estimation of the conditional density of the 30-Day Eurodollar interest rate, weekly, January 3, 1975–October 28, 1994*

\multicolumn{6}{c}{SNP tuning parameters}	\multicolumn{2}{c}{Objective function}	
L_u	L_r	L_p	K_z	K_x	l_θ	$s_n(\hat\theta)$	Schwarz
1	0	1	0	0	3	−0.68717439	−0.67711329
2	0	1	0	0	4	−0.68910651	−0.67569172
1	1	1	0	0	4	−0.97324818	−0.95983338
1	2	1	0	0	5	−1.05383519	−1.03706670
1	3	1	0	0	6	−1.10456091	−1.08443872
1	4	1	0	0	7	−1.12721105	−1.10373515
1	5	1	0	0	8	−1.16777523	−1.14094564
1	6	1	0	0	9	−1.17026140	−1.14007811
1	7	1	0	0	10	−1.17372354	−1.14018655
1	5	1	2	0	10	−1.20305457	−1.16951784
→1	5	1	4	0	12	−1.25419099	−1.21394660
⇒1	5	1	4	1	17	−1.27719264	−1.22017976
1	5	1	4	2	22	−1.28353119	−1.20974981
1	5	2	4	1	22	−1.28060865	−1.20682728

Note: L_u is the number of lags in the linear part of the SNP model; L_r is the number of lags in the ARCH part; L_p is the number of lags in the polynomial part, $P(z,x)$. The polynomial $P(z,x)$ is of degree K_z in z and K_x in x; by convention, $L_p = 1$ if $K_x = 0$. l_θ is the number of free parameters associated with the SNP model. The data set is $\{y_t\}_{t=16}^{1035}$, with 15 initial values reserved for lags. The symbol → indicates semi-parametric ARCH; ⇒ indicates non-linear non-parametric.

tion is termed the "semi-parametric ARCH score." From table 9.1, however, it is seen that the further expansion to $K_x = 1$ is warranted, which is evidence that the semi-parametric ARCH model does not capture all features of the data. The SNP model with $L_u = 1$, $L_r = 5$, $K_z = 4$, $L_p = 1$, and $K_x = 1$ is the best under BIC of all models considered. The score from this preferred specification is termed the "non-linear non-parametric score."

Evaluation of graphic output can help assess the nature of the adequacy of the fit. The middle and bottom panels of figure 9.1 are time-series plots of the one-step conditional means and conditional standard deviations from the non-linear non-parametric score generator evaluated at each data point. This model is seen to do a good job of tracking the mean and volatility over the sample period.

This cut at the data generates two score generators for the SDE to confront. The semi-parametric ARCH score contains 12 indicators that the SDE must match to zero as closely as it can, while the non-linear non-parametric score contains 17 indicators.

5.4   Estimation of the SDE

We examine three basic specifications of the SDE (44). The first is

$$\mu(V, \alpha) = \alpha_0 + \alpha_1 V, \tag{53}$$

$$\sigma(V, \beta) = \beta_0 V^{1/2}, \tag{54}$$

which is the well-known square-root model of Cox, Ingersoll, and Ross (1985). In what follows, the specification (53)–(54) is termed linear square root. The second specification is the more general constant elasticity of variance (CEV) setup of Chan, Karolyi, Longstaff, and Sanders (1992)

$$\mu(V, \alpha) = \alpha_0 + \alpha_1 V, \tag{55}$$

$$\sigma(V, \beta) = \beta_0 V^{\beta_1}. \tag{56}$$

(55)–(56) with $\beta_1 \geq 1/2$ is termed the linear-CEV specification. Motivated by Conley et al. (1995) and Ait-Sahalia (1996a), we also consider the CEV diffusion with a non-linear specification for the drift

$$\mu(V, \alpha) = \alpha_{-1} V^{-1} + \alpha_0 + \alpha_1 V + \alpha_2 V^2, \tag{57}$$

$$\sigma(V, \beta) = \beta_0 V^{\beta_1}. \tag{58}$$

(57)–(58) is termed the non-linear-CEV specification. One reason for considering non-linear specifications for the drift function is the evidence from Pfann, Schotman, and Tschernig (1996) that non-linearities in the conditional mean play a role in resolving some of the key empirical puzzles of the term structure.

Conley et al. (1995) present sufficient conditions for the existence of a stationary solution on $(0, \infty)$ when the drift function is a truncated two-sided series expansion and the diffusion function is of the CEV form. Interestingly, they find that, under suitable restrictions on the parameters of the drift function, a stationary solution exists even in what might be termed the high volatility cases where $\beta_1 \geq 1$ in (56) and $\beta_1 \geq 3/2$ in (58). In estimation, none of these conditions is imposed. As discussed in subsection 4.4, the EMM estimation method incorporates a stability penalty to force the fitted parameters to generate stationary simulated data so long as the auxiliary model itself is stationary, as was checked in subsection 5.3 above.

To implement the Platen strong order 1 scheme, we scaled time so that one week equals 0.10 units, i.e., $h = 0.10$, and divided the interval $[t, t + 0.10)$ into 100 equispaced intervals. We generated realizations of length 51,000 and discarded the first 1,000 to attenuate the effects of transients, leaving $N = 50,000$. Experimentation showed the results were quite insensitive to various other choices for S, e.g., $S = 50$ or $S = 75$, and also insensitive to the choice of N so long as $N \geq 30,000$. Other experiments showed that the results hardly change if a weak order 2 scheme is used. Labeling one week as 0.10 units of time reflects a particular choice of scaling of the parameters that maintains reasonable numerical stability for the non-linear optimization. With this scaling, then $e^{0.10\alpha_1}$ is the discrete-time first-order autocorrelation coefficient implied by model $dV = (\alpha_0 + \alpha_1 V)dt + \beta_0 dW$. For more general specifications, though, this interpretation does not hold because interaction effects alter the interpretation of the individual parameters.

Table 9.2 shows the results of fitting these three specifications of the SDE using the two score generators (semi-parametric ARCH and non-linear non-parametric) identified in subsection 5.3. (The computations were done using the general purpose EMM package of Gallant and Tauchen (1995b) which includes code, data, and a worked example.) The table shows parameter values $\tilde{\rho} = (\hat{\alpha}'\hat{\beta}')'$ and the objective function defined in (19) rescaled as in (26) to follow a chi-square distribution. The weighting matrix $\mathcal{J}^{-1}$ was formed using the outer-product-of-the-gradient as given in (32). As seen from the table, the linear-square-root specification fails to account for the semi-parametric ARCH score; it is overwhelmingly rejected. Interestingly, though, by increasing β_1 from 0.50 to within the range 0.90–0.95, the linear-CEV specification essentially can fit the semi-parametric ARCH score. For $\beta_1 = 0.95$, the p-value is just over 1 percent. The top panel of figure 9.2 shows the quasi-t-ratios, defined in (43) above, for the linear-square-root specification; the middle panel shows the quasi-t-ratios for the linear-CEV specification with $\beta_1 = 0.90$. As evident from the top panel, the linear-square-root specification has a great deal of trouble accounting for both the scores of the ARCH parameters and the scores of the Hermite parameters, which govern deviations in the error density from normality. On the other hand, the linear-CEV specification essentially fits the semi-parametric ARCH score, a finding consistent with that of Koedijk, Nissen, Schotman, and Wolff (1995) for monthly data.

Fitting the semi-parametric ARCH score, though, is not the same as fitting the data. The non-linear non-parametric score fully accounts for the richness of the data, as it emerges from a complete specification search. As seen from table 9.2, the linear-CEV specification fails to fit this score and is overwhelmingly rejected. There is evidence in favor of the added complexity of non-linear mean specification (57), which confirms Conley et al. (1995)

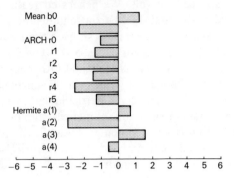

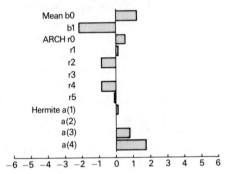

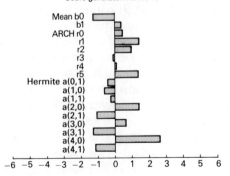

and Ait-Sahalia (1996a). For $\beta_1 = 0.75$, a criterion difference test of $H_0: \alpha_{-1} = \alpha_2 = 0$ gives $\chi^2(2) = 8.484$, p-value $= 0.0143$, while for $\beta_1 = 0.90$ the same test gives $\chi^2(2) = 12.953$, p-value $= 0.0015$.

The parameter β_1 is difficult to estimate precisely. A test of $H_0: \beta_1 = 0.75$ versus $H_1: \beta_1 = 0.90$ gives $\chi^2(1) = 7.67$, p-value $= 0.0056$, so there is considerable evidence for $\beta_1 > 0.75$. The concentrated objective function becomes quite flat for values of β_1 much higher than 0.90, though, making it difficult to pin down β_1 precisely. Values of β_1 for which the objective function differs by less than 3.84 from the value at 0.90 would be included in a 95 percent confidence interval about 0.90. Values like $\beta_1 = 1.25$ and $\beta_1 = 1.50$ would be included in such an interval.

From table 9.2, the non-linear-CEV specification with β_1 pinned at 0.90 comes very close but does not quite fit the data. The bottom panel of figure 9.2 shows the quasi-t-ratios for this specification. The only remaining difficulty is the quasi-t-ratios on the quadratic and quartic terms of the Hermite polynomial, suggesting the model might be generating data that is conditionally too Gaussian. The quasi-t-ratios are similar for values of β_1 such as 1.25 and 1.50. For the non-linear-CEV specification, the value $\beta_1 = 1.50$ is in the upper range of values consistent with the data. As a check on robustness, we explore various aspects of this fit.

Figure 9.3 provides an assessment of the unconditional density of the data. The top panel shows a kernel estimate of the unconditional density of the observed data while the bottom shows the fit to a long realization. The bottom panel is the model's prediction at the fitted parameter values, and it is seen that the model fits this dimension of the data quite well. Figure 9.4 shows the drift and diffusion functions (57)–(58) of the non-linear-CEV specification at the fitted parameter values. The estimated drift function in the upper panel shows extreme mean reversion at low and high values of the interest rate and little mean reversion in the middle, which is confirmation of the plots in Conley et al. (1995) and Ait-Sahalia (1996a).

Figure 9.5 shows volatility scatter plots, which are plots of the first difference, Δy_t, against the lagged level y_{t-1} of the interest rate. The top panel is the volatility scatter of actual data. The middle is the volatility scatter of a long simulation from the linear-square-root specification

Figure 9.2 (opposite) Barplots of quasi-t-ratios defined in (43)

Table 9.2. *Estimation of the stochastic differential equation by EMM to the 30-Day Eurodollar interest rate, weekly, January 3, 1975–October 28, 1994*

Score generator	α_{-1}	α_0	α_1	α_2	β_0	β_1	$\chi^2(\hat{\rho})$	df	p-value
SP-ARCH		0.085212	−0.009535		0.431449	0.500	42.082	9	<0.0001
SP-ARCH		0.060660	−0.005856		−0.198505	0.750	29.199	9	0.0006
SP-ARCH		0.043520	−0.003212		−0.124528	0.900	21.924	9	0.0091
SP-ARCH		0.039678	−0.002599		−0.107789	0.950	19.902	9	0.0185
Non-linear-NP		0.844394	−0.110643		0.217226	0.500	52.480	14	<0.0001
Non-linear-NP		0.252286	0.032167		0.127801	0.750	44.886	14	<0.0001
Non-linear-NP		0.180280	−0.017737		0.105673	0.900	41.684	14	0.0001
Non-linear-NP		0.138474	−0.009072		0.106227	0.950	38.893	14	0.0004
Non-linear-NP	83.891166	−29.604147	3.353859	−0.122553	0.205567	0.500	51.679	12	<0.0001
Non-linear-NP	0.301075	0.104330	−0.020774	−0.000304	0.122584	0.750	36.402	12	0.0002
Non-linear-NP	1.488935	−0.395452	0.027440	−0.000386	0.095634	0.900	28.732	12	0.0043
Non-linear-NP	0.513064	−0.086384	0.002571	0.000090	0.077414	1.000	32.590	12	0.0011
Non-linear-NP	0.889781	−0.300572	0.035812	−0.001098	0.048673	1.250	33.041	12	0.0010
Non-linear-NP	4.972764	−2.083842	0.275028	−0.010533	0.029594	1.500	32.589	12	0.0011
Non-linear-NP	13.253822	−5.662490	0.790175	−0.034622	0.011334	2.000	32.594	12	0.0011
Non-linear-NP	4.744214	−3.192985	0.669735	−0.041405	0.004157	2.500	31.771	12	0.0015

Note: The first column lists the score generator model employed in the EMM estimation, where SP-ARCH is the semi-parametric ARCH model and non-linear-NP is the non-linear non-parametric model. The remaining columns show the estimated values of the parameters α and β of the stochastic differential equation (44), where the drift and diffusion functions are defined in (53)–(58), along with the EMM objective function from estimation using the weekly Eurodollar interest rate data.

Unconditional density of one month Eurodollar rate, 1975–94

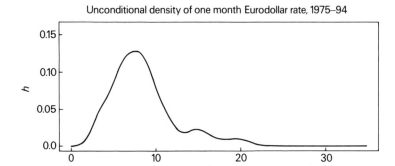

Unconditional density of simulation from non-linear SDE, beta 1 =1.5

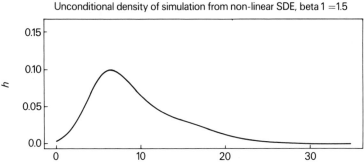

Figure 9.3 The top panel is a kernel estimate of the unconditional density of weekly observations $\{\tilde{y}_t\}_{t=1}^{1035}$ on the 30-day Eurodollar interest rate, January 3, 1975–October 28, 1994. The bottom panel is a kernel estimate from a long simulation of the unconditional density of the fitted stochastic differential equation (44), where the drift and diffusion functions are the non-linear-CEV specification given in (57) and (58) with $\beta_1 = 1.5$ and the other parameters fitted via EMM using the non-linear non-parametric score

estimated using the non-linear non-parametric score. The bottom is the volatility scatter of a long simulation from the non-linear-CEV specification. With enough patience one could simulate and plot an indefinitely long simulation, so only the outer envelopes of the clouds of simulated points matter, not their densities within the ergodic sets. The middle panel shows that the ergodic set of the linear-square-root specification is too small relative to the data, which explains why it performs so poorly. The non-linear-CEV scatter looks more like that of the data.

The top panel of figure 9.6 shows an extremely long simulated realization

Local mean, non-linear SDE with beta 1 =1.50 fit to (r1514010)

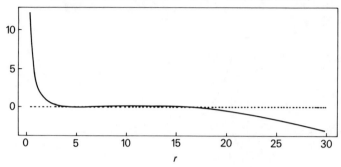

Local variance, non-linear SDE with beta 1 =1.50 fit to (r1514010)

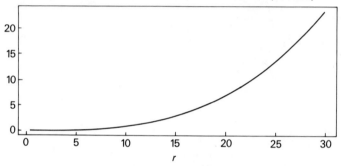

Figure 9.4 The two panels show the local mean and variance
functions of the fitted stochastic differential equation (44), where the
drift and diffusion functions are the non-linear-CEV specification
given in (57) and (58) with $\beta_1 = 1.5$ and the other parameters fitted via
EMM using the non-linear non-parametric score

(100 years worth) from the non-linear non-parametric score generator while
the bottom panel shows a simulation from the non-linear-CEV specification. The simulation from the non-linear-CEV specification is not unreas-
onable in appearance and, as to be expected, it is somewhat smoother than
the simulation from the score generator to which it is fitted.

In summary, there is considerable evidence for values of β_1 in the range
0.90–0.95 and possibly as high as 1.50, and for the non-linear mean
specification as well. The most general non-linear-CEV specification comes
close, but does not quite fit the data. The shape of the non-linear drift
function shown in figure 9.4 confirms the shape reported in Conley *et al.*
(1995) and Ait-Sahalia (1996a), which was detected using substantially
different (non-simulation) methods on different datasets.

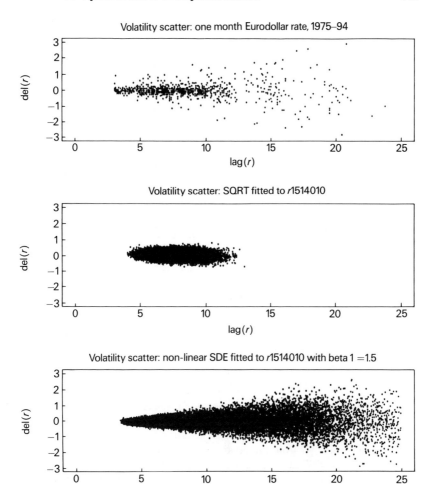

Figure 9.5 The top panel is a plot of $\Delta \tilde{y}_t = y_t - y_{t-1}$ versus $\tilde{y}_{t-1}$ based on weekly observations $\{\tilde{y}_t\}_{t=1}^{1035}$ on the 30-day Eurodollar interest rate, January 3, 1975–October 28, 1994. The middle panel shows $\Delta \hat{y}_\tau$ against $\hat{y}_{\tau-1}$ for a long simulation $\{\hat{y}_\tau\}$ from the stochastic differential equation (44), where the drift and diffusion functions are given in the fitted linear-square-root specification (53) and (54). The bottom panel shows $\Delta \hat{y}_\tau$ against $\hat{y}_{\tau-1}$ for a long simulation $\hat{y}_\tau = \hat{v}_\tau = V_\tau$ from the fitted stochastic differential equation (44), where the drift and diffusion functions are the non-linear-CEV specification given in (57) and (58) with $\beta_1 = 1.5$. Both the linear-square-root and the non-linear-CEV specifications were estimated via EMM using the non-linear non-parametric score.

Long simulation from fitted SNP (r1514010)

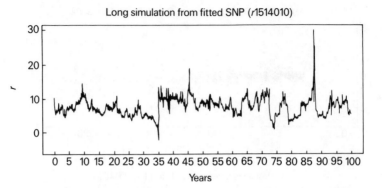

Years

Long simulation from fitted non-linear SDE with beta 1 =1.5

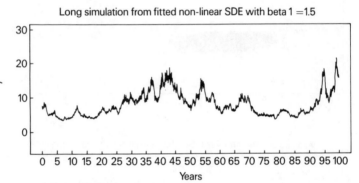

Years

Figure 9.6 The top panel shows a long simulation $\{\hat{y}_t\}$ from the fitted SNP model labeled the "Non-linear Non-parametric," where $L_u = 1$, $L_r = 5$, $K_z = 4$, $L_p = 1$, $K_x = 1$. The bottom panel shows a long simulation $\{\hat{y}_t\}$ from the fitted stochastic differential equation (44), where the drift and diffusion functions are the non-linear-CEV specification given in (57) and (58) with $\beta_1 = 1.5$ and the other parameters fitted via EMM using the non-linear non-parametric score. Each simulation runs for 5,200 periods, i.e., 5,200 weeks, or 100 years.

6   CONCLUSION

One lesson from the application is the importance of using a flexible, fully non-parametric score generator. The semi-parametric ARCH score reveals the inadequacy in the linear-square-root specification and indicates values of β_1 in the range 0.90–0.95. However, using this score alone gives misleading findings, as it suggests the linear-CEV model is adequate when in fact there is more structure to the data. The non-linear non-parametric score reveals the non-linear structure of the data. From table 9.1, this score generator is appropriate, as it is prefered under BIC to the semi-parametric ARCH score.

The remaining misspecification of the non-linear-CEV specification apparent from the bottom panel of figure 9.2 can probably be handled by introduction of a second stochastic volatility factor where (44) is extended to a two-factor model

$$dV = \mu_1(V, \alpha)dt + \sigma_1(V, U, \beta)dW_1 \tag{59}$$

$$dU = \mu_2(U, \gamma)dt + \sigma_2(U, \gamma)dW_2. \tag{60}$$

A version of this model is discussed in Koedijk, Nissen, Schotman, and Wolff (1995) and favorable empirical evidence based on a discrete-time approximation is available in Brenner, Harjes, and Kroner (1994). The latent volatility factor U can generate more exaggerated deviations from Gaussianity in the marginal distribution of V than can (44), and thus presumably should fit the data better. This specification can be estimated via EMM. Andersen and Lund (1996) undertake such estimation using non-parametric E-GARCH-SNP models as score generators. Their findings are that the volatility factor U is indeed needed to account adequately for all of the dynamics of the short interest rate.

Notes

Prepared for the Seventh World Congress of the Econometric Society, Tokyo, Japan, August 22–29, 1995. Corresponding author: George Tauchen, Department of Economics, Duke University, Durham, NC 27708, (919) 660-1812. The material is based upon work supported by the National Science Foundation. Thanks go to Yacine Ait-Sahalia, Torben Andersen, Lars Peter Hansen, and Peter Schotman for carefully reading and commenting on an earlier version and to Ravi Bansal, A. Ronald Gallant, Adrian Pagan, and Ken Singleton, for useful discussions and remarks at various stages of this research. Much of this chapter was written while I was a Visiting Fellow at the Australian National University.

References

Ait-Sahalia, Yacine (1996a). "Testing continuous-time models of the spot interest rate." *Review of Financial Studies*, 9, forthcoming.
    (1996b). "Nonparametric pricing of interest rate derivatives." *Econometrica*, 64, forthcoming.
Andersen, Torben G. and Lund, Jesper (1996). "Estimating continuous-time stochastic volatility models of the short term interest rate." *Journal of Econometrics*, forthcoming.

Andrews, Donald W. K. (1991). "Heteroskedasticity and autocorrelation consistent covariance matrix estimation." *Econometrica*, 59: 307–46.

Bansal, Ravi, Gallant, A. Ronald, Hussey, Robert, and Tauchen, George (1993). "Computational aspects of nonparametric simulation estimation." In Belsley, David A. (ed.), *Computational Techniques for Econometrics and Economic Analysis*. Boston: Kluwer Academic Publishers, pp. 3–22.

(1995). "Nonparametric estimation of structural models for high-frequency currency market data." *Journal of Econometrics*, 66: 251–87.

Bollerslev, Tim, Chou, Ray, and Kroner, Kenneth (1992). "ARCH modeling in finance: a selective review of the theory and empirical evidence, with suggestions for future research." *Journal of Econometrics*, 52: 5–61.

Brenner, Robin J., Harjes, Richard H., and Kroner, Kenneth F. (1994). "Another look at alternative models of the short-term interest rate." Manuscript, University of Arizona.

Buraschi, Andrea (1994). "The nominal term structure, stock prices and consumption dynamics with nonneutral inflation." Manuscript, University of Chicago.

Chan, K. C., Karolyi, G. A., Longstaff, F. A., and Sanders, A. B. (1992). "An empirical comparison of alternative models of the short-term interest rate." *Journal of Finance*, 47: 1209–27.

Conley, Tim, Hansen, Lars Peter, Luttmer, Erzo, and Scheinkman, José (1995). "Estimating subordinate diffusions from discrete time data." Manuscript, University of Chicago.

Cox, John C., Ingersoll, Jonathan E. Jr., and Ross, Stephen A. (1985). "A theory of the term structure of interest rates." *Econometrica*, 53: 385–407.

Duffie, Darrell and Kan, Rui (1993). "A yield-factor model of interest rates." Manuscript, Stanford University.

Duffie, Darrell and Singleton, Kenneth J. (1993). "Simulated moments estimation of Markov models of asset prices." *Econometrica*, 61: 929–52.

(1994). "Econometric modeling of term structures of defaultable bonds." Manuscript, Stanford University.

Durbin, J. (1970). "Testing for serial correlation in least squares regression when some of the regressors are lagged dependent variables." *Econometrica*, 38: 410–21.

Engle, Robert F. (1982). "Autoregressive conditional heteroskedasticity with estimates of the variance of United Kingdom inflation." *Econometrica*, 50: 987–1008.

Engle, Robert F. and Gonzales-Rivera, Gloria (1991). "Semiparametetric ARCH models." *Journal of Business and Economic Statistics*, 9: 345–60.

Engle, Robert F. and Lee, Gary J. (1994). "Estimating diffusion models of stochastic volatility." Manuscript, University of California at San Diego.

Foster, Douglas and Viswanathan, S. (1995). "Can speculative trading explain the volume-volatility relation?" *Journal of Business and Economic Statistics*, 13: 379–98.

Gallant, A. Ronald (1987). *Nonlinear Statistical Models*. New York, NY: John Wiley and Sons.

Gallant, A. Ronald, Hsieh, David A., and Tauchen, George (1995). "Estimation of stochastic volatility models with diagnostics." Manuscript, Duke University. (Available via anonymous ftp to ftp.econ.duke.edu, subdirectory home/ get/papers, as PostScript file msv.ps.)

Gallant, A. Ronald and Long, Jonathan R. (1995). "Estimating stochastic differential equations efficiently by minimum chi-square." *Biometrica*, forthcoming.

Gallant, A. Ronald and Nychka, D. W. (1987). "Semi-nonparametric maximum likelihood estimation." *Econometrica*, 55: 363–90.

Gallant, A. Ronald and Tauchen, George (1989). "Semi-nonparametric estimation of conditionally constrained heterogeneous processes: asset pricing applications." *Econometrica*, 57: 1091–120.

(1992). "A nonparametric approach to nonlinear time series analysis: estimation and simulation." In Parzen, E., Brillinger, D., Rosenblatt, M., Taqqu, M., Geweke, J., and Caines, P. (eds.), *New Dimensions in Time Series Analysis*. New York: Springer-Verlag.

(1995a). "SNP: a program for nonparametric time series analysis, a user's guide." Manuscript, University of North Carolina at Chapel Hill. (Available along with code via anonymous ftp to ftp.econ.duke.edu, subdirectory home/ arg/snp.)

(1995b). 'EMM: a program for efficient method of moments estimation, a user's guide." Manuscript, Duke University. (Available along with code via anonymous ftp to ftp.econ.duke.edu, subdirectory home/get/emm.)

(1996)."Which moments to match?" *Econometric Theory*, forthcoming. (Available via anonymous ftp to ftp.econ.duke.edu, subdirectory home/get/papers as PostScript file effgmm.ps.)

Gennotte, G. and Marsh, T. A. (1993). "Variations in economic uncertainty and risk premiums on capital assets." *European Economic Review*, 37: 1021–41.

Geweke, John (1983). "The approximate slope of econometric tests." *Econometrica*, 49: 1427–42.

Ghysels, Eric and Jasiak, Joanna (1994). "Stochastic volatility and time deformation: an application to trading volume and leverage effects." Manuscript, University of Montreal.

Gouriéroux, C. and Monfort, A. (1994). "Simulation based econometric methods." Manuscript, Centre of Operations Research and Econometrics, University of Louvain.

Gouriéroux, C., Monfort, A., and Renault, E. (1993). "Indirect inference." *Journal of Applied Econometrics*, 8: S85–S118.

Hamilton, James D. (1989). "A new approach to the economic analysis of nonstationary times series and the business cycle." *Econometrica*, 57: 357–84.

Hansen, Lars Peter (1982). "Large sample properties of generalized method of moments estimators." *Econometrica*, 50: 1029–54.

Hansen, Lars Peter and Scheinkman, José (1995). "Back to the future: generating moment implications for continuous-time Markov processes." *Econometrica*, 63: 767–804.

Hsu, Chien-Te and Kugler, Peter (1995). "The term structure of interest rates:

316   George Tauchen

systematic monetary policy and nonlinear dynamics." Manuscript, University of Vienna.

Ingram, Beth F. and Lee, B. S. (1991). "Simulation estimation of time series models." *Journal of Econometrics*, 47: 197–205.

Judd, Kenneth L. (1994). "Numerical methods in economics." Manuscript, Stanford University.

Kloeden, Peter E. and Platen, Eckhard (1992). *Numerical Solution of Stochastic Differential Equations*. New York: Springer-Verlag.

Koedijk, Kees G., Nissen, Francois G. J. A., Schotman, Peter C., and Wolff, Christian C. P. (1995). "The dynamics of short-term interest rate volatility reconsidered." Manuscript, Limburg Institute of Financial Economics.

McFadden, Daniel (1989). "A method of simulated moments for estimation of discrete response models without numerical integration." *Econometrica*, 57: 995–1026.

Melino, Angelo (1994). "Estimation of continuous time models in finance." In Sims, C. (ed.), *Advances in Econometrics, Sixth World Congress, Vol. II*. Cambridge University Press.

Newey, Whitney K. (1985a). "Generalized method of moments specification testing." *Journal of Econometrics*, 29: 229–56.

(1985b). "Conditional moment specification testing." *Econometrica*, 53: 1047–71.

Newey, Whitney K. and West, Kenneth D. (1987). "A simple positive semi-definite heteroskedasticity and autocorrelation consistent covariance matrix estimator." *Econometrica*, 55: 703–8.

Pagan, A. R., Hall, A. D., and Martin, V. (1995). "Modeling the term structure." Manuscript, The Australian National University.

Pakes, Ariel and Pollard, David (1989). "Simulation and the asymptotics of optimization estimators." *Econometrica*, 57: 1027–58.

Pfann, Gerard A., Schotman, Peter C., and Tschernig, Rolf (1996). "Nonlinear interest rate dynamics and implications for the term structure." *Journal of Econometrics*, forthcoming.

Schwarz, Gideon (1978). "Estimating the dimension of a model." *The Annals of Statistics*, 6: 461–4.

Smith, Anthony A. (1990). "Three essays on the solution and estimation of dynamic macroeconomic models." Ph.D. Dissertation, Duke University, Durham, NC.

(1993). "Estimating nonlinear time series models using simulated vector autoregressions." *The Journal of Applied Econometrics*, 8: S63–S84.

Tauchen, George (1985). "Diagnostic testing and evaluation of maximum likelihood models." *Journal of Econometrics*, 30: 415–43.

(1995). "The objective function of simulation estimators near the unstable region of the parameter space." Manuscript, Duke University. (Available via anonymous ftp to ftp.econ.duke.edu, subdirectory home/get/papers as PostScript file so.ps.)

Tauchen, George and Hussey, Robert (1991). "Quadrature-based methods for obtaining approximate solutions to nonlinear asset pricing models." *Econometrica*, 59: 371–96.

Taylor, John B. and Uhlig, Harald (1990). "Solving nonlinear stochastic growth models: a comparison of alternative solution methods." *Journal of Business and Economic Statistics*, 8: 1–17.
White, Halbert (1994). *Estimation, Inference, and Specification Analysis*. Cambridge University Press.

Index

322   **Index**

McGrattan, E. I.291–2, 300
Machina, M. J. I.177, 179, 184–7, 190, 197, 201 n.
McKelvey, R. I.48
McKelvey, R. D. II.253
MacKinnon, J. G. III.206
McKinnon, R. II.243
McLaughlin, K. II.18
Macleod, C. II.50
MacLeod, W. B. I.258, II.11, 13, 24–5
McMillan, J. II.210–32, 258, 263, III.78 n.
MacNeill, I. B. III.48
Maddala, G. S. III.151, 189
Maddison, A. II.40, 43, 46–8, 53, 55, 63–5
Madigan, D. III.145
Maekawa, K. III.55 n.
Magee, S. P. I.28–30, 42 n.
Magelby, D. B. I.31
Magnus, J. R. III.50, 55 n.
Maheswaran, S. III.264
Mailath, G. I.262–5, 270 n., 272 n.
Main, B. II.15
Mäkeläinen, T. III.48, 55 n.
Malcomson, J. II.11, 24–5
Mäler, K. G. II.148, 151 n.
Malina, R. M. II.130
Malouf, M. I.216, 223
Malthus, T. R. II.143
Mammen, E. III.189, 205
Manaster, D. B. III.266, 269
Manion, M. II.220
Mankiw, N. G. II.38, 285, III.35
Manning, A. III.111, 115
Mansfield, E. II.332–3
Manski, C. F. III.188
Manuelli, R. II.184–5
Mao, Z. II.221
Marcet, A. I.304, 306
Marcincin, A. II.211, 216
Maremont, M. II.8
Margen, S. II.152 n.
Margolis, D. II.27 n.
Margolis, D. N. III.124
Marimon, R. I.214, 278–310
Marron, J. S. III.205
Marschak, J. I.174, 177, 179, 182, 184–7, 190, 197
Marsh, T. A. III.279
Marshall, A. I.82
Marshall, W. I.48
Martin, V. III.280
Martinez, C. II.129–30
Martorell, R. II.128
Maruta, T. I.157 n., 266

Mas-Colell, A. III.185 n.
Maskin, E. I.259, 261
Maskin, E. S. II.107 n., 219, 231 n., 259, 262, 264–6, 272
Mathewson, S. II.13
Mathias, P. II.70 n.
Matraves, C. I.75
Matsui, A. I.249–50, 253, 259, 270–1 n.
Matthews, R. C. O. II.46, 51, 53
Matzkin, R. L. III.167
Mayer, C. II.60
Mayer, W. I.20–1, 29–30, 43 n.
Maynard Smith, J. I.212, 237 n., 244–5
Mazumdar, D. II.153 n.
Medoff, J. II.20–1, III.90
Mehta, J. I.222, 225
Melino, A. III.223–4, 227, 238, 279, 298
Melman, S. II.55
Meng, X. L. III.154
Merlo, A. I.56
Mertens, J.-F. I.89, 110, 158 n., 257, 271 n.
Merton R. C. III.223–4, 227, 231–3, 236, 243–4, 248, 270–1, 273 n.
Metropolis, N. III.138
Meyer, M. II.22–3, 27 n.
Meyer, R. III.124
Michie, R. II.57
Migon, H. S. III.150
Mikkelsen, H. O. III.263–4
Milgrom, P. I.157 n., 167 n., 255, 291, 295, 298–300, III.78 n.
Milgrom, P. R. I.4–5, 9–10, 12, 27 n., 87, 90, 94, 97, 102–4, 191, 210, 214, 244
Miller, J. I.214, 230
Miller, J. B. II.223–4, 227–8, 259
Miller, T. II.154 n.
Mills, T. C. II.43–4, 51, 70 n.
Milne, F. III.239
Min, C. III.149–50, 155
Mincer, J. II.329, 332, III.109
Miner, A. II.16
Mirrlees, J. A. II.4–5, 117, 153 n.
Mitch, D. II.51
Mitchell, B. R. II.51, 55
Mitchell, J. II.265, 272 n.
Miyasawa, K. I.299
Modica, S. I.152, 167 n.
Moe, T. I.48
Mokyr, J. II.50, 52–3
Monahan, J. C. III.199
Monderer, D. I.89, 132, 136, 138, 140, 162 n., 165 n.
Monfort, A. III.143, 227, 238, 241, 255, 262, 280, 285, 290

Paulson, A. II.186
Pavitt, K. II.49, 60
Paxson, C. II.170, 189
Pearce, D. G. I.87, 118–19, 124, 160–1 n., 255, II.227
Peck, M. J. II.232 n.
Peltzman, S. I.23, 83 n.
Pencavel, J. II. 27 n.
Percy, D. F. III.150
Perez, C. II.67
Perotti, E. II.265
Persson, T. II.251
Pesaran, B. III.50, 55 n.
Pesendorfer, W. I.48
Peskun, P. H. III.138
Petersen, T. II.17
Pfann, G. A. III.304
Pfeffer, J. II.26,
Phelan, C. II.186, 189
Phillips, P. C. B. II.14, 17, 36–9, 50, 54–5 n., 149, 199, 213
Piccione, M. I.93–4, 96, 98
Piketty, T. II.167, 169–70, 187
Pingali, P. L. II.244
Pinto, B. II.211, 213–14, 218–20, 252
Piore, M. II.19
Pischke, J.-S. II.23
Pissarides, C. A. III.85
Pissarides, F. II.232 n.
Platen, E. II.297
Platten, E. III.266
Pledger, G. III.167
Plott, C. I.236 n.
Podolny, J. II.17, 26
Poirier, D. J. III.128–9, 143, 152
Polak, B. II.80, 87
Politis, D. N. III.200
Pollard, D. III.279
Pollard, S. II.55
Pollitt, E. II.123, 131
Polson, N. G. III.151
Popper, K. R. I.278
Porter, D. I.220, 230
Porter, M. II.295
Porter, R. III. 64–5, 68–70, 78–9 n.
Porter, R. J. I.68, 83 n.
Portes, R. II.265, 271 n.
Posch, M. I.301
Post, R. J. II.8
Postel-Vinay, G. II.87, 97, 99
Postlewaite, A. I.272 n.
Pötschner, B. I.270 n.
Pradel, J. III.237
Prais, S. J. II.59
Prasnikar, V. I.228

Pratt, J. III.94
Pratten, C. F. II.59, 61
Preisendörfer, P. II.17
Prelec, J. I.189
Prendergast, C. II.22–3, 27 n.
Prennushi, G. II.27 n.
Prescott, E. III.143
Prescott, E. S. II.183, 191, 320, 326
Press, W. H. III.135
Price, G. R. I.244–5
Price, J. M. II.106 n.
Price, S. II.62
Pritchett, L. H. II.150
Przeworski, A. II.150
Putnam, R. I.20, 35

Qian, Y. II.219, 225–6, 248, 259, 261–3, 272 n.
Quah, D. III.188
Quiggin, J. I.183

Rabin, M. I.236
Rabinowitz, P. III.133
Radner, R. II.320, 324
Rae, D. I.48
Raftery, A. E. III.145, 155
Ramaswami, V. K. I.7
Rankin, F. I.228
Rao, N. P. II.123
Rapaczynski, A. II.231 n., 252, 262
Rashid, M. II.175, 202
Rathjens, G. II.150
Ravoteur, M. III.256, 258, 260, 268
Rawski, T. G. II.211, 213
Ray, D. II.117–18, 142, 151 n., 153 n.
Raymond, J. II.28 n.
Rebelo, S. II.38, 323
Rebitzer, J. II.16, 26
Redding, S. II.314 n.
Reich, L. S. II.48
Reimers, H.-E. III.14
Reinganum, J. II.283
Reinsel, G. C. III.38, 54 n.
Reiss, P. I.72–4, 83 n., III.74–5, 79 n.
Reiter, S. II.107 n.
Renault, E. II.223–74, 280, 285, 290
Renelt, D. II.45, 59, 63, 65, 70 n.
Reny, P. I.89, 124, 126–7, 155 n.
Rey, P. II.298, 314 n.
Rhode, P. I.258
Ricart i Costa, J. II.22
Richard, J. F. III.148–50, 158, 260
Richardson, T. J. II.232 n.
Ridder, G. III.82–125
Riezman, R. I.48